for
Pamela

So?

So if something at all
is forever the same
in London of then
and Athens of now,
I'll be looking for you
as I freely wander
on my cobbled paths
my glistening byways
in soft winter rain
of my Athens of now,
and if I tire too much
I'll just lie down and
after falling asleep
I'll be sure to find you
wherever you are.

— Tasouli

Anastassiades

Contents

Beginning

Occupation

Civil war

Later in the '40s

1950 — 1951

Styppas Returns

Falling

Appendix

Acknowledgements

Anastassiades

Illustrations

by Athena Moss

Map

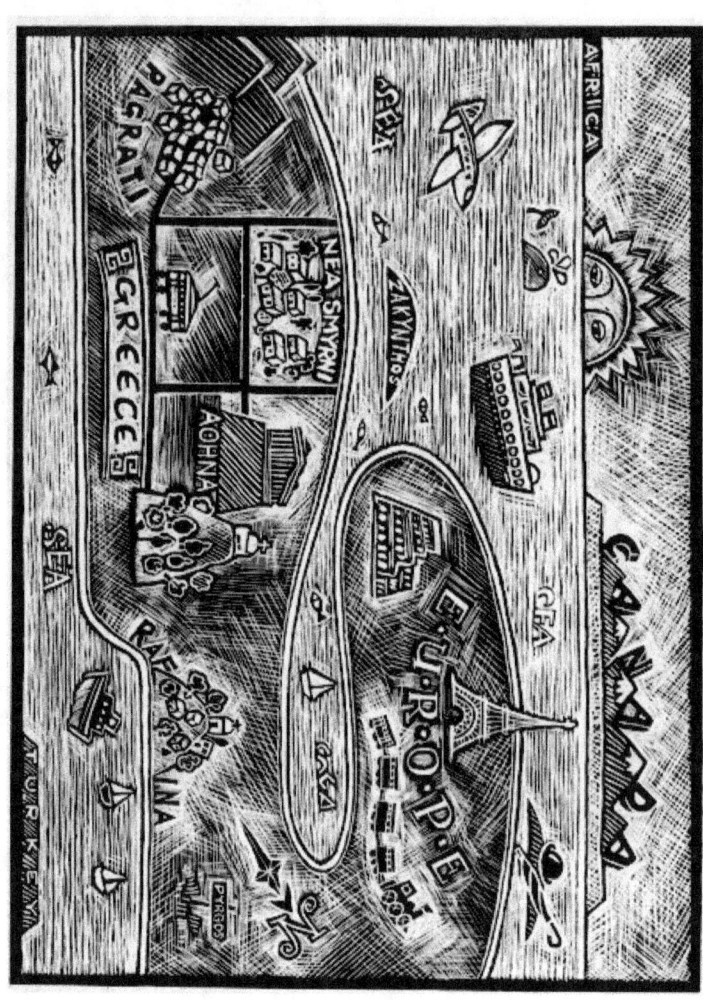

Narration

In this book, a twelve year old boy narrates his story. Born in Greece in 1938, just before the German Occupation started, he insists that he must tell his own story from the very start.

His initial narration occurs in late 1950 and covers the period from his first childhood memory until when he was about 12 years old. By then he had mastered English. He is convinced that he must be the sole narrator and that no one else can relate events as they really happened. Further, he is pedantic and a fanatic oralist, obsessed with the use of language and captivated by dreams. Yet, in subsequent years his recurrent narrations retained a surprising degree of fidelity.

His obsession with dreams and orality led me away from using the conventional quotation marks for conversation, as is often done in novels. I settled on the simplified notation of a short dash (–) after an indentation. Less intrusive for his endless imaginary conversations, the notation also seems to dictate a structure of shorter and simpler sentences for transcribing his childhood speech. I retain this notation for events that took place after the period of 1938-1950, when he was no longer a child. And as the Occupation Child's dreams and fantasies often become intermingled with reality, I felt obliged to alter or mask the names of some of the people he describes.

I was also faced with the problem of trying to convey the feeling or imagery that certain words created for him when spoken in his childhood language. For some of these words, especially ones used in his early childhood, I stayed with the Greek sounds by using Latin characters in the English context. The Latin characters generally have an accent on the appropriate vowel, to create the Greek word sound. I have to admit that a word such as *anɛmónɛs* still resonates more pleasantly in my ear than the Anglicized 'anemones'. A few fragments of Greek poetry have also been kept as in the original.

—T.S.

Beginning

A man with a white suit and a white explorer's casket was walking on the street. I think light rain was falling. I could see the man from the window of a bedroom facing towards the street. I was with my mother.

I said to my mother, pointing to the man:

– Άp`pos.

'Appos' is child-talk for *ánthropos* (man).

– Yes, Yes, anthropos, Tasoύli.

That was my name: Tasouli — little Tassos.

Later my parents told me that I would have been too young to remember something like that, at the age of one.

But I am certain that I do.

Next

I believe that my next memory is my father coming home as a soldier. I am not sure of the year. It was probably 1939 or early 1940, before the Italian invasion in October of 1940 (the war of '40). He had a long knife which I was told later must have been a bayonet, like a rapier. But I remember it had a sheath, more like a long penknife. In Greek a penknife would be called a *souyas*, but I do not remember that appellation being used. I think the sheath was made from wood, and that long knife closed into its sheath, by a hinge mechanism … like a jackknife. But maybe this was not so. This long jackknife, this sheathed rapier, was always placed on top of the high` dressing cabinet, made of varnished wood with a mirror on the door. In this way, I could not reach it.

I have tried to think of how my father was like then. I have difficulty remembering. I felt he was someone important.

Death

Then I remember my paternal grandfather dying. His name was the same as mine — Tάssos. More formally, he was called Anastάssios. This was in 1940. He had suffered a stroke. He was a very important man and was frequently visited by the doctor at home. A large bright red rubber cooler had been placed on his head. It was filled with ice. The adults said that cooling his head might help with the stroke. He was in a small room at the back of the house, with a bright window opening towards a garden. The door of the room was kept open into the main hall. He was easily visible from the hall. I remember my mother trying to keep me from going to observe him. Maybe she thought it would upset me. But I was not afraid. I was more curious.

Periodically there were sirens blaring. We had to go to underground shelters. I liked the shelters. They had handmade rag carpets (*kourelou'des*) and kerosene lamps. There were men, women and children sitting around on benches or chairs. I remember being surprised that they were not more talkative. The Greeks usually would be. Each family seemed to be in its own silent world. Perhaps they were worried about what was to come. When the sirens stopped we would go out and walk back home.

Occupation

Bastille

I remember many things about the German Occupation (*Katochi'*). It would have started in the spring of 1941 and continued until October 1944. During the Occupation, my parents, my father's three brothers and my father's mother, my Giagiá (grandmother) Sophia, all lived together on the first floor of a two-storey house, in a district of Athens called Pagráti. We had moved to Pagrati from Nea Smyrni, from the house that my grandfather had died in. My grandfather, his wife Sophia and their four boys had all escaped during the destruction of Smyrni (Smyrna) in Asia Minor in 1922. Nea Smyrni was the district where most of the refugees from Smyrni and other parts of Asia Minor were concentrated. The house I remember in Nea Smyrni was a large one-storey house, un-crowded by other houses, and with lots of light and sunshine coming in through large windows in all the rooms. The image I have of the house in Nea Smyrni is that it was made of a light or white stone. The house in Pagrati, which we rented, was on a small street and the houses or apartments were much more densely built, close to each other. It was near the main *platea* of Pagrati, platea Plastira (named after Nikolaos Plastiras).

The house had a hallway leading to the street, which was also shared by a family in the upstairs flat. There was a small garden in the back of this house that extended from a cement courtyard, and an iron spiral staircase went up from the cement courtyard to the apartment on the second floor. However, there was not much sunshine in the little garden because there was a tall wall belonging to the apartment building next to the Bastille, which was two or three storeys high. This wall was made of older worn brick, with plaster coming off the brickwork. It had a grey color and blocked the sun getting in. On the other side of the small courtyard there was a lower stone wall separating us from other apartments with back windows and little balconies with flowers or plants. Our dining room was at the back of the house and faced the little garden and the wall. *Yiayia* (grandmother) Sophia did not like the sunless back of the house and the wall. She would complain:

– Why did you bring me here, in this Bastille?

The nickname stuck and we would often refer to our house in Pagrati as the 'Bastille'. It was kind of a humorous code that the adults used.

– I will see you on Saturday at the Bastille, they would say.

I soon learned about the real Bastille. I was proud to have our house named after the famous Parisian prison.

I think the reason the family moved to the Bastille in Pagrati was to improve their chances of finding work and also to get to work more easily, for those who had something to do. Pagrati was pretty well in central Athens while Nea Smyrni seemed a more distant suburb then. Mostly there was no regular work. The family structure was pretty tightly knit, so if anyone had work all family members would be helped. Everything seemed to be shared.

In addition to my parents, my grandmother and my three uncles, there was one other person who was almost like family. She was *Kyrá* Maria. 'Kyra' is used like 'Mrs.' but in a colloquial, semiformal and respectful form. She was always referred to as Kyra Maria by everybody, including me. She would never be referred to by any member of the family using her last name (which I do not even recall) or without the 'Kyra' appellation before the 'Maria'. She was my grandmother's faithful household assistant. Kyra Maria would help with many of the heavier jobs, such as the washing of everyone's clothes which was then done entirely by hand, and all kinds of chores. Yiayia Sophia had somehow found Kyra Maria, who was previously a nun. She had left the nunnery, apparently did not have a close family, and became an important attachment to ours. Yiayia Sophia used to say that she was a good and kindly woman, a saintly woman. Kyra Maria would always refer to my grandmother as "Kyri´a Sophia" (Mrs. Sophia). The distinction between Kyra and Kyria is socially non-trivial, with the latter being the correct, formal appellation most commonly used with a last name. 'Kyria Sophia' is a form that can be used to denote respect and familiarity at the same time. I don't think that these social niceties are much adhered to now, in the modern language of urban Greek Society. Perhaps they helped maintain a structure within the family especially during the Occupation. From my point of view, I remember thinking that Yiayia Sophia was important in the family, since she had her Kyra Maria who she commanded. Of course, Kyra Maria would help all members of the family, and she paid particular attention to me, but it was also clear to me who her boss really was.

A main gathering place for Yiayia Sophia, Kyra Maria and, often for me, was the dining room at the back of the Bastille. As it faced the tall, grey wall it was always dark, but also seemed more protected and somewhat mysterious. In the summer the dining room was cool and in the winter a *magáli*, a three-legged brazier, was often lit in the evenings. Wood charcoal burned slowly in the open *magali*. A long, circular, dried orange peel was always placed among the hot coals. It was thought that this prevented noxious fumes from forming, especially, carbon monoxide, the adults would say importantly. The magali with its charcoal and slowly burning orange peel smelled really nice. I could sit there for hours listening to Yiayia Sophia and Kyra Maria talk in slow, low tones. Sometimes I would be treated to a fairy tale and on occasion, in the autumn, a few chestnuts would be put on to roast on the magali.

It was there too that the most important work of the household would be done — the preparation of the food. Because of the scarcity of almost everything, food was prepared from scratch. I can't remember if flour was rationed, but we had enough to make a type of pasta. They most often made what is now usually bought as *orzo*. A clean white linen bedsheet would be put on the dining room table. The mass of dough, in a heavy earthenware pot, would be pulled into thin, snake-like extensions, with the palms of their hands. From these snakes Yiayia Sophia and Kyra Maria would make the orzo. Their fingers would move almost faster than the eye could see, as they would spin out the individual, oval, orzo grains one by one. Each little pile they made of spun-out orzo grains would be added to a slowly growing little hill on the white linen on the table. I would be allowed to try to make some orzo grains, but I was never very good at it, so I was mostly content to watch and listen. Next day, the orzo would be cooked. It was cooked with whatever was available, perhaps some tomato, some onion done slowly in olive oil. It was always most delicious.

The men would rarely come in the dining room during these sessions. They were generally engaged in political discussions, in the living room, in the front of the Bastille, perhaps trying to get news on the illegal shortwave radio. My mother used to hover in and out of the dining room, as she also participated in the political discussions with the men in the front of the house. She was, after all, the only young woman in the household and kept her hand in everything that was going on.

Sometimes in the Bastille, the adults became glum and radiated a feeling of fear. This feeling of fear in my parents and other family members created a unpleasant sensation in me. It is difficult to describe — was something in the pit of my stomach and my legs became weak. I still have it today when something bad is happening, but I am not sure it is exactly the same. I could not tell how other children in the family felt as I was the only child there.

A family lived upstairs from us in the Bastille. The father was said to be a retired army Colonel. He talked very little. His wife talked all the time. They had two teenage children, a boy and a girl. The girl, who was older than the boy, was friendly and played the piano. The boy was often away and not at all friendly. It was not clear what he did. They seemed to be fairly well-off considering it was the German Occupation.

Language of Hunger

Hunger was the most pervasive thing I remember during the Occupation. We were always hungry. Being chronically hungry, close to starvation, is very different than the average person in today's Western world saying "I am hungry". The latter usually means one might have a hunger-like stomach pang that was not there a few hours ago. It is likely to go away after one has eaten enough. What I remember of chronic hunger was a very different feeling. These were not the familiar hunger-like pangs of the generally well-fed of today. Rather, it was a feeling of emptiness. Continual emptiness. And one never felt really well. This feeling unwell was there all the time. You would only notice that you felt better if you had something in your stomach. Even if it was very little.

Of course, there was no meat. If anyone had any meat at all he would immediately be suspected as a collaborator. The Resistance would likely get him or his family sooner or later. Even bread, the staple for the Greeks — that without which life could not really continue — was in very short supply. It is difficult today, in the Western world, to convey the meaning of bread as it was then. Yes, bread was the staple. Yet 'staple' implies that you might have other things to eat that are not a staple. But bread was often the only thing we had to eat. And bread, the staple, was the last thing that remained before starvation. It was the very last thing that stood between life and slow death by starvation.

The demotic Greek word for bread is *psom,* the affectionate diminutive being *psomáki*. As a child during the Occupation my big daily question was:

– *Mamaka*, do we have *psomaki* today?

Having even a little psomaki meant everything. And she would always say:

– Oh yes, Tasouli, we have lots of psomaki today.

But what she would do is cut what she had of the loaf into thinner slices, so it would appear more. I knew she did this, but I was happy that she made the bread seem more for me … ever, ever so happy. For I knew then that I would not die that day. I would live.

Now, English nouns do not ordinarily have diminutives such as suffixes or prefixes. Except for contracted names of persons, in many cases. In Greek, affectionate diminutives are very common, especially in child's talk. So, *psomaki* literally means a 'little bread'. But it also takes on an affectionate connotation as one might say a 'little boy'. In those days of great shortage, I would say "Mamaka, could I have a little more psomaki, please?" If she said yes, it would mean to me that my dear little Mamaka would give her little boy a little more bread, so her little boy would live and not die.

In written English "… a little more bread" does not contain an affectionate element in the word 'bread'. Of course in English speech, under similar circumstances of hunger, one might say "… a little more bread, please" with a certain tonal emphasis on 'bread'. The voice inflection could then be used to introduce an element of affection for the bread itself. But in Greek, both written and oral, it is the affectionate diminutive suffix of the word *psomaki* which contains the key emotional element. For it implied to me affection deeply ingrained into that piece of bread. For Occupation Child, the psomaki represented no less than the affection of the child for his mother and of the mother for her child.

There is still more to psomaki. For it can also refer affectionately to a loaf of bread. A whole, un-sliced loaf was the only form of bread that existed. And the daily allotment would be one loaf per family. That is, if loaves were available at the neighborhood baker. If the loaves ran out for good, life would run out.

For me and the people around me during the Occupation, the notion of a loaf of bread being equivalent to a day of life was part of everyday speech. If somebody was very sick and expected to die soon, the conversation I would hear might go something like:

– He doesn't have many loaves left any more.
– No, maybe enough for a week or two.

And I think people still used that analogy after the Occupation ended. It remained ingrained.

The taste of the loaf of bread that kept us alive is difficult to describe and comprehend now. It was not only hunger that made it taste so good. I am sure of that. The wheat was still harvested often by scythe and ground mostly locally. That flour was then shipped to the starving city and made into loaves of bread by the local baker. The allotted loaf even in the worst days of the Occupation was still warm from the oven, shortages and all. One chewed the slice with its thick crust and soft core. It started to go down into your belly and your hunger, your fear … that terrible fear would subside. It was as if you fell asleep on your mother's bosom, safe, warm and with a full belly. Your Mamaka loved you. There would be lots of slices from the loaf that day.

Your Mamaka had said so.
And you loved your Mamaka.
So it had to be true.

And it was always my mother, my Mamaka, who fed me what food there was for me. My father, my *Baba*, probably heroically starved most of the time so I could have a little more. But I think I used *Mamaka* a lot more when speaking to my Mother than *Babaka* when speaking to my father. I am not sure if the diminutive affectionate appellations I used to address each of my parents relate to who actually fed me. Maybe it had more to do with their personalities and how I perceived them.

During the Occupation, in Athens animal protein of any kind was very short. I recall that some of the corner grocers still had some slabs of salted cod kept in wooden barrels, probably from Canada. But it would have been a treat to have salted cod. There was some powdered milk and we seemed to get powdered eggs from time to time. The greatest hunger was in 1941-42 (*mégas limós*), when hundreds of thousands died.

Omonia is a central piazza in Athens. The electrical train from Kifisia to Pireus had its main station under the Omonia platea. There were vents from the Underground to the surface. There, children in rags would gather during the cold Athens winter trying to keep warm by huddling together over the vents of the Underground. They seemed to be abandoned and were starving. Some of them were dying and sometimes one had to step over the dying ones to get across the platea. Many had big swollen bellies. I remember one winter day, my mother took me to the *Cineac* (an indoor movie house) near Omonia and we had to go through these kids. My mother, pulling me by one hand, tried to cover my eyes with her other hand, so I would not see them. I remember thinking my mother's gesture was unnecessary. I had already seen the kids before and I was curious about them.

The dying children would talk to me.
They were begging, I suppose.
I wanted to ask them why they had no psomaki.
No psomaki at all it seemed.
But I was dragged away.

Blockos in Pagrati

During the Occupation we were essentially without communications. Very few families had a telephone even before the war. Radio and newspapers were strictly controlled. Censorship was everywhere. People were afraid to say anything in a public place. The person next to you could be an informer or, worse, a Gestapo agent.

But in our neighborhood, we had the urchins — the street urchins of Pagrati. These were rough street kids, mostly in rags and always hungry, probably from very poor families or, perhaps, no families. They seemed to come out of nowhere, out of the street shadows. They seemed to know everything that was going on in the district. Particularly they knew about the movements of the Occupier.

The German-Gestapo system for keeping control during the Occupation was fairly simple and efficient. Suddenly German lightly armed vehicles and soldiers would descend unannounced on a part of a district and totally surround one or more blocks. This part of the district would then be effectively isolated from the rest and no one could get in or out of the blocked area. Presumably they would act on some intelligence about the Resistance or other subversive activity. The adults in the Bastille were saying that there would be house-to-house searches. The residents would all have to line up outside in the street and that the Gestapo would always be a part of these blockades and searches. Some people would just be taken away, generally never to return. Sometimes individuals would be shot on the spot, probably as part of a retaliation program or simply to keep the population terrified. We were lucky. Our own house was never part of a blockade.

However, we were warned by the street urchins about blockades elsewhere in our district. The urchins would suddenly appear shouting *blockos sto Pagrati, blockos sto Pagrati* (blockade in Pagrati, blockade in Pagrati). I suppose the urchin warnings would give one a chance to try to move or hide anyone who was part of the resistance or who the Gestapo might be specifically looking for. I remember the adults would always look afraid when the urchins would come to our street shouting their warnings.

Their shouting also gave me a feeling of excitement. I wanted to go out and be with the urchins so I too could shout *blockos sto Pagrati* and be important and warn people. Of course, if I told that to my parents they would never let me and instead restrict me more. So, I never did.

Torture

The adults were always whispering about someone we knew, or somebody who had or was being tortured. Most of the torture was thought to be by the Gestapo or the police, but also by collaborators torturing Resistance members and the Resistance torturing captured collaborators. When the adults were talking about torture their fear showed, and I would get the unpleasant sensation. It was more the way they talked about torture than what they described that caused me to have the unpleasant sensation. A common torture technique was to use a garden hose to inflate the rectum with cold water under pressure. The pain is supposed to be very intense. I imagined the hose to be made of dull-red rubber. This was a common color for garden hoses then. Finger nails were also pulled out regularly and gradual amputations were said to take place. Another technique the adults talked about was that people were made to sit on a block of ice without pants. After a while, the pain became so unbearable that people would confess anything.

There was a woman who was a distant relative named Alexandra. She used to come around the house and I remember her well. She was a middle-aged woman, rather quiet with a lot of fuzzy, grey hair. She was always nice to me. She was some kind of an intellectual, perhaps a writer, but I am not sure. She talked in a quiet voice too, but when she talked to me what she said seemed clear and agreeable. Alexandra was captured. The adults said she was captured because Nazi collaborators had it in for her. She was tortured. My family thought that she was tortured by the collaborators but they were not certain. Maybe it was the Nazis. They said her body was found on a garbage pile. Her breasts had been cut off. Somebody said that garden shears were used.

Finding Alexandra on the garbage was a weird and unpleasant image for me which also confused me. One person I knew had breast cancer but I cannot remember if it was Alexandra or not. Breast cancer would not have been very common then and somehow I had the image of something large in the breast like an orange. Maybe one of the adults had said something to that effect, or it is a later image that I have superimposed in my mind. I remember the reason for my confusion: were Alexandra's breasts cut off with the garden shears because she had breast cancer? Some of the images from my child's imagination that I see now, like Alexandra, seem dark with green shadows. But there are some bright colors, like the orange. The images of the adults in the rooms of the Bastille are gray colors but individuals are clearly distinguishable. I easily recall the expressions and gloom of their faces. I have to think harder to recall what their voices sounded like. When I do sometimes recall, I am not sure if the voices as I remember them were from the period of the Occupation or from a later time.

In hushed tones they would discuss who might have been responsible for the disappearances, the tortures and the killings. In Alexandra's case opinion was divided. It could have been the Gestapo, but someone would have had to be an informant. Leaving her body on a pile of garbage was thought to be more likely the work of the police working with collaborators. They were often thought to be responsible for murders of this type. Of course nobody trusted the police then or for decades after. It was the organ of the Occupiers. The seeds of what was to come, in some ways much worse than the Occupation itself, were already being deeply planted. The adults seemed to sense that.

But who really committed these murders? This was a question that preoccupied me. It was also a question that the adults, who usually knew everything, could not answer. It was all innuendo and fear. The worst fear was that it was us, the Greeks themselves, who were responsible — it could be either the collaborators, or the Resistance. If the murdered person was a leftist — then it was collaborators or right wing groups in the Resistance. If it was a rightist or a collaborator — then the communist Resistance could be responsible.

I started to dream about murders, but I am not certain when the dreams started. By the time I was older there was a pattern to a dream. It was very frightening. It would happen in a series of rooms, always the same rooms, the same emptiness in them, the same locked doors between them, the same lack of windows, the same terror as I wandered from one room to another. It was very difficult to unlock these doors, but I would always manage, only to find a more horrid room than the previous one. The rooms had no furniture, but there were low, wooden cupboards, close to the floors and it was what these cupboards contained that I was forced to discover. I was forced by someone, but I cannot remember now by whom, I cannot see a face or hear a clear voice. The color of the dream was a dark yellow. Maybe the yellow color came from the poor illuminated light in the windowless rooms. But where were these terrifying rooms, and why were they so familiar to me?

First, I thought I had made up the rooms in my imagination. But gradually I placed them in a real location. Across from the Bastille, towards the top of the street there was an apartment building. It probably had only four or five stories, but it seemed very high to me. A moat separated the apartment building from the street, so the first or basement floor was below the level of our street. Our street more or less sloped downward from the apartment towards the Bastille. When one looked towards the apartment building, one could see ivy on its walls, but the walls were a dark yellow, with patches of plaster falling off. The whole apartment building seemed a dark yellow. There was a family I knew in this apartment and my mother knew them. I think they were a 'nice' and educated family, and they had at least one child, a boy about my age. I used to go over to the apartment building and play with that boy. Our games were always nice and I do not remember ever being frightened. Yet, the frightening series of rooms were in the basement of that apartment building. The ending of the dream was always the same. I was forced to open the cupboards and inside I would find a dead body. I can't remember if it was the same body each time. But finding the dead body was not the most horrifying part. It was the accusation of who had committed the murder. I cannot remember who the accuser was; maybe it was the police, the same police that were capable of doing the killing. But I was certain of one thing: I was convinced of the identity of the murderer.

> *It was I.*
> It was I, and I knew it with absolute conviction.
> Then I would awake from the nightmare, frightened. Usually I could not get back to sleep.
> The reality of the dream was absolute.
> *It did not happen.*
> I would try to convince myself of that.
> Right after been woken by the dream.
> *No, it is real. It is real, it is real ...*

The recall of each step of the nightmare was crystal clear and stark. It was reality. The terror of me having done it remained, even when I stayed wide awake until morning.

For a few years I tried to change the ending of the nightmare by consciously trying to guide my thinking. After my fright would have somewhat subsided, I would stay awake trying to think of scenarios that could change the outcome.

> *Who else could have been the murderer?*
> I would tell myself that if I could find out the circumstances of the murder, maybe the ending

would be different.
Maybe I could insert people I did not like into the nightmare.
Maybe I could insert the police, the Gestapo, collaborators in my dream ... please, anyone!
But it was to no avail.
It is I and I alone who was guilty.
Did I really commit these murders?
Maybe this is the reality.
Perhaps I am just trying to cover it up even now.
I am just trying to suppress the real memory.
The nightmare stayed unmodified, I think, for many years.
Then it went away.
It has not come back.
I am hoping that narrating it here will not bring it back.

Color of freedom

The adults always talked about freedom. It would come when we got rid of the Occupiers. We had a large radio made of polished brown wood with ivory knobs and a magical little green light. I thought that the radio was the most beautiful thing in the Bastille. It made crackling noises and had shortwave reception. It was illegal to receive any shortwave broadcasts from non-occupied countries or clandestine radio. All radios had to be taken into the police and be 'sealed' to prevent that kind of reception. The seal had to show on the radio. If someone was caught receiving illegal broadcasts they could be interrogated, tortured or even shot. But somehow we were getting shortwave reception in the beautiful wooden radio. It was mostly from the BBC short wave broadcast and the reception was very crackly. Family members did not understand English very well and did better in French, but it was only the BBC service that got through. When the broadcast would come everybody would be called around the grand radio with the beautiful controls and the magical little green light. The sound had to be turned right down in case collaborators or police in the street, or maybe in the apartment above, heard something and became suspicious. Between the incessant crackling, the low volume and the foreign language, little seemed to be understood. But every bit of what did get through was endlessly discussed and debated. It did not matter in the end, as the critical turning point in the War finally came. When we learned that Germany had attacked the great Soviet Union we knew that freedom would come. The adults were saying that the Nazis could never defeat the Soviets — in spite of all the Nazi propaganda touting great German victories. Later, we learned that the great America had also entered the war. It had been expected by us. It was just delayed. The adults became even more certain that the Occupation would end and freedom would come.

I thought a great deal about what freedom would be like. It was probably because the adults talked about it so much. I knew it would be wonderful because of how the adults spoke the word and their expression when they did. But I did not understand what the word meant. At some point I developed an image in my mind. It was a beautiful clear day with an unbelievably blue, blue sky that never went away. That was freedom. Every time that I heard the word this is what I imagined. I am not sure how I got that beautiful almost unreal bright deep azure blue color in my mind. Maybe I had seen that color somewhere in Greece on a summer's day looking at the then still pristine sea. It was more the color of a magical child's sea. Most likely I had dreamed that color. I remember, after the Occupation, being mildly surprised that *that* color did not appear. But I could still visualize the color when I wanted to.

Little girl

The Bastille was entered from a hallway from Anthipou, a small street in Pagrati. The hallway had a heavy door made of black iron lattice and semi-transparent glass. If one came into the hallway from the street, the inner door to the Bastille was to the right, which also had semi-transparent glass. A set of stairs further along the hallway led upstairs to the home of the Colonel and his wife. Further

13

along, at the end of the corridor another door opened into a cement courtyard, leading to our small garden. From the cement courtyard there was a circular iron stairway, painted black, that went up to the Colonel's apartment. The hallway was never well lit and even in the summer it was dark and always cool. The floor was made of a dark, polished stone-like material with bits of gravel and marble, common in hallways and floors in those days. It felt cool in the summer and cold in the winter.

Sometimes in the hallway I would find a little girl. I never knew where the little girl came from or how she got in. She did not belong upstairs and could not have come from the enclosed courtyard. She must have come through the front door of the hallway, which was not locked during the daytime and was heavy to open. The little girl was a bit unkempt and looked hungry but never asked for food. She was not too active and would mostly squat and did not jump or run, the way children do. She seemed to want to play but I could not figure out what kind of game she wanted to play. I think my mother and grandmother knew about the little girl in the hallway and I was allowed to play with her. At least I would not be out in the street, where I was generally not allowed to play during the Occupation. I don't know the age of the little girl. She was younger than me, maybe about three. The little girl wanted me to squat near her, which I would do. She wanted to show me her pippi. I was reluctant but did not move away because I wanted to play with the little girl. Finally she convinced me. Because she was squatting I had to put my head on the hard, cold hallway floor. There were little things hanging from her pippi. I had not seen a girl's pippi before, not having a sister, so I was not sure if this is how it should be. I can't remember if we did end up playing a child's game, but I think she was content. Later, I told my mother about the little girl and her pippi and the little things hanging. My mother was very angry.

– You are never to play with the little girl again.
– Why, Mommy, why?

I thought she was a nice little girl even though a bit strange.

– She is a dirty little girl that comes from a bad family.

My mother had a way of saying things in a tone full of implication and accusation that always made me feel very badly. I didn't understand why I would have been allowed to play with the little girl in the first place, if my mother knew she was from such a bad family.

– Why?
– She has worms, worms, worms, she hissed.

I felt badly because my mother was so angry and I did not know what I had done wrong. Could I catch the worms just by looking at them? And how did I know these were worms hanging from the little girl's pippi? My mother had not seen them to confirm that they were worms.

Maybe all little girls' pippi looked like that.
The next day the little girl did not come in our hallway.
I never saw her again.

Joujoukos

Yiayia Sophia had been married to my paternal grandfather, who was a great man when they lived in Smyrna, and who had the red rubber cooler on his head when he had the stroke. She said she had a cat phobia for many, many years. I loved my Yiayia Sophia and she loved me. She loved me so much that she agreed to let me have a cat — in spite of her terrible cat phobia. I called the cat Joujoukos.

All Yiayia Sophia asked was that Joujoukos was not to rub against her or try to sit on her lap.

– Cats give me the creeps, she would say.
– Ohh, the creeps Yiayia.
– If Joujoukos even touches me, all the hairs of my skin stand up.
– But why, Yiayia Sophia?
– I don't know. I have had it for years.
– But why, Yiayia Sophia?
– I told you, I don't know. I think it started after I had the children.

I was satisfied. That is just how Yiayia Sophia was. The cat phobia had started after her having my father and his brothers. It had nothing to do with Joujoukos. I knew she would faithfully put the best scraps in Joujoukos' dish, always making sure that the cat was at a safe distance away from her.

Joujoukos was a popular name in the Bastille. It was a made-up name that reminded one of something cute and cuddly. It also reminded people of *soujoukakia*, the incredibly tasty oval ground meat creations of Smyrna that Yiayia Sophia excelled in making. I don't think I had tasted *soujoukakia* during the Occupation (unless it was in the late stages) due to the shortage of meat, but Yiayia Sophia's soujoukakia would be talked about with great reverence.

One day Joujoukos became very excited. He had smelled meat being cooked and disappeared to investigate. We had all smelled it! It was the unmistakable aroma of meat being fried and it came from upstairs where the Colonel and his wife lived. Of course meat of any kind would be generally unobtainable, except through the black market or worse. A piece of meat large enough and of sufficient quality to fry, like a steak, would be an unthinkable luxury. Frying during the Occupation was often done on little table-top gas stoves, similar to today's camping stoves, called a *gaziera*. The *gaziera* was said to be dangerous. A few had exploded, badly burning people around them.

Suddenly, from the Colonel's apartment there was a huge commotion and racket. There was shouting and swearing and a great loud crash — shouts to turn the *gaziera* off, that it had been knocked down, and something about fire. We ran out on the cement courtyard to see what the commotion was. The Colonel's wife was out on the top of the circular iron staircase waving her slipper, while the Colonel could be heard swearing and banging his walking stick.

All of a sudden Joujoukos flew through the air, past the Colonel's wife, with his jaws locked on a piece of meat — a steak, no less. Apparently the cat had to make a quick decision. He could either go through the Colonel's wife and her thrashing slipper, or go back through the Colonel and his heavy walking stick, or jump from the top of the iron staircase, two floors down onto the cement courtyard. Brave, brave, incomparable Joujoukos chose the latter. Being a cat he landed on his feet, never letting the steak go and shot through the back door of the hallway and out the front door, both of which happened to be open.

The commotion had also attracted a number of neighbors who stuck their heads out of back windows or came out on the little balconies from the apartment buildings facing the back of the Bastille. Joujoukos had knocked down the lit gaziera with the hot frying pan and the sizzling steak. Somehow he had managed to grab the steak.

– Thief, thief, THIEF … , screeched the Colonel's wife.
– Kill that cat, shouted the Colonel in his heavy voice.

He was used to giving orders. Even if it was to no one in particular.

Kyra Maria was the first on the battle-scene from our side, and immediately raised the alarm.

– Kyria Sophia, KYRIA SOPHIA … , she shouted in a voice that could be heard across the neighborhood.
– Come quickly, they are going to kill Joujoukos; they are going to kill our cat … !

She was squealing at the top of a voice that made the windows rattle. It is not clear where the saintly woman had suddenly found a voice like a wartime siren. I guess the nuns had prepared her

15

for all contingencies.

Yiayia Sophia was on the little cement courtyard in a flash. Her response was instantaneous and magnificent. She put her hands on her hips and looked straight up at the Colonel and his wife. Her index finger started to wave.

– YOU, she shouted. You have nearly injured my cat. This cat, which I love as much as my own children! This lovely cat, which I pet all the time.

There was a brief moment of stunned silence from the Colonel and his wife. They had heard chapter and verse about Yiayia's phobia. From Yiayia Sophia herself.

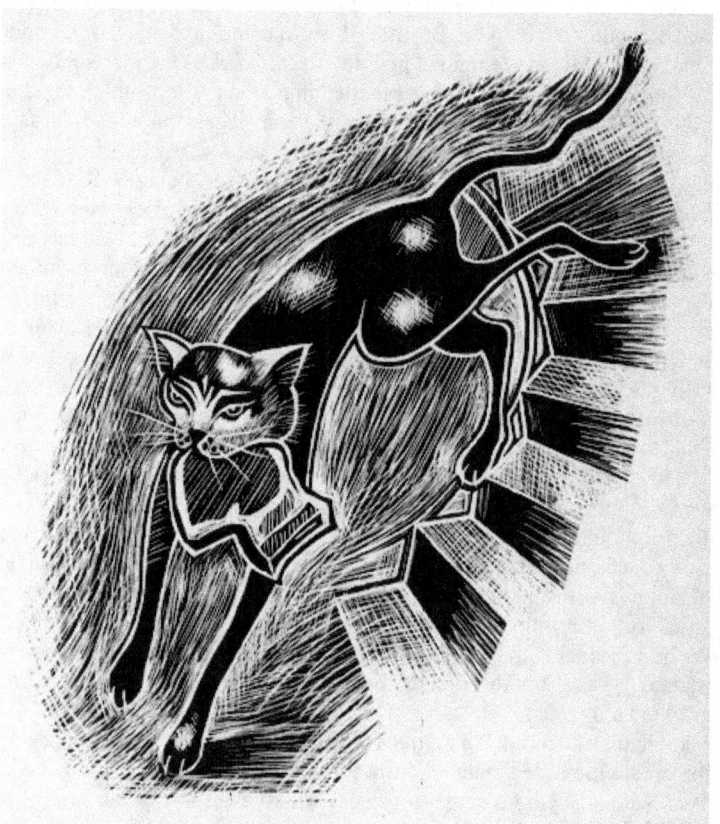

– What right do you have abusing my cat?

Yiayia Sophia continued to shout, having obtained a strategic advantage and now waving her finger ever more pointedly at the enemies of Joujoukos.

– Oh yes, yes, chimed in Kyra Maria, this wonderful cat that sits on Kyria Sophia's lap. Kyria Sophia who has lost her husband and is a wartime widow. And this kind cat who keeps her company when she has no one else …
Then the commentary from the watching neighbors started to come in, with increasing volume.

– It is not fair to abuse a cat.
– Especially a cat that is such a good cat, that sits on Kyria Sophia's lap. Who after all is a wartime widow …
– It is shameful to beat a cat that has done nothing wrong.

The chatter increased. Being able to get meat, let alone a steak, during the Occupation was never mentioned once. Praise of Joujoukos and the physical affection Yiayia Sophia lavished on him dominated the loudly exchanged gossip across back windows and balconies.

It was game over! The Colonel and his wife retreated mumbling and slammed their door shut.

But it got better still. Joujoukos, with the steak never leaving his mouth, had run into the street, bee-lined for the closest wooden telephone post, right across from the Bastille, scampered up and perched on the cross bar among the electrical connectors. There he surveyed his kingdom and feeling sufficiently out of danger, started chewing on his possession. A number of neighbors came out and watched in admiration. The commentary continued to flow.

– What a brave cat!
– We should have more cats like this.
– Yes, we need cats like this!
– Especially during these times!
– For sure. Especially during this Occupation!

Of course the word spread that this was really my cat. I remember a feeling of pride almost overwhelming me. My Joujoukos, Joujoukos mou, Joujoukaki mou! Unbelievably, Joujoukos and I had carried out a stroke against the black market.

Collaborators be warned! I was now somebody in the neighborhood. For who would not recognize the owner of Joujoukos? I no longer needed to feel inferior because I was not allowed to go with the urchins. Joujoukos and I had done our bit against the Occupation.

Family

My father was the second oldest of four brothers. There were no sisters in his family. My father, his three brothers, my mother, Yiayia Sophia and I all lived together in the Bastille during the Occupation. All the brothers were professionals but there was not much work to be found during the Occupation, so a lot of time was spent together at home in the Bastille. As the only child in the household, there must have been a lot of attention lavished on me. However, for me it was normal. Perhaps because of this, I loved my uncles. The four brothers always had animated discussions. There was competition among them as to who could solve a problem best or who was the most important. This also seemed normal to me.

Yiayia Sophia had later told me that, my grandfather, the great man of Smyrna, had decreed that each of the four boys would train in a profession that represented the four pillars of the Greek state. I am not sure if the decree was issued before the catastrophe of 1922 or after. The pillars were: engineering, the armed forces, mathematics, and medicine. The pillars were to be erected in that order, which was according to descending age of the boys. My father entered an academy for the armed forces (the Navy actually) at a very young age. Quite by chance, he escaped a career in the Navy and went into agriculture, but this is another story.

The oldest of the uncles was Stelios. He had bright blue eyes that darted around and he was interested in everything. He was a civil engineer. I was told that he was the first of the family to get a job before the war, but I don't think he had a full time job during the Occupation. Stelios obviously thought that my young age should be no barrier to learning all kinds of things particularly if they were to be found in an old, illustrated encyclopedia that we had in the house. So, he taught me, with great animation, the names of the planets, names of the great biologists that were in the encyclopedia (Darwin, Lamarck, Cuvier, etcetera) and of the great painters. Soon I was able to recognize the pictures of the planets, and of the biologists and the painters in the encyclopedia. I would parrot their names, as I don't think I could read yet.

Stelios had tuberculosis when he was young which affected both shoulders, so he was not able to lift his arms over his head. He had a unique way of lifting things and pointing because of this. He also could not serve in the war because of his disability, so he was around the house throughout most of my early childhood. It seemed to me that he had the most encyclopedic knowledge and amazing memory among the brothers. He knew about every artist, writer and poet in Greece, and abroad it seemed. He wrote stories and little poems and even had a drawing exhibition in the Bastille.

Stelios' room was next to the dining room and this is where the drawing exhibition was held. His room faced the wall so his window looked towards the small cement courtyard. This was the same courtyard where Joujoukos, the great Resistance hero, had fallen while holding the steak in his mouth. This room was also a bit dark, but this was ideal for the exhibition as it turned out. For this was no ordinary drawing exhibit. It was made up of pen and ink drawings that were caricatures of wartime political figures. I am not sure how many of these caricatures were by his own hand and how many contributed by friends. They satirized mostly the Occupation and the war and were quite cutting. Lots of friends would come around to view the caricatures and comment while the exhibit was running. So, it was just as well it was in a back dark room, so it would not attract much attention. One caricature I remember best. It had amusing profiles of Hitler, Mussolini, Stalin and my mother. The caption read something like 'decisive leaders'. I thought my mother might be mad but she loved it. Everybody thought it was quite funny. Her reputation of being a bit of a dictator was widespread among friends. I remember my father exuding pride over the caricature.

Yianis, the second youngest among my uncles had become a mathematician. I remember less of Yianis than the other uncles during the Occupation in the Bastille. He may have stayed there only part of the time and may already have been working at the University of Salonika. Later he became well-known in mathematics and rose to become president in that Institution. He was always very nice to me but I do not remember being very close to him. He married Toula, who was lovely. Toula also taught Greek literature in high school and was a most favorite aunt. She was a blue-eyed blonde who was always smiling and really nice to me. Toula had a beautiful, trained operatic voice. I loved to hear her sing. She would sing usually after supper. After she had finished I would always ask that she sing another song or aria and she would always oblige. I am not sure if it was during the Occupation that Toula would come to the Bastille regularly or if it was after the war. Toula had studied music and operatic singing at the Odeon in Athens, the premium music school. Much later she had told me that the great opera singer Maria Callas was a classmate of hers in the Odeon and that she used to get better marks in singing than Callas, who apparently was not that good a student.

Maria, who was usually called Litsa, was my mother's first cousin from the island of Zakynthos, where my mother was also born. Litsa was also studying in Salonika but used to visit the Bastille regularly. However, most of her visits were after the Occupation, when Yianis and Toula were already in Salonika. Through her years in Salonika she became very friendly with Yianis and Toula and would always have news about them. Litsa was also a favorite aunt as she was quiet, considerate and self-effacing to an unusual degree for a Greek. She was quite a bit younger than my mother and I felt she was the closest person to my age among the relatives. Litsa was studying biology in Salonika and had become infatuated with a well-known professor in Biology there. This man's name was an alliteration of a common spice. So the adults would often make a pun of it when asking Litsa for an update of the real or imaginary affair. Litsa was always good-humored about it. She would spend endless time gossiping with mother about Professor Spice and what sounded like his multiple love affairs. I was allowed to sit in through much of this gossip, although I did not understand a lot of it. I remember feeling very grown-up when Litsa would visit again and I would ask her if she had any 'spicy' news. She would always smile and include me again in the update. That is also why I liked her so much.

Thales was the youngest of the four brothers. Tall and good looking, and highly personable, he was perhaps my most favorite of the uncles. He had a really easy manner and talked to me as if we were equals, or as if I was grown-up. That is why I liked him so much. He must have liked me a lot too because he became my *nonós* (god-father). As that he had special responsibilities towards me. Thales had finished medical school and had specialized in otolaryngology, so he looked after quite a few children. I had the feeling that my father did not consider Thales to be all that great. A physician in those days was considered to be low down in the pecking order. In this competitive family of highly achieving professionals, a 'doc' was well below a great civil engineer, and even further below a great mathematician. However, it was Thales that often managed to bring home the few essentials during the Occupation. It was what he brought home that probably kept us all from starving. At a time when the currency had totally collapsed there was virtually nothing to be bought. Even hundreds of millions of *drachmas* would buy very little of what little there was to buy. But people would always find a few vegetables, perhaps a few eggs or cheese, to compensate the doctor for his medical service. They would find whatever was needed especially if it was their children who were sick. My recollection is that Thales would continue to bring in food items after the Occupation, during the Civil War and even after that.

Thales had a very close friend, who was a school mate of his in medical school. His name was Abraham and he came from one of the old, well-established Jewish families of Athens. Tall and good looking, like Thales, Abraham also had that confident easy manner and spoke to me on equal terms. So Abraham became a favorite too. I would follow Thales and Abraham around and listen to their endless discussions in the Bastille. A regular important event was when the illegal broadcasts of the BBC news would come on over the short wave radio with the magical little green light. Abraham understood English, French and German better than the rest of the family so he interpreted the crackly broadcast with more confidence. Abraham was fearless and he may have joined the underground but I am not certain. In any case, this would not have been discussed in front of me in case we were arrested and tortured. I remember the discussions when the first news about putting the Jews in camps first started coming out. At least I think I remember the original discussions, but what I remember may have been reinforced in later times. In any case, Abraham and Thales did not believe these first reports.

Thales and Abraham would always round out each other's pronouncements, nodding in agreement as sometimes each completed the other's sentence.

– It makes no sense to waste precious resources in the middle of the War by building camps to exterminate people, isn't that so, Thales?
– … they could have just as easily exterminated them by working them and starving them to death, Abraham.
– For sure, Thales, they could easily starve them to death building autobahns and railways …
– … and munitions factories.
– … and chemical factories.

Everybody in the Bastille seemed to agree that the Nazis were cruel enough to carry out the exterminations of whole populations. But it seemed totally un-German and illogical for the Germans to waste scarce resources to do so. And if there was one thing the Greeks were certain about Germans, it was that the Germans were not illogical.

At one point Abraham came to the Bastille with strange news.

– Some Jews from Salonika are buying tickets for work camps in Germany. They say there is work and food there.

Not too long after the strange news about the Salonika Jews, the normally confident and animated Abraham reappeared in the Bastille looking terrified. Apparently the Gestapo was carrying out systematic arrests of Jews everywhere in Athens, and his family was a well-known one. He was asking us to hide him in the Bastille. Everybody agreed that this was no easy matter. If we were found out, we would be lucky to be just shot and not be tortured before being extinguished. And, of course, I was particularly worried that we would be prime suspects because of the action of the brave Joujoukos. There could be collaborators already targeting us. Plus we were pretty close to starvation ourselves, so feeding another mouth was also a problem.

Just when things started to look really bleak, someone put forward an improbable idea about Abraham. It might have been Thalis. Over the next few days this idea became the focus of discussion in the Bastille. It had to do with *Pyrgos Vassilissis*.

Pyrgos Vassilissis

We were lucky during the great hunger. My father had secured a position as a wine chemist in a large former Royal estate, Pyrgos Vassilissis (Queen's Tower) that was used like the State Experimental Farm. So during the later years of the Occupation we divided our time between the Bastille and Pyrgos. It was a beautiful area, outside of Athens, with wooded hills and farmland. There one could get local vegetables, eggs and honey. There was no meat, and there was a shortage of bread. But compared to the great hunger in the city, it was like a paradise and one could get to it from Athens by bus. However, Pyrgos Vassilissis had been taken over by the German army and one had to go through checkpoints at the entrance and show papers to get into the compound.

The German checkpoints did not prevent relatives and friends to often visit us and stay over at the little country house provided for us. I think the main reason they visited so much was to get a bit more to eat. When they stayed over, there were not enough beds to put them up, so mattresses were put on the floor where they slept, often side-by-side. These sleepovers were my favorite time as it was the closest thing to a party I had experienced. One aunt in particular, Maricha, always made a big fuss of me as she had no children or husband at the time. Maricha was very jolly and entertaining. She lived in an Athens working class district, Kokinia. She was big and plump with reddish hair and had a loud, pleasant laugh. She wore pyjamas for the sleepovers during the winter. It was unusual for women to wear pyjamas then. She would dance and sing on the mattresses in her pyjamas and tell stories and show me how to do shapes with lead that we melted on the coals of the fireplace. Much after the war we heard that Maricha had her first baby when she would have been in her fifties, which was some kind of a record then.

There was another cat that adopted us in Pyrgos Vassilissis who used to come to our little house when we were there. It became my cat in Pyrgos and she would follow me everywhere, but I have forgotten her name. The cat would always be there waiting at the little house for the Greek guards, at the entrance to the estate whenever we came by bus from Athens. We would never see her at the German checkpoint. Initially we thought the cat was there every day, maybe because the guards fed her. But the guards said no. The cat only came on days we were supposed to come and patiently waited. It was puzzling because our schedule was not that regular, although we would always discuss in our little house when we would go back to Athens and when we would return to Pyrgos Vassilissis. The cat would start to rub herself on everybody's legs when these conversations would start. I was of the opinion that the cat understood our conversations. But maybe there was some other clue we left about our return that we were not aware of.

It was at this time, when we were going to-and-fro from Pyrgos that Abraham came to stay with us in the Bastille. The discussion of where to hide him kept up for days. The adults said that there was a risk in hiding him in the Bastille but having to cross the German checkpoint in Pyrgos seemed a greater risk. Yet so many relatives and friends had crossed the checkpoint without any problem. Finally, it was the lack of food in Athens that forced the issue. We took the chance and Abraham was taken to Pyrgos by bus. He crossed the German checkpoint with only a cursory look by the guards of his ID card and papers. He sailed through with the rest of us. This should have been a clue that there was something strange about the Germans at Pyrgos. But I think the adults were so relieved to get Abraham through that they did not bother to discuss why he got through so easily.

A few meters down the gravel road from the German checkpoint, there was the slightly dilapidated little, old Greek guardhouse for the Pyrgos Vassilissis. There were a couple of Greek guards who greeted us. As usual the cat was waiting with the Greek guards.

– She was expecting you, said a guard with a smile.

I looked at the guard. It was unusual to see anyone smiling during the Occupation. So, I asked him.

– How could she know?
– She just knows …

POWs

It was very odd. Inside the Pyrgos compound the Germans had set up a concentration camp. It had barbed wire all around it and wooden housing for the prisoners in the concentration camp. There were a few armed German guards here and there, but the whole operation seemed fairly lax. I would stand outside the barbed wire and the guards did not seem to care. Most of the prisoners were unshaven and in disheveled army uniforms, but seemed very friendly. Some would wave to me and wanted to show me pictures. They were mostly pictures of their kids often my age. A few would have some candy they wanted to give me which they handed to me through the barbed wire. The German guards watched all of this with apparent disinterest and never tried to stop me. They never bothered to speak to the prisoners either. I knew that the prisoners were certainly not Greeks and I figured out they did not speak German. They were Italian soldiers!

I knew that we had been fighting the Italians in the snows of Albania not that long ago and that they were the allies of the Germans. There were lots of ditties ridiculing Mussolini and the Italian invasion that we kids had learned by heart. Also, my father and his brothers had been fighting on that front after all. They had even told the story of how Thales was nearly shot, after the Italians were defeated and the Greeks finally surrendered to the Germans. Thales who was an officer in the Greek Army had decided to keep his pistol side-arm. This was in violation of the terms of surrender which required that all soldiers had to be disarmed. His brothers tried to convince him to give it up, but he objected. He was always full of bluster and pride.

– I am an officer of the Greek Army and the general surrender order does not apply to officers' side-arms, he insisted.

Just then armed German military police on motorcycles whipped up to where Thales was standing with his brothers, shouting and waving their guns. They were enforcing the surrender order. My father and Yianis had said that they thought that Thales would be shot on the spot. But he wasn't. The armed Germans just tore off his pistol from its holster, threw it on the ground and rode off shouting in German. So, why were the Germans being kind to the Greeks while keeping all these Italian soldiers, their Axis allies, in a concentration camp?

At around that time I made a startling discovery. Near the little house we were allotted there were typical farm buildings. There was a large farmyard where a few chickens were wandering about and a large barn. I would often go into the barn and explore. On one side there was farm equipment but most of the barn was taken up with piles of hay, some of it in bales but mostly loose. I loved to climb on the loose hay and lie about and daydream. The cat would often follow me and curl up and purr. No one ever seemed to bother me up there. I was in one of my favorite hiding spots in the loose hay when I suddenly saw them. Unshaven and in untidy uniforms they were unmistakable — two Italian prisoners of war. They looked as if they were from the same bunch that was behind the German barbed wire fence and were offering me candy. I was startled, but they looked absolutely terrified. They did not speak, just looked at me with pitiful eyes. I ran back home as fast as I could and shouted to my parents my discovery.

– Mama, Daddy … there are Italians in the hayloft. I found two Italians in the hayloft.

I was astonished that my parents did not seem surprised. They just looked worried.
It turned out they knew already. They just didn't want anyone to hear.

– Shh, shh! Be quiet.

They explained to me what I had already guessed that these were Italian soldiers who were held as prisoners of war by the Germans and we had to hide them. If the Germans found out that we were hiding their Italian prisoners bad things could happen to us. I do remember wanting to ask how come my father and his brothers were fighting the Italians a little while before and now we were hiding them but I never got the chance. My parents were clearly preoccupied with what to do now. I figured that they would restrict me in the house so I would not go gabbing about my discovery.

But I was really surprised with what my mother next said to me.

– What you have to do is to take food to them.

She was always the decisive one, while my father more or less nodded.

– Food and drink … twice a day. Nobody will suspect you since you are always wandering in and out of the barn.

So, that became my job. I would bring the Italians some bread, cheese, tomatoes and some Pyrgos wine. Occasionally there were a couple of hard boiled eggs. I tried to hide the stuff when I would take it, but no one seemed to pay much attention to me. The Italians did not seem surprised to see me bring them food. They just gobbled it all down while I watched them in silence. They were not talkative like their fellows behind the barbed wire in the concentration camp.

I was very proud of my job. It was the first time in my life that my parents had given me a responsibility, instead of just protecting me. I was taking it very seriously. One problem that I never figured out completely was whether the Italians were good or bad. They certainly seemed good to me, especially the ones in the German concentration camp, who would give candy and show pictures of their kids. So why were my father and my uncles fighting them before? And why did we learn these ditties ridiculing Italy and Mussolini? I remember turning all of this over in my mind but not being able to figure it out. I think that I had some vague notion about them being bad before and being good now, but I am not sure.

Also, I imagined that feeding the Italians was something important I was doing as part of the Resistance during the Occupation. There was no doubt that this was good because everybody said how bad the Occupation was. Also, I had a special feeling of pride that made me feel good, because taking the food was a task I was doing by myself. It was not like the Bastille incident when the incomparable Joujoukos stole the steak, and I was lavished in glory simply by being his master. Here, the Pyrgos cat did not play a part in resisting the Occupation. She would just follow me around to the barn, even more than usual, maybe because she saw or smelled the food I was taking to the Italians. I would actually try to swoosh her off as I did not want to be given away. But she was very persistent, and in any case, she had been following me around before.

After a few days the Italians were gone. I asked my parents but they would not say what had happened to them. It was all very hush-hush and I never saw them again.

Execution

I am not sure if I was actually there for the beginning of this event as I tell it. Perhaps I was told about it enough times that I got to think I was there from the very beginning. But for what followed later, I was most certainly there and I remember vividly what happened. Like it was yesterday.

It all began with an action by a Resistance cell outside the compound of Pyrgos. A German patrol was ambushed and shot, killing several German soldiers. The response to this kind of action was pretty standard during the Occupation. Assuming the Resistance fighters could not be caught, which was the usual case, there was retaliation against the local population in the neighborhood or location where the action happened. It usually went by a standard formula. For every German soldier killed there would be x number of Greek civilians executed. The Resistance would then issue statements that for every Greek executed, x number of Germans would be killed. And so, this horrid little game would go on and on. The German retaliation method was swift and efficient. If the Resistance action was in a densely populated area, there would be a *blockos*, where lightly-armored vehicles and soldiers would isolate the city section in question. Then they would do a house-to-house search and line up mostly men on the street. Often individuals would be asked to step forward and after a cursory questioning, the required number would be executed on the spot. Others would be selected and be taken away, presumably for much worse treatment.

So, the expected thing happened after the Resistance action in Pyrgos. The Germans lined up a whole bunch of Pyrgos workers for the preliminary questioning. This was in front of the administrative buildings and production facilities of Pyrgos. These buildings were on one side of a stone-laid courtyard. They were mostly stone buildings with wooden verandas, maybe built in the late 1800s or early 1900s. I liked these buildings a lot and used to wander through them. There were wine production facilities and other interesting agricultural machines, store rooms and old offices. There was always a nice musty smell about. My father had a little office in those buildings and worked in the production control Labs, mostly for the wine. He also had a supervisory or administrative position in Pyrgos, having a University degree in Agriculture, and would often be found in the little office. I would regularly visit there. On the opposite side of the stone courtyard from the buildings there was a high stone wall, separating the buildings of the compound from the rest of the farm. It was against this stone wall that the workers, mostly farm-hands, were made to line up.

My father was not asked to line up. Presumably the Germans suspected that the workers would be most likely to be associated with the Resistance cell. It seems they thought that the administration would be less likely to be part of the Resistance than the workers. For some reason my mother was also there. Maybe it was by chance or she had heard about the situation and ran over. Our little house was very close by these buildings and she would have run there in a couple of minutes. My father was standing outside looking at the workers lined up. He turned to my mother.

– I am going to line up with the workers.
She started to shout.
– Are you crazy?
– I can't … if they are made to line up, I have to line up, Dinaki.
But she wasn't giving up. She was now screaming at him …
– They will be shooting people in the lineup any minute now! What is the matter with you? In front of your own son … do you want to leave an orphan?

His head fell on his chest and he would say nothing. Of course, he lined up. The thought flashed through my mind that I would become an orphan. Maybe like the ones in Omonia, with the swollen bellies … Then a strange thing happened.

These German soldiers did not follow the usual protocol and shoot the required number of suspects right away. Instead their Officers were saying that they suspected that some of the farm-hands were part of the Resistance cell that had carried out the action against the patrol. I am not sure how the Germans communicated with the Greeks. My parents did not speak much German or English and I doubt the Germans spoke much Greek. Maybe they spoke in French, still the *lingua Franca* in much of Europe. Maybe there was a translator. The discussion went something like this.

– Some of the workers are part of the Resistance. We will take appropriate action to protect German troops.

This was announced by a tall, stern German Officer. He was probably the commander or in charge of security. Well-groomed, with polished black leather boots and belts running across his chest and middle, he was all business.

My father was standing all meek and silent, lined up with the farm-hands against the stone wall. But my mother had somehow managed to get herself in front of the lineup. Her manner had totally changed. She was no longer shouting. Her voice had become calm and reasonable as she spoke to the German officer.

– No, no there are no Resistance people inside Pyrgos.

She sounded very convincing, stretching to her full, plumb height of just under five feet. But the German officer in command was unimpressed.

– We are very suspicious. There are far too many workers in the farm for an operation of this size.

My mother continued in her best soothing voice.

– Well, it is wartime. People are starving. They come here to work for a bit of food and very little pay.
– There is war in Germany too. We would never have that many people for an operation of this size.
– We Greeks, are of course, not as efficient as you Germans …

By then she must have been practically cozying up to the Officer, black eyes all a-flutter, the center of attention. She was always fearless and brimming with confidence in critical situations. She would have barely come up to the chest of the tall German officer, but she had captured the psychological commanding heights. She seemed practically ready to give orders herself — a regular little Greek Hitler!

The German officers continued to show doubt as they continued to discuss the situation among themselves. And then, even more strangely, no order was given to shoot or take away any of the people lined up. Nobody was executed on the spot as was the custom. After more discussion and questioning, the farm hands were allowed to leave the wall and they sheepishly wandered off to their chores. My father went up to my mother who was still talking to several German officers who had by then gathered around her.

These German Officers

Apparently the end result of the conversation between my parents and the German officers was that they decided that it would be a good idea to meet socially. No doubt my mother had managed to convince them. It was meant to build confidence and try to avoid more episodes like this. A few days later, a group of three or four German officers came to our little home in the evening for a social visit. I think it was a week-end. They came to the garden in front of our house and sat down in *chaises longues* and chairs, in an outdoor veranda at the front of the house. My parents and I sat across from them with our backs to the house. It was a beautiful, mild Greek night. Our jasmine vine, intertwined over the little veranda, was in full bloom. A large, bright moon had come out, so the lit kerosene lamps were hardly necessary. The smells of the jasmine vines and other flowers in the garden and the veranda were sweet and delicious. My mother served them wine and nicely arranged local farm-food goodies. Conversation and pleasantries seemed to flow easily, although I did not understand anything that was said. It might have been in French. The radio played music in the house which the Germans seemed to like.

I remember them distinctly going into a relaxing mode. As if by signal, the German officers started to take off their heavy black belts, with their service revolvers in their leather holsters. Then they laid them on a window sill, two or three meters across from where they were sitting on the veranda. It was their way of showing that they were relaxed and being friendly. We were no longer the occupied, nor they the occupiers. They were just German friends visiting and enjoying the beautiful weather and Greek hospitality. It would undoubtedly be like that one day.

Then it started to happen.

Inside our little house, which until then was silent except for the music, there were stirrings. One by one people started to come out and sit in the veranda. They were our usual group of relatives and friends, up as guests for the weekend. Food remained very short in Athens and there was always some farm produce to eat in Pyrgos. Of course, when the German officers first arrived the house guests fell quiet, but as they heard the relaxed conversation and with the Germans putting away their pistols, they figured they could come out and join us on the veranda. Out came Thales, maybe then Stelios and Maritsa was there, I think. Last of all, out came Abraham.

The German officers froze. I was sitting across from them and I could see them throwing furtive glances towards their pistols now on the window sill, separated by Greeks. They probably figured that this was another trap. First, the ambush of the patrol outside of the Pyrgos compound, and now the officers themselves were sweet-talked by the treacherous little woman with the dark eyes into walking into another trap. Should they make a go for their pistols? Were these people coming out of the house armed, or were others with submachine guns inside the house ready to mow them down? The ruthless Greeks were even using a child to trick them into putting their guard down. Shameful!

But, of course, it was not a trap. The relatives and friends took a little wine and picked at the nice goodies as politely as they could, considering they were always starving. Soon the Germans could swallow their saliva again and the polite conversation was reinstated. More wine. The Germans started to relax again. And Abraham spoke German — fluent German. Conversation became very animated. Later on that evening and for the next few days, I found out what the conversation was about and why it had become so animated. It was politics they were talking about — wartime politics. And these Greeks, mostly leftists, and these Germans were agreeing! What could possibly be the subject of agreement? Hard to believe, but it was Hitler. These Germans were adamant about it.

– Hitler had to go!

The Greeks could only nod in amazement. They tried to broaden the discussion, but the Germans stuck to the topic.

– The conduct of the war was unprofessional under Hitler.
– He and the Nazis were leading Germany and Europe through a disastrous course.
– Germany had a great deal to offer Europe, but it was not Hitler and not Nazism.
And as for the Gestapo, they were worse than pigs.
– They should all be shot.
– Professional officers should conduct the war and settle the peace.
– The Gestapo would most certainly never be allowed into Pyrgos Vassilissis. Not if they valued their pig-like lives.

The Germans stayed on quite late and left in an apparently excellent mood, with my mother making sure they had all picked up their belts and pistols.

In the ensuing days there was much discussion in the house as to who were these Germans that occupied Pyrgos Vassilissis. It was known that the German operation in Pyrgos had primarily to do with communications. A little later my parents said that they had found out that Pyrgos served as a major wartime communications center for the Near and Middle East. But the command, what was the command? Who gave permission to these Germans to talk like that about the Fuhrer without fear? The name Rommel had been mentioned, but we did not know exactly what that meant at the time. One important matter was that the Gestapo was not allowed in. It turned out Abraham was hiding in a key centre for German communications and happily circulated among the German army officers. It was probably the safest place in Europe for him to hide. It was the Gestapo that really hunted the Jews and they were not allowed in. These Germans probably could not care less what he was. This is likely the reason for the cursory check of papers when he went through the German army checkpoint, in spite of Abraham's name. And that is probably why we saw the paradox of German officers, who were possibly conservative and nationalist, and a leftist Greek Jew agreeing in politics, especially on the disposal of Hitler, right in the middle of the war.

Later in the Occupation we lost track of Abraham. It was thought he had joined the Resistance, where he likely had connections before. During the Civil War some said he went to the Soviet Union and then possibly to Israel. By joining the Resistance, I guess, his chance of survival would have been the same as any other Greek that joined. A little different chance than the conservative, ghettoized Salonika Jews, that he so often talked about, some of whom had even bought one way train tickets to Auschwitz!

We also lost track of the German Officers and the men who worked in Pyrgos Vassilissis. I have often wondered how many of them would have survived the war.

Anemones

In the spring time Pyrgos was beautiful. The rolling hills were covered with pine, with little valleys and openings full of aromas of wild thyme, myrtle and dozens of the other wild herbs and flowers of Attica. Honey bees and butterflies were everywhere. My mother would often take me for a walk from our little house into the hills and valleys. We would find a little spot near the pines on a hill and watch the movement in the valley. They would move like ancient animals, crawling along the side and bottoms of the valleys, turning around and then changing directions again. They had greenish or brown colors that seemed to match the countryside. These were German tanks on maneuvers.

We would sit and watch them, it seemed, for hours on end. Sitting with my mother close by I felt very safe. We were never bothered by the Germans who were generally directing the maneuvers from the other side of the hill. One could make them out in their uniforms and military, capped hats, watching the tank maneuvers through binoculars. The tanks would seem to move in different ways, depending on what the vegetation and terrain was like. Just past the edge of the pine forest it was mostly wild scrubs, aromatic herbs and green grasses. There, the tanks would seem to go up and down, mostly bumpety-bump. As they went further down into the more level valley the tanks would enter the seas of wild flowers — reds, purples and whites. And there the tanks would seem to float.

The seas of wild flowers were mostly anemones. My mother loved the anemones. The sound of saying 'anemones' resonates more pleasantly in my ear when it is pronounced in Greek. *Anemónes* may be derived from *ánemos*, the wind, like flowers of the wind or maybe because the petals of anemones are taken so easily by the wind. When my mother would say it she would pronounce it by lengthening the 'o' like *Anemóónes*, making the sound of the flower seem more exotic, more beautiful and mysterious. I think she liked to see the spectacle of spring colors, the sea of flowers. For me it was different. I loved the individual flowers, but not so much the red colored ones, which are like poppies, and are often called *paparounes*. The *paparounes* covered fields in red color, which I thought were rather common looking from close up. The *Anemónes* always created a special feeling in me. But I was very fussy about the kind of anemones I really loved. These were the blue or blue-purple varieties. When I looked really close up, by lying down and putting my eyes close to a flower, I could imagine the world become magical. I don't know why I loved this color so much. I think I would sometimes dream that color and when I woke, I wanted to fall asleep again so I could dream that color again. But most often I could not. I was given a set of coloring pencils and my favorite coloring was when I mixed blue and purple, and I managed to make it look like the color of my blue or blue-purple anemones.

There is an old black and white photograph where my mother is pointing towards something and I am attentively looking in the distance. After the war she had said that she was pointing out the German tanks on maneuvers. Perhaps it was spring time and the fields were full of anemones and poppies and aromatic shrubs and herbs. I imagine that my father must have taken the picture, but I do not remember him being there.

The other favorite season for me was the autumn. Although, I liked all of the seasons, it was the smells of the earth that were most intense in autumn, and often in the winter, that I remember so well from my childhood. The colors in the Greek autumn were muted yellows, and fallen leaves would cover the wet earth but usually not form a thick ground canopy. The smells of the earth … why were they so intense? It is difficult to describe in words the smell of the Greek earth as I remember it, in its almost aromatic mustiness. It seemed to continue even as I wandered through the paths of Pyrgos, and not fade from my consciousness. Even a light rain, just glistening in the mosses, the barks and the yellow leaves, seemed to bring it out even more. And it would persist and persist and never be lost during my adventures. The smell of the earth would change, as I passed through pine trees, thyme and oregano bushes and other herbs whose names I do not recall. But underneath there was always a consistency in this almost addictive, deep smell of the earth.

There were many temptations that could make me stray to the fields of Pyrgos. Beautiful butterflies, insects of all descriptions, trees with great hollows and rocks with strange mosses. But one of my favorites was the beehives. There was a full beehive colony in Pyrgos with an older beekeeper and a couple of young assistants. My father would also show up frequently among the beekeepers. He taught them about scientific bee-keeping although he had never kept bees. But he was the educated Agriculturist and everybody listened carefully. They were all dressed with beekeeper hats from which fine netting came down to protect their faces. They had the smoke generators so they could blow smoke, clear out the bees and lift the covers of the hives to inspect inside. Occasionally they would be stung on their hands but not too often. Initially I too would wear the beekeepers protective gear, but the bees still bit me on my hands and arms. But it did not bother me. The adults thought this was peculiar. It did not bother me at all, and soon I would not wear the headgear protection. Unless I was very close to the beehives, the beekeepers would then make me wear the head gear. It was not unusual for me to have four or five bites when I was near the beehives, sometimes more than that. Then one day I got bitten by a giant bumble bee. I was emboldened because the bee bites did not bother me and got very near the bumble bee while it was buzzing around a beautiful blossom and tried to play with it. I had a terrible reaction with my arm going all red and awful. When I got stung a second time by a bumble bee, I got a similar kind of reaction. So, I learned to stay away from bumble bees.

In the fields of Pyrgos we would sometimes see rabbits in the fields. I think they were mostly hares. Soon after I learned how to write, I wrote a story about a little hare. I cannot remember the exact period when I wrote the story, but it might have been after the Occupation, as we continued to go to Pyrgos for some years after. I am sure the little rabbit was in Pyrgos and played in the fields of the anemones, but I no longer have the story. I thought it was a very long story because I wrote it over many, many days. Each day I would write a few lines, I think, but it would be about something different that the little rabbit would have done. These were all the adventures that the little hare had. I colored the book with my favorite color, which was a deep blue-purple. But the hare was white (maybe it was a rabbit disguised as a hare). The story starts with this good little rabbit at a time when there was a war between rabbits and dogs. The little rabbit wanted to be a soldier but found it too hard and too tiring, so he had to rest and soon fell asleep.

My mother for many years after would like to relate the story to me and anyone else who would listen. She would be very proud that her son had written a story at such a young age. She would say that the story was actually about me, because this is how I was in real life — frantically play, play, play, work, work, work and then fall asleep in happy exhaustion. My father, as usual for these types of conversations, would not say much and just smile and look admiringly at my mother.

The version of the story that survives was finished on September 11, 1947, but I cannot remember when it was started. I think I recall that most of the elements of the story were from an older version written by me when I was much younger in Pyrgos. It was typed by my mother, I think from my handwriting. For this typed version she must have made suggestions, considering the words and phrases used.

– What a good little rabbit this is, Tasouli.
– Yes Mamaka.
– And he does not go to play where he is not supposed to.
– No Mamaka.

~

I was not allowed to stray from the trodden paths and play in the fields.
But I had seen them.
I had seen them from afar and seen them close by.
Boys who were thin from hunger, with listless eyes.
Never begging, just looking, always looking.

Anastassiades

They were staring at me walking.
They were staring at me walking with those eyes.
Why were they looking on how I walked?
Never resentful, nor threatening they went on looking.
In the fields and valleys that I was not allowed to go.
They were looking for scraps left by the Germans, bits of metal.
Old or broken parts, broken off from a vehicle or tank.
Anything, anything they could use or sell.
And they hobbled about, some on a rough-looking crutch.
Supporting the stump of a leg.
Some had learned to work with one arm.
And you could see the stump of the other.
It was the mines.
Everything was mined.
The valleys and fields were mined.
Even ploughed fields were mined.
My mother had said so.

– Why are the boys without arms, without legs in the fields, Mamaka?
– They should not have been allowed to go.
– But, Mama, they are still in the fields. You said there were mines there.
– They are ignorant, from ignorant families.

My mother made me unhappy. She would upset me when she talked like that. The boys in the fields were from ignorant families. They got punished. But then, I had two arms and two legs. I was not from an ignorant family.

Montessori

During the latter part of the Occupation I went to kindergarten or pre-school. I don't remember the exact dates, but it was in 1943 and part of '44 I think. I think my father still had a connection in Pyrgos, but this pre-school was in central Athens, maybe in Kolonaki, or nearby. The school was run by a family of very serious educationalists, who were close friends of my parents. Their name sounded a little like rabbit in Greek and I named them the Laggi′ — the hares. I thought they actually behaved like rabbits. They were serious, but kindly, totally dedicated to the task at hand: to educate very young children by the best educational methods and equipment available. The Laggi′ also looked a bit like rabbits. They were chubby, with rabbit-like faces and noses. When they talked they would make little downward motions to discover this by ourselves — through structured play. I remembered how I suffered. Mostly from boredom. I could not get uneven rectangular-shaped pegs to fit into boards with polygonal holes.

The chief Mr. Laggós was examining me very thoughtfully in front of my parents.

– He is very advanced in concepts, you know.

Mrs. Laggina was agreeing equally thoughtfully, making little rabbit motions with her head.

– Oh yes, you can see he is conceptually advanced.

The chief Mr. Laggós was now exuding quiet gravitas.

– Of course the family environment is terribly important in spatial conceptualization.

Mrs. Laggina was not to be outdone. She was now nodding and smiling, as she chorused in.

– Terribly! You know, terribly!

The toy board really looked expensive. I now think it was probably made in Italy, or Germany, maybe France. Of course, I would have higher conceptualization coming from such a family of such close friends and, of course, I should have a more advanced toy.

After a few unsuccessful tries, I jammed the polygonal peg in question into a hole of my liking and I hammered it in with another peg, when no one was looking. The rabbits inspected the result, making little rabbit movements. Their continued silence was annoying. No one slapped my hand or told me off for nearly destroying the expensive educational toy. That was *verboten*! No, instead the educationalists had to figure out how to induce this barbaric child to self-educate. They brought to me a much simpler toy board. Mrs. Laggina was very thoughtful now.

– You might be more interested in these shapes and concepts.

They kept using that word 'concepts'. I had no idea what concepts meant, but I was not going to ask. I knew that I had been downgraded, and only one of the Laggos was paying attention to me now.

Things were definitely improving! I promptly tried again to jam what was now a clearly square peg into the round hole of my preference. I had hidden my jamming instrument and it came in handy. I got a feeling of satisfaction when I finally jammed the peg in. Mrs. Laggina took the board away. She went to the other side of the classroom and I could see her trying to un-jam the peg. She couldn't.

~

I had another early educational experience outside the Public School system. It was music lessons. I can't be certain that they took place entirely during the period of the Occupation and they may well have extended after that.

My father's first cousin was George Tzanetakis. He was also a favorite uncle of mine and he was married to Ellie, also a favorite. Ellie had a sister Chrysoula, who taught music professionally. Chrysoula was also a professional smoker and spinster. Since just about everybody smoked in those days, she must have smoked a lot to have made an impression. She smoked incessantly. I think she was also a bit nervous or neurotic. Various attempts had been made to find a suitable match for Chrysoula but all to no avail. She was unmarriageable. But I think she liked me a lot and I liked her, at least initially. My parents said that Chrysoula had an excellent reputation as a music teacher. The problem was that Chrysoula was also made fun of by the family at large. I think she was an easy target mostly because of her neuroses and behavior. So, I would go to see Chrysoula in the Tzanetakis home for my piano lessons with mixed messages. I quickly discovered that Chrysoula was no disciplinarian. There were lots of heavy curtains and old furniture in the Tzanetakis home and I would quickly find one of my favorite hiding places, while Chrysoula would try to recover from the stress of trying to teach me by having a cigarette. Since she practically chain-smoked, most of my allotted time with her was spent in games of hide-and-seek, rather than the music lesson.

I don't think Chrysoula ever told my parents what a little brat I was, and if I did mention the hide-and-seek games (which I do not remember if I did) I was never disciplined for it. After all, it added to the amusing repertoire of stories about Chrysoula. Also, had not my parents' Montessorian friends, the all-knowledgeable rabbits, unequivocally decreed that the only permissible way to teach a child was through structured play? Chrysoula surely was not a Montessorian, at least not a real one. If she would have been, making fun of her would simply not have been permitted. So, I never actually learned to either read or play music.

Gianakis

I did not have many friends to play with. But occasionally Gianakis and his family would come to visit in Pyrgos. Gianakis and I were similar in many respects. We were the same age, the same height and had some of the same attitudes. We still see each other from time to time. Gianakis' mother, Poupa, was a classmate of my father's at the University in Athens in Agriculture. It was unusual for girls to enter that field in those days and I think she was either the only girl or one of very few in the class. But that qualified Gianakis to play with me. I thought Gianakis was the pushiest kid I ever met. He was confrontational about everything. Worse still, he seemed to have no clue that he was that way. On the other hand, I think I was getting used to having my own way. More or less. Gianakis was totally impervious to anything I would say or any suggestions I would have about the games we would play. We would often fight. Fight as hard as kids of our age could. I would get upset after these scraps. Never Gianakis. It was as if nothing had happened. As if we never had the fight.

One day in Pyrgos we were walking and play-fighting on a byway in a countrified area lined with tall trees. It was autumn and the yellow leaves covered this wide path or road. I have a distant memory of an old cistern, made from ancient stones, with mosses on them, nearby. There was nobody else around. Gianakis was being particularly obnoxious. As usual, a fight broke out. I think we started to wrestle and then throw stones at each other, at close quarters, but neither of us had been injured. Nobody really won either, but Gianakis, as was his habit, behaved with total disregard about our fight and was going on as if nothing had happened. I was certain I was right over whatever it was we fought over, and he was wrong. Maybe I had got the worse of that fight, although we were usually pretty even. Being even would make me also angry. There should be a winner and a loser. It was just not fair, particularly since he was wrong, wrong, wrong! A rage came over me. I could not see clearly and it felt like a curtain came down over my eyes. I had never felt that absolute, overwhelming, nothing-else-mattered kind of rage. Gianakis was impervious to my rage which made it worse. I was totally driven by the immense rage. I resolved to kill Gianakis. I was going to kill him good and do it right on the spot.

Since the rock fight with smaller stones did not settle matters, I looked for the biggest boulder I could find. Gianakis was no longer interested in stones and was looking at something else that had absolutely nothing to do with the matter in hand. I found the stone I wanted near the cistern. It was wide and flat, old, moss-covered and very big. This would surely kill Gianakis. The stone was so big I could barely lift it. In order to kill Gianakis good, I had to lift this huge, flat stone over my head which would flatten Gianakis. I got it over my head and ran towards Gianakis. By the time I got near him my arms were hurting. All I had to do now was throw the stone, which was still over my head, and I would flatten him like a bug. I gave one mighty last effort. I let go my Cyclopean rock, but my arms by then were too weak and they never moved much from being over my head. The stone landed squarely on top of my head. It split my scalp, and my eyes were instantaneously covered with a curtain of red. Except, this time it was my blood. Gianakis regarded me with mild disinterest. I don't remember any pain. Just not being able to see too well, because of the blood, and maybe feeling a slight sense of dejection. I said I wanted to go home, which we did, he never commenting, either then or subsequently. As far as I could tell he never carried any malice, feeling of victory, gloating or just even saying that I deserved to have my head split. I had just happened to split my head in the normal course of events. Nothing had changed between him and me as far as he was concerned, or so it seemed. This was the first time I ever had a major split on my scalp, causing blood to pour out.

Thief

This story, from an earlier time in Pyrgos Vassilissis, almost seems to be coming out of a mist, but the location and events are very distinct in my mind. I am sure it took place at an earlier time than the Execution or German Officers stories. We had not yet moved to the little cottage in Pyrgos, with the garden in front and the jasmine vine, where the German Officers sat on that magical, moonlit night. This earlier house in Pyrgos was much bigger, and had two levels. We lived on the upper level. There were stone stairs going up the back of the house to the second floor. The structure looked impressive from a distance. It was made from white-looking stone, or was whitewashed, and there were some neo-classical columns in the building, supporting balconies of the second floor. There were big verandas on the ground level. But the ground level seemed big and vacuous and I don't think it was inhabited. It was used as storage for supplies. Staples like grain and olive oil were stored there and I think it was guarded. A number of farm workers were always around doing various jobs. They would frequently go in and out of the ground storage level, carrying heavy sacks on their backs or on wheelbarrows. Around the house the soil had been cleared a long time ago and turned into flat fields of hard level clay, probably old threshing fields. There was a solitary tree that had been allowed to stand on the thrashing fields around the house. It was an old tree, probably an oak or a plane tree. From a distance the house looked majestic and the tree stood out.

My father was the boss or supervisor of all of the farm hands milling about. They were a rough-looking lot — uneducated, thin and sinewy and with hungry eyes. They seemed to follow whatever orders my father gave them, but mostly they seemed to have their own tasks and went about their business.

One morning the farm hands had caught a thief. He was prowling around at night, they said, trying to get into the storage area where grain and olive oil were kept. He was brought around the thrashing fields, with his hands tied up behind his back with a heavy rope. He also had some kind of a noose around his neck with the same rope. The rope was white and seemed very strong and wide to me, twined from knitted kemp. The thief had old blue overalls and a dirty ragged shirt. He was thin, dirty and unshaven — like the farm hands, but worse. There was talk among the farm hands of how he should be punished. In the end, he was tied up to the tree on the thrashing fields. The rope went many times around his body and the noose was left around his neck. I never heard him say anything. Finally, the farm hands went and got my father to decide on the punishment of the thief. I was very afraid that I would have to see what they would do to the thief. But on the other hand, if my father was ordering the punishment for the thief what he did must have been very bad. I knew he tried to steal grain or oil because he was very hungry. My mother, who would normally cover my eyes from seeing bad things, never even tried to get me off the thrashing fields or send me inside. Of course there was no point calling the police. They were mostly pro-Nazi and, in any case, not likely to bother to come into the Compound for simple thievery. And if the thief had been with the Resistance and they recognized him, or if he was on their list, that would likely be the end of him. The farm hands were very obedient in whatever my father told them to do. While he was telling them, they would all bow slightly to him in acknowledgment of his superior authority. They would address him in the plural, while he would talk to them in the singular. The thief was beaten with the rope for a very long time. The farm hands took turns because it was tiring. He remained tied up to the tree in the thrashing fields during the beating. He never made a sound. He never cried. He was left tied up on the tree during the night. In the morning I did not see him. He was gone and the farm hands were going about their business. I asked what happened to the thief. Nobody would tell me.

Barbarians

At that earlier time in Pyrgos, when we lived on the upstairs floor of the two-storey house, we were often visited by a bachelor. He always came on his own from Athens on the bus. I have now forgotten his name, although it was a familiar name to me for decades after. He was a typical bachelor of that era. Although resources were meager and the hunger had not subsided, he always maintained a distinct propriety and a civilized old-world behavior. I think he visited regularly because one could get a little more to eat in Pyrgos than in Athens, but he never showed any hunger. He was invariably well-dressed as befitting a middle-aged to older gentleman of the time. I remember him mostly visiting in the winter. A nice old tweed jacket, with leather patches on the elbows, a matching knitted vest and tie, and cuffed trousers from good material, and shined leather shoes were his uniform. He smoked a pipe. I remember his pipe well. It was curved, made of beautiful shining wood, older and comfortable — just like the bachelor himself. The aroma of the tobacco he lit in the pipe was beautiful. None of my family, or other people I knew, smoked a pipe. It was all cigarettes. But the bachelor emanated this wonderful musky, reassuring smell not just from his pipe but from his tweed and, it seemed, his being. His speech was the same. He spoke in quiet modulated tones, a little unusual for a Greek. He used only the *Demotic* Tongue, never getting into the curlicues and the difficult to understand phrases of *Katharevousa*. And he used it simply and beautifully. I understood everything he said, even when he was speaking to my mother and father about all kinds of topics. His manner and speech were just very reassuring to me and I loved it. But we all liked the bachelor a lot, especially my mother who would always make a fuss over him and always tried to serve him a little extra food. He would always eat it correctly and slowly, never permitting the food to take precedence over the conversation.

The bachelor was some type of literary man. I am not sure what exactly he did for a living. During the Occupation, of course, with jobs dwindling right down, literary types especially had very little work that they would actually get paid for. But literature flourished. Some of the best poetry and prose in Modern Greek was written during that period. I could not read or really understand poetry or literary prose at that age, but I was already used to the rhythm of poetry. My Uncle Stelios, in particular, who was the most literate of the four brothers, would often read poetry in the Bastille. One of his most favorite poets was Kostís Palamás, whose poems had beautiful diction, economy of phrase and a deep romanticism. A number of the Palamas poems had a theme related to individual or collective freedom, and were very popular during the Occupation. Some readings by Palamas were even public, and it was apparently touch and go where there would be massive arrests. Another favorite of Stelios was Constantíne Caváfis. I liked listening to Stelios reciting poetry from the whole anthology of Greek poetry, often from memory, even though I did not understand a lot of it. Palamás seems to hardly be known now among young Greeks I have talked to. George Sefe´ris and Odysseus Ely´tis, both of whom have been awarded Nobel prizes in literature, are justifiably widely lionized now. They were less popular in the Bastille household during the Occupation, if my memory serves correctly, even though Sefe´ris was born and grew up in Smyrni.

But our bachelor in Pyrgos also read or recited poetry from many poets. It would often be done after dinner, I think around a small coal fire in the winter. Maybe we had some chestnuts or toasted a little bread. The bachelor would always light his curved pipe during these occasions, which added to the wonderful smells in the house. There were many poets whose poems the bachelor read during his visits to Pyrgos. But there is one, above all else, that made an indelible impression on me. It is by Caváfis and it is called 'Waiting for the Barbarians'.

I can't say that Caváfis was overwhelmingly popular during the Occupation and it is difficult also for me to explain the apparent resurgence of his popularity nowadays. There are many, many translations of his poems into English, and they keep coming. Almost everybody that has read Cavafis is fascinated by him, especially if they can read him in Greek. I have read in prefaces of his poems that Cavafis translates really well into English and because his themes are so universal, he crosses languages easily. His poetry has certainly some modern themes, including some beautiful poems that are clearly homosexual. I remember not long ago in an English second hand bookshop I picked up a volume called 'Modern Greek Poetry: From Caváfis to Elytis'. It was by the excellent Greek translator and commentator, Kimon Friar. The bookseller, seeing the title, told me that "he shared the sentiments of Caváfis". I was sure he meant the gay sentiments of Cavafis. I did not answer him, because I got mad at his comment, which I considered ignorant, and I did not think he deserved an answer. On the other hand, maybe our ever-so traditional, encyclopedic bachelor of Pyrgos was also gay. But few would dispute that Cavafis is much more than just 'a gay poet'. If there were to be one word, and there isn't, that categorizes his poetry one might say that he is a poet of despondency. A sense of mourning of that which has been lost is the main theme that runs through so many of his poems. Yet his sly humor keeps popping up in little unexpected turns. The more one rereads Cavafis, the more one discovers. Born in Alexandria and going back to die there, having spent long periods in England, he has something to say about the decline of something of value that was, more clearly and yet more indirectly than any poet that I certainly know. And that something of value was Hellenism itself. Cavafis has reputedly referred to the destruction of Smyrni as "the destruction of the Race". Some think he meant the Ionian Race and, thus, the destruction of the last real remnant of Hellenism.

Of course, as a young child I would not have known or understood much or any of this. So why would the Barbarians of Cavafis make such an impression on me? After all, the bachelor read many poems and yet this one became my absolute favorite. I would ask him to read it every time he came and once he read it, I would insist that he would read it over again. My parents have told me that I was too young to pronounce properly τους βαρβάρους του Καβάφη (the barbarians of Kavafi) and I would say τους βαβάρους του Βαφή (the babarians of Vafi).

After "the babarians of Vafi" had been read a couple of times I was happy and ready to go to bed. Some nights after I had gone to bed I would stay awake repeating in my mind the rhythm of the Barbarians. I could imagine the scarlet embroidered togas, the amethyst-studded bracelets and the glistening emeralds of the poem, all in beautiful colors.

I would lapse into a conversation with myself. And a Voice would say:

– Hey Tasouli, you were there.
– But the barbarians did not come. They are no more.
– It does not matter, they will come again.
– Will it be a long time?
– No, not too long, Tasouli.
– Will they come when we have freedom?
– For sure, when the Occupation ends.
– And will there be psomaki to eat?
– Oh, yes. Lots of psomaki. Lots of psomaki, Tasouli!

Civil war

Insurgents

My recollection of the end of the Occupation was that it came quite suddenly. I cannot remember how many days after the Germans had pulled out of Athens that the Resistance fighters appeared, but it did not seem very long. I have tried to avoid reading accounts of the events at the start of the Civil war, so that my childhood memories would not be influenced too much. At Liberation, I do not remember much in the way of celebrations in Athens or rejoicing in the Bastille. Maybe the adults knew better what was happening in Greece and were preoccupied by events.

My first memory of this period was our house being occupied by the Insurgents. This I remember very well. They had taken over nearly all of Athens. They were victorious; they had fought hard all through the Resistance and they had won. Their attitude was confident and they radiated this. Many of them had beards and uniform-like clothes, with belts full of bullets crossed on their chest. They were quite young mostly. They were also very polite. They invariably addressed my parents and my uncles and, of course Yiayia Sophia, in the plural. More polite than the young people one met in Athens. They said they were mostly from villages from different parts of Greece and had joined the Resistance during the Occupation. I told them about Joujoukos' exploits and they smiled and said they had not heard of a cat joining the Resistance before.

The reason they occupied the Bastille was that they said it was in a strategic spot, although I did not think so. It was pretty well in the middle of a small street in Pagrati. But maybe the flat terrace over the top level, above where the Colonel lived, gave them a good view. From there you could see a great distance all around. I would often go up the winding iron staircase, which went up the back of the house to the rooftop terrace. I often wanted to go up there to watch the sunrise, but most of the time I would not succeed as I would not wake up in time. The few times I did it, was unbelievably beautiful. The fresh clean smells of eucalyptus, pine and the Attic earth still permeated Athens then.

The Insurgent boys never came into the house proper. They had set up in the hallway and I think they also had a lookout on the rooftop terrace. In the hallway they had laid down their sleeping blankets, all neatly folded during the day, their guns and ammunition. A large machine gun had been set up in the front of the hallway. They seemed to have their own supplies of food, but they got water from the tap at the back in the garden. I think there was a small toilet in the front of the house, near the hallway which they used, making sure they closed an intermediate door, so we were not disturbed. From time to time Kyra Maria and Yiayia Sophia would make extra orzo pasta with tomato and olive oil and offer a few servings to the Insurgent boys. After a few polite refusals, they would gobble it all down, with all the country thanks and complements mostly to Yiayia Sophia.

Prisoners

The Insurgents thought they had essentially won the war in Greece. Virtually all of Athens was under their control and they had massive popular support. They also thought that they had the full material and military support of the victorious Soviets. But it was not so. Behind the scenes Stalin, Churchill and Roosevelt had made a secret deal. Greece was not to join the rest of Eastern Europe and become part of the Soviet sphere of influence. It was to stay with the West. So, British forces landed in the port of Pireus. Their orders were to engage the partisans and prevent Greece from going Communist. After the British landed with a massive force, at the end of the Occupation, there was a period of relative quiet and then heavy fighting broke out throughout Athens.

I do not remember hand-to-hand fighting in our street, but one could hear guns and explosions close and far. Some of the Partisans were wounded. I do not remember any dead ones being brought back to the Bastille, but the lightly-wounded ones all came back. Thales mostly took care of them, cleaning the wounds and putting dressings on. The first-aid station was our main bathroom, where there was running cold water. At least, there was most of the time. We always had to boil water in the little gaziera to wash the wounds. Then, patched up, the Insurgent boys would go out to fight some more.

I can't be sure how long the Insurgents occupied our house but it was quite a few weeks, maybe months. As the fighting intensified and the Insurgents had brought their wounded for treatment, they also brought to the Bastille a small group of captured British prisoners. I think they were all officers, who came with tattered uniforms, but still very British. They were also lightly wounded. They were brought in the first-aid station — main bathroom. A couple, I recall, had superficial face wounds that had more or less dried up.

I was assigned special responsibility for those with the facial wounds. The reason was that I was the razor-boy. Safety razors were available then in Greece, but with the years of occupation, it was difficult to find new razor blades. So, razor-boy's job was to sharpen used safety razor blades. It is a skilled job. One needs a drinking glass with a cylindrical shape. The safety razor blade is put inside, more or less flat against the inside of the glass and then slightly angled, so the edge of the blade is against the glass. Then using the index, and maybe the middle finger depending on the size of the glass and one's hand, the blade is moved from edge-to-edge against the glass, which gradually sharpens it. If one persists in using just one glass, then the inside of the glass becomes a bit rough with repeated use, which helps with the sharpening. Ultimately one has a pretty decent safety razor blade again for a good clean shave. And a good clean shave was essential under the circumstances. What else would a lightly wounded British officer, who had the misfortune of being taken prisoner, want more than a good shave and a wash, so he would not appear scruffy to his captors? So, I stood beside the English officers, sharpening their safety razor. They seemed to be familiar with this trick and showed me how to improve my technique. We provided the soap and the shaving brush, and water was boiled for them. Then, my most important task was done and I was able to watch the British prisoners shave. They all seemed very tall to me, with their heads practically touching the low bathroom ceiling. However, this was a most excellent vantage point from which I could observe if my sharp safety razor blade was getting too close to the wounds on their face. I had to be especially vigilant as they shaved under their chin and their throats. They could not see under their chin and their throats too well because they were too tall for the mirror over the sink. If it looked dangerous, I would warn them with a tug on their uniform, and the shaving went well, without further trauma. The Brits looked quite happy and I was rewarded with some British candies. They were harder, and less sweet than what I was used to. But they were very flavorful and tangy.

These British prisoners had their own smells. They smelled of nice tobacco and other unusual musty smells none of them unpleasant. Their smells were closer to my bachelor in Pyrgos and different than the Italian prisoners in Pyrgos, who smelled mostly of sweat, inside the barbed wire. In later years I came across the same smell among the Londoners. The English were not as talkative as the Italian prisoners, but they were very pleasant. They smiled after having told me something, which I generally would not understand and which they would repeat and smile again. I suppose they were telling me little jokes or making amusing comments or else they were trying to speak to me in Greek, which I also did not understand with their funny accents.

I am not sure how long the British prisoners stayed in the Bastille. I think it was just a few days. Most likely they slept in the hallway with their captors, the Insurgents. And like the Insurgent boys, the British were very polite. And politely and quietly one day the Insurgent boys approached my Uncle Thales.

    – Mr. Thales, excuse us.
    – Yes, what would you like boys?
    – Mr. Thales, we have received orders.
    – Orders?
    – Yes, Mr. Thales. Orders from headquarters.
    – What orders, boys?
    – Excuse us, Mr. Thales, but we will have to execute the English prisoners.
    – What in the world for?
    – For retaliation, Mr. Thales.
    – Retaliation?

– The English have executed some of our boys, Mr. Thales.
– But we don't do these things, we are not Barbarians!
– No, Mr. Thales, we are not Barbarians.
– And you are supposed to represent the people — you are our popular Resistance.
– Yes, Mr. Thales, we are the popular Resistance.
– Then you can't execute prisoners, boys.
– No, Mr. Thales, we can't execute prisoners. Excuse us, Mr. Thales. Headquarters said we have had hundreds of casualties. And tortures of our people. And executions.
– But the commanders at the headquarters are supposed to be communists and we are all to be working to build a better society. We can't start a new society with executions of prisoners, can we now boys?
– No, Mr. Thales, we cannot start like this.
– How can the commanders call themselves communists, with orders like this? The British are our allies to fight fascism. It is outrageous, you cannot just shoot them. I will not allow it! I looked after you all.
– Yes, Mr. Thales. You looked after us very well when we were wounded. We will not shoot them, Mr. Thales.
– Good. You are talking sense now.
– We will decapitate them, Mr. Thales. These are our orders, Mr. Thales.
– Decapitate them?
– Yes, Mr. Thales. To save bullets. We are all running short of ammunition.
– You can't decapitate prisoners in our home. In the Bastille!
– No, Mr. Thales, we cannot decapitate them in your home. That would be impolite. We will decapitate them in the garden.

I knew exactly how the Insurgent boys would decapitate the English prisoners. They would use a long knife, like my father had brought back from the front. It had the wooden sheath like a long pen-knife. Now I knew what the wooden sheath was for. It was to hold the knife to cut their throats first and then for the rest of the decapitations. Maybe it was even the same knife that my father had brought back from the war. I wondered if the heads of the English would still look clean-shaven, on the ground in our back garden.

A couple of days later the British prisoners were gone from the Bastille. The Insurgent boys did not seem to know what happened to them. I checked a few times in our little back garden, walled all around as it was, but I could not find any English heads.

The spanking

During the beginning of the civil war, when the fighting was heavy in the streets of Pagrati and the rest of Athens, I was not allowed to go out. Even the Insurgent boys, camped in the corridor of the Bastille, would tell me to go inside. But during the lulls in the fighting, some lasting only a couple of hours and some much longer, I could hear other kids in the street and I badly wanted to go outside and play with them. So I devised an escape strategy. I knew if I went out of our front door, through the corridor, the Insurgent boys would almost certainly tell my mother. Going out in the garden was of no help, because of the wall all around it. To go out on the street, I would have to go through the front door. But there was one other possibility. It was to go out through one of the front windows facing the street. The street sloped, more or less from North to South I think, and the way the Bastille was built, on the slope, the windows facing the front were some height from street level, even though we were on the first floor.

However, there was a little ledge on the outer Bastille wall, maybe half a meter from the street level. The ledge also sloped down, more or less parallel with the street. So I figured if I could climb out a front window, I could hang onto the outside of the flat window sill and reach the ledge with my feet, from where I could jump onto the sidewalk of the unpaved street. What made it easier was that the window sills were often made from a marble slab in Greek homes of the period. The construction of the Bastille was no exception. The marble slabs were often used for flower pots, although there were no flower pots on the marble slab of the bedroom window facing the street. Now the marble slab protruded a little past the wall, so I figured it would be easy to hang onto this protrusion of the window sill to reach the wall ledge. All Greek homes had wooden shutters outside of the glass windows. The shutters opened outside over the window sill and they had horizontal, sloped openings and were generally painted a nice deep, hunter green. They were made to fold outward, vertically in two parts on hinges and had a heavy cast iron catch so that they could be securely locked on the wooden window frame. The shutters were pulled shut for my rest after lunch, a daily ritual. However, they were generally not locked. Of course the adults also took a rest after lunch, but less so in the winter than in the summer. This was an important point because I slept in the same room as my mother and my father, the front bedroom of the Bastille.

So, my escape plan started to develop. The critical elements were: it would have to be during rest time, my parents should not be taking the ritual rest that day and there should be a lull in the fighting. It was never working out. Usually at least one of my parents would come in after lunch to lie down, at least for a while. Finally there was a day when neither of my parents came into the bedroom to take the rest I so despised. The only problem was that the fighting outside was going on and there was a lot of small-arms fire nearby. Now I should explain that the Bastille had sort of a strategic location. Our street was between two hills, one on the southern end and one on the northern, with the Bastille more or less in the middle of the street. That is probably why the Insurgent boys picked it as a good location to keep an eye on both hills and to fight from. The hill to the north was behind the old Olympic stadium, built for the first modern Olympics, and closer to Zapion and the Royal Palace. The top of the hill had been taken over by British troops and Royalist Greek forces, such as they were — which was not much at that point. The southern hill was still held by the Insurgents. The main dog fight was between these two hilltops with small-arms fire and a couple of machine guns, although there was a bigger explosion from time to time. But I could also hear kids playing games on the street, from my little rest prison in the bedroom. That did it for me. I unlocked the shutters and made a break for it. I got to the edge of the window sill and hung down to find footing on the wall ledge. I had miscalculated — probably something to do with the way the street sloped down. I hung on for a while but ultimately I had to let go. I landed on the broken-up sidewalk, scraped but intact. Free at last! I could hear the voices of my street mates in the lower part of the northern hill playing some kind of a war game. I headed up the hill as quickly as my legs would take me and joined them. It was heaven.

The game was already under full steam. Comments were flying back and forth as some kids imitated the speech of the Partisans and some of the British. It was mostly what they had heard from their families and other kids. Some of the comments were political or social, but the kids would switch back and forth. Gradually we divided into two gangs, fortified ourselves behind some big boulders and a stone-throwing fight started. Which gang each kid joined did not seem to be much related to who they imitated or even supported. It was more to balance out the teams, with the age of the kids and the good and weaker rock-throwers. Like a street pickup football game. The stone-throwing fight was going quite well as there were endless loose stones in the Athens hills. It was really quite exciting and absorbing because the actual fighting would continue in fits and starts throughout our stone fight. Our own play-fight became modulated with the real fire-fight. Sometimes our stone-fight would intensify when the firing intensified and sometimes we would hide behind the boulders until the firing subsided and then start the stone-fight again. An unspoken rhythm seemed to develop in the game. Somehow we all knew what to do. Maybe we had leaders in the two gangs who told us when to throw stones and when to hide behind our boulders, but I do not recall this. I was overwhelmed with the exhilaration of the two interwoven fights.

Suddenly, I was grabbed by the scruff of my neck. I looked behind me and there was Thales. He was ducking very low, as he was so tall, to avoid the bullets. He was furious. He slapped me on my bottom repeatedly, as hard as he could, I thought. Strangely, I felt absolutely no pain. Not even a little sting. I guess I was too preoccupied with the stone fight and all the excitement. But I was really surprised. My Uncle Thales slapping me! My very own *nonós*! Unheard of. And why was he so mad?

– Why are you slapping me? I complained.
– Are you crazy? Are you out of your mind?, he shouted.
– Why? We are just playing a game.
– Game! You could be killed.

I was incredulous. We boys had told each other innumerable times that it was totally safe in the lower part of the hill. The Partisan boys from the other hill were firing at the British, dug in at the top of our hill.

– But the Partisan boys would never fire at us, Uncle Thales.
– You are crazy! What if they miss-fire and hit you?
– The Partisan boys are crack shots. They never miss.

By then I was being dragged unceremoniously down the hill by Thales, my own *nonós*. I briefly glanced back at my old gang to see if they made humiliating gestures or expressions. Fortunately, they were engrossed in the stone fight. They had hardly noticed my exit.

– And what if you were hit by an English bullet?

He was by now dragging me by my shirt, but he soon picked me up in his arms, still ducking and running.

– The English are also excellent shots. They would never fire near children.

It all seemed so logical and safe to me. But, obviously, not so to Thales. Finally, we made it to the front door of the Bastille. Only a few of the Insurgent boys were there, to man the machine gun, if necessary. Maybe the rest were on the rooftop or had joined the fight from the other hill. A couple of the boys still left in the hallway cast a disinterested glance at Thales and me going in.

Escape to Nea Smyrni

I think it was over the next few days that the family decided to leave Pagrati. The Insurgent boys had said that the battle for Athens was not going well as tens of thousands of heavily armed British troops kept coming in. There was no help from the Soviets or the Yugoslav insurgents, which they had expected, they said. The fighting could degenerate into house-to-house battles in the most contested districts of Athens. Pagrati was one of them. The family made the decision to go to Nea Smyrni, then essentially a suburb of Athens where apparently there was no fighting. Arrangements were made to stay with relatives on Yiayia Sophia's side, who I will call the Tzeds. How the Tzeds were contacted for these arrangements was a mystery to me. It just seemed to happen. There were hardly any public telephones that worked and we certainly did not have a private telephone. Of course, we had no automobile and it would be dangerous to drive in one, in any case. Pagrati to Nea Smyrni was a walkable distance that could take a couple of hours. There were also trams and some buses, but I do not recall if they were running during that part of the Civil War. I think that maybe someone going to Nea Smyrni got word to the Tzeds. The adults thought it would be best to go on foot, but in any case we had to wait for a lull in the fighting.

It was early on a Sunday morning. The weather was bright and clear and very crisp. You could see your breath in the morning air. There were church bells ringing in the distance, but otherwise it was dead quiet. No guns and no people in the street. I am not sure whether during other Sunday mornings there was no fighting or whether it was just that morning. Maybe the Insurgent boys had told Thales that there would be no fighting that morning, or maybe we just took a chance. In any case, we had a few belongings that would be carried and we said goodbye to the Bastille. We did not lock anything. There was no point. The Insurgent boys were still in the outside corridor. They would have to use the bathroom, which was inside the front door opening into the corridor. We left so early that the Insurgent boys were still mostly sleeping. Maybe a couple of them acknowledged our escape with a wave.

It was a long walk to Nea Smyrni. We took back streets, avoiding main thoroughfares and *plateas*. But we hardly met anybody. As we approached the outer parts of Nea Smyrni everybody's mood seemed to lighten. We went past the Alsos of Nea Smyrni, the little wooded park, with lovely smells of pine. We passed the church of Agia Fotini meant to remind people of its famous namesake, which had been destroyed in the real Smyrni during the burning of the city in 1922. As we got further into Nea Smyrni we noticed a big difference from Pagrati. It had to do mostly with the houses and their gardens. Pagrati was largely built up by apartments usually of two to four levels, and gardens were often not very prominent. The whole district looked crowded. Nea Smyrni had mostly single home dwellings with big, well-kept gardens that one could see behind low stone work enclosures, supporting open lattice iron-work. Their trimmed gardens with rose bushes, jasmine vines, lemon and bitter-orange trees and the mature grape-vines growing over trellises made me feel that all was still well. In the warmer seasons there would be flowers growing everywhere. The storied gardens of the Smyrni of old flourished once again in the fertile land of the new namesake.

Finally we reached the house of the Tzeds. Mrs. Tzed was a sweet woman, who was a teacher and ran a private school. Her first name was Elenitsa (little Eleni); to me she was always Aunt Elenitsa. The classrooms of her school were connected to the house. They had wooden desks and inkwells and blackboards. The main hallway of the house was like a school hall. It was all complete with drinking school fountains separated from the outside with semi-transparent glass. There was a good-sized schoolyard in front of the house. But the classrooms were empty. I never saw students during the period we stayed with the Tzeds. I think Aunt Elenitsa said that they had very few registrations because of the civil war and they closed the school for a period. They were quite optimistic it would flourish again. Uncle Tzed was very different than Aunt Elenitsa. He was a bureaucrat and very rotund. He was also a well-known glutton. In better times he loved to have great tables laid for a dozen guests. His favorite was roasted piglet with huge servings of roast potatoes and rice pilaf. It was said that during the pre-war times (and after the war also) he would have several of these animals served to the guests, on great platters, along with a hundred hard-boiled eggs. I don't know why the hard-boiled eggs still stick in my mind. He ultimately developed diabetes and was forced to diet. After that he did not look like the same happy, round man. He started to develop unhealthy looks and his flesh sort of hung from his face and neck and arms. He reminded me of a partially inflated balloon. He died from complications due to diabetes and suffered a great deal. But the family gossip was that most of his suffering was because he was not allowed to pursue his gluttonous hobby.

The Tzeds had two children, Aliki (Alice) and Theodore, who were my cousins. Theodore was my age or a bit older, I think, and Aliki was younger. Theodore was very studious and looked it. He had heavy glasses and a personality to match. He talked a great deal about his studies, how to study, how to get better marks and how to sit the exams of the future. But he also pressured me about this and that, and would try to influence me. In later years he became interested in girls and always had some sexual angle, mostly fairly crude. He seemed to have sex on the brain and was preoccupied with it, in what now seems to me a pretty juvenile way. I think my mother had told me he was "a corruptor". I cannot remember in what context she said this. My Yiayia Sophia said Theodore was "a great Jesuit". In Greek calling someone a Jesuit is not entirely complementary. It can imply someone who is two-faced. I asked Yiayia Sophia if that is what she meant, but she just repeated "Theodore is a very great Jesuit". There was a tone of admiration in her voice.

While we were at the Tzeds, I slept in a small dark room beside the classroom. I cannot remember if anyone else slept in that little room. In any case, the days were short and darkness came early, so there was plenty of opportunity to converse with myself. *The Voice would come out and keep me company.*

– Hey Tasouli, what do you think of Nea Smyrni now, it would say.
– It's OK. At least I have Aliki and Theodore to play with.

– Theodore hardly plays. He is all about studying and how to get ahead.
– True. But there is lots of space here. And this big empty schoolyard. And the school fountains. And the empty classrooms.
– It is all the houses and nice gardens of the other relatives here. Isn't that why you like Nea Smyrni?
– Yes, they give me treats when I go to visit them.
– How come you remember where they lived? You were pretty small when you left for Pagrati.
– I just remember.
– Is that why you wandered all by yourself here, in the middle of the Occupation.
– I remembered where Uncle Vironas' house was. So, I came to find it.
– So, what made you come to find it?
– Because Nea Smyrni was where I used to live.
– But it was a very long walk when you were small.
– I just wanted to explore.
– Explore?
– Just explore. First the street near Bastille and then the next street. In the direction of Nea Smyrni.
– Are we going to explore more, Tasouli?
– Sure, tomorrow after I wake up. But where did you come from?
– Don't you remember? From Pyrgos, 'the Babarians of Vafi'.
– Of course I remember. I always remember. But I am sleepy now. I have to go to sleep. G-night.
– Good night.

I think we stayed in Nea Smyrni with the Tzeds only a few weeks. The British had poured in — in overwhelming forces. The war had not gone well for the Partisans, and they had retreated from most of Athens. Everybody said that Stalin and the Yugoslavs had not helped the Partisans, as they had expected. They were not fighting over Pagrati anymore, so it was safe for us to return. I can't remember if we walked back or whether we went by tram or bus.

When we arrived in the Bastille, everything was exactly as we had left it. Nothing seemed to have been disturbed. The beds were still made, all the cutlery and plates were in their drawers and all the clothes were hanging in the closets. But there was a note, scribbled in schoolboy-like writing pinned on the bed in the main front bedroom. It was from the Insurgent boys. It said "Excuse us, but we have taken the binoculars as we don't have any. We have also taken two blankets. Excuse us. They say it will be cold in the mountains where we are going to fight now. We have very few blankets. We will return the binoculars and blankets when we come back after the Victory".

But there would be no victory for the Insurgent boys; there was no return. Many of them would be killed in the mountains. Stalin, Churchill and Roosevelt had decided how to divvy-up Europe. Greece was to be with the West, while the rest of Eastern Europe was to be under the Soviet Union. The ugliest phases of the Civil War were just beginning. It would pit household against household, village against village, and sometimes, brother against brother. The blood-letting would go on and on. The adults seemed to sense that all of this was going to happen and they only spoke in muted tones. For me it was a depressing time, since I was always influenced by how the adults felt and what they said around the Bastille.

Also, Joujoukos had disappeared during our absence from the Bastille. I guess his stomach was more important to him than loyalty. I asked everyone I met in Pagrati about him. No one in the neighborhood had seen him or even seemed to know who Joujoukos was. How could they have forgotten so soon the great hero of the Resistance! But I had not forgotten. I knew Joujoukos had left the Bastille because he was hungry. He would have been at least as hungry as I was in the early days of Pyrgos, when I would ask my mother if we had *psomaki*. No matter, for I would often talk to Joujoukos. He would invariably answer, because cats can do these things. Sometimes he would answer in cat language and often with a loud purr. And of course, cats can see invisible people. Everybody knows this.

The Goose

During the early part of the Civil War people were still very poor. What paper money people had was not worth much. Sometimes to get something one would exchange it for something else. One day Thales appeared with a goose. He had been given the goose instead of money because he had removed the tonsils of a boy who was very sick. The tonsils were full of pus and they thought the boy could die. This was a live goose which was not too friendly. She was put in the back garden of the Bastille. She could not escape from there as she was surrounded by the back walls of the other apartments. Initially the goose would hiss at me and try to bite me. Gradually she got used to me and I would talk to her. But she would never answer back even though I had a lot of interesting things to say. She was preoccupied with pecking at the ground and gulping down whatever bits of leftovers we put out for her.

– Where was your house before, goose?
– ...
– You have not seen Joujoukos by any chance?
– ...
– Joujoukos the cat — the great hero of the Resistance. I would go on to relate Joujoukos' exploits at great length.
– ...
– All that happened right here, goose. Right where we are!
– ...
– We went to Nea Smyrni, goose. To escape all the fighting in Pagrati. Have you been to Nea Smyrni, goose?
– ...

By then Yiayia Sophia would look through the back window of the dining room, facing into the walled-in garden, and would shout,

– Enough talking to the goose! Be careful, she will pick and bite you. Come in now.
– I am trying to teach her how to speak, I would protest.

But, of course, I knew she would not talk. Not like Joujoukos. She was a bird after all. Nevertheless, I got to like the goose. I got to like her quite a lot. And that is where the problem started.

The adults had another conversation going on about the goose. It was mostly around the dinner table in the back room of the Bastille. I was not sure if the goose could hear it through the window. Probably she could not, as dinner was always after dark and the goose was already asleep.

– In Zakynthos, in the winter, they do them boiled with herbs. It is delicious. Very tender and it gets rid of the fat, my Mother would say.
– And the fat can be saved, for making sweets with flower and sugar and egg yolk, added Kyra Maria.
– And stuffing it with chestnuts and apple, and roasted slowly in the oven is to die for, said Yiayia Sophia thoughtfully. It is how they did them in Smyrni. The recipe is even in Tselemendes.
– But roasting would be difficult in our small oven, said Kyra Maria. And we do not want to give it to the baker to do it in his big oven. You never know what might happen. And people will start to talk.
– No matter how we do it, it will be delicious, said Uncle Stelios. The goose is certainly the most tasty of all domesticated birds. This is well-known by all authorities on the subject.
– And we have not had meat since before the Occupation, said Uncle Thales. It will taste absolutely phenomenal.

I was sitting there listening to the dinner time conversation with great interest. I started to imagine that the goose would have the most beautiful taste I had ever experienced. And since it was a large goose, there would be all the meat you could possibly want. It would be the feast of all feasts. Unbelievably tasty, unbelievably tender, unbelievably filling my stomach. Then I started to think about my conversations with the goose. Admittedly, she never responded but I had got to like her.

– How could I eat someone I liked? And what if one liked that individual a lot? Like, loved them. And if you could eat a goose that you liked a lot, could you eat a cat that you liked even more? And what if you really loved the cat, would you eat it? Certainly I could never eat Joujoukos. On the other hand, the goose was the most delicious thing I would ever taste. Everybody said so.

I went to bed late that evening. I could hear the adults talking in the dining room of the Bastille. They were still discussing the goose and how to cook it. Yiayia Sophia was in her element. It was as if goose had become a staple in the eating habits of the Smyrni of old. It was cooked in all kinds of delicious ways. One would be led to think that the *whole* of the Ionian civilization was created around cooking the goose!

Gradually I started to fall asleep. *I was half-awakened by a familiar Voice.*

– Hey Tasouli, it sounds like that goose will be absolutely delicious.
– Yes, Voice. That is what all the adults say.
– All the different ways of cooking it.
– Whichever way, it will be fantastic.
– But don't you feel sorry for the goose?
– Not really. I just want to taste it.
– But Tasouli, you were talking to the goose.
– She never answered.
– That is no reason to eat it, Tasouli.
– It would be different if she could talk.
– So you figure if someone talks to you, you should not eat them?
– Yup. If they have language you should not kill them.
– Even if you don't understand the language? Like Joujoukos.
– But, Voice, I *do* understand Joujoukos' language. So I would never kill him.
– So, what if you do not understand a language? Like English.
– You mean like the English prisoners?
– Yes, Tasouli. The Insurgent boys were ordered to cut their heads off. Right in the back garden. Where the goose is right now.
– Well, they did not have their heads cut off in the back garden. I looked for English heads and there were none. I even searched the bushes and underneath the iron staircase.
– I know that Tasouli. But you helped shave their faces and their throats. So it would make it easier if their throats and heads *were* cut off.
– You know too much Voice! I was only looking at their throats while they were shaving because it was the only part that I could see. The English towered above me. So I had to look up and tug on their pants if they looked like they would cut their throats or under their chin while shaving.
– Still if their heads were cut off, it would be easier if their throats were shaved. And you don't know if they understood you any more than the goose understood you.
– It is not so, Voice. The English prisoners understood some of what I was saying to them. They showed me how to better sharpen the safety razor in the glass.
– Maybe they did it just so their throats and heads could be cut off with less trouble. The English are like that, Tasouli. If something unpleasant has to be done, they try to make it easier.
– Well, the goose did not try to make it easier to have her neck cut. So, she is different from the English. Also, the goose would not speak at all but the English did. And even if she had spoken,

goose language is different from English language.
– So which is better, Tasouli? Goose language or English language?
– I don't know, Voice. It depends if you are Goose or English.
– But don't you feel even a little bit sorry for the goose, Tasouli?
– Well, maybe a little. But it will be such a delicious goose. I am going to dream all night about how good it will taste.
– G'night, Tasouli.

I did dream all night about the goose feast. I had gone to bed late, in any case. Initially my dreams were all about the different ways of preparing the goose. I dreamed that I tasted them all the ways it was prepared. Each recipe was more delicious than the next. Then, somehow the English prisoners started to get mixed up in my dream. The goose took on an English head. So, when the goose's neck was cut this little English head was rolling around in the garden. The goose was running around without a head on, which was on the ground talking in incomprehensible English. That dream awoke me and I could not go back to sleep for a while. The Voice was gone so I was all by myself. I guess the Voice felt there was nothing more to talk about and it had gone to bed. It was probably fast asleep.

The following day I woke up late. A most interesting smell was coming from the kitchen. The goose was already in the pot. With herbs! It had been killed and cleaned while I was still asleep. I did not even bother to ask who had assassinated my goose. I suspected the saintly Kyra Maria. The nuns had probably taught her everything, including how to cut the heads off chickens and geese. Once the suspicion entered my mind, I started to also wonder if the English prisoners ended up in the monastery where Kyra Maria came from. Maybe their necks were cut off there, since the Insurgent boys of the Bastille were too timid. But no matter what, for now I was overwhelmed with happiness and expectation about tasting the goose. I told myself that I would no longer have to talk to the stupid animal or have to worry about the fate that I had known awaited her. Instead, the most delicious meal in the world was already being prepared. Soon we would all sit around the table and eat and eat and eat the wonderful tender meat, all to our heart's content.

The passing of the day seemed very slow. Bastille was buzzing with expectation. Yiayia Sophia and Kyra Maria had set up a special table, with the best dishes we had. It was all laid out formally on a beautiful linen tablecloth that I did not know even existed. It had been embroidered by some spinster relative of Yiayia Sophia from Smyrni. Even the design of the tablecloth was flowers and some kind of generic birds. Yiayia Sophia said they were Smyrnian geese. To me they looked more like peacocks. To go with the goose, a big pot of rice had been prepared with a lovely tomato sauce.

The great feast started. Cutting up the goose was difficult. Uncle Stelios, with the most encyclopedic knowledge said that geese were the most difficult of all birds to cut up properly. It had something to do with the type of dark meat in the muscles of the geese. This phenomenon was well known among biologists. Thales was assigned to cut up the goose. He was the most qualified, being an ear, nose and throat surgeon. Every member of the family was finally served a piece of the goose, but not without an insignificant struggle. Orders were given that no one was to start until we had all been served. There was excited chatter all around the table. Finally everybody started together.

It tasted very weird. I tried to chew my piece but I could not. I attributed this to my small size and to the very special properties of the goose that Stelios knew all about. Then I noticed that all the adults were chewing and chewing on their pieces without much more success than me. Gradually the excited chatter was replaced by silence.

– I can't eat this meat with my false teeth, said Yiayia Sophia.
– It is impossible to eat it, don't you think so Phoebus? said my mother.
– Yes, it is very tough. I had never heard my father disagree with my mother.
– It must have been a very old bird they gave me, said Thales sheepishly.

Stelios just looked depressed, with his intelligent blue eyes darting from side to side, trying to figure out some biological or mechanical explanation for the state of the goose. Kyra Maria said nothing. Not even a suggestion that she could take the decimated carcass to the nuns.

This had to be the biggest disappointment of my life. After all the work-up, the goose was un-edible. It was un-edible even after all the shortages of the Occupation. Fortunately, there was the rice with the tomato sauce. I filled up on this, making myself think of how good the tomato sauce tasted. Now I did not feel the least bit sorry for the goose. I resented her.

School in Pagrati

During the Occupation and first part of the Civil War a lot of schools were closed, I believe. I was told that our own Public School in Pagrati had been closed. I am not sure if the buildings were used for something else or there were not many available teachers or the whole public education system had gone caput. In any case, sometime after the end of the Occupation, our Public School reopened. Due to a shortage of teachers and classrooms, our own grade one class was immense. I think there were about one hundred children in that class. I think it was made up of just the grade one kids, but I cannot be sure that kids from other elementary school classes were not with us. I spent the first three years of my public school education here, from 1944-47.

We were all in one large vacuous classroom with huge windows. The students' desks were made of heavy iron bases and heavy old polished wooden tops. There were ink stains and old initials, names and slogans carved or starched on the old desk tops. These were long desks with a wooden bench which was part of the desk. There would usually be three or four students to each desk. It was considered the lap of luxury if you were lucky enough to get a desk with just two students. There were inkwells in all of these desks. I can't remember when we first started to use the wooden pens with the iron pen-nibs, but it was relatively early on. I think we had only two or three teachers that taught us everything in those classes. Because of the size of the class, the seating system was reversed. The students that paid most attention, or who were better nourished or cleaner sat in the front row. Some kids were more or less in rags. The ratty-looking students were given desks further away from the teacher. Generally the rattier and more malnourished the kid, the further back in the class he sat. The rattier kids in the back rows certainly paid less attention and were more restless and noisy. The less obedient they might be to the teacher's commands to be quiet, the more likely they were to be moved further and further towards the back. The system had the advantage that at least some kids would learn something and with good behavior one could move towards the front of the class. I don't remember anyone questioning this system or even imagining it could be anything else. That is what it was. I was with the 'good' children and was assigned a desk either in the front row or second row. I think we had separate classrooms for boys and for girls but I am not completely certain. Boys and girls certainly mixed during recess.

There was a large elevated wooden platform in the front of the class for the teacher. The teacher's desk was there and also a large blackboard on wooden legs on the platform. The learning process was simple. The teacher would give the lesson in a voice that would carry to the back of the class. Sometimes he would write stuff on the blackboard. Then he or she would call on children to recite part of a lesson, usually from the previous day, or that day. He would start with children in the front rows and work towards the back of the class. Obviously only a small proportion of the class would be tested any one day. Once the student was called, he would have to mount the wooden platform, facing the teacher who was generally sitting down at this stage. The student would then be asked a question and told to speak loudly. If you got the answer correctly, a second, a third, and up to usually half a dozen questions would be asked before you would be allowed to return to your desk. That was assuming you got all the questions right. If you goofed up the answer, you were given a second and sometimes a third chance. If you missed all the chances you were punished in the front of the class.

The teacher had a long ruler and you were asked to put your hands out, palms up. The teacher would then hit you hard with the ruler in the palms of your hands. It stung quite a bit and a lot of students cried. Nearly all had tears in their eyes, although they tried to hide it. It was a status symbol whether or not you cried or had tears. There would be giggling or other noises by the class in response to one's reaction to the punishment, but the teacher would ask for silence. More importantly, if you did not cry or show many tears you would be complemented and admired at recess by other students. If you failed the tear-and-cry test you would be teased, or worse, much worse, be disregarded. There was, however, a secondary strategy to the punishment that could affect your status at recess. It was to avoid being hit in the palms of the hands altogether. To do this you had to suddenly and very quickly pull in your extended hand, palm up, just as the ruler came down. It had to look involuntary, whether it was or not, or else one got it really good. Then you tried to repeat it with the other hand. If one managed to get 2/2, i.e. withdraw both hands, then the teacher would have to stand up and smack you on the legs with the ruler. Since all boys wore short pants (and the girls short skirts) no one escaped ruler contact with bare leg skin, if the punishment got that far. Actually, getting hit on the legs was not too bad. It did not sting as much as on the palms. Also, you could angle the legs a bit and slightly deflect the shot. But best of all, the teacher had to work harder, standing and often having to bend to get the legs. These maneuvers of the teacher were extensively discussed at recess. Anyone who managed to make the teacher look silly by trying to hit one's legs was admired and praised at recess and sometimes even after school.

The teaching program at Pagrati elementary school was pretty straightforward. We were taught mainly reading and arithmetic. I can't remember if history and religion were introduced at early primary school level or if these started later, like in grade four. Sometimes all of the students in the school would assemble together in the schoolyard and get talks on cleanliness and health.

What I remember about arithmetic most, is having to memorize the multiplication tables. We had to recite them over and over again until they became a cant with a rhythm of their own. This rhythm has stayed for life. Even today, when I am stuck without a calculator I fall back on the rhythm of my Pagrati elementary school multiplication tables. I cannot replicate that rhythm in English, so I still solve a visual multiplication problem made up of Arabic numerals using the Greek cant of my childhood. How well one had mastered the tables was readily apparent to the whole class by how many or few hits with the ruler one got. Of course, as we progressed with multiplication of higher numbers of the decimal integers, like the 8s or 9s, it became progressively more difficult to do the cant as one had to think back to the multiplication tables of lower numbers. So big markers for us were the rhythms of 7 7s is 49, 8 8s is 64, 9 9s is 81. To get around the pure rote of the multiplication table cants, we had to instantaneously respond to the multiplication product of any two integers up to 10 and later up to 12. Problems of all sorts using addition, subtraction or multiplication became second nature, as one got punished if they were not solved on the spot.

Then division was introduced and we learned long division and carrying over the differences. By then, we had mastered the multiplication tables and were being hit a lot less. The way we were taught division was to write the dividend on the left and the divisor next to it on the right. The two numbers are separated by a vertical line, connected to a horizontal line which is under the divisor, like a 'T' with the top on its side on the left. The quotient (or its first approximation) is written under the divisor, while the remainder(s) is written under the dividend. As far as I can tell this is the reverse of what children were taught in the Anglo-Saxon world, including Canada. The former convention is still the only way I can do long division with pencil and paper. I have no idea why these two conventions are in reverse. Learning division brought into our teaching the concept of *incommensurate* numbers, for remainders that would go on and on. We would be called by the teacher to go up on the wooden platform and do examples of long division in front of the class, on the blackboard with a squeaky piece of chalk. Kids that had trouble with the long division would make the chalk squeak more and this would annoy the teacher. If the kid persisted in making the chalk squeak because they got stuck or flustered with the long division, they would be hit on their legs with the ruler. The teacher would not hit them on the palms of the hand because then they would have a reason to not be able to complete the solution on the blackboard as they would say that their hands stung too much, or they would cry. But then the teacher would start to look ridiculous trying to hit the kid that could not do the long division on the legs, as the kid would expertly move his legs. The kid would finally be ordered off the platform, where the blackboard and the teacher's desk were, and back to his seat. But as the kid got off the platform, a murmur of approval would rise among the giggles, for the kid had made the teacher look ridiculous. The teacher would have to ask for silence, and if the kid that could not do the long division had played his hand to perfection, then the teacher would have to ask for silence repeatedly and even start shouting. That kid would then be much complemented and even lauded at recess. Often the kids that could not do long division very well came from poorer, less educated families. So it seemed to me that not being able to do long division but ending up having the teacher ridiculed provided some kind of reward for being poor and coming from an uneducated family.

Later on in my education, I cannot remember students being hit any longer with the ruler for making mistakes in long division. Perhaps by then the teachers considered us as having mastered the elements of math. Or maybe by the time we got to mastering long division, the memory of the Occupation was already starting to recede and punishment with it. Or hitting students was becoming less popular for other reasons; perhaps it had something to do with the classes becoming smaller. And to this day I still wonder about the meaning of incommensurate numbers, which were such an important part of our long division exercises. Do these never ending quotients really have a meaning in the physical universe? Do they mean anything at all? Or will they actually end after a few more steps? Maybe these kinds of questions occur less and less to kids in modern schools with the wide availability of calculators and computers. Or maybe it did not occur very often to kids then either. Maybe most of them thought that long division was invented as another way of torturing them. Or maybe some even thought it was there to provide them with an advantage in the cat-and-mouse game with the teacher. At least, through the physical punishment it often generated, it gave them a way to salvage some self-respect and even pride.

Reading, writing and grammar were the other major preoccupations. Writing was all about penmanship, using the wooden pen and the iron pen nib. A lot of it was copying the elementary grade book we had. In those days Greek was not monotonic and all the breathing sounds of vowels and the different accents had to be mastered. While Greek is relatively easy to pronounce, and as it is much more phonetic than, for example, English, the Greek grammar is a killer. By comparison English grammar is trivial or a walk in the park. Worse still for us kids, the fight was still raging between the proponents of *Katharevousa* (the purified Greek language) and *Demotiki* (Demotic Greek). This fight took political dimensions that are difficult to comprehend nowadays. *Katharevousa* was the language used in the legal system, to a large extent was still used in most of the newspapers, in politics and political and other government announcements. Apparently it was used even among some conservative, upper class families. It was an artificial language introduced some time after the Greek revolution of 1821 and was meant to reflect the glories of ancient Greece and the language of the Bible. But it was not spoken very much in the street, where *Demotic* held sway. Just as importantly *Demotic* was used by the vast majority of the most popular and influential literary novelists and poets, with only a couple of exceptions that I know of. Broadly speaking, the political Right, most conservatives, the King and the army generals supported *Katharevousa*, while the political Left in Greece, including the anti-royalists and communists, supported *Demotiki*. This political split was not just an academic debate. It played a role in the Civil War, further dividing Greek allegiances and psyche. Subsequently, it continued to divide Greece into the time of the first Papandreou government, especially with respect to what should be taught in schools. The language issue in primary schools became a major cause for the fall of that Government and the subsequent takeover by the dictatorship of the Colonels in 1967. For us kids, after Occupation, these divisions were only too palpable. Our school books and some of the teachers used Katharevousa, particularly as part of the more formal language learning. But if the teachers got mad, or if they punished us during recess, they would do it mostly in Demotic. I think more often a 'mixed' language was used, neither pure demotic nor Katharevousa. The end result was a confusing approach to the language affecting verb and noun endings in the different tenses, and also sentence structure.

I had a lot of difficulty in reading initially. The system we were taught was by syllabication. Verbal spelling, as in English, is not used in Greek. Spelling, in the sense that it is most commonly used in English is, in fact, meaningless since Greek is so largely phonetic. In Greek the word is simply pronounced and then one may add, if it is not clear, how a vowel sound is written. For example, one could specify if an 'o' sound is written with an omicron (ο) or an omega (ω), should it seem ambiguous. It is a little more complicated with the ĕ sound, where three Greek letters (ι,η,υ) make the identical vowel sound as do also some combinations of vowels (οι, or, ει). The grammar prescribing when to use these vowels or combinations is difficult, and is likely a remnant from ancient Greek. However, it should cause no confusion in the pronunciation that a child is learning since these vowel designations all have the same sound in modern Greek, namely ĕ. In fact, mastering the syllabication system should actually be much easier in Greek than in English, since the former is more phonetic. So, I don't know why I had this real difficulty in reading out words. All I knew was that I wanted to read very badly but I could not. The sequence of letters did not translate somehow in my brain into the spoken words. My mother tried to help me (she had trained as a school teacher) but it was to no avail. I tried and tried and tried … day after day, after day, after school, every day. After many weeks, it seemed, I was just not getting it, not improving. I tried to syllabicate and syllabicate and syllabicate anything I could get my hands on, but I still could not read.

Then, all of a sudden, one day I could read! I could not read one minute and the next minute I could read, or so it seemed. It was one of the most profound experiences of my life. I felt a huge elation. I was certain at that moment that I could master anything. No adversity could defeat me. I started to read manically. I read everything I could get my hands on. I had been given all kinds of children's books that I could not read before, but which I could now read. Many of them were children's adaptations of the classics from foreign languages. I read translations of Molière's plays, *Gulliver's Travels*, *Les Misérables*, the Hans Christian Andersen stories and *Pinocchio*. These were all in illustrated nice, thick paperback editions, where one had to cut the attached pages on the top or the side with a paper cutter. Each page that I cut would then produce a surprise, a little treasure, maybe a pen illustration or even a colored woodcut print. Woodcut prints were still popular in children's books at the time and they all seemed unbelievably beautiful to me. And I read these illustrated books and reread them, over and over again, so excited was I that I could read. I came across one of these childhood books of mine (Molière's plays) not long ago. As I reread it now in advanced adulthood, the flashback of the language in the story I knew so well came flooding back, almost word for word.

Another big problem I had in primary school in Pagrati was fleas — ordinary house fleas. During the Occupation fleas were considered to be not only a nuisance and a sign of overcrowding and poverty, but also as dangerous for carrying typhus and even the plague. I am not sure if there was actually much illness from them, but typhus was talked about quite a lot. Of course, we did not have antibiotics then. So, with the opening of the schools, public health measures were taken to combat fleas. Boys were obliged to have their hair cut really short, like a very short crew-cut. We were then all made to line up in the schoolyard for flea inspection. The line-up and inspection, every couple of days, was a big part of our week. The instruments of inspection were a very fine-tooth comb and a red and blue marking pencil. The boy's head would be inspected and combed by a teacher, looking for fleas. If any were found on the head of the student, the teacher would try to kill them between the ends of the markers, leaving a tell-tale blue and red mark. The more blue and red marks a child had on their head, the more they would be humiliated. The idea was that the parents would know, so they could bathe and isolate the infected child. Girls were subjected to the same routine, except they did not have to cut their hair short, and they also ended up with blue and red marks. I actually never had fleas, as far as I know. My problem was that my mother resisted having my hair cut very short as required by the school. I remember the exchanges with the teachers, over my hair. They generally took place in the schoolyard, in front of everybody.

> – We do not have fleas in our family, she would say to the teachers in her usual combative manner and loud voice.
> – All of the boys have to have their hair cut short, the teacher would reply.
> – Not my son. He will not be humiliated with the short hair. He is not a prisoner of war.
> – It is just a check for fleas.
> – Do you think I do not check my own son?
> – But all the families are supposed to do it.
> – I am not going to have my son treated like that. I will take him out of school.

– As you wish, Mrs. Dina, as you wish.

A small crowd of students would gather around to watch the combat. My mother never seemed embarrassed, just haughty and accusatory of the system, the teachers and their backward thinking. The funny thing was that other students never seemed to react to the argument, either for or against, and they never made fun of me. They would simply go back to their groups or games once the argument ended. I kept my hair longer than the crew-cuts and no one seemed to pay much attention.

Also, part of the post-Occupation public health measures was supplementary nutrition for all school-age children. I think this program was later promoted by Queen Frederica, the wily and very visible wife of King Paul. It was said that Frederica ruled the roost. I remember a large, framed black and white picture of her dominating the hall where we had to go to get our nutritional supplement. I think it was a Boy Scouts hall or something like that. The Boy Scouts were also promoted as a paramilitary organization to resist communism and keep the youth straight during the later stages of the Civil War. There was a line-up after school and we all had to swallow cod-liver oil and drink a glass of milk. The cod-liver oil was generally considered the more distasteful of the two, even though the milk was made from milk powder mixed with tap water, and was never cold. For the cod liver oil, we had one of two options for taking it. One was to swallow a tablespoon of it, which was fed to us by a nurse with a red cross on her cap. The same spoon was used for all the kids, which does not seem very hygienic nowadays. Alternately, you could be given a piece of bread on which a spoon-full of cod-liver oil was poured. and then you chewed the bread with the oil. I preferred the latter. In either case you had to open your mouth and show it to the nurse, to ensure that it was swallowed and not just kept in your mouth to be spat out later. Queen Frederica observed me at all times from her framed photo. Even after her husband died she continued to exert significant influence through her son to the end of the monarchy in Greece.

Caterpillars

The second educational experience I had outside the public school system occurred sometime after the Occupation. I can't exactly remember the time, but it was well after I had started Public School. In any case it was relatively early in my education, and had to do with learning a foreign language. The Laggi educationalists had decreed that learning a foreign language should be started early when the child's mind had not been fully molded. So, I was sent to a private teacher to learn English. Our Chrysoula also knew languages, but primarily French, and there was some reluctance to have me sent back to her after the unsuccessful music lessons. So, an unrelated woman, a private teacher was found. I disliked that woman from the start. She was officious. I disliked learning English even more. She tried to teach me the English (Latin) letters, and I was supposed to learn them in writing form, mostly lower case. What I found most annoying was that letters like 'mnwu', particularly if joined together in pen writing, looked to me like caterpillars.
    – They look like caterpillars, I protested.
    – Caterpillars? Caterpillars? Ridiculous. I have never heard that before, said my officious lady.
    – They are odd and squishy and you can't tell one from another, I said, showing her some samples of my penmanship on the lines of the prescribed writing exercise book.

In desperation she tried to show me once more the proper penmanship to make the different caterpillars appear distinct from each other.

    – How ugly too, I thought. How horribly ugly, when compared to the elegant lower case Greek letters.

Pronunciation was even worse. Nothing was pronounced as it was written. Why write 'why' in that absurd way? Surely it should be written as 'houái'. Even the first letter of this inscrutable language did not have the 'α' sound in it, like in a civilized language. Why in the world, was the first letter of the English alphabet 'a' pronounced as 'εë'?

– Where was the 'α' sound, I asked.
The teacher had no explanation.
– Because that is just how it is, she said.
– But the first letter should have the 'α' sound. It is not an 'ɛ́' and it is not an 'ë'.
My protests went unheeded.
– The first letter is pronounced 'ɛ́ë'. You have to learn it like that.
– But what about a written word with the 'α' sound?
– Like in 'house'.

She said it with great satisfaction. She then wrote it out for me. I dully inspected her writing and looked doubtful.

– It has the 'α' sound in 'ha', she intoned almost triumphantly.

There was something very mysterious about this Tongue. Even the first letter of their alphabet has two different vowel sounds and it does not have the vowel sound it is supposed to have, I thought.

I had to find a hiding place and try to figure out if the teacher was making it all up or if this language was really as mysterious and nonsensical as she made it out to be. Fortunately, I had trained well under Chrysoula and there seemed to be lots of hiding places in this obnoxious teacher's house.

– Where is the letter 'α' in 'house'?, I thought looking for the best hiding place. Surely it should be pronounced phonetically as 'hoou´sɛ' or 'hoousɛ˝'. And if you actually wanted to say 'house' it surely should be written as 'haouz' in Latin characters or 'χάουζ' in Greek characters.

I was quite convinced that I was correct and the teacher had got it wrong or was at least misinformed. I then had every right to hide from her, I figured. The curtains looked like a pretty good hiding place. While hiding behind the curtains, I thought that this teacher was not going to be as patient as good old Chrysoula. Also my parents had said that contrary to Chrysoula, this teacher expected to be paid regularly. So I was hopeful that since we had so little money, my period of bondage would be short.

The living room where I had my lessons had lots of heavy curtains, all drawn, covering the windows as well as parts of the walls. The sunlight was not to be allowed to come in, which was not that uncommon in certain Greek homes of the time. The dense, double curtains kept the heat and dust out, both of which were plentiful in Athens of the time, and were hung so they were a bit separated from the walls. So my hiding area was extensive and I could move behind the heavy floor-length draping without being easily detected. The teacher had given up hunting for me. I could not hear her fussing about in the living room. She was going to get paid anyway.

I wondered if it was just me that did not like the way English was written. No one else had mentioned it. Not my uncles, not my parents, not other kids.

– *Hey Tasouli, why are you hiding?, a Voice nearby said.*
The Voice was male and sounded familiar and it came from somewhere behind the curtains where I was hiding.

– Is that you Dad, I whispered.
– No, but …
– Shh, the teacher is going to find me.
– No, she is not.
– How do you know?
– She won't bother. She is going to get paid anyway.
– How do you know?

– Didn't you just say that?

– I didn't think I did, Voice. But sometimes I talk to myself.

– Hm. You know, there are others who also don't like the way English is written.

– Oh yeah?

– There is someone by the name of George Bernard Shaw. He wants English to be written phonetically. You know, like Greek is phonetic.

– "Ssso"?

– No, 'Shaw'. I will spell it for you. S-h-a-w.

– The w is a caterpillar. I'll have nothing to do with it!

– But this man is a famous British author. Irish, actually. He writes plays. He says he will put a lot of money aside to make English writing phonetic.

– Oh! I remember. My Uncle Stelios mentioned him.

– I know.

– You seem to know everything Voice.

– In any case, Shaw is not going to be successful in making English phonetic.

– Too bad.

– You can't win them all!

– But Voice, English has too many letters in any case. 26 compared to 24 for the Greek.

– They are actually Latin letters used in English.

– I know that, Voice.

– But Greek has extra letters for both the o and ë sounds.

– I hate all those extra letters too. You need to learn all the grammar to know when to use them.

– It was like that in Ancient Greek. So you would know if you were writing about a woman, or a child, one or many, and so forth. Maybe they also pronounced the o different from the ω. And for the ë sound in modern Greek, like in ι or υ or η or οι or ει, maybe each had different lengths or intonations, or something, a long time ago.

– I know. I've been told this before. It is all very fine, but in modern Greek there is just one sound for o and ω, which is o. And there is only one sound for ι, υ, η, οι or ει, which is ë.

– So?

– So, phonetically you would only need 21 Greek letters.

– But then you have the compound Greek sounds, like ντ together to make d and γκ to make g.

– So?

– So, you would use a few more combinations of characters for a phonetic Tongue, if you were to use just Greek characters.

– Hm. You might have to throw a few English, I mean Latin, characters in to make it simpler. As long they are not caterpillars … What is your name, in any case?

– Styppas.

– That's funny. That is my name too. Styppas … Dad, that is you, hiding behind the curtains! You have come to pay the teacher and you are playing a trick on me!

– No, I am not your dad. Not really.

– Yeah. You are right Styppas. My Dad does not play tricks. And the jokes he tells are about serious and important things. I often don't understand his jokes. Still your voice is familiar.

– We met before.

– Where?

– First, back in Pyrgos. The Barbarians, you know …

– Oh yeah. Now I remember. I was pretty small in Pyrgos.

– And then in Nea Smyrni. During the start of the Civil War. And I talked to you about the goose.

– Oh yeah, that I know! But are you the same person?

– The very same.

– I was not sure. I thought your voice sounded different than the voice in Pyrgos. And I am not sure about Nea Smyrni, or even Pagrati.

– It is because you have grown.

– But why would your voice sound different if you are the same?

– I will have to go soon, little Styppas. You better go and find the teacher.

I stepped outside the curtains. There was no one there. I could hear the teacher in the kitchen.

– She is in the kitchen making coffee and having a cigarette, Styppas.

– I didn't think she smoked.

– She said I drove her to start again. She smokes Papastrattos number one. But she does not smoke like Chrysoula.

– Yah … I know.

– You say you know to everything, Styppas. Come out of the curtains. We can play a game.

– Even if I could come out, you wouldn't see me.

– Why? Are you invisible?

– Kind of.

– If you are invisible, like a spirit, I will get Joujoukos to talk to you. He can also see you.

– Joujoukos?

– For sure! Cats can talk to spirits and see invisible people. And this is Joujoukos-the-brave. You know. The famous Resistance hero.

– Bye Tasouli.

– Bye Styppas.

I went to look for the teacher in the kitchen. She was having puffs in rapid sequence from an aromatic cigarette, Papastratos number one. She had made herself a Greek coffee in an individual, 'atomic', little coffee pot. She was trying to drink from a tiny coffee cup but her hand was shaking.

– Tell your mother and father that I can't give you any more English lessons. And tell your father I want to be paid.

She was all agitated and kind of stuttering.

This had turned out to be a pretty good day! It looked like I was winning the battle against the hated caterpillars and unpronounceable words in this barbaric language. And I had found a new friend. Well, sort of new, I guess. On my way home I told Joujoukos, as I talked to him regularly. He was very pleased and purred loudly. Less so my parents when I finally told them that the teacher would not give me any more lessons and wanted to be paid. My father went out to pay her. He did not look pleased.

War games

Once the Civil war was fought in Athens, our gang games developed further. Our gangs became more distinct and defined by neighborhood or even part of the street. We would gather with other members of our gang on one of the two hills, which would then have become *our* hill. Our weapons improved. We graduated beyond simple stone throwing. We nearly all had rubber band slingshots, so our range of lopping small stones and pebbles at the opposition greatly increased. The rubber for the slingshots was lifted from abandoned tire tubes of mostly German vehicles. Another weapon was the top of tin cans. We collected these assiduously and stockpiled them. When we were fighting our friends in another gang at a relatively close range both gangs would take cover behind boulders or perhaps behind walls of a partially demolished building. These types of fortification made stone throwing by hand pretty well ineffective. The slingshot might allow the occasional ricochet of a lucky shot but these were pretty feeble weapons against a well-fortified opposition. But when we brought in our stockpiles of tin-can tops the complexion of the conflict changed. By throwing the tops of the tin cans underhand, with a Frisbee-like motion, the can tops could be made to curve, and with the right gust of wind even start to come back. In this way the rival gang was no longer safe behind their fortifications and could be cut by our little sharp-edged flying saucers. If the rival gang finally abandoned its fortified position and went elsewhere the fight was generally considered a success due to our tin-can-top offensive, and we celebrated appropriately. The possibility that our rivals were simply bored and were looking to play elsewhere never entered our thoughts. We had simply won an important territorial victory. An advance scout team would then be sent to explore the previously occupied, and now liberated territory.

The gang's biggest technical advance was our catapult. It was an engineering marvel and the only weapon we had that ever caused serious damage. I should add that we never had guns. Although guns, hand grenades, bullets and the like were frequently found in our post-Civil War wanderings, I don't remember any of our neighborhood gangs having guns. I think the police and paramilitary organizations took a pretty grim view of that and, in any case, our gangs did not have criminals. I do not remember any stealing, planning to rob anything, and drugs were unknown. In fact, Athens was a very safe city from the point of view of ordinary crime. It was like that before the Occupation and the Civil War, and the deprivation especially during the Occupation did not seem to have changed this. Our catapult, however, came close to bringing in the police. And the police would never come in unless there was serious damage. To be fair, it was bigger boys that conceived and constructed the catapult. I was younger and pretty well in the periphery of the older boys, only helping here and there if asked.

To make the catapult, a small tree with a V in its lower branches coming off its trunk was chosen. It was conveniently located on the smaller hill on the South side of our street. The tree was trimmed so all that remained was the rooted trunk and the V-like two lower branches. Two wide rubber bands, about a meter-and-a-half long were securely attached near the top of each side of the V and a sac was rigged to the free ends of the large rubber bands. The whole apparatus was like a giant slingshot, which was almost impossible to draw right back even with two boys pulling. To draw back the giant slingshot we had adapted a *tambour* crank apparatus for drawing water from an old well. The sac could then be held back with a rope put over a secured hook. So, a big boulder could be loaded in the sac, and on command the rope would be let go. It took a few tries to get it right. But then it was glorious. A couple of the shot-off boulders actually flew over the houses of the street and landed on the opposite hill where our rivals were supposed to be. There was no doubt now that we had artillery superiority. Unfortunately one boulder did not make it all the way to the other hill. Instead it hit a tall cement electrical pole at the other end of the street near the hill towards which we were aiming. The pole was damaged near the wires and the ceramic insulators and the electricity in the neighborhood went off. Fortunately the electricity going off was a common event and no one paid much attention. The repairmen, when they came after a couple of days, were puzzled about what had caused the damage.

As the fighting in Athens receded in our memories, so did the gangs and the war games. The same kids got reorganized in other kinds of competition. The Northern hill near our street had quite a bit of wind especially in late autumn and was ideal for flying kites. We kids were very competitive in our kite flying, just as in the war games. Basically, we made two types of kites and we made them from scratch. One was the Athenian and the other was the Smyrni (little Smyrnian). They were very different in construction and aerodynamically. We never bought kites. I am not sure if one could even buy them ready-made at that time. The chief ingredients were cane (reed), oil-paper, string and paper glue. Cane was always around and the rest were either available around the house or borrowed from other kids or, as a last resort, inexpensively bought from the local corner store.

To make the Athenian, one had to split the cane longitudinally into lengths. A cane of the desired length, usually about two centimeters in diameter, would generally yield three equal widths sufficient to construct the Athenian. The three split segments would then be carefully arranged so they crossed in the middle and secured with string, so the ends of the cane segments formed a hexagon. Sometimes a fine nail would be driven carefully through the center so the cane segments would not split. Then the ends of each segment were scored on the side and string was securely looped around the end of what should now be a perfect hexagon. The oil paper was then cut, so it would fold over the strings of the edges of the hexagon and glued, so we now had a hexagonal kite of paper, string and cane. Then came the key measurements for the construction of the yoke. Without making the yoke exactly right, the Athenian would not fly properly and one could be totally humiliated. I will not reveal the technique of making a perfect yoke as I considered this to be a trade secret when I was a child. More balancing followed for the yoke of the tail. The tail itself was made of string and fine paper strips, often multicolored whose length and weight had to be critically adjusted for the tricks and fights of the Athenian. With a large spool of strong string, wound in a spindle-like fashion around a piece of wood, and the correct knot connecting the spool string to the yoke, we are ready to fly. I am describing the basic version of the Athenian. However, all kinds of adaptations and decorations could be made. For example, finely cut strips of paper, cut like a tooth comb, could be secured with string all around the margins of this type of kite, which made it rustle loudly in the wind. Kites were often decorated with favorite football team ensigns. Messages could be sent up the string to the kite, written on a piece of paper cut in the middle, which the wind took all the way up to the yoke.

These Athenian kites were the best for flying the highest and were also the strongest and most stable. With a relatively long tail and proper yokes and balance, they would only be limited by the length of string to how high and far they could fly from our hill top next to the marble Olympic stadium. But in spite of the stability and grace of the Athenian kites, war games would break out. Usually if you could bring down another child's kite with your own kite, the other kite became your prize. In practice the other kite and often one's own were destroyed, so the win was more of a matter of pride and bragging. To change one's Athenian kite from a stable, high flying kite to a diving, fighting kite, the simplest adaptation was to shorten the tail sufficiently. But if the other kite was big, stable and the other kid had a huge length of string, one would generally not be able to have kite-to-kite combat. The other kite would just be flying too high to be attacked. One could of course wait until the other kid started to bring their kite down and attack it then, but this was not considered sportsmanlike. In any case, with the Athenian kites I made I preferred just to fly them and send up messages rather than fight. But other kids would try to attack my kite. Overall, war games where one Athenian kite was attacking another was a bit of a waste of time, because of the stability of these contraptions. Also, if you lost your own kite while attacking another Athenian then it was really humiliating. Kids would mock and make fun of you, so you would be jeered off the hill.

But Athenian kites had a vulnerability during the kite war games. And their Achilles' heel was the Smyrnaki. This type of kite could not fly high like the Athenian and was much less stable. They were made primarily to dive and to do fancy dips. Their construction was simpler than the Athenian, but trickier to get right. To make a Smyrnaki, one had to bend a strip of cane, attach a straight strip on each end of the bent piece and secure the ends of the straight strips to each other with string. The frame then looked like a narrow piece of pie. After the frame was covered by the oil paper and glued around the edges, the yoke was made just from one piece of string, tied to the ends of the bent piece of cane where it was secured to the straight pieces. The tail was directly attached to the angle made by the two straight pieces. The Smyrnaki would usually attack the string of the Athenian, tangle it and hope to pull down the Athenian if it was not too big and flying too high. The Smyrnaki also had a secret weapon (not used by all of them) which could bring down the biggest Athenian in the world, with a little luck and a lot of skill. This made them respected and feared, if they were flown by knowledgeable hands. The secret weapon was a safety razor blade, sharpened in a glass exactly as I had done for the English prisoners. The razor blade (or often more than one) would be inserted in the bent piece of cane, facing up. This gave the Smyrnaki a very sharp cutting edge on top. A skillfully executed dive across an Athenian string and the Athenian would wave bye-bye to its owner, released to fly off in the distance before it gradually came down. Actually, all of these kite-war games were carried out in a fairly civilized manner; older kids that had large, elaborate Athenians that flew off in the far distance were respected. No one would attack those kites that were generally considered to be works of art. Also, the previous stone-throwing gangs did not stick together and were unrecognizable in kite flying. On occasion we would have kids that would try to cut down any kite and not respect the unspoken rules. But they would not be from our neighborhoods in Pagrati.

At some point after the Civil war, I was given a very big present. I cannot remember what grade I was in, or even whether I still went to school in Pagrati. I do remember that I was asking for this present for a very long time, maybe many months or even years. It was a real football of my own. Street football (soccer) was very big in our neighborhood, as all over Greece. It was the number one sport. For practical purposes, the only real sport. So, having my own football raised me way above the other kids in the neighborhood. The football I was given was made from real leather. It was of a standard size, just like the professionals. Initially the leather was a little hard but with usage it gradually became softer leather, which was a lot easier to kick by quick feet. All of the football we played was on the street. There were no fields, no grass, no pitch. Smaller streets in Pagrati were not paved at the time. Ours and the surrounding streets were no exception. Nowadays an unpaved street may bring images of soil, maybe hard soil, but soil nevertheless. Not so the unpaved streets of Pagrati. Their surface was mostly stones. Not flat stones, but irregular, often sharp stones. That is why the ball got worn out and became softer soon. Any fall on these sharp stones of granite and limestone left one with serious scrapes and often blood pouring out from knees and elbows alike. Since it was my ball, I obviously chose what position I would play. I chose goalie. I am not sure why. I suppose it gave me good control of my ball and I could demonstrate that I was fearless, thus deserving the ball. I would dive to make saves falling right on the sharp stones of the road. My favorite side to dive was to the right, probably because I was right handed and I felt more secure in protecting myself from scraping. Nevertheless, I was always bleeding from the dives, which gave me further status and recognition. I still carry the scars, mostly on my right knee. My right knee-cap is twice the size of my left.

Baker's dozen

At the lower end of the street where the Bastille was, there was a cross-street with a large chestnut tree. This street seemed like it was in a depression in the ground and I remember it as being dark, compared to the bright street that we lived on. I think because of the small hill nearby and the orientation of that street, it seemed darker, and the chestnut tree shaded the sun. On that street there lived a baker. The baker's shop that housed his oven was directly across from his house. The baker and his family were very poor. During the Occupation, if he had not owned the oven, the baker's family would surely have starved. The main reason the baker's family were so poor was that there were so many children. There were twelve. This was a very high number for Greece, even for that time.

I was friendly with one of these twelve children and I knew a number of the others, but I would get confused between them. They mostly dressed in rags and seemed soiled by dirt. Their dirt was dark, like you might see on somebody working in a mechanics shop or even black like the coal-man who delivered the charcoal in our district. The baker's shop and oven was of similar dark color. The oven burned charcoal and maybe that is where the dark soot came from. Sometimes I would go with the baker's boy into their house. The house was like a half basement and it was also dark and small. There were hardly any windows and there seemed to be crowded bunks everywhere in their living space. One would often see kids or adults lying in the bunks, although I could never make out very well who was in any one bunk because of the darkness. By comparison, the Bastille was like a Crystal Palace. People on the street said that the baker was very honest. They said that he refused to cheat customers in the weight of the flour required to make the standard loaf, in order to try to feed his family. No one had ever seen a potato or a vegetable missing from the tapsia (the circular, large metal baking dishes) that customers gave him to bake in his charcoal oven. Of course, during the Occupation these were the only things that the baker baked, in addition to the standard-weight loaves of bread. The loaves were distributed by rationing, through government stamps, usually by half or quarter loaf, depending on the number of family members. They would be carefully weighed out during the years of the great hunger.

After the Occupation and the Civil War the monarchy was reinstated in Greece by plebiscite and, about that time, a large framed picture of the King appeared in the baker's shop. There was mild curiosity about the baker's politics in the neighborhood, but this was soon superseded by much more vital gossip. The gossip swirled around deaths in the baker's family. These deaths appeared to occur regularly year in and year out during the Occupation and the Civil War in this very large family. It was usually one of the youngest children of the brood. They were the most susceptible to malnutrition and diseases of early childhood. The curious thing was that the neighborhood was left with the impression that the baker's family did not change very much in size, although no one could say with certainty how many children there were at any one time. They all looked kind of alike, in their rags, in their dark dust, and their resigned expressions, and anyone that went into their house could never tell how many kids lay around in the darkened bunks. Also, the baker's wife always looked the same. Always dressed in the same stitched up old dress, made from different pieces of cloth and loose fitting, it was hard to tell when she was pregnant. Plus, it was said, that with so little to eat the babies were always born small, so she never had a big belly. I guess that is why these were the ones that were most likely to die. Then a story started to circulate as to how all of these deaths were related to the births, and why the King's framed picture had appeared on the bakery wall.

It turned out that the palace wanted to encourage large families in Greece. It had something to do with increasing the size of the race. The King would have a bigger kingdom and Greece would become a more important nation. But Greek women were cautious and generally well-educated about reproductive matters, even those that did not get very far in school. So most of them knew how to say "no" and the population was not growing very fast at all. Certainly not as fast as the Nationalists wanted. So the Palace announced an incentive. Any woman that gave birth to a thirteenth child, would have that child baptized by the King (most likely someone from the Palace in the King's name). This would make the King godfather of that child, which means quite a lot in Greek tradition. All kinds of presents and gifts would be forthcoming from the kingly godfather, including maybe a long-term subsidy. But there was a small catch. The interpretation of a woman giving birth to a thirteenth child required that this child be born alive, and more importantly that there would be another twelve *living* children. Also, if this last of thirteen children died, it would presumably no longer be the godchild of the King as it no longer existed, and all subsidies and presents would cease. Well, it turned out that this desolate baker's family had pinned their hopes for some years on having the King baptize their thirteenth child. It seems that this, or something like this, was an old pre-war custom in any case. So, when one of their children would die or looked like it might, Mrs. Baker would get pregnant again in order to keep up the numbers. The problem was that the deaths occurred with monotonous regularity, year in and year out, and by necessity so did the pregnancies. Bets would go around the neighborhood as to whether this would be the year that they would reach the magical thirteen. All kinds of factors were weighed for both the chances of birth and death. It was pretty morbid but everybody seemed to enjoy handicapping the living kids, the appearance of Mrs. Baker's belly, how worn she looked and what the oven business was like. But finally, victory for the bakers became undeniable. Word spread around the neighborhood that Mrs. Baker was pregnant this time with twins. What made it particularly sweet was the general consensus that this might be the last time Mrs. Baker would be able to get pregnant, as she was starting to get on in years. Feverish preparations commenced in the baker's abode to receive his Majesty — their godfather. There was much joy in the family of the baker. They told the whole neighborhood. Their troubles would be over, the King and the palace would take care of them into their old age. They were certain now to become relatives of the Royalty, even if another child died. And living conditions would improve, there would more food!

That year two of their children died.

But for me, things were going along generally pretty well during that same period. The situation in my school in Pagrati had improved. The teachers were no longer frantically searching kids' heads for fleas with blue and red pencils and the very short crew-cut was no longer compulsory for boys. As a result my mother did not have as many fights with the teachers. School class size had declined, as more classrooms were opened, but they were still pretty big. From time to time my parents talked of moving me to a "better school", but as I would have to walk quite some distance, any move was delayed until I became a little bigger. Yet there was one thing that continued to bug me in school. It was grammar; the impenetrable, complicated Greek grammar that I found impossible to fully master. Of course, the fact that we were also taught *Katharevousa* and spoke *Demotiki* did not make matters any easier. But the main problem for me was how to write words correctly, in this essentially phonetic Tongue. I seemed to never be able to totally comprehend the rules of when to use ι, υ, η, all three having the identical sound of ë. Maybe they were not meant to be comprehended and had their origin in a distant antiquity. Even when to use, οι or ει, which also have the sound ë, I had some difficulty with. But the rules seemed clearer for these. I always had to ask how such-and-such a word is written. "Is it with a ι, or an η"? In Greek 'spelling' has no meaning as it is used in English, since it is phonetic and the only question about "how to write" a word has to do with the ambiguity of the character to be used for the ë or o (i.e. o or ω) sound. Having mastered reading and reading voraciously did not really help my problem, which continued to challenge me and frustrate me. On the plus side, my English lessons had been restarted with another teacher who was not as fanatical about the caterpillars or smoking. My parents also became less fanatical about sending me regularly for lessons, so this inscrutable language became a little more tolerable.

To walk to school in Pagrati, I had to go past the baker's shop and the great chestnut tree. I was often preoccupied with the grammar problem of writing the ë or o sounds correctly coming back from school. One day there were a bunch of kids, mostly older, throwing stones around the chestnut tree. I had not seen a good stone fight for a while, so I stopped to look. It turned out that the kids were not actually having a stone fight. Two groups had gathered on each side of the great chestnut tree and they were trying to knock down chestnuts with the rocks. Because they were bigger kids they could throw bigger rocks and with high velocity. They were getting lots of chestnuts down by this method. Half thinking about the insoluble problem of the grammar, I bent down to pick up one of the chestnuts. There was a dull thud in my head and my vision became all red. I had been hit by a rock thrown by a big kid who totally missed the tree. The biggest kid in the group stopped all the stone throwing and came to see how I was doing. I think they felt really badly for having hit me. Maybe it was just because it meant one of them was such a bad shot and had missed the chestnuts altogether and it was not altogether clear who had thrown the rock that got me. In any case, I went home. It was the second time my head had been cracked, the Gianakis incident being the first. At home, the bleeding was stopped with cold compresses and pressure, but my head continued to hurt and I had to lie down.

I must have fallen asleep before the prescribed afternoon rest period, with my accident and the intractable grammar problem still swirling in my brain. *The now familiar Voice came on.*

– Hey Tasouli, you cracked your head again, I see.
– Yes, is that you Styppas? My head hurts too much and I still do not want to open my eyes in case it hurts more.
– Yes, it is me. But, I guess you were not looking when you bent down to pick up the chestnut.
– True, I was thinking about the cursed Greek grammar and why there are all these symbols just to make an ë or an o sound.
– And you still think you want to eliminate all the Greek vowel letters, except one for the α sound, one for the ë sound and one for the o sound?
– For sure. Like I said, 21 letters would be OK for the Greek alphabet.
– And you still hate the English caterpillars?
– Not as much now.
– You are still pretty opinionated! But I guess you are not too small now to want just 21 letters in the Greek alphabet or to dislike the caterpillars.
– So what if I am opinioned. Dropping off the extra Greek vowels of the ë and o sounds makes sense.
– You should try out a 21 letter alphabet.
– Sure. I will try it out next time you visit, Styppas.
– Maybe you will not have a headache then.
– Styppas, my headache is already better. I guess all the talk about language has taken my mind off my head. And I think I must have had my rest without knowing it. I think I will ask my mother if I am allowed to go out and play.
– What would you play?
– What about a little game of football? Just you and me. Out on the street with my football.
– I don't think I could play football. My knee hurts from time to time and it is hurting me now.
– Oh, which knee?
– The right. I hurt it a long time ago playing football.
– How did you do that?
– I scrapped my knee cap badly diving for the ball. When I was small.
– That is funny.

– What is funny?

– I was just thinking how come both of our right knees hurt from playing football. And from scraping the knee cap diving for the ball.

Movie theater

In Greece movies were shown outdoors in the summer. They were very informal and usually noisy affairs. The outside environment was always beautiful, with the outdoor theaters often in little parks with jasmine bushes and high hedges. We sat often on straw-matted wooden chairs, on flat ground covered with fine crushed stone or marble, separated from houses and the street usually by a tall hedge. The movie would not start until after dark, which was quite late in the summer. Everyone talked and smoked. Kids ate candy and smaller kids ran around. No one would ever say "be quiet". The sound track was pretty loud and could be heard around the neighborhood. The movies of that period were mostly black and white and were either romances or comedies. Many were silent, with subtitles, which was another reason why no one bothered to keep quiet. In between conversation with subtitles there would usually be music and other sound effects. It never rained in the summer, so the outing to a movie was always a success. The fact that the reel broke frequently and had to be re-stitched on site by the projector-man did not bother us in the least. We were totally used to it. Quite often the movie would just repeatedly flash because of all the previous stitching and then just go dark. But in the Athenian nights with all the excitement and activity in the audience no technical glitch really seemed to matter. The movie coming on and off, the loud sound track, the talking, little kids running about were all interwoven together.

In the winter, there was only one movie house we went to — the Cineac. This seemed rather luxurious compared to the outdoor summer movies. Cineac was near Omonia, the major commercial center of Athens. Cineac had plusher, more comfortable seats and a big screen. The reel did not break as much as the outdoor movies, but often enough. In front of the screen there was an orchestra pit. There musicians would gather and play an accompanying score for the silent movies. During the Occupation, and I think also after, the musicians would play quite often as many of the movies were pre-war silent films. I loved to hear the musicians play, although they smoked also, as did most of the audience even though it was indoors. I suppose there were a lot of unemployed musicians then, so what else would they do but smoke a lot? "News of the World" would always be shown first. These were accompanied by a very loud, triumphant voice of the announcer and rousing, military-style music. The News always reflected the views of the government in power. During the Occupation there were lots of battle reports and German military parades. During the Civil War we saw lots of reporting on the King, Queen Frederica, British and American news and the like. Laurel and Hardy (called in Greek "the fat-one and the thin-one") and Charlie Chaplin (Charleau) were very popular and my favorites. Peels of often uncontrolled laughter would ring out of the audience right through these comedies. Wild clapping would break out when Charleau would succeed in overcoming a vile adversary. Often there were cheers over political content, especially in the Charleau films. These would be directed against the pro-German government during the Occupation. You might also hear cheers against the rightist-Royalist governments during the Civil War. It was hazardous to cheer against either of these regimes, even though one would say they were just cheering for Charleau. People seemed to let go in the movies, although they knew they could be watched by the secret police or informers. There seemed to be an exhilaration in the movie crowd, massed together, that I have not seen elsewhere. There was both a feeling of safety and of greater freedom of expression within a packed audience in a darkened movie-house. For me, the excitement came more from the audience reactions than the movie content. And when Charleau would be threatened by a nasty coming at him from behind, huge warning shouts and instructions would rise from the audience, sometimes seemingly in a single voice.

– Look out Charleau! Look out!

– He is behind you, Charleau. He is swinging a stick … duck, duck!

– Damn it. The bugger got you!

– We warned you, Charleau, we warned you.
– Yeah, we were all shouting to warn you, Charleau. We were all warning you!
– What is the matter with you? Don't you listen?
– Get up now!
– Get up and punch the bugger back, Charleau!
– Bravo! Bravo! You got him, Charleau. You got him!

An occupied race had found its voice, in its own demotic tongue, in the Cineac movie house.

~

– *Did you like the movie, Styppas?*
– You should still be asleep, Tasouli.
– How do you really know my name, Styppas?
– I just do. Why are you wandering about?
– I was awake and I didn't have anyone to play with.
– But how did you find me?
– I don't know. I just did. Or maybe you found me.
– But Tasouli, I am in Kingston and you are in the Bastille.
– So what?
– Also, it is the wrong time for you.
– No it is not. It is early in the morning. Nobody is up and around yet, because everybody is still asleep in the Bastille. That is why I had no one to play with. I looked for you and could not find you. So, I went looking for you. That is, if you did not start looking for me first.
– But it is late here. It is well after midnight.
– That is OK, Styppas. Some people sleep in the day and work at night. Uncle Stelios told me that is what they do for some Engineering jobs. And Thales said it for doctors in hospitals working at night.
– I know that. It is not the kind of time I am talking about, Tasouli.
– As usual, you know too much, Styppas. But you never answered me if you liked the movie.
– Which movie?
– Why do you ask which movie, Styppas?
– Because I saw a movie also. Here in Kingston.
– Oh I know, Styppas. You saw "Kill Bill"?
– Yes made by Quentin Tarantino.
– "Kill Bill" was not made by Charleau, Styppas?
– Of course not.
– Why not?
– Different times mostly.
– But you never took me to see "Kill Bill". You took Pamela.
– How did you know about "Kill Bill" and Pamela, Tasouli?
– It was all in your dream, Styppas. And I could clearly see it. Nice colors in "Kill Bill". Charleau is always black and white.
– Tasouli, you are starting to know too much.
– I don't know as much as you Styppas. You know nearly everything. Except what you forget. Did you like "Kill Bill"?
– Yes, I did like "Kill Bill". But the audience was all quiet mostly. They would not cheer, like in Charleau.
– Why would they not cheer, Styppas?
– Nothing is real for them in a movie. It is just a movie.
– But Charleau is a real hero. Like Joujoukos. That is why they cheer Charleau too.
– But "Bill" and the girl are heroes too and the audience still did not cheer them like Charleau, Tasouli.

59

– Maybe they did not think that "Bill" and the girl were like Joujoukos, Styppas.
– They would not know Joujoukos, Tasouli.
– Why is that?
– They are not in Pagrati, Tasouli. They are in Kingston.
– Where is Kingston?
– Never mind. It is where I fell asleep.
– If they do not even know Joujoukos in Kingston, what do they know Styppas?
– Altogether other things. They would not even understand you, Tasouli. They speak English.
– Ah, the caterpillars!
– That's right. The movie was in English.
– They are English — like the English prisoners?
– No, Tasouli. They call themselves Canadians.
– But they speak English, Styppas?
– In Kingston they do. Mostly.
– How come they speak English if they are not English?
– Some of their ancestors were English.
– But what is their race now, Styppas?
– They say they don't have a race. Mostly.
– How can you not have a race, mostly? Everybody is supposed to have a race. Just to have a language of your own.
– How so?
– You know, Styppas … we speak Greek and we are Greeks. The English prisoners in the Bastille spoke English and were English. The Italian prisoners in Pyrgos spoke Italian and were Italian. The German officers in Pyrgos spoke German and were Germans.
– You've been thinking about these things, Tasouli?
– Yes, of course. It is just normal. You can't have a language of your own without a race of your own. You can ask Yiayia Sophia, or Uncle Stelios or Joujoukos.
– Joujoukos?
– Sure. Joujoukos speaks Catish because he belongs to the Cat race.
– Tasouli, you've gone off in a tangent about language and race. The conversation started about the audience in Kingston not cheering "Kill Bill", unlike the audience in Cineac who would cheer Charleau.
– True. Because Charleau was of our Tongue, of our race.
– Charleau is not Greek.
– The movie was silent. You know that, Styppas! But the subtitles were Greek, and so were the orchestra and the audience. Charleau is one of us. Everybody says this. He was one of us especially during the Occupation.
– What does that have to do with the Kingston audience not cheering "Kill Bill"?
– How can "Bill" or the girl be one of them in the audience, if they have no race that they can all belong to? How can they really cheer "Bill" or the girl? They do not even speak a language they can call their very own.
– True, Tasouli. But maybe cheering Charleau in Cineac had little to do with language and our own race. Maybe it was all about the Occupation and oppression.
– They didn't have the Occupation in this Kingston of yours, Styppas?
– No, not at all.
– No wonder then they do not cheer or laugh loudly, Styppas!
– But there were a few rowdy kids in the movie house that laughed and made noise and text-messaged all the time. They never had seen the Occupation, either.
– But, this text-messaging, you talk about, is it like a language of their own among the rowdy kids. Is that not so, Styppas?
– Probably, Tasouli.
… but listen, I will have to get out of this dream or change dreams. Otherwise, with all the talk never ending, I am afraid that after I wake up I will not be able to go back to sleep.

– That is OK, Styppas. I can now hear the adults moving about in the Bastille. I will go and explore and see who is up. I think it is Uncle Stelios. He always gets up earliest since he is the oldest. And then my father.

– Just one more thing, Tasouli. How did you really find out what I was dreaming?

– I have started to figure you out, Styppas.

– That isn't how it should have worked, Tasouli. But, I guess you have grown up quite a bit. How old are you now? Eight?

– I've just turned nine, Styppas.

– Nine, already! Are you then going to try an example of writing just with 21 Greek characters? Like you said you would last time we met. You know, when your head was cracked when you bent down to pick up the chestnut.

– What I said, Styppas was that I would try it next time you visited me. This time, I think I found you. So, I visited you. You did not visit me. So you have to visit me for me to try the 21 letter alphabet.

– You are starting to get annoying, Tasouli. And you are becoming pedantic.

– How can being correct be annoying? If it is correct it should not be annoying. But what is pedantic?

– Like too detailed, insisting on precision all the time. Tasouli, you better go and check out the adults waking up in the Bastille. I too can now hear Stelios in the bathroom.

– OK, I'll go in a minute. But I think I will like being pedantic, Styppas. So will Stelios and my father. Thales will mostly laugh. I will try pedantic on all of them today. Of course, Yianis will like pedantic most of all since he is a very serious mathematician. But he is living in Thesaloniki now — with Toula. So, he will not know yet about me becoming pedantic. But I will tell him when he visits the Bastille and he will have lots of questions about whether I have really become pedantic. I will have to prepare on how to answer all of his questions.

– You are boring me with all your plans for becoming pedantic.

– Sorry about that, Styppas. But I am very proud of trying to become pedantic. I promise that I will work hard at it.

– Goodbye.

– Goodbye, Styppas. Sleep well.

I lie half awake and then fall asleep again and start to dream not about "Kill Bill", but about Cineac and the musicians in the orchestra pit in the subdued light and the black and white images that flashed on and off from the antiquated projector. The dream seems to float along on top of dark blue waves of a winter Mediterranean Sea. The flashes of the screen images reflect off the waves and I can see clearly what is good and what is bad in the world of the Occupation Child.

Later in the '40s

Maraslion

When I was in grade three in Pagrati Elementary School, my parents made the decision to move me to the Maraslion Academy in Kolonaki. So, I started grade four there and stayed until I finished grade six. Maraslion had a reputation of being one of the better schools of Athens. I think it had in its full name the word 'Experimental', perhaps because it also trained teachers in new teaching methods. Maraslion was hugely different from Pagrati Elementary School. The class sizes were much smaller, with only about 30 kids per class compared to the vastly greater numbers in Pagrati. We had to wear cutsie little tunics over our shorts and shirts, which came to about the length of the shorts. The tunics were a dark royal blue with a nice white logo. I can't quite visualize what the logo said but it was something about the school. Girls wore a similar tunic over blouses and skirts. We had individual desks and only occasionally would there be two children to a desk. The desks themselves were also different from Pagrati. No more of the immensely heavy, unmovable desks made of solid cast iron lattices — black like a crow with the indestructible oak desk tops an inch thick. The heavy benches, without a backing, were long enough to accommodate four kids. Our desks at Maraslion could be moved around. They were made of a lighter, likely hollow metal. The wood was also lighter both in color and weight. There was even a shelf underneath the desk where we could store stuff. I think our classes were mixed but, strangely, I do not have clear recollection of where boys and girls sat. I do remember that contrary to Pagrati, the desks were arranged in a much more haphazard manner. The end result was that one had a good view of the teacher from wherever we sat. It was this more uneven arrangement of the desks that seemed to drive a teaching system that was like day and night from Pagrati.

For example, the teachers in Maraslion rarely, if ever, hit the students with a ruler. And because there were a lot fewer students in each class it was possible to test each student individually in a more persistent way. This was both good and bad. In Pagrati, you had to stand on the wooden platform when asked a few simple questions. You either got them right and got off the platform unscathed, or missed them and got hit with the ruler before climbing down, all flushed but with lots of sympathy or even admiration from your classmates. In Maraslion, the teacher would ask a question and students who thought they knew the answer would put their hand up. The teacher could pick one of them and test them, more or less in rotation. If some students hardly ever put their hand up for a particular topic, the teacher could ask one of them to try to answer the question. In either case, if the student got the answer right the teacher would go to the next question. If the answer was wrong, the teacher would then give a clue or ask a simpler question on the same topic. This process could go on and on, until either the student got a simple question right or was totally humiliated by getting everything wrong and reduced to a confused or blabbering state. There was no option to just give a smart-aleck answer, get hit with the ruler and get it over with, but with your head held high with the glorious approval of your classmates at recess. It was that honor code in Pagrati Elementary that made one feel so, so good on occasion. Not in the Maraslion Academy! If one got the answers repeatedly wrong other students would start to get restless, giggle and one would become the focus of the whole class. This giggling could then carry on during recess, a punishment much worse than getting hit with the ruler. One thing that the teacher would never accept was an "I don't know" answer. This point turned out to be a critical one in my later education and attitude towards schooling.

The major issue in education, during my years at Maraslion, was language. The fight between *Demotiki* and *Katharevousa* continued to rage. The two versions of Greek were markers for which side of the Civil War families were on. Certainly, someone who openly supported Demotiki could be considered as a Communist sympathizer, Anti-Royalist and the like. As a child in school, I was always very careful not to make any comments about language. You never knew what another child might say to their parents and what could then happen to me or my family. My biggest fear was not that I would be expelled from Maraslion, if it was found out that my family supported Demotiki. It was that my family would be arrested and tortured and exterminated and that I would be left an orphan, with a big, swollen belly. Just like the abandoned kids in Omonia, during the Occupation.

But now there was enough food to prevent big swollen bellies. And, once, my mother had somehow allowed me to taste a salami sandwich. I had never tasted anything so incredibly delicious. Sandwiches were uncommon in Greece and I don't think that pre-sliced bread was even available. But the salami in this sandwich made me think that I was absolutely in heaven. I can't even remember who made this salami sandwich, but it would not have been my mother. It must have been an important friend because I was allowed to eat it, and it must have been in the important friend's house. I begged my mother time and time again to make me a salami sandwich which I could take with me during the excursions and picnics that were organized by Maraslion. It was to no avail. Salami was dirty. You could not tell what dirty meats were used to make it. I was never to be permitted to taste it again. Not in my whole life.

I can't remember what I was given to take with me during these excursions and picnics of Maraslion. It was clean, healthy food. I hated it because all I could think about was a salami sandwich. To make matters worse some kids had salami sandwiches. I tried not to think about it during our trips to the country and played the various organized ball games in the playing field. But we were usually not the only school at those outings. One time there was another school outing near our school group. The kids had green jackets with their school logo and they stuck more or less together as a group. They seemed fairly quiet. Much more quiet than us. We were playing football and the ball was accidentally kicked towards the kids with the green jackets. I went to retrieve the ball. Then I noticed something extraordinary. Most of them were eating salami sandwiches. I could smell the salami. I wanted to stay close by the kids with the green jackets, in case I was given a salami sandwich. But they were not at all friendly, although not rude either. They just ate their salami sandwiches and kept looking at me and the other school children from Maraslion. Soon I was called back by the teacher, as I had got the football.

– Who are those children? I asked the teacher as I returned the football.
– They are just orphans from the orphanage.
– But, they are eating salami sandwiches, I protested.
The teacher just looked strangely at me and repeated:
– I said, they are from the orphanage. It says so on the logo of their green jackets.

Since then I started to have this association with Demotiki and the salami sandwiches. It was a rather peculiar association, for Demotiki was the language of the street and Katharevousa the language of the privileged, and yet the orphanage kids had the priceless privilege of being allowed to eat salami sandwiches. Also, they did not have swollen bellies, like the orphans of Omonia during the Occupation. Over the next few days, I noticed that I was losing the fear that my parents would be taken away and I would be left as an orphan, because they supported the Demotiki. After all if they were taken away and exterminated, with the rest of my Bastille family, I would probably end up in an orphanage and there I would be given lots of salami sandwiches. I started to feel badly about this and did not tell anyone. So, my fear that they might be taken away if I started to speak in favor of Demotiki gradually returned.

If fact, the Demotiki was entirely used in Maraslion and I do not remember any of the teachers trying to teach us in Katharevousa. I think that at least some of our text books were in a *mihtí* (mixed) language, especially some of the grammar and history books. Of course, for religious studies we had to understand biblical Greek which was not very difficult, and in the last year at Maraslion, I think, they introduced classical ancient Greek which was much more difficult. So, there were actually five types of Greek we had to at least be familiar with: Demotiki, Katharevousa, this 'mihtí' version, biblical Greek and some ancient Greek. Even though Conservative forces dominated the political landscape of the late 1940s, including bringing back the King, my impression was that Demotiki continued to make quiet progress in the street and even in at least some schools, such as my own.

Recess at Maraslion was in a large schoolyard, with mostly a cement surface, surrounded by school buildings and some shrubbery. One building, across from the main building with the classrooms did not seem to be used very much. I think it may have been the original older, stone building of the school which housed some offices. On a couple of occasions I went inside that building during recess and what I found really surprised me. A whole floor was full of equipment: microscopes, weighing scales and other fancier machines, whose purpose I did not know, all new-looking, nice and shiny but not used. When I asked what this was all for, I was told it was for experimental labs and it had all been purchased from Germany before the war. It looked very solid, good quality stuff. Apparently it was to be used to train teachers, but seemed to be set up for students. I don't remember this equipment ever being used by the students during the three years I was there.

The bottom of the schoolyard opened down, through two or three stone-laid steps into a larger football field with a reddish clay-soil surface. On the left, as one came down from the main schoolyard there was a gym, with a high roof but it was open towards the football field as there was no wall on that side. The other three walls of the gym were studded with horizontal wooden handles, as ladders for climbing and the like, as well as gymnastic equipment of various sorts. There were mattresses for tumbling and exercise horses. The exercise ladders and other gymnastic equipment attracted only small groups of students, while the football field became the main battleground for the boys. It was there that everything about being a boy was decided. There would be a gym teacher who acted as a referee during the football matches, but I do not remember actually ever being coached. The main role of the gym teacher seemed to be to prevent bloodshed. He did that by blowing his whistle and shouting a lot. The bigger and older boys would dominate what was essentially a continuous scrum. I don't think the gym teacher ever insisted on playing positions or on passing the ball. Being smaller and younger, especially when I first went to Maraslion, I got pushed around a lot and hardly got to kick or dribble much with the football. I really hated being assigned to this inferior position in the pecking order. The big boys scored the goals and they were the ones everybody paid attention to. I just had to suck it up, lick my wounds — both mental and physical (scrapes and scratches mostly) — and go on to the next class, or head off home if the football scrum was the last activity of the school day.

During recess at Maraslion, boys and girls seemed to form their own groups and did not mix very much. I had befriended two or three boys and we tended to play together during recess. One of those boys was Frank; he was quite different from all the other boys and stood apart. Frank was very tall compared to the other boys in school. He was certainly the tallest and very tall indeed for a Greek child who would have grown up through the Occupation. Greek kids that were very young during the Occupation never grew very much, having not enough food to grow on, even for the well-to-do. Frank was not Greek and he did not grow up in Greece during the Occupation. He was French. I think his father was high up in the French Embassy in Athens, maybe even the Ambassador. Also, Frank was different from the Greek kids in other ways. He was pale looking and his white skin contrasted with the generally darker, sun-tanned Greek boys. He had mild-looking, washed-out blue eyes behind spectacles, I think, although I am not 100% sure about the spectacles. But the biggest differences were in his manner and his speech. Contrary to the more aggressive manner of the Greek children, Frank was more placid and he would respond to a pushy comment or even a shove or a kick in this detached manner that he had. If the other kid or kids continued being aggressive towards him, he would still be inclined to make a general comment, a little off topic perhaps, but he would never return aggression, which was considered to be a 'must' both in the schoolyard and on the street. Frank's Greek was also fairly heavily accented with French. I think his Greek was generally correct, but the way he pronounced words, putting in a lot of 'z' and 's' sounds and not rolling his 'r's in the typical Greek way made him sound like a sissy. But he would always be engaged in whatever was going on in the schoolyard and was never just standing by himself. We explored together the building where all the teaching equipment was being kept. Frank seemed to know what everything was for. And when someone asked us what we were doing there, Frank was able to talk about the teaching equipment in a way that made this person simply nod and leave us alone. I was impressed.

Frank always had some innovative idea that he was trying out. It was usually something to improve an activity or a game and he always explained it slowly, thoughtfully, in his mild, French-accented and yet convincing manner. One day, during recess, he was insistent in showing me a new physical education trick. We were with some other kids in the schoolyard with the cement surface, rather than the football field with the red clay surface. The idea of the trick was that I would bend forward, put my arms between my legs and Frank, who would be standing behind me, would give a good hard pull on my hands. One would then be expected to do a flip forwards and land on their feet. He said he had tried it many times and it always worked. I was a little doubtful at the beginning but he convinced me. Frank told me to put my hands and my head between my legs. I put my hands between my legs, still thinking about the Demotiki and the salami sandwiches. Frank grabbed my hands and gave them a hard pull from behind. My forehead came down like a hammer on the hard cement of the courtyard.

The resulting dull thud was more encompassing than the one I remembered from the giant flat stone I had dropped on my head; it was more numbing than the stone thrown at the chestnuts of the chestnut tree which also accidentally hit me on the head. I had difficulty getting up from the pavement. I looked up through the familiar curtain of red blood coming down over my eyes. I could see Frank's mild blue eyes staring at me looking totally terrified. I tried to reassure him but I don't think that I was making coherent sounds. They tried to get me up and finally they succeeded, although I was pretty wobbly. The blood kept pouring out, which was making me more wobbly. Fortunately the famous Evangelismos Hospital was practically next door to the Maraslion. I was walked over to the Emergency Department, where I was promptly stitched up. I hardly felt anything, maybe a few tiny pricks. The blood soon stopped. I no longer felt wobbly. It was amazing how much better I felt, except my head hurt a little. This was the third time that my head was split. Surely it was the most important time, as I had to have stitches. People said I had five stitches. They said this with awe, I thought. I was proud to have had that many stitches. I started to think: Frank had not tried the trick on the mattresses for gymnastics in the gym, or even on the red soil of the football pitch. For some reason he had tried it on the hard cement courtyard of our school.

– You did not put your head between your legs like I told you, he said, still looking upset and practically ready to cry.
– No, I was thinking about something else.
– What could be so important?
I did not answer.
– And your legs were all rigid. They did not bend.
– I told you I was thinking about something else.
No way would I reveal that I was thinking about the Demotiki and salami sandwiches. I would be regarded as a total sissy.

I carefully considered my situation. It was impossible that Frank, with his mild blue eyes and non-competitive personality would have tried the flip trick on the cement out of wickedness or malice. No, instead it had to do with all these little details that make up life and could change it in an instant. That is why I have tried to relate these little details. Every little detail has meaning in the story, some which come up later in important events.

I went home that day with my stitches and thinking about how the little details determine fate. The walk from Maraslion, up in Kolonaki, to the Bastille, down in Pagrati, was a long one. In those days the river of Athens, the famed Ilysos of antiquity, still ran uncovered through that part of the city. If fact, Ilysos in the late '40s was nothing more than a big ditch which most of the time had a small trickle of dirty water running through. There was lots of garbage on its fabled banks, where the nymphs no doubt cavorted in antiquity. To cross it I had to go out of my way, across a bridge and then gradually find my way to Alsos Pagratiou, the little park of Pagrati, and then get into the district of Pagrati itself and finally take the streets that led to the Bastille. Before I entered the Alsos, I would have to go through a rough, partially inhabited area, with old cans and other garbage lying around. Of course, garbage then was nothing like garbage now. There was virtually no organic waste, since almost everything of animal or vegetable origin was consumed. Also, there was no plastic in the garbage and there were no discarded clothes. But there were metal cans. And I would normally carefully choose one of these cans. I do not know what made me choose one can over another. I think I tried to choose a newer can that had not rusted too much. But I knew very clearly why I would start kicking a can at about this location. I did it every day coming back from school. This area, and further into the Alsos, was full of big rough kids. They looked like they belonged to gangs. I was an obvious target. They would always start to make fun of me and would want something. I also knew why I was a target, what with my long hair and my cute little blue tunic with the embroidered Maraslion logo. The tunic was over a nice clean white shirt and short pants. There were no other kids like me in that district. A target to be sure! Many times they would threaten and chase me and I would run as fast as I could. I was afraid they would beat me up or worse. I was terrified. Then, one day, I figured I would look tougher if I went casually through their territory, apparently preoccupied with kicking a can. I also took off my tunic and held it in my hand or put it over my shoulder. Strangely enough, the kick-the-can trick seemed to work. At least, most of time. I did not seem to be as much of a target, although I was still chased from time to time. Nevertheless, I was never free of these gangs. I figured that once I had left the deserted, garbagey no-man's land and entered the Alsos, where there were a number of adults sitting or reading papers, I would be safe from the ugly kids and their gangs. That was not always the case. The adults seemed to pay no attention to the young gangsters, who would often chase me through the Alsos and sometimes jump out from the bushes trying to get me. When I was nearly through the Alsos, near the Pagrati neighborhoods, these rough kids would disappear and I would be safe once again. Of course I would arrive home all sweaty and my mother would cross-examine me demanding to know in her suspicious, accusatory manner, why I was so hot. Of course, I would never admit my tortures.

The day when my head was split by Frank, I figured that I would be really in for it from the rough kids. I did not feel at all strong and I did not think that I could run fast. As luck would have it, I found a very shiny, new kicking can that day in the no-man's land. I started to systematically kick it, approaching the Alsos with the young gangsters hanging around as usual. I tried to concentrate on the can and pretended not to look at the young gangsters. They seemed to be plotting some particularly nasty trick and were grouped together talking conspiratorially. I figured that at least some of them would come after me. But for some inexplicable reason, none did. They simply glanced at me and almost nodded. To this day I still don't know how I escaped so easily in my weakened condition. Maybe it was the shiny can. Or my split head with the stitches. Or they were too much into their own plots. But surely they saw me and I thought I detected nearly a nod. Maybe even a nod of recognition. It was one of the few times that I did not have to run. When I got home, my mother did not ask me why I was sweating because I was not. I explained to her that Frank had split my head and the circumstances. Surprisingly she was not at all mad. I thought that again there was almost a nod of understanding if not approval. After all, Frank was from a very good family, the son of the French ambassador or something. She even seemed impressed I had been stitched up at the famous Evangelismos. No running to the Maraslion to fight with the teachers, as had been the case for Pagrati Elementary School and the flea searches of the kids' scalps. My head was split and sown-up by important people. I had arrived!

I stayed up late that night, savoring my exploits of the day. How easily had potential disaster and humiliation turned into a double victory! The tough kids in the Alsos had let me pass without threatening me and perhaps even nodded, and my mother's attitude was one of pride. Yet my head was split probably because of my stupidity. How was poor Frank to know that I had not tucked my head in properly and my legs became stiff when he performed on me his well-rehearsed trick? All because I was thinking about Katharevousa and Demotiki and all the political conflict over language and who would dominate and who would be oppressed or even eliminated. And if my parents and my family were to be eliminated for supporting Demotiki and I ended up in an orphanage, would I really be given salami sandwiches? It was in this state of a mixture of satisfaction and ambivalence that I finally fell asleep.

~

– *So, you split your head for a third time, Tasouli,* said the familiar Voice.

– I am glad you came to visit me, Styppas. I have a lot to discuss with you. Especially about Katharevousa and Demotiki. You know, that it was the real cause of having my head split.

– Oh, I know alright. But much more important events than splitting your head will happen in the future, over the conflict between Katharevousa and Demotiki — like a democratic government falling and the rise of a dictatorship.

– As usual Styppas, you know everything. But the language conflict was the reason for having my head split now. And I must explain to you how Katharevousa and Demotiki are related to splitting my head.

– OK then, explain it if you insist.

– I have not told anyone else.

– And why not?

– I am really too embarrassed.

– My lips are sealed. I couldn't tell anyone else you know, even if I wanted to.

– Oh. In that case here is what happened. You see I am afraid to say that my parents and family are all pro-Demotiki. I am worried that they might be taken away and tortured or even terminated.

– That wouldn't be that unusual these days.

– Yes, but then there is the problem of the salami sandwiches, Styppas.

– Salami sandwiches?

– Yes, I dream and fantasize about them because I tasted one once and it was so, so, so good.

– So?

– So these children from the orphanage were all eating salami sandwiches …

– Oh, I get it Tasouli. You thought that if you told people that your parents were pro-Demotiki you might end up as an orphan and then you would be able to have lots of salami sandwiches. So your legs went all rigid while Frank was trying to flip you because of the conflict.

– Oh, thanks Styppas. Thanks a lot.

– For what?

– For not making me explain it all. I am not embarrassed now. But I have something else to tell you.

– What?

– You are now visiting me here in Bastille, rather than me visiting you when you are in Kingston. And that is important.

– How so?

– Because visiting me in Bastille is for the events that happen to me here, but finding me when you are in Kingston is for events that happen there to you.

– You are becoming more and more pedantic and splitting hairs.

– Thanks, Styppas. I know that splitting a hair is very difficult, because it is so thin. Still, this time you are visiting me in Bastille which would be different than if you found me when you are in Kingston.

– What does this have to do with the topic of conversation?

– Each time you visited me in Bastille, we talked about things happening to me, but when you visited me in Kingston we talked about things that happened to you, Styppas. Like the "Kill Bill" movie you and Pamela saw without me.

– You have certainly become more pedantic and just a little annoying!

– Oh, thanks again, Styppas. I have been working hard at becoming pedantic. But does being annoying make one better at being pedantic?

– Probably.

– That is good then. Because I can work at both together.

– So, now that I have visited you here in Bastille rather than visiting you in Kingston, are you going to try out 21 letters of the Greek alphabet? … To see if they would actually work?

– That is a most excellent suggestion, Styppas. I think you are also becoming more pedantic on the visitation question.

– Don't be condescending. It is annoying.
– Is 'condescending' like pedantic?
– Not really.
– But if annoying makes you be better at pedantic and condescending is like annoying, then condescending should also make me better at pedantic. Is that not right Styppas?
– There is certain logic to it, annoying and condescending as it might be.
– Thanks again Styppas. You have taught me a lot tonight. I will try to be pedantic, annoying and condescending all at once.
– Goodie, goodie! Are you going to try out the 21 Greek letters or not?
– What should I try them on?
– On something you really like. Like the Barbarians … you know, the Cavafis poem.
– OK. This is easy. These would be the first two lines of the Barbarians in a stripped-down phonetic, monotonic, language with just 21 Greek symbols. I'll write it out for you and then recite it:

Τι περιμένουμε στιν αγορά σιναθρισμένι;
Ινε ι βάρβαρι να φθάσουν σίμερα

– It looks a bit odd, but it sounds OK. I like the monotonic.
– We've also done away with these awful breathing sounds, circumflexes and the like, Styppas. That is good. Anyone should be able to read it now.
– Well, in a few years they'll adopt monotonic in any case. What about the last two lines?
– Here you are:

Κε τόρα τι θα γένουμε χορίς βαρβάρους.
Ι άνθροπι αυτί ίσαν μιά κάπια λίσις.

– I kind of like it once you get used to the look of just one kind of ë and one kind of o.
– It is as if one is getting rid of Greek caterpillars.
– It is ultra, ultra demotic, Tasouli. Your parents and uncles would be toast if they started to support this kind of hairy[1] demotic.
– Nothing but salami sandwiches for me, Styppas.
– Very amusing. But tell me, Tasouli, you didn't want to learn the English tongue because you hated the caterpillars and the way the Latin letters make up the sounds in words? And on top, you hated your first English teacher and would hide from her all the time.
– Yep.
– And what if the English teacher was nice and made you feel good about the caterpillars and the sounds.
– But she wasn't.
– But what if she was?
– That might be OK. The new English teacher does not bug me as much.
– Did either of the English teachers ever try to teach you Greek poetry in English?
– Never! No way!
– Here, then. Try out the first two lines of the Barbarians in English.
– Can't be done Styppas. You'd be insulting Cavafis. My Uncle Stelios would even agree.
– No, Uncle Stelios would think this would be real interesting. He translated whole books and so did Yianis. I will read it for you, since you will massacre the English with your caterpillar obsession. Here goes. The first two lines of the Barbarians:
What are we waiting for, all gathered in the agóra?
For the barbarians shall arrive today.

And the last two:

And now what shall we do without barbarians?
Those humans were some kind of a solution.

– Doesn't sound too bad. But nothing like the Greek. Did you do the translation all by yourself, Styppas?
– No, I based it on a previous translation by a man called Kimon Friar. I changed a few words.
– What did you do that for?
– I am not sure. I think to see if my changes give a better flavor of the original.
– So what did you change?
– Like in the first line, Friar says "What are we waiting for, all mustered in the forum?"
– So, why is "… all gathered in the agora" better than "… all mustered in the forum"?
– Your English is suddenly improving, Tasouli. I thought that σιναθρισμένι, in proper Greek συναθροισμένοι, was closer to "all gathered" than "all mustered". Same for "forum" and "agora". It is closer to the original. In English the word 'forum' is more commonly used than 'agora'.
– But does it *sound* better, Styppas, in the language of the caterpillars?
– I am not sure, Tasouli.
– It might be a waste of time. You either like the sound of it or not, just reading it.
– True, I think. In any case, I better go and get some sleep too.
– Are you going to sleep in your hiding place in Kingston, Styppas?
– That's where I am going. G'night Tasouli.

Athens then

Even during the Occupation, the Civil War and in the later '40s, Athens retained her character and beauty. There were very few private automobiles and a surprisingly good public transporation system. Trams were everywhere. These were big, heavy yellow affairs with solid old wooden seats, some made of polished narrow planks that seemed indestructible. I am not sure where they were made. Perhaps in the Soviet Union or maybe that was later. There were 'No Spitting' signs in the trams made of glazed porcelain-like material, which also seemed indestructible. Of course, everybody suffered from the great hunger during the Occupation, as well as fearing tuberculosis, particularly after the War. When people coughed or spat they would do it in a handkerchief. Usually in a large, white linen handkerchief.

Trams and marbles

I loved the trams. I got on them for free. But I was also afraid of them. Often they did not say clearly where they were going and they just had numbers. The drivers were pretty gruff and the conductors gruffer. I was often afraid to ask passengers for they would look at me as if I was stupid or inferior and talk to me in a dismissive manner. I was always intimidated. So, I would not ask where the tram was going. Instead I adopted a different practice. I would not ask — I would pretend I was busy with my little school-satchel, which carried my books and my marbles. My marbles were very important. In Athens, most boys would have marbles. But they were very different marbles from what I later had in Canada. Nearly all of the marbles of Athens were made of hard-baked clay or some kind of stone and stained with colors that were not very bright, mostly red-brown shades. So they were not at all like glass marbles. They were called βόλοι (vóli), probably derived from *volí*, like a throw or a bullet. The *voli* of Athens were inexpensive and could be bought at any corner store. But they could also be won on the playgrounds at school or on the street. I greatly prized my vóli since I had won most of them. But I prized above all my lead vólos, which was larger and was used as the main shooting volos. This king volos was a glass marble, with colors inter-winding in the glass. It was very beautiful — perhaps one of the most beautiful things I had ever seen.

It is curious that voli are called marbles in English, even though marble was uncommon in England, but common in Greece. Possibly it means that voli were made of marble or stone among the English in the distant past. But Pamela recently assured me that during wartime in England she and her friends played with colored glass marbles. They did not play with stone or marble voli. And instead of a lead glass marble, their king marble was a 'blood alley'. I did not know this then, for if I had, I would have surely asked the English prisoners in Bastille. If the English prisoners had confirmed that English children played with colored glass marbles during the War, when we played with voli, I would have considered it an exorbitant privilege. But it would not have totally surprised me. After all, everybody, in Athens knew that most of the English were Lords. The children's books about England that I had were full of stories about big and little Lords. The Lords must have been as common as the marbles of London then.

So, on a bright winter day as I was riding the tram, which I had caught in the Platea at Pagrati, I had my satchel over my shoulder containing my marbles, my most treasured possession. In addition to my schoolbooks and exercise books I had a small, cloth-bound reading book in English, all about Lords and Ladies of various ages and sizes. I think I may have come directly from an English lesson when I got on that tram. My intent was to go to Syndagma, where my father's office was, and visit him in the office. I think it was late Saturday morning and most offices worked on a Saturday. Surely, I would be treated to pastry in the fine pastry shops that lined Syndagma square of Athens. But my mind was on my marbles and particularly how beautiful my lead glass marble looked in the cool winter sunlight. The heavy tram clunked and clanged past Zapion and past the columns of Olympian Zeus. The tram would then turn right, past the Royal Gardens, and I would be at the top of Syndagma, across from the Parliament buildings and the old Palace in just a few minutes, where I would get off the tram. From there it would take me only a few minutes to cross Syndagma square and be in my father's second floor office which overlooked the square. Syndagma was always full of people, dressed in their winter clothes, many strolling but most sitting in the cafes that lined Syndagma, and drinking coffee, endlessly discussing the politics of the day or a hundred other topics. Some would be eating pastries. They would sit there for hours in the winter sunshine, until it got too cool and then they might go inside the pastry or coffee shops or finally go home. Once I got to my father's office I would have to go through the usual polite re-introductions to colleagues and co-workers in the office. Then I was sure my father would take me to the pastry shop and we would sit outside facing the square. I would have the most delicious pastry and admire my king glass marble which would shine and be unimaginably beautiful in the winter sunshine.

Then, just as the tram had gone past the columns of Olympian Zeus disaster struck. The tram should have turned right onto Queen Amalia's Avenue, but instead it made a wide left, starting to leave the Olympian Zeus behind and to the left, turning towards Syngrou Avenue. It was heading the wrong way! I was going away from Syndagma, away from the familiar coffee shops, away from the tomb of the unknown soldier, away from the Royal Gardens. Instead it was heading rapidly towards Fix, the massive brewing company building in the direction of Nea Smyrni and Faliron. I panicked. I tried to explain my plight to some passengers but no real voice came out. They regarded me with mild, disinterested curiosity. The conductor was further down the tram and he was engrossed in counting and recording his tickets. I knew that if I interrupted him, he would be angry and shout at me. I had to make a quick decision, as the Olympian Zeus columns and the Royal Gardens had started to recede in the distance. The trams then were open at the back and one would get off by first getting on an iron platform and then going down the corrugated iron stairs. A strong iron hand rail was along those iron stairs. I hung onto the hand rail and went down to the bottom stair. The tram was still picking up speed and the buildings started to look a little blurry. I took my heart in my hands and jumped!

I hit the cobblestone pavement and the tram lines really hard. I never anticipated the force of impact. I got scraped very badly. Fortunately there was not much traffic even though another big tram was thundering down towards me. The driver jammed the brakes and the big tram came to a screeching halt in a hale of electric sparks from the wires, of shouting and abuse by the driver. I noticed my arms and legs were bleeding already, but the bleeding, the narrow escape and the driver's abuse were pretty minor compared to the real disaster that befell me. My marbles, my beautiful marbles, flew out of my satchel and spilled all over the tram lines. Many of them had gone into the tram lines. But my wretched schoolbooks and the English book stayed in the satchel. My first and only thought was to try to recover my marbles. In an instant the driver was out shouting more abuse at me and was joined by the conductor who had a very powerful voice. Passengers were also coming out of the tram joining in the chorus of how stupid I was interrupting the tram and causing havoc. Where were my parents? I must have been deranged to jump off a moving tram and more deranged still to try to pick off marbles from a tram line. I had to leave most of my marbles in the tram lines and then watch the tram go over them. But there was one bit of consolation. I had managed to save my beautiful, lead glass marble.

I stumbled over to the sidewalk, nearly being hit by a couple of taxis and I elicited the usual torrent of verbal abuse by their drivers. I headed towards Syndagma on foot. Finally, I limped up the stairs to my father's office. My father seemed preoccupied but noticed my scratches and bleeding. I said that I had accidentally slipped in the Royal Gardens and I got no further questions. I got no special pastry treat that day. Everybody seemed preoccupied. I do not remember the return home.

That evening, in bed, I was hoping that Styppas would come and visit me so I could tell him about my lost marbles and my disaster. He would have some ideas and maybe he could even tell me what to do — he knew everything. But Styppas did not come. I think I fell asleep waiting for him to come. *Finally, I went looking for him. He had already told me about his hiding place.*

– Is that you in bed, Styppas?
– …
– Styppas! Styppas! Wake up; I have something important to tell you.
Two blue-green eyes regarded me blearily.
– You startled me, Tasouli. Styppas is not here.
– Where is he?
– He is gone to Toronto. He went last night and will not be back until tonight. What are you doing here so early?
– Oh, that is you Pamela! I thought it was Styppas. Disaster befell me and I wanted to tell him about it.
– What kind of disaster?
– I lost nearly all my marbles, Pamela. Except my lead glass marble.
– At least you did not loose your blood alley.
– What is a blood alley?
– Your lead marble.
– Why did you call it that?
– Because my lead marble was big, black and with blood-red streaks. The most beautiful of all marbles.
– And did you play and win at marbles with your blood alley, Pamela?
– Oh, yes! In England, in London. A long time ago. When I was a little girl.
– When you were a little girl … It must have been a very long time ago.
– Don't be cheeky!
– And did you try hard to win?
– It was blood in the alley.
– You fought in games of marbles?
– Hard, in the gutters.
– And in the alleys?
– If they had gutters.
– So, your marble games were in the gutters.
– Always.
– And you fought with other girls over marbles?
– Girls and boys.
– Not many girls play marbles in Athens now.
– But they did in London then.
– And did you win many marbles.
– Lots and lots.

Anastassiades

– And what about the Lords? Did they play marbles and win?
– I never met a Lord.
– But my English storybooks are full of Lords.
– Not in my London then. Not in my Southern London, in Mitcham, where I lived.
– And do you think there are Lords now in your Southern London, your Mitcham?
– I doubt it.
– Maybe just in your mind when you were a little girl.
– Maybe …
– And girls and boys play marbles in London now?
– I am sure.
– In the gutters with blood alleys?
– Oh yes. Just like then.
– So was the London of then like the London of now?
– Oh no, so different then than the London of now.

– But marbles and gutters
blood alleys
and Lords of the mind
in London of old
in Mitcham of yours,
is that still the same?

– Yes … you make me smile, Tasouli. No easy task this time of the morning.

– But if marbles and gutters
blood alleys
and Lords of the mind
in London of old and London of now
are ever the same,
then the London of old
is that not the same
as the London of now?

– Do you really believe it, Tasouli?

– Why, if marbles and gutters
blood alleys
and Lords of the mind
are ever the same,
your places of play
in London of then
and London of now
are also forever the same.

– So?

– So if something at all
is forever the same
in London of then
and Athens of now,
I'll be looking for you
as I freely wander
on my cobbled paths

my glistening byways
in soft winter rain
of my Athens of now,
and if I tire too much
I'll just lie down and
after falling asleep
I'll be sure to find you
wherever you are.

– But much has changed from wartime London then, Tasouli. There is plenty of everything now.
– In Athens too, a lot has changed since the Occupation. Yet, I looked for Styppas but found you instead. And you listened to my disaster with my marbles and books in my satchel, Pamela.
– But you saved your blood alley … sorry … I mean your beautiful lead glass marble.
– I did save it! And learned it was like a blood alley. I have my beautiful lead glass marble under my pillow. I can feel it in my hand.
– Maybe then, marbles and gutters, blood alleys and Lords of the mind are ever the same Tasouli.
– Yes, they are ever the same. I will now win back lots and lots of voli with my lead glass marble, my blood alley. Just like you did, Pamela, in your London of then.
– Of course you will Tasouli. Can you let me go back to sleep now?
– But I just want to say, Pamela, that I could never win all these voli back if I had not learned about your blood alley. And I have only learned about the blood alley because …

London of then
and London of now
are forever the same
as Athens of now
for marbles and gutters
blood alleys
and Lords of the mind.

– But how can you make
the then be the now
even just for the marbles
the gutters
blood alleys
and Lords of the mind?

– But I found your hiding place, didn't I Pamela?

Visiting Mrs. Tougias

In the Athens of my childhood, the old district of Plaka was much as it had been for generations. Nothing at all like now, full of tourists, restaurants, souvenir shops and the like. Old stone houses lined the cobblestone streets, vines with well-maintained grapes ripening, a few little general supply stores now and then. Old Athenian families still lived there, in the quiet, by the marbles of the Parthenon and the ancient Agora. Many of the pathways inclined sharply on this the most sacred hill of ancient Athens, and one had to climb the well-worn step stones. In the spring, Attic wild flowers grew in between these stones and everywhere among the antiquities below the sharp cliffs of the Acropolis, where the remains of Classical and Hellenistic houses are found. On visits or walks during moonlit nights Plaka seemed to me totally magical. There were only a few electrical lights and many of the stone houses used kerosene lamps. The air was clear and one could see the stars and galaxies dominating the pristine Attic sky.

Later in the '40s we would sometimes go out to eat in the *tavernas* of old Plaka. In the summer we would eat out late at night and children would stay up late. The food in these tavernas seemed to be unbelievably tasty, even though I think most of it was simple with little meat, as there were still shortages in meat. But fish of all varieties seemed to be plentiful. The beautiful, fresh, simply grilled Mediterranean fish of Athens … ah, it was never to be matched by what was caught in the Atlantic or Pacific Ocean, and which I learned to eat years later.

In the winter, I was not taken out much to eat in Plaka but I listened to the stories of the adults who frequented the old Plaka tavernas. Many of these tavernas went underground in the winter, some in old caves. It seemed full of mystery to me. These stories were spun in winter evenings in the Bastille, by Thales and his inseparable cousin Rikos, now that Abraham had disappeared. Wintertime in Athens added a special dimension to their tales. For the rain fell in Plaka in a different way than it did in other districts. Maybe it had to do with the old cobblestone streets, the stone buildings and the Byzantine roofs, where mosses grew and black cats appeared. Each cobblestone glistened in its own way in the winter rain. As the evenings came earlier, the few street lights were lit and yellowish lights from house windows appeared one by one. The rain gave a new texture to the Plaka cobblestones as reflections of light would come from the side and the stones would become magical. Thales and Rikos would tell of how the *bon vivants* and gourmets of the time would fan out night after night, checking the tarvernas of old Plaka. They would gradually taste all of the barrels of wine that had been cracked and sampled the menus. Once they agreed as to the best barrel of wine they would then congregate in that taverna to eat and drink late at night and into the morning. Then they would regularly visit that taverna until that barrel was drunk or they got tired of the menu. And the cycle would be repeated in other tavernas again and again until the warmer weather returned in early spring and the rhythm of visiting the underground tavernas changed. They would laugh and joke about their own exploits and their almost mythical buddies. I could hardly wait to grow up so I could also go on these winter jaunts.

But I did go to Plaka fairly frequently to visit Mrs. Tougias. She had an old, large stone house on Adrianou St. in Plaka, which still exists but is now a garishly lit tourist shop. I can't remember whether I always went to Mrs. Tougias with an adult. Often it was my mother I think. But when I was inside I had the freedom of Mrs. Tougias' house. It was dark, with high ceilings and mysterious large back rooms that I loved to explore.

In one of these cavernous rooms, I think it was an attic, I would often find a naked woman. Usually her back would be half turned towards the door. She must have been about my mother's age and had a forbidding, somewhat pained expression on her face. I think there was illumination from a roof sky-light, or an electric light if it was dark, making her body stand out. I was not used to seeing naked women, illuminated or not, and I had a vague sense of uneasiness. Perhaps it was the projecting light that made angles and curvatures of her back stand out so much. If my mother was with me, she would make me feel particularly uneasy with little non-permissive motions full of implication and accusation that made me feel very badly. It reminded me of how she behaved when I told her about the little girl that I had found in the corridor in the Bastille, who wanted to play with me, but had the worms in her pippi. But in Mrs. Tougias' house, I had found a fully grown naked woman who showed no interest in wanting to play with me. But her forbidding, somewhat pained expression did not make me feel badly like my mother's motions full of implication or accusation. Nevertheless, I would have preferred that the naked woman had smiled and said something nice or funny to me.

Mrs. Tougias would often come in the room with the naked woman, and sit on a deep-cushioned chair. She would keep as quiet and still as one could imagine. If one made any noise at all she would give you a really strict look and silently do the 'shhh' sign with her index finger pressed to her lips. Mrs. Tougias' silence sign seemed to counteract my mother's looks of implication and accusation that made me feel that I was guilty of having done something unspeakably bad. Mrs. Tougias was a patrician old Athenian, wearing her gray-black hair in a tight, neat bun, and dressed in a black dress, well-cut and of good material, as she was a widow. She had all the old world manners, so not permitting noise in front of the naked woman made me think that I might be in school or, in a church, or something like that. This seemed to soften the bad feeling my mother had created that I

74

had done something terribly wrong. Also, I knew that later Mrs. Tougias would be treating us to all kinds of preserves and homemade sweets.

But there was one other person in the room with the naked woman. He was not always clearly visible from where I usually stood or sat. Sometimes he was standing in the room shadows, behind a board on a wooden stand. That is why I did not see him the first time I saw the naked woman with the light shining on her. The person in the shadow was George Tougias, Mrs. Tougias' somewhat strange and eccentric son. He was quite a bit older than me, had thick glasses and a pronounced limp. He was not very sociable. He was studying to be a painter at the Athens academy and Mrs. Tougias took everything he did very seriously. George was the brother of my Aunt Toula, who was married to my Uncle Yianis the great mathematician of the family. At this stage in his career George Tougias was doing neo-classical paintings of human bodies. So, the naked lady was a hired model for the young painter. But of course, I did not know all of this when I first started to observe the naked woman. But it was not always the same naked woman. There was at least one other, much thinner model whose back George painted. With time, over many visits to Mrs. Tougias, I became used to the models, Mrs. Tougias and George's idiosyncrasies and even my mother settled down and stopped making her little accusatory motions. George Tougias went on to become a respected and fairly well-established painter in Greece, whose paintings were shown in international exhibitions. He moved from neo-classical to totally abstract paintings. A number of his abstract paintings still hang in our extended family's houses and apartments.

But it was not only George's naked models that caused me trouble. There was also a very stylish, thin young woman, who lived mostly in Paris. To me she was Auntie M. She favored elegant tight black dresses and very dark glasses to match, even at night time. The family in Bastille sort of made fun of her. I got to like her and she would talk to me quite a bit when I saw her in Athens. She would often wear a low-back stylish dress, often black, when we were out eating in the evening in outdoor Tavernas. In that kind of dress her shoulder bones and spine would stick out prominently.

– Bones for the dogs, bones for the dogs, Tasouli! She would point to her bare back in a humorous but somewhat self-depreciating manner.
– Oh, no, Auntie M. You look very nice, I would reply truthfully. I really liked her vampish looks and that she was different from the other adults. I felt really grown up sitting beside her and she created an unusual, pleasant sensation in me.

I had really no idea why Auntie M would be living in Paris. But my family said she was a *décoratrice*! The whole family used that term, with a certain tone of mystery and awe. 'Decorator' doesn't convey the mysterious occupation — the English translation just doesn't give credit to the feeling *la décoratrice* created, especially the way they pronounced the word. The image I had of Paris, with its brightly lit main streets and small dark alleys lined with large, imposing buildings was mostly from the short news reels I had seen in the Cineac. *La décoratrice* in my imagination fitted perfectly there. I could see her in the slinky black dress, framing those coordinated shoulders and back bones for the dogs, floating in and out of purple and velvet-green wall drapery she had arranged in her vampish *décoratrice* style, in this immense 18th century Parisian house. She would beckon me to come near her and somehow we would float away together through the draperies and small dark alleys of Paris and into the luminous Champs Elysée.

– Feel my bones, she would say in that endearing manner. Bones for the dogs, showing off her low cut back.
– Oh, no Auntie M. Your back is very nice.
– Really? You could caress it then, if you like.

Ambivalence struck me. Surely my mother would not like this. Not at all. I would do her bidding. It was a most delicious sensation, like I had never experienced before. Her back did not feel like dog bones at all! Her skin was beautifully smooth and silky and almost creamy in quality. She seemed to know it.

– You like the feel of my back, don't you, Tasouli?
– Very much so, Auntie M.
– You could stay here and feel it forever.
– But I would have to go back to the Bastille. And what about Uncle George?
– He is in Athens, but we are in Paris. Just you and me.
– Just you and me.

What was I to do? Stay with Auntie M with the beautiful skin that felt so good over the dog bones, or go back to the Bastille? My mother would make me feel really bad, the way she would look at me and by what she would say. And my father worse still, by not saying anything about such matters. Maybe Styppas could help me. But not likely. He was more interested in Katharevousa and Demotiki and caterpillars and "Kill Bill" and the like. None of my uncles, not even Thales, would help. They would all think it was my mother's and father's problem. And none of them would be happy with me going off with Auntie M in Paris and spending all my time feeling her smooth skin. After they all had made so much fun of her with her dark glasses and dog bones. Then it struck me … It struck me suddenly — Pamela! Pamela, who knew about marbles and gutters, blood alleys and Lords. I had to find her immediately.

~

– Auntie M, I have to go. I have to find Pamela and ask her something.
– Who is Pamela and what could you possibly want to ask her?
– It is whether I can stay here with you or go back to the Bastille.
– Ridiculous, just childish ambivalence!
– What is ambivalence?
– Not knowing what to do, silly. You are here with me now. Just you and me in Paris. No one in the Bastille can make you feel as nice as I can, Tasouli.
– But my mother will be very mad. I will never be allowed to play again.
– You can play with me for ever and ever.
– But Pamela can help figure out what to do.
– Ridiculous — this Pamela! Auntie M's dog bones all protruded in a menacing way.

I dove behind the heavy velvet curtains. Auntie M was scurrying around trying to find me, but I was well trained in hiding behind curtains. My hate of caterpillars had made me an expert in this, and Auntie M had used a lot of heavy curtain material. I could hear her making exasperated noises and hissing sounds. But she could not find me.

I lay motionless for a long time. I had my eyes closed but I started to look for Pamela. I retraced my steps to where I had found her before. There she was snoozing again under the bedclothes besides an open window with a cold winter breeze coming in. She looked so comfortable and warm. But there was no time to lie beside her and feel the nice warmth.

– *Wake up, Pamela, wake up!*

Green-blue eyes peeked at me just above the bed-clothes.

– What is it this time Tasouli?
– I am in big trouble.
– You usually tell your troubles to Styppas.
– He is more interested in language and this is nothing like it.
– So, tell me.
– Before I was struck by disaster, now I am struck by ambivalence.
– Which is worse?
– Ambivalence — much worse.

– So, why do you think I can help you?
– 'Cause you know all about marbles and gutters, blood alleys and Lords.
– … alright.

I knew now that she would listen to me. Her arms were out of the bed-covers and she half sat up, adjusting her pillow.

– It is very cold in this room, Pamela. There is blowing snow outside and it must be many degrees below zero. Can I close the window?
– I don't like the window closed. I like the fresh air and it is warm under the duvet.
– Can I come in under the duvet?
– Oh … alright.

I crawled under the duvet and tried to sit up like Pamela with my back against the huge, dark wooden head board but the upper half of my body stuck out. It was still freezing cold, so I crawled right in so just my head stuck out above the duvet. She looked at me with a little smile.

– Better, Tasouli?
– Oh yes, Pamela, much better.

It was absolutely, deliciously warm as the cold winter blowing snow raged outside the open bedroom window. Pamela seemed to generate the kind of warmth that made me have no fear that the warmth would ever run out. It was a sensation that I had not quite felt before. The nearest was when I would lie down in the fields of Pyrgos close to the 'Ανεμόνες', and I would watch the blue or blue-purple varieties I really loved and imagine that the world became magical. I was quite happy to lie here in the warmth under the duvet, and not say anything at all.

– So, what is this ambivalence that struck you, Tasouli?

I explained my situation with Auntie M, her dog-bones and the silky skin of her back that she said I could caress forever if I stayed in Paris. And on the other hand, how badly my mother would make me feel by what she would say and how she would say it. And that my father would make me feel worse still by not saying anything at all.

– What do you think I should do, Pamela?
– Why would your father make you feel worse, if he does not say anything?
– It is the way he looks, without saying anything. He is an Archeomarxist, you know.
– An Archeomarxist?
– Oh yes! They are very strict. No partying. No enjoying yourself, unless defeating others in political argument. No gambling. No getting drunk. Anyone that does these things is very inferior.
– And caressing Auntie M's bony back is like gambling and getting drunk?
– For sure. Worse! And I do not want to feel very inferior. I'm very afraid I will.
– My father sometimes also made me feel badly, and he was no Archeomarxist.
– How did he do that, then?
– From time to time he would turn ugly. Usually if he drank too much. And then my mother and my sister would be afraid.
– And what would you do, Pamela?
– I would not show fear.
– And what would your mother and sister do?
– They would just be afraid. My sister would cower.
– But you never cowered?
– No. I would confront him and talk to him.
– And what would he do, Pamela?

– He would gradually come around. He would then be OK.

– I wish I was not afraid. Not afraid that I will be inferior.

– You will always be afraid of something, Tasouli. The main thing is not to show it.

– Does Styppas not show fear?

– Not very often.

– But is he ambivalent?

– Often.

– I want to be like him.

– You must now go back to the Bastille and show no fear. Auntie M and you in Paris was just a dream — a fantasy.

– I know, Pamela. But I am afraid my parents would find out.

– They can't find out. Not unless you tell them.

– I will never tell them, Pamela … I will keep it a secret. Just between me and you. And you do not tell them either, OK? A pact? For ever and ever.

– … alright … ever and ever, Tasouli. Now … goodnight.

Steptonakis' store

In another old district of Athens not too far from Plaka, near the ancient Thesion, my Uncle Steptonakis had a general store. But Steptonakis was not my real uncle. He was married to my Aunt Paraxia, my grandfather's sister, so he was related through marriage. We often went there to visit because, after all, Paraxia was a blood relative and was from Smyrni. Steptonakis' store had everything. When I say that his store had everything, I mean it had everything that a child could wish to explore. The building that the store was in was of very old, stone construction. It had ancient, worn down, old floor boards, many of which were partially or totally missing. I had to really watch where I stepped; otherwise I could easily go through one of these thin, half-rotten boards and disappear forever into Steptonakis' dark underworld. I had never been allowed to visit this underworld. Steptonakis would periodically disappear into his Haydes and ultimately reappear, carrying vats of olives, slabs of dried, salted cod or other mysterious goods or implements. He would always be out of breath after visiting his Haydes. He was a short, rotund, bald man with spectacles and was perpetually in a bad humor. He would hardly even acknowledge my presence, let alone talk to me. On the other hand he did not seem to mind my exploring the store, as long as I did not try to descend into his Haydes. The main part of the store occupied an open space of what must have been a floor-and-a-half or even two floors in height. In any case, the old, dirty poorly-lit ceiling was a very long way up. Parts of the ceiling plaster had fallen off, exposing the old wooden lattice-work used to support the plaster. But about two thirds of the way up to the ceiling there were decrepit wooden platforms attached to the walls and supported by wooden stilts. They went right around the store, which had an area of probably a regular house, like you could fit in easily about four large rooms. Just as decrepit were the ladders that led up to the platforms from the wooden floor. These platforms were full of old storage bins, wooden barrels, pulleys and winches and other strange devices. The barrels and bins were nearly all empty. I had never seen Uncle Steptonakis going up the ladders to obtain wine or oil, or anything else. He would keep a slightly disapproving eye on me as I explored this strange world of the wooden platforms, but he never asked me to come down so I had free rein.

Customers that visited Uncle Steptonakis' store were few and far between. Among those few that came by, I rarely saw anyone that bought anything. And the occasional one that did, would not buy anything ordinary, like olive oil or salted cod or wine or vinegar or slabs of green soap. Instead they would get some strange paper-wrapped packages that appeared from nowhere. It was a mystery how the store kept going.

Steptonakis and his peculiarities were the cause of much merriment and gossip in the Bastille. He was a hypochondriac, although he had a number of real ailments as well. So he would be visiting doctors all the time. But generally he did not like their advice, so he would not follow it and complained continually that such-and-such a doctor did not know anything, or was a charlatan. A lot of the advice was about what he could and could not eat. I think he may have had diabetes or thought he did. Ultimately he would find a doctor who would give him advice he liked, generally advice that would suit his eating habits. This would then be the greatest doctor in the world. At least he would be the greatest doctor in the world for a time. But before long that doctor would also join the ranks of the incompetents and the charlatans. The search for another suitable doctor would then start all over again.

The old street that Steptonakis' store was on sloped down, and the house where they lived was attached to the store on the downward side. Because of the slope, the back of the store opened through a door and one had to go down two or three stone steps, into a little wall-enclosed, paved courtyard. This courtyard, with its plants in large clay pots and its jasmine climbing bush, lead to the Steptonakis' old, poorly-lit house. There Auntie Paraxia, their peculiar son Rikos, and the more peculiar tiny little dog, Sweetie-pie, all lived with Steptonakis. That is how they were when I first remember them. But this was the kingdom of Auntie Paraxia. When in the house, Steptonakis seemed to disappear into the dark shadows of the old walls, silent as a mouse. At the time I knew Auntie Paraxia, she was a massive woman, twice the size of Steptonakis it seemed, with round, black-wire glasses framing her dark eyes. She easily towered a head and a half above him, although he was very short, barely taller than me. Our family in the Bastille gossiped that Paraxia thought she had married well below her status and looks. There must have been something to this, as old family photos from Smyrni show her as a statuesque, strikingly good-looking young woman. And of course, she was a younger sister to my grandfather — the very great man from Smyrni. In any case, the Bastille gossips said she complained all the time, although I don't remember her ever complaining in front of me. Instead, she seemed fixated on Rikos and the little Sweetie-pie. When we visited she would treat us to a preserve sweet on a little green iron table in the little courtyard, or inside the house during winter months. Then all she would talk about was either Rikos or the little Sweetie-pie. Darling Rikos was also a short boy. In fact, he was called by his cousins and friends "Rikos the short" and he had the dark poppy eyes of his mother.

That little dog was as obnoxious and tiny as he was vicious. As soon as he would see me he'd show his sharp little teeth and growl in a high pitched tone. His eyes, which looked a bit like Aunt Paraxia's and Rikos' — all dark brown and pop-eyed, would go glassy and wild. Then he would attack. Sweetie-pie invariably would go for my lower leg, above the ankle, since that is all he could reach. I wore shorts winter and summer, like other Greek kids then, and Sweetie-pie bit me badly enough to draw blood on several occasions. I was very afraid of this tiny, little dog. I did not *become* afraid of him. I think I *was* afraid from the very first time I saw him. I tried to remember Pamela's advice and show no fear. But I could not. Fear, horrible cold, nauseating fear would run over me on the sight of Sweetie-pie. It seemed to come in waves. I was sure Sweetie-pie sensed my fear and that is why it would attack. But I could do nothing about it. I began to believe that even if I mastered the art of showing no fear, he would still attack. This just caused more fear because there was nothing I could do.

Worse still was the adults' attitude towards the obnoxious little dog. Aunt Paraxia totally defended him by telling everybody what a fine and obedient little dog he was, and by implication that I did something to annoy him or stir him up. Of course, I had done nothing of the kind. Even after the little Sweetie-pie had drawn blood and his little teeth marks clearly decorated my lower leg Aunt Paraxia never disciplined the little dog. She never even took him away from the yard, where he would usually attack me, and put him in another room. All I got was tincture of iodine from Steptonakis' store to put on my leg. It stung like hell. And my mother's attitude was neutral at best, even though she was always telling me to stay clear of dogs because of rabies. Rabies was very bad. You would die from rabies. It was a horrible death full of screaming pain she said.

One day we were sitting in Aunt Paraxia's little garden having a sweet, syrupy fruit preserve and a cold glass of water. Sweetie-pie was on the other side of the garden with his crazy eyes starting to become glazy. He was figuring out how to attack me. It was not so easy because we were sitting by the round little iron table, where the sweet dessert was served, and I had put my legs up high on the supports of the table making it hard for the little dog to reach them. Furthermore, my mother was sitting between myself and the vicious little beast. Aunt Paraxia was sitting on the other side of the table. I decided to play my trump card.

– Mother, will I catch rabies? Sweetie-pie has already bitten me today.
My mother just looked vague and uncomfortable. Aunt Paraxia looked absolutely horrified,
– Rabies, my Sweetie-pie to have rabies? Impossible! Isn't that right Dina?
– Oh yes, Tasouli, you could only catch rabies from street dogs. They are abandoned and can have all kinds of very bad things. You must never go near them. Sweetie-pie is not like this. He is not like an abandoned dog, is that not right Paraxia?
– Horrors, of course not. He is the best cared-for dog in the world! In Smyrni we were so particular about our dogs.

I supposed my mother had gone as far as she could. Even to imply that Sweetie-pie might have anything in common with Athenian street dogs, from which he could catch rabies, could result in a major family conflict that would last for years. After all Paraxia was from one of the best families of Smyrni, the capital of the great Ionian civilization. My mother was only from Zakynthos and an agrarian family at that. If my mother had gone over the line, she would be told that she was just of peasant stalk even though she married Phoebus. But, in fact, my mother had won that little exchange. Marrying Phoebus, the great agriculturist and Archeomarxist was no match for poor Uncle Steptonakis, the general store owner. Paraxia knew it. She knew it only too well. Marrying below her status was the bane of her life. Paraxia did not dare to pursue the discussion on the superiority of Sweetie-pie over other dogs. It was clearly just code for who was superior — Paraxia or my mother? Paraxia had been humiliated since my mother had raised the comparison of Sweetie-pie to street dogs and she did not dare to respond the way she would like to. If she did respond by commiserating with my mother about her agrarian, peasant background, my mother would commiserate right back about Paraxia's marriage to Steptonakis. Paraxia had started serving-up great gobs of the syrupy preserves and even took out a box of chocolates from Steptonakis' store reserved for special occasions. My mother had been brilliant! I basked in the victory and glanced over at Sweetie-pie, who clearly was sensing my newly enhanced status. I looked straight at Sweetie-pie's eyes, pointedly chewing on a couple of the chocolates and licking my lips as much as I could. Sweetie-pie seemed to lose interest in my leg. His eyes started to look normal.

But then, safe from Sweetie-pie, replete with sweets, I started to ruminate about the Athens street dogs. So, rabies came only from abandoned dogs. Nearly all dogs you saw in the streets of Athens were abandoned. So, you catch a horrible death because a dog was abandoned? It figured. It went along with everything else my mother had said about kids without families or bad families from which you could catch bad things. Maybe street dog-rabies was just as bad as poor little girl pippi-worms. The only problem about catching rabies from the abandoned street dogs that I saw in the streets of Pagrati and Nea Smyrni and Plaka, or in Zapion, was that they never attacked me. Their eyes did not have the glassy, crazed look of Paraxia's Sweetie-pie. The street dogs would just follow me, hoping I would give them a scrap of food. These were starving dogs, mostly skin and bones. But later I started to figure out that they would follow me not just because I might give them a scrap. They must have been able to smell that I had no food scraps. They followed me because that is what street dogs do. If I swooshed them off with a stick or picked up a stone, they would put their tail between their legs and retreat. If I swooshed without a stick or stone they would just back off a couple of paces. Sometimes they would half lie down protecting their bottoms. I think the females were more prone to do this. If I talked to them, then they would start to wag their tails and be all friendly. I could see it in their eyes. They even understood what I said to them. I was sure they did. Or, mostly.

So why was it, that the street dogs never showed any interest in attacking me while Sweetie-pie always did? I could not believe that Sweetie-pie was just born more vicious than all the kinds of street dogs that I had seen. There must be some other explanation. I just knew there was something in me that Sweetie-pie sensed. If it was fear, then what really caused me to have fear? And why did I not have fear with the street dogs? If anything, I should have been more afraid of all those loose street dogs than this tiny house-dog. There had to be some reason why Sweetie-pie induced fear in me while street dogs did not. My mother and Paraxia were now engaged in a long conversation which did not interest me any more. The relative safety and comfort of my situation now, the victory of my mother over Paraxia and my belly full of sweets started to take its toll. I was almost dozing off, when I heard Aunt Paraxia reiterate again.

    — In Smyrni, we took very good care of our dogs. Not like the Turks, you know Dina.
    — For sure, Paraxia, not like the Turks.
    — The Turks let their animals run around in the streets. They are inferior, you know Dina.
    — Oh yes, Paraxia. Inferior.

Then all of a sudden it struck me. That was it! That was the solution to the puzzle of why there were attacks against me by Sweetie-pie but not by the street dogs. I must be inferior. Inferior — just like the Turks. I was not an important agriculturalist or an Archeomarxist, like my father. I did not even understand what an agriculturalist or Archeomarxist was. Worse still I had absolutely no desire to be either. And Sweetie-pie was sensing my inferiority. After all Sweetie-pie had been trained by Paraxia to be a superior dog, a dog like they had in Smyrni … So, a dog with superiority sensed the inferiority in someone who was inferior, but dogs that were inferior and starving did not. It was all relative. Why had I not seen this before? It now seemed so obvious. But I did not like it. I did not like it at all.

Then, I started half dreaming of what it must have been like in Smyrni with the superior dogs of the Greeks and the inferior dogs of the Turks. Of course, the Greeks and the Turks lived mostly in different districts of the city. Yiayia Sophia had said so. A district would be called a *mahalas* in Turkish. Yiayia Sophia talked all the time about the *ano mahala* (upper mahala) and *kato mahala* (lower mahala). The Greek words 'ano' and 'kato' were always intermingled with the Turkish word 'mahala'. It gave almost a dreamy ring to Yiayia Sophia's narration about the *mahalades* and all of their sounds and smells. I could see the street dogs of Smyrni wandering around the *mahalades*, just as free as the street dogs of Athens. But of course, the street dogs of Smyrni would be mostly Turkish dogs. Aunt Paraxia had said so. But if I wandered around with them, like I did with the Athens dogs, would I be like a Turk? I knew it — to wander around the dreamy city of Smyrni with the street dogs, through the small back streets, through the French and Jewish and English mahalades, on cobblestone passages shining from a fine warm rain, I would have to turn into a Turkish boy. In this way the Turkish dogs could understand what I was saying to them.

When we returned to the Bastille, I would relate to the adults all of this. I could hear the conversations now:

    — You can't turn into a Turk, Tasouli, Yiayia Sophia would say. After the great Catastrophe … Why would you want to do that?
    — Just so I can talk to the street dogs of Smyrni, Yiayia.
    — Dogs are just dogs. They do not understand any one human language more than any other.
    — Greek dogs understand me, Yiayia. And I speak to them in Greek. So Turkish dogs would best understand me if I spoke to them in Turkish.
    — You have a mind of your own. You will become a philosopher. Yiayia Sophia would always say what I would become depending on the conversation.
    — You should learn some Turkish if you go to Smyrni, the logical Stelios would offer. You do not have to become a Turk. Many Greeks spoke Turkish and Turks spoke Greek in Smyrni. And all kinds of other languages.
    — Yes, Uncle Stelios. Does Turkish have caterpillars?
    — Of course. Turkish script is now in Latin letters. The same as English and French. Since Kemal.
    — Oh yes. I knew that. But I hate caterpillars. You know! But if I was a Turk I would not hate them. Right?

Then my mother would cut in, with a worried face all full of implication,

– Why are you saying these things? You must be upset about something. Who upset you? She was forever the psychologist finding causes of harm for her little son.
– No one upset me, mama. I just started thinking after Sweetie-pie bit me again why the Athens street dogs never bite me. And Auntie Paraxia and you were discussing dogs in Smyrni. Remember? That is what set my brain on the Smyrni street dogs.
– Somebody has upset you. I know that. I am your mother. Don't you think so, Phoebus?
– Perhaps he is planning to go to Smyrni to start a great socialist revolution among the Turkish proletariat, my father would say. The street dogs are just a cover. Lenin in Zurich used similar ruses. My father was often ironic like this. But not everybody would laugh.
– Oh leave the boy alone, Thales would finally intervene. Tasouli, if you want to go Smyrni and become a Turk, so the street dogs can understand you, there is nothing wrong with that! Thales' easy smile and manner made it seem entirely possible. Everybody would laugh. But my mother would still have that worried, suspicious look … something else was bothering her little boy and he was not admitting what it was.

Rikos — I have only a vague memory of Rikos during the early times when we used to visit the Steptonakis. It must have been early during the Occupation. I think he was perhaps in his early twenties. He was sullen and did not speak much and seemed to sit mostly in the shadows of the dark Steptonakis house. I have no idea if he worked at all, but I suspect not much. If he was supposed to help his father in the store, he spent a lot of time trying to avoid it. Later he went to University and spent endless years there, getting his degree, supported by his parents. This was not that unusual for Greece. Getting into University was very hard based on guillotine-like National exams at the end of high school (*gymnasio*). It took a huge effort and expense of preparatory private school during the last years of the gymnasio to have a good chance of getting into University. If you did not get in, you became essentially forever a blue collar individual. If you got in, you became white collar. That did not mean that you automatically got a better job than a blue collar worker. You may not do much at all and your parents would continue to support you. Also, you could keep failing or not taking University courses and there seemed to be no time limit to how long you could stay as a student. The latter was the situation with Rikos for many years. Finally, Rikos did graduate to much rejoicing. I do not think he worked very much after graduation, although I recollect that his degree was in chemistry.
Rikos, in fact, evolved. He evolved into a professional dandy. Often dressed in an immaculate white silk suit, with the most fashionable Italian pointed matching leather shoes and contrasting ties, his personality changed from that of a sullen young man in the Steptonakis house to an absolutely outgoing type in company. His loud, infectious laugh could be heard continuously when he was around. He and Thales gradually became inseparable after Abraham disappeared during the war. But underlying Rikos' now effervescent personality there was a terrible secret. The secret was not a true secret. It was just something that no one really liked to talk about. Rikos had a disease. A disease he acquired in childhood. It was said in the Bastille that it was because of his disease that Paraxia and Steptonakis were so permissive towards him and that he was never disciplined. That is why he was not made to work in the store and why he was allowed to go on and on at the University, while his parents kept giving him money. Maybe it was the disease and its bad prognosis that made him such a vital character as he grew up. Maybe that is why he succeeded so brilliantly as the professional dandy, *bon vivant* and top socialite of the family … the highly entertaining and lovable personality that made the Bastille resound with joy the instant he passed through the door.
But what remains most in my memory about Rikos was his intensity in being what he was. Rikos' eyes were always intense. Paraxia was good looking in the old pictures, but I would not call Rikos really good looking. But his eyes had that shining intensity. Every movement, every clever remark, every joke had that red-hot intensity as if that single moment was the most important moment of his life, and everybody else's life too. When he was still young he had a totally bald head, which seemed to suit the immaculate, fashionable way he dressed and made his eyes seem

more prominent. He was quite a ladies' man. The girls apparently really liked him. Maybe it was the intensity in everything he did. And being totally bald in Greece seemed to be no disadvantage with the girls. As long as you had hair on your chest and you were not too white. All of the ancestors on my father's side were bald and mustachioed in the old photographs — the men that is. My father was very white, with blue eyes and little hair on his chest. He joked that he had a classmate in school that was missing a leg and the little Phoebus was never sure whether it was worse luck to lose your leg or to be too white and hairless. But that was an Archeomarxist joke. Maybe being too white and hairless is what drove him to become one. When Rikos and Thales got together they never told Archeomarxist jokes, except to make fun of my father's strict morals. And then the jokes were very carefully told and were subtle and teasing as they did not want to chance his wrath. But when my father was not around the Rikos-Thales jokes were often about girls and pretty colorful at that. Particularly since Thales was also a looker and very popular with the girls. Rikos and Thales became inseparable, and continued to play a big part in Tasouli's life, especially later in the '40s.

Many years later Rikos got married. He married M. Yes, M of the dog bones and the naked back that I fantasized about in a Paris I had never been to. They seemed to be very well suited to each other. Everybody said so. Rikos seemed very happy and the little jokes about everything and everybody, the happy outings with long dinners, in the warm Athens evenings in the tavernas, continued on and on. Surely, this charmed time would never end I thought. These were the immortals. All I had to do was grow up a little more, understand the jokes a little better, drink and eat more like them, and I would be as happy as they were.

Then Rikos died. M said they were in bed, Rikos in his usual joking mood before they fell asleep. When M woke up in the morning Rikos was dead by her side. His childhood disease was rheumatic fever and apparently he had a huge heart. He and Thales knew he could die, but they did not expect it so soon and so suddenly. He died in his fashionable, pure silk pyjamas.

Sunrise in Pagrati

While I lived in the Bastille I always had a special desire. This was to be allowed to go up the spiral iron staircase, that the incomparable Joujoukos flew by when he exposed the black marketers, and spend a lot of time on the rooftop terrace of the second floor of our apartment building. Normally, I was not allowed to go up that steep spiral staircase by myself. In any case I would often get dizzy when I tried. So I would generally obey and climb down when I was called back. Gradually my mother would take me up more and so would Kyra Maria when there were chores to do up on the terrace such as hanging the wash to dry. However, my dizziness when climbing the heights of the winding stairs never went away completely. The dizziness would become worse if I looked over the low retaining wall that was all around the second floor terrace. I had developed *illingos*. Many people told me that *illingos* was a common affliction, so I was not too worried about it. Except that I thought that I had a very bad case of it. Illingos is like vertigo, but it sounds worse. It is like a fear of heights. It was horrible. Any time I looked over the low retaining wall illingos would start in an instant. I felt that I was going to fall, and it was as if the street below had a giant magnet pulling me down. I had to use all of my strength it seems not to fall, yet I knew it was ridiculous since my feet were firmly planted on the terrace. Sometimes I would get the vertigo component of the illingos and everything would spin, like a vortex that was spinning me down. Down and down and down to my death. But it was the most horrible nauseating death, full of conflict since I knew I could defeat it by logic and yet I was unable to. It was the total loss of control that made it so horrible, and made worse still because I loved to go to the rooftop terrace.

If I stood back a little from the retaining wall I did not get the illingos but the view was more distant. Still, you could see all of Pagrati, the local hills and the mountains of Athens. There was very little pollution in Athens then and on clear days one could see far, far away. The highest buildings in the area would be mostly two-storey apartments and many of the houses were single family dwellings. If I were allowed, I felt that I could stay there for hours watching the view and the goings on in the world below. I would gingerly move towards the retaining wall and see how close I could get to the edge before my enemy the illingos would get me. The closer I could get the more delicious the view, as one could look directly down. But the closer I got the worse the horrid illingos. It became a game I learned to play. Different parts of the veranda, with different views also had different degrees of illingos as one approached the retaining wall. Generally, the more spectacularly attractive the view, the worse I had the illingos. There did not seem a spot that I could find in the whole of the veranda where a breathtaking view was not associated with a breathtaking fear and the illingos. Why was it like that? You would think that there would be a little oasis, a little special space in the whole of the wide rooftop veranda that I could see a view that would excite my heart and make me marvel without the horrid fear, the dizziness and falling into the abyss. The little oasis, the little space of respite did not exist. My situation seemed hopeless. People I asked about the illingos said you were not easily cured from it. It was most often a permanent condition. Stelios who knew everything anyone had ever written said the reason one could not be cured from illingos was that it was based on a primeval fear. The great Sigmund Freud had researched it and found it was all about a conflict of having a death wish. I did not know I had a death wish but Stelios said everybody had one. In other words I was done for. Just as I suspected.

But, actually, I still had a ray of hope. The secret reason I had gradually convinced my mother to let me go to the rooftop veranda was that I would be allowed to sleep there overnight. Perhaps by sleeping on the rooftop veranda, making it like a summer bedroom for me, the illingos would diminish. Sleeping on the flat veranda-like rooftops during the hot summer nights was common in Athens then. The cloudless, relatively cool nights were magnificent. The Athens sky would shine with all the stars and one could see the nebula. It was all in the illustrated big book my grandfather had written on popular astronomy: *The Sympan* — the Universe. In *The Sympan* it said that no other atmosphere in the world was as pristine and clear for observing the stars as the night sky of Attica. That is why the ancients made so many observations on the stars and the movements of the planets. But that was so in olden times before electricity and a lot of people came. Nevertheless, a mattress, some sheets and maybe even a blanket and a favorite pillow made it heavenly. And it was totally safe. Other kids I talked to often slept on their rooftops without any trouble. No one had ever heard of a mishap from sleeping on roof verandas. But my mother was very cautious. Anything could happen to her little boy up there. Why there could be wild cats or bats or even beggars or gypsies wandering around the rooftops. None of that really fazed me. Also, I had a secret reason, within the secret reason of trying to diminish my illingos: I wanted to see the magnificent colors of the Athenian sunrise in Pagrati. In the summer the sun rose so early, that I was almost never up early enough to see it rise. And from the Bastille on the first floor, the rising sun was barely visible.

Surprisingly, my mother agreed in spite of her reservations. So, on the great appointed night we went up to the rooftop which was already laid out with bed mattresses and old sheets and blankets. My mother had decided that she too would sleep on the rooftop. It was a very warm summer evening even by Greek standards. Kyra Maria had done most of the work carrying the mattresses and bedding to the rooftop veranda. She was not going to miss out sleeping on the rooftop either. So, here we were. After dinner, which was late in the evening during summer months, my mother, Kyra Maria and I climbed up the winding staircase and got into our individual beddings on the mattresses. My mother had the most bedding, as she took no chances of catching cold even though it was still so warm in the late evening. She was from Zakynthos after all and Zakynthians were very careful about not catching colds she said. Kyra Maria's mattress was closest to the entrance from the winding staircase. No wild cats, or bats or beggars or gypsies would get past her. She was well trained on how to repel all such nuisances by the nuns of the monastery. I had put my mattress and the bedding on the east side of the veranda, so when I woke up to see the early sunrise I would not disturb anyone else. I could enjoy the magnificent panorama all by myself. I don't think there was a moon that night and the galaxies were shining brightly in full panoply. Kyra Maria was sleeping like a top, snoring lightly, dreaming of repelling wild cats, bats, beggars and gypsies, no doubt. My mother slept lightly, in case her little boy was attacked by vermin. I could not sleep. I felt that I must study the galaxies, just like they were written about in *The Sympan*. So, I stared and stared at the stars but could not identify one group from another. Also, I did not want to fall asleep in case I missed the sunrise. But finally Morpheus struck.

I woke up startled and in a cold sweat. It was a nightmare that I often had before that woke me.

At least the stars were still shining so I had not missed the sunrise. But the end of the nightmare made me feel queasy and unsettled. It was always the same ending and the frightening result was always the same. It was the 'falling dream'. I would fall off a cliff or something high and then fall and fall and fall in a horrid, uncontrolled way, my heart fluttering and racing. This time it was all intertwined with falling off the rooftop veranda no doubt, but still somehow there was a cliff in my dream. I hated that dream because it was so frightening. I knew I would crash at the end of the fall and something unspeakable would happen on impact. I would then wake in the instant before the unspeakable happened and jump up all startled from the bed. It was always the same pattern. Stelios the expert in everything had mentioned that the falling dream was very common in humans. Maybe it was related to the illingos. But this did not help me at this time. I felt all upset and anxious. I had no one to talk to. Both my mother and Kyra Maria were now happily snoring. I tried to settle myself as best as I could, focusing on the galaxies as hard as my bleary eyes would let me. Soon I fell asleep again.

– *The falling dream again startled you, Tasouli?* It was a relief to hear the familiar Voice.

– Oh Styppas, is that you? I am so glad you came. Everybody else is asleep and I have no one to talk to.
– The falling dream is very frightening. I have it too.
– Oh yes? … Stelios said it is very common.
– And did Stelios say how one can get rid of it?
– No. It is something inside humans he said.
– Too bad. I'd really like to get rid of my falling nightmare. After it wakes me, most often, I cannot go back to sleep again.
– Me neither, Styppas. Except for tonight when I fell asleep again after the nightmare.
– But you had stayed up all night looking at the galaxies so you would not miss sunrise in Pagrati. So you were very sleepy even after the nightmare.
– As usual you know everything, Styppas.
– Well, you must make certain that you wake up so you do not miss the sunrise.
– I would never do that, Styppas. I have been preparing as hard as I can to watch the sunrise over Pagrati. As hard as I have been preparing to become pedantic.
– That is one thing I came to talk to you about. You seem to think that I told you to become pedantic.
– Oh yes, Styppas. I am very enthusiastic about becoming pedantic you know. I even told Pamela that you wanted me to become pedantic.
– Don't I know it!
– I know you know it, Styppas, because you know everything.
– That is not what I meant when I said "don't I know it!"
– But "don't I know it" is the same as "I don't know it", is that not so Styppas?
– No, when I said "don't I know it!" it was an exclamation meant to be sarcastic.
– Can you be sarcastic and pedantic at the same time?
– It isn't easy!
– Oh. If it is not easy and I am still studying to become pedantic, I should not be sarcastic. It might be too difficult. I should master pedantic first.
– You practically already have!
– Thanks Styppas. But I think I still have quite a lot of work to do before I become very good at being pedantic.
– I don't think I'll be able to stand it! But I am visiting you also to talk to you about something else. It is actually the main thing I want to talk about.
– Since you visited me, rather than me visiting you, you are supposed to talk about things happening to me, rather than things happening to you.
– You are already a master at being annoyingly pedantic!
– Thanks again Styppas. You did talk about the falling nightmare which was happening to me.

But it had also happened to you. What is the main thing you come to talk about?

– Language, actually. Although I nearly forgot with your insistence at showing me what progress you made at being pedantic.

– You usually want to talk about language, Styppas. But that is OK because I do too. So if you are visiting me rather than me visiting you, it is still OK. Especially if it is about writing and the English caterpillars. And when you first visited me you said Bernard Shaw wanted to make English phonetic.

– Yes, but he did not succeed.

– I remember you saying this. Uncle Stelios also said it. So, what happened?

– A lot of money was made from one of his stories that was turned into a successful stage play, called "My Fair Lady". But all of the money could not be used for legal reasons.

– How come you know all of that?

– I just do.

– Not even Uncle Stelios knows all that you know about Shaw.

– He couldn't know about "My Fair Lady".

– Oh, Uncle Stelios remembers everything!

– He could not remember this.

– Why?

– Never mind! They finally had a competition about how to make the English Language phonetic and the man who won came up with a whole lot of new sound symbols. They called this phonetic English 'Shavian'.

– Ssssavian?

– No. Like named after Shaw — 'Shavian'.

– Were the sound symbols caterpillars?

– No, Tasouli. More like worms.

– How many of these worms are there.

– Many.

– More than 21?

– Many more.

– But that's no good, Styppas. Last time we had cut down Greek to just 21 sound characters. For Cavafis' Barbarians. Remember?

– Oh, I remember alright.

– So what will happen to the many-worm English?

– Nothing much really. Like before, 'Shavian' will not catch on.

– Too bad in a way. I prefer worms to caterpillars. They would not curl up as much to make mnuw … right?

– Right. But I have some more bad news for you.

– Oh, oh …

– There is something called the International Phonetic Alphabet. They call it IPA. You can make the sounds of all languages.

– But that is good.

– Yes, but it is very complicated. Especially in the way consonants are made.

– How many consonants can there be.

– Many it seems in different languages. Depending on where you make the sound and how you make the sound.

– So you are not decreasing the numbers of letters?

– Not really, there are many more sound symbols than alphabet letters in IPA.

– But that is no good. We took a lot of trouble to read Cavafis' poem in just 21 letters.

– Yeah, well IPA will only work because of the computers they will have in the future.

– How do you know that, Styppas?

– I just know.

– I know you know everything Styppas, but *how* do you know?

– Never mind.

86

– You are always saying this. You are not telling me everything. But what are computers?
– They are like electronic brains.
– Oh yes, Uncle Stelios has talked about them. He said they will be common in the future. Although the Germans already had some. To keep track of prisoners and the like.
– The Germans like to count everything.
– But do you really need all these sound symbols? Why can't you have just the 19 sound letters?
– I don't know. It is a very big field. It is called linguistics.
– It does not make sense to me, Styppas. A consonant is a consonant and a vowel is a vowel. And you write each only in one way — one letter for each consonant and one for each vowel. Our teachers taught us this at the very beginning.
– I told you … I don't know. Maybe it is to make it easier for English speakers to make the sounds of other languages.
– First time I hear you saying "I don't know", Styppas. Uncle Stelios would never say "I don't know". He always had an explanation for everything.
– Maybe that is why Stelios and your father have terrible fights sometimes.
– Oh yes, Styppas. You know that too! When my father gets into a fight he becomes very angry. He could kill with his eyes. Especially if Stelios' explanations did not conform to Archeomarxist principles.
– Was Stelios afraid when your father got very mad, Tasouli?
– Oh, yes Styppas. And Yianis too. Everybody would stay clear when my father got very mad. Until his eyes softened and he became calm. But sometimes he would hold a grudge for days to come.
– I wonder why he became like that … Listen Tasouli, it is getting late for me. I have to go back to Kingston.
– OK, Styppas. G'bye.

I woke suddenly but could not open my eyes. Styppas was gone. All I could see was a bright yellow light through my still closed eyelids. Everything felt very warm. I wondered why I could not open my eyelids and where all the bright yellow light was coming from. I made a huge effort and opened my eyelids just a little. I jumped up in total shock. It was bright sunshine — that is why there was this yellow light through my eyelids, that is why the warmth was everywhere. It hit me — it was a great disaster for me. Staying up and watching the stars, waiting for the sunrise, the falling dream and all the conversation with Styppas about linguistics had made me sleep through and then way past the sunrise. It must be mid-morning now. I had totally missed my much anticipated sunrise over Pagrati. Missed it totally! I felt depressed and humiliated. I looked around the rooftop veranda and the beddings of my mother and Kyra Maria were gone. The flat tiles of the rooftop were getting hot on my bare feet. I stumbled down the winding black iron staircase to the back yard and entered the coolness of the Bastille through the kitchen. Kyra Maria was busying herself there.

– Ah, Tasouli, I was just going to the roof to get you.
– I slept right through the sunrise, Kyra Maria. It is terrible.
– You were sleeping so soundly in the morning; your mother and I did not have the heart to wake you.
– You should have woken me. I did not want to miss the sunrise.
– I thought about it, Tasouli, because I am up before sunrise every day.
– But why did you not wake me, Kyra Maria?
– First, you were watching the galaxies most of night, so you must have been very tired.
– But how did you know? You were asleep during the night, Kyra Maria. I heard you snoring.
– The nuns taught us to keep half an eye open even when we snored.
– Half an eye for wild cats, bats, beggars or gypsies?
– Half an eye for everything. But I would have woken you if you were not having a dream early in the morning, before sunrise.
– I had the falling nightmare, Kyra Maria.

– Oh, the falling nightmare. And then you were talking a lot in your sleep.
– That was Styppas.
– Styppas? You mean your father? Which Styppas?
– No, Kyra Maria. It is a different Styppas. He knows everything. Even more than Uncle Stelios. He even knows the future.
– Pa, pa, pa, pa, pá! Don't say things like that.
– Why are you crossing yourself, Kyra Maria?
– To ward off the evil spirits. Those that come from the future.
– But I do not want to ward off Styppas. He knows a lot of interesting stuff. But he sometimes gets really mad at me.
– It isn't natural, Tasouli. It is not natural to imagine someone who is so real. And who can foretell the future? — Pa, pa, pa, pa, pá! I will light a candle for you and say a prayer.
– But what do you do to ward off wild cats, bats, beggars or gypsies, Kyra Maria? Do you cross yourself and say a prayer and light a candle for them too?
– No, no, no. For those you either feed them or give them alms.
– And what was the sunrise that I missed like, Kyra Maria?
– It was like every other sunrise. Like every other morning.
– That is not so bad then … I thought I had missed the most beautiful sunrise in the world.

~

Rafina then

    During the burning and destruction of Smyrna, Yiayia Sophia, her husband Anastassios and the four boys — Stelios, Phoebus, Yianis and Thales — barely escaped with their lives. This was what the Greeks call the great catastrophe of 1922 when the ancient civilization of Ionian Hellenism in Asia Minor suddenly ended after thousands of years. There is much written and there is still a great deal of debate as to what parties were really responsible for the great catastrophe, which came during the last days of the declining Ottoman Empire and the rise of the modern Turkish state under Attaturk Kemal. The refugees from the cities, towns and villages of Asia Minor who survived ended-up on the shores of Greece and had to be accommodated. The Greek government tried to resettle the refugees in areas that resembled their own environment in Asia Minor before the catastrophe. One such settlement was in and around the tiny fishing outpost of Rafina, on the eastern coast of Attica, south of Marathon. The refugees who were settled there were mostly from the thriving town of Triglia, north of Smyrna.

Triglia was a small Greek town in a beautiful narrow valley leading to the Sea of Marmara (Marmora) just south of Constantinople (Istanbul). Fruit trees, fertile fields and mulberry trees lined the little valley which was in the district and town of Brussa, famous for its production of silk. I don't think that Triglia had much of a port but then neither did Rafina back in the 1920s. The first allotments went to the refugees from Triglia, but a number were left over and they were then distributed to refugees from other parts of Asia Minor, particularly from Smyrna. So it was in Rafina, during the period immediately after 1922, that my Grandfather, the great man from Smyrna, was given an allotment. It was there that he and his wife and sons and their friends spent many summers before the Occupation Child was born. It was there that Yiayia Sophia exercised her influence even more than in the Bastille. It was there where she finally settled, a widow now, after the Bastille broke up as her boys left with their women for other neighborhoods, other cities, other more distant lands. And it was there that the Occupation Child spent his post-war summers, those hot, idyllic, never-ending summers of Rafina.

Apparently the first opportunity for an allotment for the great man was an area in Rafina facing the sea, near the cliffs that form the back of today's port. But the great man traded that magnificent spot for an allotment a little higher up, on the outer border of the village settlement that had more distant and imposing vistas. It turned out to be an unfortunate choice, as his once dominating vistas are now blocked by apartment buildings. On each of the allotments that were assigned to the refugees a little house, of maybe 50 square meters, had been built by the Greek Government. These houses were of a similar design. The green painted wooden front door of our house opened into a small living room used also as the dining room. To the side on the left a door opened into the kitchen that was equipped with a space for either a coal or a gas stove. At some point an ice box was obtained, made from varnished pine on the outside and lined with tin on the inside. Blocks of ice were delivered in the summer, which were placed in the tin container inside the top of the ice box, allowing the cover to be closed tightly. These ice boxes were life-savers in the hot, long summers with temperatures rising to over 40° C. Behind the kitchen and the living-dining room were two bedrooms, one with a larger bed and a regular bed and a smaller bedroom, with a little bed. This smaller bedroom with a window and a door opening towards the garden, was dubbed the *dammaki*. I am not sure what *dammaki* exactly means, but it had a lot of meaning for me, because I was often allowed to sleep in the *dammaki* by myself. A little bathroom came off the kitchen. It had a toilet and a little sink. A bucket was filled with water and poured in the toilet after each use. After swimming we washed off the salt with a rubber hose attached to a garden tap. Like other similar houses, a small cistern was dug out below the little bathrooms that served as an absorptive sewer. These cisterns or culverts worked very well as the amount of waste was small and most absorptive sewers rarely if ever needed to be emptied. There was no central sewerage in Rafina and I think it may still be the case now. The smelly crud from each apartment building has to be sucked up very frequently from the cement-lined cesspits by immense container trucks and emptied elsewhere.

It was the overall construction of these little allotment houses that made them so endearing and so durable. Their Byzantine tiled roofs had a beautiful golden red color especially in the beginning and the end of the day. The overlapping tiles were set on pine planks from the local Pendeli evergreen forest and supported by elegant, thin cedar tree trunks, all cut by hand. The Occupation Child could sit for hours admiring the woodwork of the roof, especially in the dammaki. The roof of the house sloped fairly sharply, so the outer part of the roof of the dammaki, at the side of the house, was certainly not high. In fact it was low enough so that I could almost touch it if I stood on the small ranch bed that was sometimes put in the *dammaki* next to the outer wall.

One particular summer afternoon I was allowed to take my nap in the dammaki and I woke from my slumber and went to speak to my Mamaka. No real reason. I just wanted to speak to my Mamaka. A little later, again for no apparent reason, she wandered into the dammaki. Like a flash her slipper was in her hand and in a single motion she crushed it. I was just entering the dammaki myself at that instant. It crunched and squirted a bit. It was a scorpion. And it was a fairly large one at that. It looked like an elongated crab, really more like a crawfish. It was on the wall that separated the dammaki from the rest of the house and sitting on the same side as I had my pillow probably about 15 centimeters or so from my face. My mother frantically inspected me. She found a little bite on my left ear lobe, which would have been the side towards the wall if I was sleeping on my back. There was a little redness and nothing else. I had not noticed pain or anything else. My mother concluded I had been bitten by the scorpion. She immediately dragged me around the neighborhood to get the opinion of the locals that knew about such things. She was terribly anxious.

– My Tasouli was bitten by a scorpion. What should we do?
– Mrs. Dina your Tasouli is too well to have been bitten by a scorpion.
– He was bitten I tell you. He was bitten. I killed the scorpion myself on the wall of the dammaki.
– Well, where is the bite?

So my slightly red ear was demonstrated to the neighbors.

– This is no scorpion bite, Mrs. Dina. There would have been a much bigger reaction. We have even had young children die from scorpion bites. But they are not at all common.
– I tell you it is a scorpion bite. I am his mother. Who else would know if my little boy was bitten by a scorpion!
– Ok, Mrs. Dina. If you say so. Maybe then he has a resistance to scorpion bites.
– A resistance? A resistance … that is it. He could have developed a resistance.
– Did he ever have a snake bite?
– No, no of course not. Do you think I would allow my little boy to be bitten by a snake? What kind of a mother do you think I am?
– We were just asking Mrs. Dina because some say one can develop resistance to scorpion bites if they were bitten before by a snake.
– But Mamaka don't you remember all the bee bites I used to get in Pyrgos? And they never bothered me. Except for the giant bumble bee bites, I had big reactions to them.
– There you go Mrs. Dina. Maybe he developed resistance to the scorpion bites from the bee bites. You can rest easy about Tasouli. And we will go back to our chores.
– Is that so?

My mother was clearly not satisfied. After all, these Rafina neighbors were just ignorant peasants or fishermen. What would they really know about scorpion bites and how one can become resistant to them? She had to appeal to a higher authority. Fortunately, a little later in the early evening, Thales came in from Athens. He had barely crossed the threshold of our garden when my Mother was already badgering him.

– Thales, my good Thales finally I can get a sensible answer.
– To what Dina?
– To what? Tasouli got bitten by a scorpion and you calmly ask 'to what'!
– But Tasouli looks so well. He doesn't look like he was bitten by a scorpion.
– I saw the scorpion with my own eyes. I killed the venomous creature on the dammaki wall just centimeters from my Tasouli's face. And Tasouli had a bite right on his little tender earlobe.
– And, Uncle Thales, I did not react to it. The neighbors say I must be resistant to scorpion bites. They said that maybe I got the resistance from all the bees that bit me in Pyrgos.
– Is that so?

– That is what I also said to them, Thales: "is that so?" I am so glad that finally a medical authority agrees with me.

– So who told them about Tasouli being bitten by all the bees?

– Tasouli himself did.

– But did they really believe Tasouli was bitten by the scorpion?

– No they didn't my dear Thales. Can you imagine … the ignorant peasants!

– So, Dina, it was only after they said that they didn't think that Tasouli had a scorpion bite that the whole bee bite resistance business came up?

– Exactly, my dear Thales. Exactly. What ignorance!

Thales flashed his quick everybody-is-right conciliatory smile and winked at me.

– They probably had no idea my dear Dina, but I read in a Medical Journal just the other day the discovery that bee venom cross reacts with scorpion venom.

– So it was just a lucky guess they made?

– Absolutely, my good Dina. Absolutely. There is no way they could have known.

So everybody was able to now relax. No one seemed to be thinking about the scorpion. Except for me, that is. I had my own theory. I figured that the scorpion actually did bite me. But just a little. So my mother was at least half right. But what would be the point of trying to poison me when I was asleep? He could not eat me. So maybe it was just a little trial bite without much poison injected. On the other hand I liked the idea that I had been made resistant to scorpion bites from all the bee bites. As the hot summer day was gradually turning into a comfortable summer evening we sat in the garden and watched the dimming rays of the sun reflect off the walls of the little Rafina house. Refreshments were being passed around. The now rose-colored walls of the house made it look like a safe haven, strong and reassuring and magical.

I think the walls of these little initial Rafina houses were made from local sand and rock and generally white-washed on the outside with lime to almost a sparkling white. Each little house was built on the corner of a sizeable garden allotment, maybe ten times the area of the house. The gardens were generally fenced in by white-washed, low stone walls with iron trellises on top of iron gates nicely painted to match the doors and wooden window shutters of the houses. The gardens of Rafina were the gardens of Eden. In every garden there would be a *climataria*, the well-kept grape vine trellis, providing shade in the summer, usually outside the front door in a little garden veranda. A jasmine tree-bush would often be nearby sometimes even entwined with the *climataria*, with the aromas of its white flowers permeating the cooling evening. We had fig trees and pomegranate trees full of fruit towards the end of the summer and into the autumn. Almond, orange or lemon trees were everywhere. The fruit trees were often interspersed with elegant tall, deep green cypress trees or a few mature pine trees. In our garden we also had some pistachio trees that regularly gave a fine crop of fresh pistachios, and also productive pine trees from which I could gather the pine cones and crack and eat the rich white pine nuts. And of course, olive trees were always there producing enough olives for a household. I don't know why such small areas of land produced so much and so consistently in Rafina. Perhaps it was the ever-fragrant red clay soil that had also supported the evergreen forest or the endless sunshine.

Even in the early glory days of the Occupation Child, the great pine forest from Pendeli extended down into the small valley of Rafina, and wild thyme and the myrtle and the Attic flowers and the evergreens were everywhere. The aromas of the evergreen forest and the wild herbs and flowers were as intense as the buzzing honey bees in the ravines. We used to follow the paths in these ravines protected from the blazing summer heat of the late morning. Down through these shepherds' paths we would find our way, to go swimming in the pristine beaches and the azure-blue sparkling waters of Rafina. And the sea was a treasure trove of fish and little crabs and cockles and every manner of sea life. We would swim and play, and play and swim until the sun had got so hot that it was time to go back up through the cooling ravines, where the smells were now intermingled with the heat of the day, creating different sensations than the morning descent. And in a state of delicious physical exhaustion we would reach the protective coolness of the little house. A little wash with the brackish Rafina fresh water, hot in the garden tap initially but soon stinging cold, and we were ready for lunch. And what delicacies Yiayia Sophia always prepared for us! How we thought those meals tasted better than anything on earth. And the discussions and jokes until finally it was time for everyone to lie down for our short late afternoon nap, the invariable siesta of the summer months. And how easily that little break, that refreshing sleep in the heat, changed the very structure of time! How, when we woke from our slumber, a new day seemed to emerge as the day started to cool. The little walks, or sitting in the garden enjoying a refreshing bitter cherry cold drink and maybe talking about going to a little Taverna later. But these were plans for much, much later in the evening. The siesta, the changes in the smells of the garden and in the rhythm of our daily lives made each day seem like it extended into two, perhaps even three summer days. These childhood summers in Rafina went on and on and never seemed to end.

Concrete

All of that is long gone now. The seemingly endless pine forest has long been destroyed, first in favor of marginal farming and then for the sake of uncontrolled development. Apartment buildings are everywhere, and the parking of automobiles is often bumper-to-bumper, helter-skelter on the small and larger streets, including sidewalks and street corners. The occasional little house from the 1920s, with its Byzantine-type tiled roof and enclosed garden still lingers, squashed between the endless apartment buildings. But it no longer evokes, for me at least, the intense memories and smells of my childhood Rafina. It is more of a sad reminder of what used to be. And yet, sometimes as I meander in the small remnants of the old primeval pine forest by the cliffs of the sea in the winter after a rain, the smells of the sacred soil arise again and awake the ancient memories. The Rafiniotes used to talk about progress in Rafina. How an expansion of the port, better roads and automobiles would bring them better lives. I rarely hear that anymore and a few old-timers that retained the old houses sometimes refer to the apartments, that their children want to build and put them in, as their 'cement prisons'. Often I have wondered: if the catastrophe of 1922 had never happened, and the Greeks had continued to live in Triglia and in Smyrna and the other towns and cities of Asia Minor, would they have been as adept in destroying everything of beauty and nature as they did in Rafina? The cement prisons seem inevitable now in Athens, Smyrna, Rafina or even Triglia. "For what?" these few old-timers would say in Rafina now, "for what, do they have to put me in the cement prison endlessly watching the flashing tube? … for what? … for a few talents of silver?" Maybe some Turks are saying the same things in modern Smyrna (Izmir) or even in Triglia (also called *Zeytinyaği* — the olive orchard). For concrete has been the great destroyer of language and race, the great dominator but also the equalizer.

I remember now how an old man in Rafina, still living in a little original house with the Byzantine-tiled roof, was relishing the sound of his own speech, his freedom and his race. And as he brought forth the imagery of the cement prisons and their television sets, his old, crackly voice seemed to sing out to me what had really been lost in the cement:

> And in these prisons of concrete
> for Greek and Turk alike,
> the tube reflecting from the walls
> with children buggy-eyed
> the language gist rings hollow
> color of freedom fades
> the race it's become meaningless
> only cement remains.

And the old man was right, for in Rafina the gist of language and race were very different from now. For us it was Yiayia Sophia, above all, that kept the rhythm of language, the color of freedom and the meaning of the race clear and pulsating. Dressed in plain black, right down to her underclothes it seemed, winter and summer, with a black cotton kerchief perfectly wrapped around a perfectly combed bun, she was the epitome of the widow for life that the decency and the conservatism of Greek society then required. But underneath that stereotyped image she was very different. Her kindly but sharp brown eyes framed in the horn-rimmed glasses never missed a thing. She had a saying for everything and managed the family more by indirect day-to-day persuasion rather than an overall master plan.

Yiayia Sophia read avidly every bit of political, social or cultural news in her favorite daily newspapers, which she communicated to all with plenty of her own commentary. Her political sympathies were, in some respects, typical of the refugees from Asia Minor. She was an immense admirer of Eleftherios Venizelos, the great and most famous prime minister of Greece and the originator of the 'great idea': a Greece that would include also the ancient Ionian Greek cities in Asia Minor and Constantinople. She would have been pleased that the new airport of Athens is named after Venizelos and that it is close to Rafina. She still would analyze in great detail all the events that led to the 'great catastrophe' attributing fault and credit to the King, Venizelos, various generals, the European Powers, Attaturk Kemal and the like. Her main objective seemed to be to convert me to her views of historical events and to an extent I think she succeeded. How these views played out with her children, particularly with my father Phoebus, is a different and more complicated story. It is part of the 'prehistory' of what actually happened to make my father so silent about his early years.

Perhaps somewhat surprisingly, Yiayia Sophia did not seem to be against Attaturk Kemal, even though he was the architect of the 'great catastrophe' and the 'destruction of the race'. I never heard her attacking or even criticizing Kemal. I do not even remember with certainty if she thought that he was responsible for the burning and then the massacres of Smyrna, which is a commonly held view among Greeks. These events of 1922 were still a relatively recent memory for the Asia Minor refugees. Rather, when she got going she had some positive things to say about Kemal; particularly about the emancipation of women, his creation of a secular state, limiting the influence of religion in Turkey and his overall intellect. I had the impression that she felt she could say these pro-Kemalist things to me, which she might not say so openly to others.

She was also a total and unrepentant supporter of Bonaparte, Napoleon the Great, as she always referred to him. She firmly believed that Napoleon, by opposing and defeating the anti-democratic Imperialist forces of Europe, carried out a massive stroke in favor of liberty for the common man. According to Yiayia Sophia this feat was only matched by his humbling of the church, especially the Catholic Church, and thus releasing much of European humanity from ignorance and oppression. This may seem odd as she had been trained by Catholic Nuns, who taught her pretty good French, and ended up with a full qualification from the Nuns as a teacher. Having a teacher's diploma was a rare qualification for young women in Asia Minor, or anywhere for that matter, in the 19th Century. I never did ask her if the Order of the Nuns that trained her were also secret Bonapartists.

The Saint

Bonaparte aside, Yiayia Sophia covered her bases very carefully. From time to time I was sent on a very secret mission.

– Tasouli, she would say in a very quiet, conspiratorial voice when no one was listening.
– Yes, Yiayia Sophia.
– Tasouli, you know that Auntie so-and-so is very sick.
– Yes, we were all talking about her at dinner last night. Why are you whispering?
– Because no one must find out.
– No one must find out what, Yiayia Sophia?
– It is only you I can trust, Tasouli.
The way she said it made me feel that I was the only person in the world worth something.
– Of course you can trust me, Yiayia Sophia.
– You must not tell anyone.
– OK, Yiayia Sophia. But what is the big secret?
– … shh! Keep your voice down.
– OK.

I would start to whisper like her.

– Here are a few drachmas.

The coins would appear out of her little black soft leather wallet with the shining metal clip. Somehow she never seemed to be separated from that wallet.

– What am I to do with the coins?

– You must go Agios Nicholaos and light a candle. For Auntie so-and-so.

– Sure, Yiayia Sophia. But why is it so secret?

– If they find out that I sent you to light a candle, they will think I am religious … They will ridicule me.

– Oh, you mean my father and my uncles.

– Of course. They will all gossip and say that I am full of superstitions.

– Like Kyra Maria?

– And worse still! Because I'm supposed to be educated.

– So what if they gossip, Yiayia Sophia. They will not criticize you, will they?

– Oh, yes, they will. Your father especially, Tasouli, he will start the criticism.

– Because he is an Archeomarxist?

– He will carry on and on with the endless analysis. And then the others will start to laugh. I know they would also be making fun of me, underneath it all.

– I will go now, Yiayia Sophia.

– Bravo, my Tasouli, she would say petting me on the head. You will become a great scientist.

So, off I would go to Agios Nicholaos on my most secret mission with a few puzzles whirling in my head. First, what exactly was I to do with the drachmas? I knew that some of the little coins should go in the Agios Nicholaos iron box that was beside the candles. But there was no set price for candles. One could leave any number or size of coins or none at all. Taking a new candle from the stone candle repository under the Agion Nicholaos icon, one stuck it in the sand of the large metal candle-stand container, after lighting it from the already-lit candles in the container or an oil lamp illuminating an icon. It was better lighting like that because the candle was then lit with sacred light. So, I gradually became convinced that putting some money into the iron box and lighting the candle were two distinct and not necessarily connected operations. I thought that one should not have to put down money to get a candle if one was very poor. At the same time the poor seemed to frequent churches more, often bringing in some relative or sick looking kid to be helped by the Saint or the Virgin Mary. They were always putting coins in the iron box then lighting candles and crossing themselves a lot. Second, there was the problem of the way Yiayia Sophia gave me the coins. It was as if some of them were for me, for doing her bidding, for keeping the secrecy, for doing the little chore, although she would not actually say so. But it was implied. So, I never knew what to do. How many of the coins should go to Agios Nicholaos and how many, if any, to me? And then, if I kept any of the coins was I betraying my father and uncles twice over? I knew Yiayia Sophia was right about them ridiculing any religious belief as superstition or pure ignorance. Even more complicated was that she agreed with them in discussions about religion … that it was all superstition. But then she seemed to make these exceptions for sick Auntie so-and-so. And what if the exceptions happened to be right, what then? How would Agios Nicholaos and God regard me if they saw me putting either no coins or just some of the coins in the iron box near the candles? So, when I first started these little excursions on behalf of Yiayia Sophia I would usually, but not always, end up putting all of the little coins in the iron box, even if there was nobody around. You could never be too sure about these saints and God — particularly if it was a case of divided loyalties. The saints and God seemed to thrive on divisions, disagreements and conflicts. I already knew of this from my Religion classes at Maraslion. We had to learn about the endless religious Councils that the Byzantines and the Roman Popes kept calling because of conflicts over dogma and the related bloody wars. All considering, it is amazing that these dubious, secret little excursions, to light candles in so-and-so's name on behalf of Yiayia Sophia, always turned out well for me.

Perhaps it was because I always loved the walk over to Agios Nicholaos. It was about a 10- to 15-minute walk from our house through the high part to end of the village of Rafina. There were only a few whitewashed houses with their beautiful gardens en route. Agios Nicholaos was a tiny little chapel, probably only about ten square meters, at the edge of the spectacular cliff that made up the eastern border of Rafina. It commanded the straights between the eastern part of Attica and the long island of Evia. Agios Nicholaos was only made a chapel after the Occupation. During the war there was a German fortification and observation post built at that site. The site was chosen exactly because of the commanding position it held as a lookout. The walls were immensely thick and made of reinforced concrete, apparently built to German specifications to withstand the heaviest bombardment from the Allies. The story was that, at the end of the war, the local Rafiniotes tried to blow it up, as they did with all remnants and reminders of the Occupation. However, this structure seemed to withstand all the attempts to dynamite it. Finally they gave up, figuring it would be too expensive or dangerous to use enough dynamite to blow it up. It was then that someone had the idea to convert it into a chapel. A little spiral was built, made also of thick cement with a cross on top and a simple, Byzantine-type open arch for the church bell. The whole tiny chapel was always whitewashed with lime, sparkling in the sun, and the wooden door and window shutters were painted with a soft water-color azure-blue, to remind one of the sea and the sailing boats. It was sanctified to Agios Nicholaos (Saint Nicholaos) the protector of seafarers and fishermen. It was an instant success and remains so to this day. Hundreds of weddings, christenings and the like have been performed in this tiny chapel and the open spacious paved church yard, with the magnificent vistas.

Roughly a generation after the story of the Occupation Child in the late 1940s, one of the baptismal ceremonies performed in the little chapel of Agios Nicholaos was for three children. The oldest, Amandina, who was by then five, complained bitterly about having been dipped starkers into the baptismal cistern and coming out all wet and oily. She put on a major screaming exhibition, while everybody made encouraging little noises and giggled at all her objections, which made her scream even louder. Fion, who was barely a year and a half, thought the whole thing was rather amusing and Philip, just a few months old, regarded the dipping with a certain amount of distant curiosity. It was all done outside of the little chapel, which was far too small to accommodate all the god parents, relatives and the like. The officiating priest thought he was directing a major Hollywood movie, giving continually loud directions to the various relatives holding cameras, without ever seeming to interrupt his psalms and cants. He was very well practiced. The background of the beautiful sparkling blue sea on a warm summer day and the whitewashed little chapel was certainly a worthy background for any movie. Yiayia Sophia sat on a wooden chair throughout the whole thing with a tiny little smile on her face. Everybody said that the group baptism, having brought all three kids, their parents and grandparents across the wide seas, was really for her sake. After all she was very old then and could die at any time, so there was a wave of sympathy in her favor. Of course she had never said that she wanted her great-grand children baptized, individually or all together. To have said anything like that could have started up the gossip again that she was religious. No way was she going to give an opening to her sons to criticize her as a religious, superstitious old woman. Instead she had said that it was their parents and grandparents who wanted them baptized. Curiously this included her son, the Archeomarxist, who had lots of theories and lengthy convoluted arguments as to why baptism was a core value of the Marxists. After all, it solidified fraternal and comradely feelings among relatives for what could then sprout a greater revolutionary purpose. Baptism *was* proletariat solidarity! The absence of any real proletariat around did not seem to dampen his enthusiasm. Yiayia Sophia said nothing; her main concern that she not be seen trying to exert any influence on this matter. She just sat in the wooden chair, whose seat was woven with dried reeds by the gypsies, simply savoring another little victory in the bright sunshine of Rafina.

Getting back to my most secret missions for Yiayia Sophia, as the Occupation Child in the 1940s, I remember how the walk to Agios Nicholaos would always give me a sense of elation, when I returned.

– Did you do it? Did you light the candle?

– Oh yes, Yiayia Sophia. Just as you said.
– You will become a great scientist, Tasouli … she would say patting me on the head again.

I could never figure out why I would become a great scientist just because I had been essentially bribed to light a candle for so-and-so at Agios Nicholaos.

– A great scientist, Yiayia Sophia?
– Oh, most certainly. You will even win a Nobel Prize! Here you take this.

She would pass me a few more coins, to which I would initially object but would always take in the end. Her bespectacled smiling brown eyes, would then light up. She had just won another little victory over her sons — including my father; perhaps, especially over my father. I had no idea why accomplishing Yiayia Sophia's most secret mission made me feel good. I never thought about it much. Maybe it was the walk to Agios Nicholaos itself that was elating. But it was not that alone. Maybe it was also the promise of becoming something great, although I had no idea what she really meant. Or maybe it was the little monetary reward at the end of the mission. I soon discovered that I got this reward whether or not I had left all of the coins she initially gave me to the venerated Saint, for lighting a candle in his sanctuary. Thus I learned that you could share a little with the saints, without any readily apparent retribution at least in the short-run. Looking back, I think Yiayia Sophia made me feel good because she was a master at adding positive psychological effects — I think it would now be called "value added". And it worked. It worked invariably. Whether it was for a most secret mission, or one of the less secret missions that she would also send me to accomplish.

The Anatolian

Sometime during her years in Rafina, Yiayia Sophia acquired a helper. She was more like a faithful accomplice. This was Kyra Ourania. What Kyra Maria was to Yiayia Sophia in the Bastille, Kyra Ourania was to Yiayia Sophia in Rafina. Even more so. For the roots of Kyra Ourania run deep into Asia Minor, while I don't even know what Kyra Maria's roots were. And while my memory of Kyra Maria's exact physical appearance has faded with time, Kyra Ourania's image is as clear as if I am looking at her now. She was striking. When Kyra Ourania was on her feet, which was nearly always, she was bent over at nearly a right angle. Maybe a little less, but her back essentially formed an obtuse angle of about 100 degrees with her legs. The angulation was fairly low down in her spine and was totally fixed. As a result she had to keep her neck extended when she was standing in order to try and look straight ahead. She was thin as a rake, with strong, long sinewy arms that radiated capability through her gnarled hands. It seemed that there was nothing that Kyra Ourania could not do in house and garden alike. But what made her appearance so striking was not so much the extreme hunching of her back but her eyes. They were big, inquisitive and of a pale but somehow bright blue color. This kind of striking eye color seems to be a trait of many of the Ionians from Asia Minor. About half of my father's side of the family have this trait, and one sees it frequently in Rafina today among the descendants of the original refugees that settled there after the great catastrophe. It is rare among Turks and other peoples of modern Anatolia, as far as I know. These bright inquisitive eyes of Kyra Ourania were set in a face covered with wrinkles. She had always been wrinkled like this, as far as I can remember. But her wrinkles were not the usual wrinkles of aging. They were thick and leathery, more like people get when continually exposed to the elements for years and years. And, indeed, that was the story of Kyra Ourania. She came from a farming background in Triglia and when they settled in Rafina, she was given a garden to cultivate. This garden had fruit trees and some grapes and vegetables of different kinds. She managed to take care of her family through this garden, although she was quite young then. The only problem was that the garden she was given was down in the most low-lying part of Rafina, near a swamp. Back in the early 1920s, swamps like that were full of malaria. So, the young Ourania suffered badly from malaria but somehow she still managed to take care of her family. But it was not malaria that made her an extreme humpback.

She developed a fever that was of a different kind than the typical fever of malaria, which she already had. The young Ourania had caught meningitis. It was apparently bacterial meningitis and it was not clear if it was tuberculous. In any case, this all happened much before the era of antibiotics and she gradually got worse and worse. Finally, it was believed that she would die and she was left to do so in a little dark side room, because the light bothered her so much. This side room was far from the main part of the Institution where she was in, a hut really, with only a ranch cot and a Turkish toilet dug into the ground. It was a way of isolating infectious people that were condemned to die. They say that after many months in the tiny dark hut with just a dirt floor, close to death, her pale blue eyes became luminous and very inquisitive. Just like Phoebus' did before he died, far away from the Rafina of his youth. But young Ourania did not die. She did not improve quickly either, but rather stabilized, and her fever started coming down slowly. After many months she was able to get up from the ranch cot. But when she did get up she was bent over at nearly a right angle. The deformity of her back had become permanent, and so had the inquisitive look in her eyes. She had also been cured of the malaria. Amazingly she married, managed a pregnancy and outlived her husband. By the time she became Yiayia Sophia's accomplice-helper-Anatolian slave and girl-Friday, Ourania was already a widow. She had certainly earned her title of Kyra Ourania and everybody's bemused admiration.

It was a mystery what hold Yiayia Sophia had over Kyra Ourania, who helped her with everything and did all her bidding. She certainly did not pay her much, since Yiayia Sophia basically lived on a widow's pension from the great man of Smyrna. What money Kyra Ourania did get from Yiayia Sophia was in the form of a few coins now and then, similar to what I got for performing her bidding. I know this for a fact because many a time I was sent to Kyra Ourania's — just a couple of houses down the street — with orders from Yiayia Sophia as to what job or chore Kyra Ourania was to perform and given just few coins which I had to pass on to her. The little bit of change was similar to what I got from Yiayia Sophia for lighting the candle in the venerable Saint's little white chapel. Of course, I never took a cut from the change I took to Kyra Ourania, like I did on occasion from the Saint.

Whenever the question was raised by some adult as to why Kyra Ourania did all these things for her, Yiayia Sophia would put on a slightly mysterious little smile.

– She is from Asia Minor you know, she would say.
– But so is just about everyone else in Rafina, Yiayia Sophia. And they don't all behave like they are your bondsmen!
– But she was originally from Anatolia, deep Anatolia.

The little smile would broaden on Yiayia Sophia's face. The questioner would look like he understood. Everybody knew of the association of deep Anatolia with a harsher life, of habits of serfdom bordering on slavery that were still held there and of the hardened inhabitants, compared to the more urbane and educated Greeks of western Asia Minor.

As for me, I always liked Kyra Ourania. She always treated me with a mixture of deference, kindness and a certain type of friendly formality. But she certainly never seemed servile. Not one bit. Maybe she was from the deepest of Anatolia, but she was nobody's slave. Certainly not Yiayia Sophia's. I thought that Ourania treated Sophia with the same friendly formality as she treated me. Yet she could not have missed the point that, in her later years, after Yiayia Sophia's boys had left the Bastille, their own mother had to retreat to Rafina. It was her last defense, her last domain. A move like that for a mother, especially a widowed mother, was unusual for Greek morals and tradition then, or even now. A move so unusual, in fact, that it must have jutted out like a primeval rock among the uniform, traditional family structure of Rafina. But Yiayia Sophia was nobody's slave either. And every time the question was raised by some adult, as to why Ourania did all these jobs for the older Sophia, and every time the patently false explanation was given that it was just because Ourania hailed from the deepest Anatolia, a small victory was won by Yiayia Sophia. The boys should not have let their widowed mother go and live by herself in a summer cottage in Rafina. Especially in the winter. But Yiayia Sophia was adamant. She had to have her independence. This was a very contentious issue. For, in the winter the damp cold was penetrating and the winds blew and blew harshly. Yet the boys' widowed mother was by herself in a little country cottage.

Rafina was famous for its winds, blowing down mostly from the north and the east. I was told that the cold winds were an important topic of conversation all the way back to when my grandfather ruled the roost in Rafina. Even a special expression had been coined by an old friend of my grandfather's, Mr. M, to describe their strength.

– Good morning Mr. M, the great man would say, with a slight tip of his fashionable, straw fedora with the black hat band.

He retained the civilized manners of Smyrna. Even though they knew each other very well they would address each other by *Mr.* and then the family name employing the polite plural tense.

– Good morning, Mr. Styppas.
– The wind has started again, Mr. M.
– Ah, Mr. Styppas, when these winds of Rafina start they can uproot even the horns from the goats.
– Uproot the horns from the goats, Mr. M.
– Uproot the horns from the goats, indeed, Mr. Styppas.

A little smiling wrinkle would appear in the bespectacled eyes of Mr. M. He had confirmed once again that the great man not only liked his expression about the Rafina wind uprooting the horns of the goats, but had adopted it. His description of the winds of Rafina would now surely become famous. And he was the originator. It had already been a very good morning for Mr. M.

There were plenty of goats in Rafina then and I always looked for a goat whose horns had been uprooted. I had never found even one. I never stopped looking. But before I had heard the story of how Ourania had got her hump, I often wondered if it was the proverbial Rafina winds that had bent her over. After all, there were plenty of pine trees that were bent over exactly as Ourania because of the strong winds. And the wrinkled, weathered skin of Kyra Ourania looked a bit like the bark of the pine trees. Sometimes in a dream, the bent-over Ourania and the bent-over pine trees would become all entangled. As I meandered through pine groves and forest, the pine trees would look at me with those curious pale blue eyes. It was not an unpleasant dream — just a bit odd.

But the bent-over Ourania never liked the expression about the wind uprooting the horns of the goats. She would clearly signal her slight dislike, if somebody mentioned the expression, through her eyes which became momentarily disinterested. So I would never say the expression in front of her. Ourania kept goats herself and I figured she did not fancy the idea of her goats having their horns uprooted. But what she seemed to admire was the independence of Yiayia Sophia and her determination to keep her own small domain. In the winter, Ourania would always gather a little wood for the small, cylindrical, top-loading, black cast iron stove that had been installed in our Rafina cottage. Together they would sit near the lit stove for hours. They sat on a large wooden chest, whose top could open on hinges in two sections. This chest was kept closed against a wall near the small rough wooden table that served as the dining table. It contained all kinds of interesting old clothes and papers, and I always wanted to be present when they planned to open it. But the main function of this wooden chest was to double up as the chesterfield in the little dining-living room. It was also the favorite resting and nap place for Yiayia Sophia. It was in a strategic position as it faced the front door, so no one could go in or out without Yiayia Sophia knowing what was going on. The chest was covered with a thin mattress and on top of that would be one or two *kourelou'des*. *Koureli* means rag and these popular coverings were made from rags, generally of old clothes but they could be from bedding, from almost anything. The *kourelou'des* were also used as carpets, especially in the winter when one's feet got cold walking on the ceramic tiles that made up the floors of the little house. Now, of course, they are considered as 'folk art' and they can be expensive to buy from the markets. These *kourelou'des* took some skill to make, particularly in selecting what rags to use where, how to cut the rags and how to mix the colors of the rags. Ourania was particularly good at making kourelou'des and often she would busy herself making one when she would sit and keep Yiayia Sophia company in the long winter evenings. A little toast or a few chestnuts might be placed on the iron concentric rings that made the top cover of the stove, and they would quickly roast. At other times the well-worn pack of cards would come out. Then Ourania seemed to be content to watch Yiayia Sophia play one game of patience after another. Yiayia Sophia would always tie in some unlikely event, like winning the National Lottery, to the game of patience coming out. When the game, as usual, would not come out Yiayia Sophia would say:

– Well, Ourania, this hand of patience did not come out again. We'll have to buy another ticket for the next draw.
And Ourania's pale blue eyes would shine, among the deeply etched wrinkles.
– No, Kyra Sophia, it did not come out. Patience is a difficult game. It usually does not come out. We'll have to wait for the next draw.
– And when is the next draw, Ourania?
– In two weeks, Kyra Sophia.
– Ah, two weeks. Here, Ourania. Here, take the money for buying a ticket for the next draw.
Yiayia Sophia would reach into her black money pouch. Then she would hesitate momentarily and hand Ourania a little more money.
– Might be better to buy two lottery tickets this time, Ourania. I have a feeling the next patience hand will come out.
– Oh, it would be better to buy two tickets, Kyra Sophia. Particularly if the next hand does come out.
– If the next hand comes out and we win the lottery, we will live like Kings, Ourania.
– Even better, Kyra Sophia. Like Queens.

There was an aspect of the relationship between Yiayia Sophia and Ourania that puzzled me. It was when they started talking to each other, in a low confidential tone, sitting together on the wooden chest that was covered with the thin mattress and the kourelou'des. Yiayia Sophia seemed to do most of the talking. I never knew what exactly they said to each other, for when I got within earshot the conversation would cease or the topic seemed to change to something that was suitable for my ears. I don't think it had anything to do with me directly, but I've suspected it was about other family members. I thought it was most likely, about Yiayia Sophia's late husband, and her children. After these secretive conversations, which I had inadvertently interrupted, and after Ourania was gone Yiayia Sophia would often start some general discussion about what great a man her husband was. Or about things her boys did in childhood. It was as if she was giving me a child's version of what she had been saying to Ourania. Or, at least, I thought, a different version of the same topic. Did these recollections make up her version of my father's childhood, about which he had been so silent? Of course, I cannot be sure if what she was telling me was even the same topic as her secretive conversations with Ourania. No matter what these secretive conversations were about, they certainly do not point to a servile relationship of Ourania towards Yiayia Sophia. No, this was no peasant from the deepest Anatolia that paid homage to the educated and higher class Smyrnian woman. Yet Yiayia Sophia often appeared as a non-religious liberated woman at the turn of the 19th Century. Sophia the Bonapartist, Sophia the Venzelo-phile, even Sophia the secret admirer of Kemal who had lifted the veil of ignorance from the Anatolian women. This part of Yiayia Sophia always came out in conversations with her children, particularly when the Archeomarxist was around. But then she might send her trusted Tasouli to light a candle to help ensure a little blessing from the Saint. Just in case. And she might have a secret discussion with Ourania who was thought to be deeply religious, as befitted an Anatolian peasant. But Ourania never wore religion on her sleeve, so no one was sure if she was truly religious. Ourania was as silent as the grave, no one had ever said that they had heard even a morsel of gossip from her mouth. If Yiayia Sophia had a secret, it was in safe keeping with Ourania. And she might even say a silent prayer for a secret sin of Yiayia Sophia, exactly as she thought Sophia would want it said. All the advantages of confession were provided to

Sophia without the shortcomings: Ourania ... the silent, bent, curious-eyed, peasant-confessor of the deepest Anatolia.

Soujoukakia

If Yiayia Sophia had a great *pièce-de-résistance,* it was *soujoukakia* ... yes, *Smyrnaika soujoukakia. Smyrnaika* conveys not only that the soujoukakia would have originated in Smyrni but somehow they were in themselves Smyrnian, with all the imagery of the hustle-bustle of that most cosmopolitan metropolis of Hellenism and the near East. Any time the words "Smyrnaikasoujoukakia" come out of Yiayia Sophia's mouth I could imagine the Smyrnian women at the turn of the 19th Century fussing around, gathering and grinding the magnificent herbs, especially fresh cumin, getting the best beef, the best tomatoes in preparation for the soujoukakia. I would start to salivate. I had the perfect Pavlovian response ingrained already. I automatically assumed that everybody else would have the same kind of Pavlovian response to the magical words. But Yiayia Sophia, the master psychologist, was not content just with a conditioned reflex. She had developed a whole scheme around Smyrnaika soujoukakia. Probably her strategy succeeded so brilliantly because hunger, the terrible hunger of 1941, was still felt in the psyche, the pit of the stomach of the Greek. Also, food was still relatively scarce. Certainly meat was. Meat of any kind was a treat. This was more so in most rural areas, where any kind of animal protein would be available only on certain occasions. Also, farm mammals could be killed only in certain seasons for fear of interfering with production, which could result in starvation the following season.

It must be difficult for many living now in the West to imagine what cooking and food conveyed psychologically back then. The notion that many foods are only seasonal has disappeared now, as they are available year-round in the supermarket. It is hard to really grasp now what it was like then to eat the beautiful, tasty produce only available during certain seasons. Above all, the memory of deadly hunger still hovered, from not that long ago. Scarcity and careful choice of what one could afford ruled behavior. Adequate amounts of food were still needed for mere survival for many. And it was tied into the survival of self, the survival of family, the survival of the race, the survival of language. Somehow self, family, race and language all came together. They all became one in the act of eating together; if one was lost, all was lost. Family structure, which seemed to me akin to staying together, was about having enough for all if we were all together, but not enough if we were separate. Somehow, that deep and unspoken component of love through absolute sacrifice always lurked in the background of preparation of what little food there was. I knew in my heart that, if it came to it, someone in the family, someone older, would be willing to starve so that I could live. But I did not think that I was in any way exceptional. I believed that this kind of sacrifice was ingrained in every family that went through the Occupation — older adults might have to die so that the children could live. You used to hear this being said all the time. Every part of the ritual of buying the food, bartering for it, cooking it, contained that implication. When the food came to the table for all to eat, I felt safe.

So, we would all be sitting together, in the little cottage in Rafina to get away from the summer heat, with the conversation going from topic to topic. Everybody was very relaxed. Perhaps the conversation might lag for an instant. At that exact instant, carefully chosen among all other instants, Yiayia Sophia would say in a dreamy, almost far away voice:

– I wonder what we should have for lunch a week next Thursday.
– A week next Thursday, Yiayia Sophia? Everybody seemed a little puzzled or maybe making a bit of fun of Yiayia Sophia.
– We are not even sure if we will be alive a week next Thursday, Mama! Stelios might say.
– I was just wondering if you would like me to make soujoukakia. A week next Thursday … Smyrnaika soujoukakia … that's all.

There would be a few general nods of having heard, and the conversation would revert to the previous topics. Surely Yiayia Sophia's question about Smyrnaika soujoukakia for a week next Thursday was forgotten a few minutes after it was said. But Yiayia Sophia had a system. A system which always worked. A couple of days later … maybe now when we were all sitting together in the evening, in the garden of the Rafina cottage under the jasmine tree, Yiayia Sophia would probe again. And again her timing would be perfect, just during a slight lull in the conversation.

– So, for a week next Thursday I will cook the soujoukakia. Do you agree, Dina?
– Of course, Yiayia Sophia, the Smyrnaika soujoukakia.
– Yes, my good Dina. You remember the Smyrnaika soujoukakia from last time we made them! Yiayia Sophia was never reticent about reinforcing alliances through one's belly.
– We can all manage to eat the soujoukakia. That is if we are still all alive a week next Thursday, Mother! Thales always had a little fatalist twist to his humor.
– Soujoukakia would be immaterial, if we are dead, Stelios clarified somewhat redundantly.

Stelios was forever the engineer-philosopher. The obvious often needed to be stated. The Archeomarxist was silent, possibly considering if this conversation would pass Archeomarxist standards. In any case, he would have been happy since his Dina had been openly praised by his mother, for not having forgotten Smyrnaika soujoukakia, which would be on the menu for a week next Thursday. A tiny, little ironic smile appeared on his lips, under his mustache. Although I thought I saw it also in his penetrating blue eyes, it was so subtle that I was sure no one else noticed. Except perhaps Dina, who always kept half an eye on Phoebus.
Another couple more days passed taking us to the Thursday before the Thursday of the making of the soujoukakia.

– So, a week today we will be making Smyrnaika soujoukakia … for lunch.

Yiayia Sophia was simply reinforcing what everybody knew already.
Now, the psychology had shifted from mere remembering the great soujoukakia day to actual interest.

– How will you make them Yiayia Sophia … with tomato sauce or plain white sauce?

My mother had asked the critical question. Being from Zakynthos, bay leaf-flavored tomato sauces in olive oil would be favored. More importantly tomato sauce is the common way to make Smyrnaika soujoukakia. I doubt there is a restaurant in Greece today that does not make Smyrnaika soujoukakia in some kind of flavored tomato sauce. Also, usually the soujoukakia were to be accompanied by plain white rice. The flavored red tomato sauce in olive oil would be served over the rice, beautifully accompanying the soujoukakia done in the same sauce.

Yiayia Sophia had to think fast. Could the upstart daughter-in-law, not even from Smyrna, but from the other end of the Greek world, the upstart who had stolen arguably the most intelligent but also the most single-minded and complex of her boys, be planning an uprising? The critical choice between tomato sauce and plain white sauce was asked in such a friendly and casual way. Only those that are very good could start an uprising in such a quiet way. These are the ones one must watch especially carefully. The issue about which sauce would be the preferred one was clearly a trick question. For one could not easily reject the favorite, traditional soujoukakia tomato sauce. Yet if the tomato sauce was chosen, would it be done in the Smyrnian or Zakynthian way? Sophia had not missed the tiny little smile under the mustache and in the eyes of the most complex of her children. Not only did Yiayia Sophia have to think fast, she also had to be careful … very, very careful.

– What would everybody like? Tomato sauce or plain white sauce?

This counter-question was not a show of democracy. It was a little strategic retreat by Yiayia Sophia to gain time, to evaluate how the game was going. The others were bound to show their hand on the critical sauce question. She had to find out where her boys stood. Were they still with their mother, or was the Zakynthian woman making great inroad in their thinking? After all, Phoebus had hardly asked her opinion about marrying Dina. Of course, from his point of view it would have been below Archeomarxist standards to do so. Yiayia Sophia considered this line of argument as nonsense, but she would have had to admit that it was unusual in those days to marry just for love, just basal attraction. Particularly without heeding the old ties of culture and tradition … ties so essential for cohesiveness among the refugees of the old Ionian civilization. And Yiayia Sophia had not forgotten the cartoon that Stelios had exhibited in his back room in the Bastille on Hitler, Mussolini, Stalin and Dina as the 'decisive leaders'. No, she had not forgotten at all! She had simply not said anything at the time. The impression my mother had made on her sons was certainly not to be ignored.

But my mother was always right on the ball in these types of discussions. She had a natural sense as to what was to her long term advantage. What would be the point of winning a concession on the type of tomato sauce for the soujoukakia, if the older woman were to trap her, and the vote went to plain white sauce?

– Plain white sauce would be nice too, Yiayia Sophia. We have not had that for a while.

My mother had started her charm offensive, setting aside the Zakynthian preference for the flavored fresh tomato sauce. She executed brilliantly, now persuasively praising the plain white sauce.

– Of course, my Dina. But, you know, we can make both. It really would not be much trouble.

Yiayia Sophia's careful defensive tactics had worked. This chess game was all about making no mistakes. When the players were of such high caliber, a small error could change the tempo of the whole game, and a brilliant charm offensive could turn into a loss. And Dina had just made a tiny little mistake in tempo. By raising the question as to which sauce should be prepared in the first place, Dina had found herself having to possibly agree to them making both sauces. Sophia's next move was obvious and Dina had not seen it. If Dina agreed that both sauces should be made, then Sophia would propose that Dina could make the tomato sauce, since she was from Zakynthos, and Yiayia Sophia would make the plain white sauce. Having a non-Smyrnian make the traditional sauce for Smyrnaika soujoukakia was bad enough. But Zankythian tomato sauces were not made for soujoukakia. They were made for cockerel or rabbit in a casserole and the proportion and types of the flavoring spices and amount of olive oil were rather different (generally increased) than for soujoukakia. The brothers would expect their mother's Smyrnian tomato sauce to go with the soujoukakia. Here Sophia would have also an immense psychological advantage. Surely only someone from Smyrni could make the classical tomato sauce for Smyrnaika soujoukakia. And who could make it better than their own mother. It seemed that Yiayia Sophia had imperceptibly managed to get the equivalent of a passed pawn in this little chess game. Dina's brilliant plain-white-sauce charm offensive was now in tatters. But my mother was not slow to appreciate the danger of an innocuous-looking passed pawn. She made an immediate decision. It was best to go for a draw.

– Yiayia Sophia, we still have a week before making the soujoukakia. We do not have to decide about the sauce now.
– Of course not, my good Dina. We would not have to decide until next Thursday. And it depends also what the tomatoes are like a week from today.

Yiayia Sophia — the master of little details, all in a couple of little sentences! First she had decided to graciously accept the draw being offered by my mother. No point winning a little chess game and worsening the real game of family relations. Also, who could tell what kind of daughters-in-law she would end up with when Thales got married, and if Stelios married? Stelios was the eldest and should have been married already, but he had not. Perhaps it was because of his disability with the childhood tuberculosis having affected his shoulders, and perhaps even his personality. In any case, it made strategically no sense to quarrel with Dina now, even though her boys had Dina down as a 'decisive leader' along with Hitler, Mussolini and Stalin. That was just irony towards Dina, and people had a way of shifting alliances in any case. So, Yiayia Sophia had managed to defend very adequately against the charm offensive. First, a draw with Dina, at this stage, was as good as a win. Second, she had once again re-enforced the expectations of the making and the eating of the soujoukakia, which was just a week away now. And third, she had hedged her bets on the type of sauce, thus giving her full control of the sauce question on the day that the soujoukakia would actually be made.

During the next few days Yiayia Sophia never changed tack about the soujoukakia. She would find ways to remind everyone of the great day that was coming. The brilliant tactical battle about the sauce was over and forgotten. Probably most family members had not even noticed what was really at stake between Dina and Sophia. Once the sauce challenge was settled all that Sophia needed to do was to continue to send little verbal and subliminal messages about the soujoukakia.

Finally the great day came. It was Thursday, and on Yiayia Sophia's insistence everyone had gone to bed the night before at a reasonable time. You did not want staying up late the previous night to affect your taste buds. On that Thursday morning Yiayia Sophia was up early, preparing. It was a perfect summer day, like nearly all other summer days in Rafina. Normally, in the summer time the swim might start at 11 or so in the morning and go on until 2 or so. We would then eat around the little table and everybody would take a long afternoon nap, getting up around five-ish, now well rested for the evening. But on that day, refreshed from having to go to bed early the night before, everybody was already up by six-thirty or seven and having their individual little Greek coffees with dry biscuits that made up the basic breakfast. Yiayia Sophia then dispatched everyone to the morning swim around nine instead of the usual eleven o'clock. Everyone that is, except me. I was to stay back to help her with the various chores related to the soujoukakia. I did not mind missing the swim. Helping with the soujoukakia was more interesting. I thought that my mother might also stay back and help, especially after the great sauce discussion of the previous Thursday. But no, Dina went along with the boys for the swim. In fact she said to Yiayia that she would make sure that no one would return from the swim until after two. Yiayia Sophia just nodded.

– Would it not be better still if I got them to come back at three, Yiayia Sophia?
– Three would even be better, my good Dina.
– Of course Yiayia Sophia. I am sure I can delay them coming back until about three.

I thought I detected that tiny little smile in Yiayia Sophia's eyes. And then my mother added:

– And of course, Tasouli can stay here to help you, since I will be on the beach keeping an eye on Phoebus and his brothers.

With these words, I was certain, the beginning of a grand alliance between Yiayia Sophia and my mother was being forged. I thought that was an alliance that the other 'decisive leaders' never succeeded in forging. But, of course, Hitler, Mussolini and Stalin did not know the first thing about soujoukakia. How could these poor dictators ever be expected to succeed?

For me, the only thing that was missing was Joujoukos. He would have been in his element. Even his name, Joujoukos sounded like soujoukakia. Perhaps the story of soujoukakia evolved because of naming Joujoukos after soujoukakia. I consoled myself by daydreaming that Joujoukos actually lived in the soujoukakia. Yes, I could see him there physically being in the soujoukakia, with his eyes and moustaches all smiling, anticipating the taste. Then, as I was starting to become preoccupied with the problem of eating the soujoukakia without accidentally eating my Joujoukos at the same time, Yiayia Sophia called:

– Tasouli, Tasouli …
– Yes, Yiayia.
– Has everybody gone for the swim, Tasouli?
– Most certainly, Yiayia.
– Everyone?
– Yes, Yiayia, everyone. I have even checked the *dammaki* and the back garden. They have all gone for the swim.
– Good, Tasouli. We must now start the preparations.
– The preparations, Yiayia!
– The most important thing is the meat. To get lean veal. Not the milk-fed veal, but the *damalaki*.
– The *damalaki*. In between the milk-fed and the full-grown animal.
– Exactly, Tasouli. And it must be very lean.
– How are we going to get it Yiayia?
– You must go to the butcher we trust, and say it is for me.
– But which butcher do we trust, Yiayia? There are four of them in Rafina.

She named all four butchers, using names I was not too familiar with, and then started a comparative description of the honesty, politics and geographical pedigree of each. As far as I could tell each one was a bigger thief than the previous one she named. And each one had the worst Monarchist, with unspeakable anti-Venizelos politics than the previous one. And only one of them seemed to be from Smyrnian origin. For some incomprehensible reason she eliminated him at once. She went through the remaining three one more time, and decided finally on the one she had been denigrating the most. He was apparently an unrepentant Royalist and a rightist for sure, and she would not be caught dead having anything to do with him. I did not follow her logic as to why she chose him over the others. I was sworn to secrecy in any case. The name of the butcher where the meat for the soujoukakia was obtained must not be revealed under any circumstances.

– You go and tell him the meat is for me, Tasouli.
– OK, Yiayia, I am on my way.
– Three times, Tasouli.
– Three times what, Yiayia?
– The lean veal from the *damalaki* must be ground three times.
– Not once, not twice, but three times, Yiayia?
– Three times.
– But will he grind it three times, Yiayia?
– He will.
– But do you know him personally, Yiayia?
– He knows me.

So, I go down the hill, in the searing morning sun of Rafina and find the butcher shop of the Royalist. I enter and it seems pitch dark. No other customers. There is a huge black and white picture of King Paul on the wall, in an old wooden frame. The butcher is a Royalist for sure, and he is sullen and suspicious to boot. When I tell him that I want ground meat he pretends not to hear. When I say Yiayia Sophia sent me he does not seem to know her and acknowledges nothing. I am starting to get intimidated and scared. I am going to fail my mission. I did not manage to tell him the weight of the required ground meat or that it must be ground three times. I am petrified. Then I notice that he is putting a large amount of meat through the big manual meat grinder and before I can say anything, he is doing it again. And again. He knew to grind it three times, without me asking him. The meat is then all wrapped in butcher's paper and handed to me. I had no idea how much I was really supposed to get or what the price was. I give him what money Yiayia Sophia had given me, and he takes it and sticks it in the till without looking at it. He never says anything. I leave the dark butcher shop and the silent, sulking Royalist. I am slightly shaking, and run up the hill to give the soujoukakia meat to Yiayia Sophia. I tell her I did not know the amount I was supposed to get, but she does not seem to be interested either. I asked her if it is OK, and she also disregards me but seems quite satisfied with the look of the meat.

– Now, Tasouli, you must run to get fresh ground cumin.
– Fresh ground cumin, Yiayia Sophia?
– Yes, Tasouli, in the little general shop down by the Platea.
– Will they know to grind it for me, Yiayia?
– They will. They are from Smyrni.
– Do they know you, Yiayia?
– And I know them.

So, I run down the hill again to the Platea in the searing, now late morning sun. I find the little shop which, contrary to the dark butcher shop, is nice and bright. A picture of Elephtherios Venizelos, the former Prime Minister, who Yiayia Sophia had sanctified, hung in a nice bright frame. The shop was run by a woman I had seen before that looked a little younger than Yiayia Sophia.

– Hello Tasouli, she said brightly. She knew my name. I wondered what else she knew.
– I came for some cumin …
– I will grind it finely for you Tasouli. She knew about grinding the cumin.
– Thanks, I said sheepishly.
– For the soujoukakia, right? She knew that too. I nodded just as sheepishly.
– Say hello to Yiayia Sophia.
– How much for the ground cumin? She was disregarding me, already serving another customer. Then she quickly turned to me:
– It's for the soujoukakia. Good appetite! She made a dismissive motion at my offer to pay for the ground cumin.

I had got the ground cumin free, so I started up the hill again. The hill from the main platea to our house seemed particularly steep. We normally would do it no more than once a day but I was already on my second ascent and it was still morning. I was starting to feel tired and I stopped under bits of shade to rest from the blazing sun. I started to think. I could have got both the three-fold ground meat from the Royalist and the finely ground cumin from the Venizelophile in one trip. Why did I have to do two trips? I guess Yiayia Sophia was so involved in making the soujoukakia she was not thinking clearly. And we had not even got to the sauce. What if Yiayia Sophia had decided to make the important tomato sauce and I had to go down again to get tomatoes from her favorite green grocer. I would become too exhausted. Probably, I would become so exhausted that I could not even enjoy the soujoukakia. I must ask Yiayia Sophia all those questions when I got home.

When, finally, I did get home and entered our little house, it felt cool and I immediately felt better.

– Yiayia Sophia, I have got the finely ground cumin. And the lady at the shop did not take money. I got it free, I said proudly. Yiayia Sophia just nodded as if she already knew all of this.
– Yiayia, why did I have to make two trips down to the platea in all the heat? Could I not have done it in one trip? I could see a little smile behind her glasses.
– Tasouli, you did not go for a swim today.
– No, I stayed to help you.
– And you have helped a great deal. These will be the best soujoukakia ever. I felt better still and starting to get a little hungry for the best soujoukakia ever. But I was cautious. Would I have to be sent again for the tomatoes?
– Yiayia, are you going to make the tomato sauce today?
– Oh yes, Tasouli. And it is going to be the best ever.
– So, I will have to go down for the tomatoes now?
– No, no Tasouli. I already got them. Fresh, today.
– But how did you get them, Yiayia? The traveling green-grocer only comes around twice a week and he was by a couple of days ago.
– From the gypsies, Tasouli.
– The gypsies? But the gypsies do not sell tomatoes. They mostly fix chairs and the like.
– We had an understanding.
– But the gypsies only come around once a week. On Thursdays.
– We had an understanding from two weeks ago, when they fixed the seats on all the chairs in the *dammaki* and the bedroom.
– Oh, I know that, Yiayia. Everybody commented as to what a good job they did replacing the old rattan. They look like new. But what does this have to do with the tomatoes?
– The gypsies grow their tomatoes without irrigation, Tasouli. Near their caravans north of Rafina, close to Marathon, towards the mountains.
– Oh, I know about irrigated and non-irrigated tomatoes, Yiayia Sophia. My mother says that the non-irrigated tomatoes are the tastiest, although they are much smaller. In Zankynthos they much favor them for sauces and even salads.
– The tomatoes near Marathon, are probably the best in Greece this year, Tasouli. And if they are grown near the slopes they are better still.
– But how did they know to bring them this Thursday, Yiayia Sophia? The very day of making the soujoukakia.
– Like I said, Tasouli, they were fixing the chairs two weeks ago. And they said that their tomatoes should reach their peak in about two weeks.
– They must have been expensive, if they are so special, Yiayia Sophia.
– No, they gave them to me for free.
– How come, Yiayia?
– I bargained with them. If they got the order to fix the chairs in both the dammaki *and* the bedroom, they would bring over the tomatoes this week for free.
– I bet you my mother must have been happy to get non-irrigated tomatoes for the tomato sauce for the soujoukakia.
– She does not know. It will be a surprise.

Yiayia Sophia never seemed to waste a motion while she talked. She was already well into the mixing the trice-ground lean damalaki meat with just the right amount of pepper and salt and the finely ground cumin. The additions were all done in ordered stages. The order could not be changed. The mixing was all done by hand, in a big glazed, earthenware reserved for that purpose. It seemed very hard work. Wetted core of white bread fresh from the oven was added in stages, so that the soujoukakia would "go far enough" — so there would be enough for everyone. But she also admitted that the right amount of white core bread and the wetting of the bread had much to do with the right consistency. The mixing was done with both the palms of her hands as well as her fists. It seemed like kneading bread, while the conversation continued unabated.

– But Yiayia Sophia, if you had made arrangements to have the tomatoes from the Gypsies today, what was all the discussion with mother about what kind of sauce to make.
– I never said that I would *not* make the tomato sauce. It was *she* who asked if we would make tomato sauce or plain white sauce.
– Oh.
– And you know, all the Gypsies ever said was that their tomatoes should reach their peak in two weeks. So, I was not sure they would even bring the tomatoes today.
– Oh.
– But your mother handled things very well.
– Oh?
– Oh, yes. The sauce question was very important. Very important for women from Smyrni. They were very particular about the kind of sauce they made. Only certain sauces go with certain meals and you cannot mix them up. It is like an order of life and it is civilization.
– Very important, Yiayia. But my mother did not stay and help you with the right kind of sauce. She went down with my father and uncles for the swim.
– Your mother is a very smart woman. She took everybody down the wooded ravine for a long swim.
– Why such a long swim today, Yiayia?
The familiar little smile behind the glasses appeared again.
– Tasouli, after the walk up and down the ravine and the long swim they will be tired and very hungry.
– I am getting quite hungry too, Yiayia Sophia.
– Of course you are, Tasouli. You had to go down to the Platea in all the heat — twice today!

On that great day Yiayia Sophia made the Smyrnaika soujoukakia not with just one sauce, but both kinds. First a lot of the soujoukakia was made with the plain white sauce and then a second lot with the tomato sauce — the best tomatoes that could be found in the whole of Greece. Both lots were set aside, while she made the plain white rice. Enough of the tomato sauce had been made to go with endless amounts of the plain white rice.

Just when the rice was done, as if by pre-planned timing, everybody arrived from their swim — tired, hot, and hungry as bears. They all said they could smell the soujoukakia even as they were coming up the ravine. The aroma of the soujoukakia mingled with the smells of the pine trees and the wild thyme and myrtle growing along the ravine, they said. They all fell upon the soujoukakia as if they had not eaten for a week, taking both kinds of soujoukakia, but mixing the plain white rice mostly with the tomato sauce. A fresh cucumber salad and freshly baked bread from the local oven accompanied the meal. Everything was washed down with the plentiful local white wine, from the barrel, which cost next to nothing and tasted like nectar. There was a uniformity of opinion that these were not just the best soujoukakia ever, but the best meal ever. Everyone headed straight for a nap right after. We all woke up refreshed and in a very good mood around five o'clock. We were now all ready for a very good evening.

That meal of the soujoukakia in Rafina had a major impact on the family for years to come. It created a kind of competition and even conflict among the women — the daughters-in-law of Yiayia Sophia. It also created an apparently unsolvable mystery which was only solved by a new generation decades later. Ultimately, there were four daughters-in-law. Thales married Ourania, who had striking good looks, and was a classmate of Thales, also a physician. Not to be confused with Ourania, the silent, bent over, Anatolian companion of Yiayia Sofia. Yianis had married Toula, during the Bastille days and, of course, Phoebus was the first to get married to the Zankynthian Dina.

Stelios married last and was the only one to marry by sort of *proxenia*, a kind of semi-arranged marriage. In a *proxenia* the boy and girl would not know each other or, at least, not very well. A person that does proxenias, almost invariably a middle-aged woman, would first approach the girl and then separately the boy, and see if they were interested. Then a little social occasion was set up so the boy and girl could meet. The parents were kept in the picture every step of the way and, of course they knew all the details like the girl's dowry, education and schooling of the boy and the girl, and the like. These 'matchmakers' were also popular in North America but their business has since been cut into significantly by web-based matchmaking. When I say "sort of proxenia" for Stelios, it is because he ended up marrying Mimoza who was already well known to the family, particularly Yiayia Sophia. Mimoza was known because her parents were also from Smyrni and from a good family, of teachers, I think. So, Yiayia Sophia and the great man, my grandfather, knew Mimoza's parents quite well. They also initially settled in Nea Smyrni after the catastrophe of Smyrni. Mimoza used to hang around with the boys during the glory days of Rafina, although she was quite a bit younger than the boys. So, one would think that Yiayia Sophia's matchmaking for Stelios and Mimoza would have turned out well for Yiayia Sophia. But the opposite happened. They did not get along well and as the years passed their relations became frostier. It was never quite clear to me why that was the case. Yiayia Sophia would complain to me:

– I can't stand Mimoza. She does not talk. She just sits there in the *monokomato*.
– The monokomato Yiayia Sophia?
– Yes, you know. That dressing gown cut from a single piece of cloth (mono = single, comato = piece).
– Does the monokomato have something to do with Mimoza not speaking to you, Yiayia?
– She is like a monokomato herself!

But Mimoza had many attributes. She had been a top student. She was highly organized. She had an absolute detailed memory for everyone and everything. She had strong likes and dislikes and she loved gossip, much like rest of the family. And she spoke very good, precise English. In much later years, after Yiayia Sophia died, Mimoza became friendly with Pamela and she was able to fill in gaps in the Styppas prehistory. Just as importantly Mimoza made Smyrnaika soujoukakia many times … with the tomato sauce. But never once did she acknowledge Yiayia Sophia's recipe. Mimoza's soujoukakia were very good. But they would just appear from the refrigerator, prepared from the day before, as she was so highly organized. In truth, Mimoza's soujoukakia never reached the poetic heights of Yiayia Sophia's. Of course, no one ever mentioned this, and Mimoza was content to have her soujoukakia happily devoured by all present.

But much before this, the story of the Rafina soujoukakia had already played a big role in the lives of the daughters-in-law. For years after the Rafina soujoukakia all four brothers started to complain to their women. The complaint was the same, namely that the Smyrnaika soujoukakia each of the daughters-in-law made were never the same as Yiayia Sophia's soujoukakia. The implication was that their soujoukakia were inferior. Since cooking was taken so seriously, by extension the daughters-in-law were inferior in their cooking abilities. Of course it took a few years for the four daughters-in-law to all compare notes. First, each tried to improve her soujoukakia by studying the various available recipes, discussing the recipes with friends, etcetera. But to no avail. Each time they made the Smyrnaika soujoukakia the judgment was the same from their man: good, perhaps even improved, but not the same as their mother's. Certainly no match for that glorious, unforgettable meal in Rafina, which gradually began to represent in their mind all the soujoukakia meals that Yiayia Sophia had ever made. In desperation, each of the women approached Yiayia Sophia, on different occasions, and asked her for the recipe for the Smyrnaika soujoukakia. Yiayia Sophia duly accommodated their individual requests. Each recipe was in Yiayia Sophia's own hand-writing, nicely dated and given in an unsealed air-mail envelope, with the recipe ending with a polite affectionate wish of 'good appetite'. So, each of the women tried to follow the recipe exactly, each believing that they were given the 'true' Yiayia Sophia recipe. Unfortunately, the results remained totally unchanged. Each of their men reiterated the same cant that the soujoukakia did not taste like their mother's.

Except, perhaps, for my mother who, hotly reminded Phoebus that it was un-comradely to make these types of bourgeois comparisons. What could the poor Archeomarxist do but agree. The problem was that my mother was never one to try to emulate traditional recipes. It was unclear if she was incapable of doing so, or if she truly believed in the innovative little meals she prepared. The other brothers were unimpressed with Dina's innovative modernism in cooking. Thales, with his cutting humor, even coined the term *skatoloismata* (which roughly translates into 'shitty-talkies'), to describe Dina's cutie little offerings. No, for him it was either proper Smyrnaika soujoukakia or death ... liberty or death it was, and there must be no retreat or society was sure to collapse.

But things got worse with time. Yiayia Sophia had accommodated the request for the soujoukakia recipe from each of her daughters-in-law, in the order that the requests were made. These requests were often made months apart and fulfilled whenever the particular daughter-in-law might visit with Yiayia Sophia. At that time, the particular daughter-in-law was handed her recipe by Yiayia Sophia in a personalized, open, air mail envelope. The recipe ended with the terminal affectionate wish of 'good appetite'. So, by comparing notes as to what their men had supposedly said about their relative successes in trying to meet their mother-in-law's high standards of the soujoukakia, the daughters-in-law arrived at a most disturbing conclusion. Each started to believe that one of the others was given the *true* recipe of the soujoukakia, while they themselves had ended up with an inferior version. Once that kind of suspicion entered their minds there was no end to it. Jealousy became rampant. Why would one of the others get the true recipe and not themselves? Were the rest inferior? Or maybe there was more than one true recipe. So, each one would start to wonder if she would have got not only a bad recipe but maybe even the worst recipe. What had one done to be punished by the mother-in-law in this most unjust way? Was Sophia really trying to wreck her marriage? These Smyrnians were not just devious. It was said they were also unforgiving right to their death bed. But another suspicion started to enter the minds of some of the daughters-in-law. Maybe, just maybe, it was not just *her* that Yiayia Sophia hated. Maybe it was not that terrible woman-to-woman hate. Maybe it was a way Yiayia Sophia had of punishing the son she had married. One would have to find out more about the relationship of her husband with his mother. What could have led his mother to want to punish her son in this underhanded way? So, each daughter-in-law would question endlessly her husband about his relations with his mother. And this would go on and on. And so would the implicit accusations. It seemed that the jealousies would never end.

Gradually, however, as the Bastille broke up and all the couples got their own homes or apartments, the soujoukakia passion started to wane. Relations between the daughters-in-law became better. It is said that at a party, a family gathering, the idea came up to compare the soujoukakia recipes that each had received. After much discussion and reassurance from all that solidarity would rule, no matter who had got the worst recipe, they agreed to compare recipes. When they all saw their recipes, it is said that it was as if a thunderclap hit them. They could not believe their eyes. The prized soujoukakia recipes they each so treasured were identical. Not a word was different, not a punctuation mark. Once they had calmed down, they gradually agreed that they would all go back to making the soujoukakia according to their own methods, their own innovations. That horrid little 'monkey of suspicion' was off their backs. It did not really matter as much now what their husbands said. The women had been treated fairly and equally by their mother-in-law. Maybe the Smyrnaika soujoukakia recipe would now taste as good as Sophia's to their husbands. It would be made clear to all the brothers that the same recipe was given by Yiayia Sophia to all of the wives. It was very likely the true Sophia recipe and that knowledge alone should make it taste better. A lot better. Maybe, just maybe, it might taste as good as their mother's. But it never happened. Each of the brothers continued to insist that Yiayia Sophia's soujoukakia were better than any their wives ever cooked, even if they followed exactly the recipe they all possessed.

Years passed. Decades passed. The soujoukakia controversy started to fade into the background. Tasouli was no longer a child but grown up. And a young Pamela had come onto the scene. And Yiayia Sophia had grown much older. But Rafina of old still held much of its character. A few apartment buildings had been built. But the little house with its garden, surrounded now by a stone fence, was still intact. Yiayia Sophia still had her castle, her last abode. Her children did not visit her much, being busy with their jobs, their families and friends in Athens. Mimoza, in particular, was much against Rafina during that period. It was whispered that something had happened in Rafina between her and the boys when they were all very young. It was apparently some physical attribute that the young boys and their friends teased her about. Whatever had happened turned her off Rafina. And because she had an elephantine memory, Mimoza never forgot.

But now Yiayia Sophia's fortunes revived again. A new generation had arrived. They had come to visit her from across the ocean. They stayed with her during the summer. She was again the undisputed elder; the old matriarch could show her mettle one more time. Pamela did not speak much Greek then and Yiayia Sophia spoke no English. But the old nuns that had trained Yiayia Sophia came to the rescue. They had taught her French ... French, the old lingua Franca of Greece and most of Europe. Pamela's French was passable and Yiayia Sophia's very good. The old Bonapartist never abandoned the language of the nuns. I don't know if she practiced French secretly or continued to read in French. But Pamela and Sophia had no problem communicating, even if it was not in their mother tongues. Something gelled between them almost immediately. Soon they became inseparable. And the visits were to continue over the years. The topic of making soujoukakia came up again, of course. The ritual was followed in their preparation and the result seemed as good as ever. Almost nothing had been lost. But there was a small difference. Yiayia Sophia had undertaken to show Pamela how to actually make the soujoukakia. So the demonstration began from the very start. From the very first principles:

– A good cook is a clean cook. Would you not agree my dear Pamela?

Yiayia Sophia was demonstrating washing her hands in the cold Rafina water with lots of soap, carefully rinsing and wiping her hands.

– Of course Yiayia Sophia. A good cook must be a clean cook.
– And it is best to sterilize the hands after washing with a little white wine. The water is safe but one should be very careful when cooking, Pamela.
– But you washed your hands very well, Yiayia Sophia.
– Still one cannot be too careful.

And so, the full demonstration would proceed step by step. Both soujoukakia with plain white sauce and tomato sauce were made. They were consumed, after the long statutory swim with great appetite, as if the old days had never changed.

– Yiayia Sophia, they were delicious. Do you have a written recipe or do you do them from memory?
– Of course, my dear Pamela, I have the recipe written down. I will copy it for you.
– It is not necessary Yiayia. I think Dina said she has it.
– Nevertheless, I will make you a copy so you can have it yourself.

Later that evening Pamela carefully studied the recipe Yiayia Sophia had written for her. She called me over:

– Tasouli, here is something interesting. The part about washing the hands is not here.
– The bit about 'a good cook is a clean cook'?
– That's the one. It is not in the recipe.
– That is just a general instruction, Pamela.
– But did you not notice?
– Notice what?
– She was washing her hands in white wine.
– That is for extra cleanness, Pamela. She said it was because of the water.
– But the Rafina water is perfectly safe. It just tastes brackish.

– Maybe she is being extra cautious.
– Extra cautious before each soujoukaki, Tasouli?
– How so? And why are you calling me Tasouli, just like Yiayia Sophia?
– She washes her hands in wine before making each soujoukaki, Tasouli.
– It's not in the written recipe?
– No. It says to add just a little bit of wine to the whole mix.
– Do you think it would make a difference?
– None of the daughters-in-law succeeded in making them taste the same as Yiayia Sophia!
– So … their husbands said.
– So, they all said.

Later that year, we had a chance to compare the soujoukakia recipe given to my mother, Dina. It was identical to the one Yiayia Sophia had given to Pamela. Word for word. As opportunity arose, over the next few years, we checked whether any of the daughters-in-law had ever actually seen Yiayia Sophia make Smyrnaika soujoukakia. The checking had to be done carefully because of how sensitive that topic used to be. The responses had become now rather disinterested, but they were uniformly "no". And it was after that summer in Rafina, when the making of the soujoukakia was first witnessed by Pamela, that the prehistory of the family also started to become clearer. Yiayia Sophia seemed to want to provide more and more bits of the early childhood history of the family and of Phoebus in particular. Those parts that he had left out or had not wanted to talk about to his grandchildren or to old colleagues. Perhaps Sophia sensed that the stories and secrets would be safe with this newly-found female kindred soul, this Englishwoman, associated with her trusted Tasouli. Or perhaps, it was the opposite, and this was her method of ensuring that they *did* get disseminated. In either case, she must have had some confidence that these stories and secrets would not become gossip or insinuations that could be turned against her by this Pamela. She was correct in that.

Darkness in Zakynthos

My earliest memory of our village in the fertile Arcadian valley of Zakynthos was darkness. A terrible, all-pervasive darkness. I can't accurately date these earliest memories, but they must have been during the war. Probably early in the war, because I have no sense of my father being there, just my mother. Her mother was called Agelikí … Yiayia Ageliki to me. Ageliki lived on a plot of land in the dispersed agricultural hamlet of Gerakaríon, quite a distance away from the port town of Zakynthos, the *Chora*, the capital, of the island. You could reach Gerakarion from the Chora only by an infrequent old bus that stopped on demand on a dirt road. So Gerakarion was fairly isolated. The isolation added to the dependence on the hard agricultural labor. A bare sustenance of livelihood was squeezed out of the little plots of land. This was all there was and it was at the heart of existence in Gerakarion. There was no running water and no electricity. It was the lack of electricity, I think, that made my memories of darkness, especially in the winter, so strong. The only source of light in the hut-like houses I remember was a small kerosene lamp with a smoky glass chimney, turned low to save money. Yiayia Ageliki lived in a mud hut at the edge of our property. The property was made up of plots of olive trees, grape vines and vegetables. There was, also, a little grazing plot. The walls of the mud huts were made by mixing mud and straw to make a firm paste, then cut to the size of large bricks and baked in the summer sun. I think Yiayia Ageliki's hut may have had a corrugated tin roof. The floor was just leveled-out soil: the dark-red fertile soil of that part of Zakynthos. There were a couple of *kourelou'des* on the soil floor, but that was all. It always seemed damp and cold in the autumn and winter. Contrary to the vivid picture in my mind of Yiayia Sophia, I have only vague memories of Yiayia Ageliki. She sat in the darkness of her little hut. She was welcoming but I do not remember a single thing she said. When she died she was old and people marveled because she still had all her own teeth, each one in perfect condition. Apparently she used wood-charcoal dust to clean her teeth with her finger every day, rinsing off the charcoal with the crystal-clear cool water from the ancient, eternal spring at the top of the property. The daily cleaning with charcoal dust was said to be the reason for her perfect teeth.

113

Yiayia Ageliki had three daughters, Dina, my mother, Nana and Marina. I got to know Nana very well. I never met Yiayia Ageliki's husband, Theodoris, my maternal grandfather as he had died before I was born. He was said to be a very kind, hardworking man, an *agrotis* — an agrarian, a farmer perhaps in North American parlance. But *agrotis* also has a ring to my ear that is close to a peasant. After all it was not that long before the time when Yiayia Ageliki and Theodoris were children, that feudal society in Zakynthos still held sway. The feudal system gradually deteriorated and progressive reforms for land were brought in, but the deep dark poverty and the oppressive bond to the land seemed to become ever more pervasive.

Yet Gerakarion was in the agriculturally prized province of Arcadia in Zakynthos. Like the ancient region of Arcadia in Peloponisos, it evokes images of endless plenty in a lush agricultural Garden of Eden. But in the lush vegetation of this Arcadian Gerakarion I always felt a sense of unreality. This sense seemed to come over me mostly in the summer and late spring. It was everywhere and wanted to envelop you and enclose you. Perhaps this sense of enclosure was because of the bewildering, rich aromas emanating from the Zakynthian wild flowers and herbs and from the ordered, neatly cultivated plots of land and shimmering olive groves. But don't think this unreality was like a fear of lurking death, as in the much romanticized warning *Et in Arcadia ego.*[2] That idealized Peloponesian Arcadia had likely never existed, in any case. In the Zakynthian Arcadia of my childhood, I do not remember the fear of death. Not even in the darkness of the setting evening and the solitary kerosene lamp. The unreality I am talking about did not appear out of the evening shadows. Rather it seemed to come out of the bright suffocating summer sunlight and the visual images of the Zakynthian agrarians. These were sunburned, sinewy peasants, working on their plots, the men often naked from the waste up, the women covered with their kerchiefs and often dark dresses. From far away they seemed to me like unworldly small dark shadows in the pervasive light. I could only see the tops of their bodies, the lower halves made invisible by the cultivated crops and wild flowers sprouting on the elevated soil boundaries of the little plots. The rhythmic swinging of the scythe or of the heavy, angled spade was endless in the blinding heat. I could look away, or go away and come back and the same rhythm would always be there. It was as if the peasants never stopped the back-breaking labor, never stopped the cultivation of the land. They never sung while they worked. They always seemed to work in silence.

This silence during work of the peasant-like agrarians of Zakynthos that I remember during the Occupation and the post-war years must seem strange now for an Island renowned for its song. The melodic and poetic Zakynthian Cantades, with their first and second voices should have mingled in perfect tuning with the mandolins and guitars. The romantic lyrics of the Cantades, from poems of old — many of them unwritten — would have touched the heart and the lyrics would have brought a smile and refreshed the mood. So, what happened to the Zakynthians at the time the Occupation Child first got to know them? Was it just the oppression of the Occupation that had eaten their heart out and silenced their spirit and their voices? Was it the hunger and the angst of squeezing out a living from tiny plots of land cultivated by hand, with all their agrarian effort and sweat-drenched labor? It could not be that their spirit was broken by the boot of the Occupier. For the Resistance in Zakynthos was organized and apparently effective, often openly in the small mountain villages and underground in the Chora and larger villages. And the Zakynthians found their own ways to resist. There are endless stories of how they did it.

For instance when the Nazis demanded that the names of Zakynthian Jews be handed over, (these would have been just a few hundred souls), the bishop of Zankynthos handed over his own name and that of the Mayor's while the Jews were all hidden by the populace. "Take one, take us all" was the Zakynthian message. The Nazi regime in Zakynthos backed down, a most unusual occurrence. They must have sensed the solidarity of the Zakynthians. In the poverty of the Occupation, the Communist party grew strong and the horrible atrocities started. So, perhaps it was the fear of these atrocities that made people silent. It made them afraid that their little plots that provided their livelihood would be taken away, that they themselves would be taken away, by the right or the left — by communist or fascist, and be terminated. And long, horrific torture before termination, before being extinguished, was common, so that information could be obtained. Information of any kind could be used — whether true or not or whether obtained by torture, it could

114

be used. So, people would always whisper. And if the working agrarian man of the family was terminated or otherwise died, the women, children and old people in that household would be left unprotected. In the absence of a grown man, the little plots of land, making up their property could be prayed on by unscrupulous others, often relatives or neighbors. And that is why information was so important — information that could be twisted, that could be turned — starting with small seemingly unimportant things. What seems so little now was worth so much then. It was worth so much because survival was worth everything and there was nowhere to go. Not really — for it was like that everywhere. The agrarians and their families were chained to their little plots and had been so for generations … much before the Occupation.

The land had been divided and subdivided in Zankynthos for a long time. For each generation passed on the land — the only real wealth was divided among the children. Less fertile land on the hillsides was terraced with stone-on-stone to tease out a little more land, with endless labor from childhood to death. It was to no avail. The divided plots were still getting smaller. The last large holdings in the Gerakarion region were many generations ago by a great, great, great … grandfather, the great 'Papos', who remained in peoples memory. This great Papos was talked about with great admiration. I was never exactly sure when the great Papos lived. Perhaps he was the last of the real feudal lords left over from medieval times. I am not sure if he lived during the unpleasant and oppressive hegemony of Zakynthos by the rulers of the British Empire. This was the last occupation before that of the Germans during the Second World War. That English occupation left many scars on Zakynthians, many of whom were imprisoned in the *Kastro* (the Castle on the hill overlooking the Capital, the *Chora*), and horribly tortured before being executed. These methods were also applied by the English to anyone considered to be a 'pirate'. Problem was, of course, that pirates and brigands had a long and distinguished history much before the British Empire. They were generally regarded by island populations as distant cousins, since the islands were depopulated by the great medieval plagues. The repopulation of the islands would have included many such pirates, brigands and other thieves of the seas. Many of them would have then found land to settle — most likely more marginal land — in the depopulated islands. The English occupation would not have looked kindly on the Zakynthian poor who would be most likely to still have some connections with pirates. The control of the English rule of the waves had to be absolute. Anyone that interfered with this dominance of the high seas would be terminated. I wonder if the executions and killings caused any pangs of conscience to the English masters.

But perhaps the great Papos lived before the English hegemony, during the years of the Ottoman Empire, which then allied itself briefly with the Russian Empire. Perhaps he was alive even before that, during the much more benign and enlightened Venetian occupation (*Venetocratia)*, which lasted about three hundred years. The Venetians freely integrated and intermarried with the Zakynthians. It was this Venetian occupation that left the strongest cultural imprint in Zakynthos. Many of the words in the Zakynthian dialect and the lyrics of the *cantades* (cantatas) are of Italian origin. The name of the 'cantades' itself is likely from 'canto', the song idiom of medieval Italy. Poetry in Italian was not uncommon and even the National poet of Greece, Dionysios Solomos, composed some of his poems in Italian. Also, the invading Venetian aristocracy had apparently integrated to a large extent with native Zakynthian aristocracy. The names of titled and important Zakynthians (perhaps Venetian and Zakynthian alike) were recorded in the *Libro Doro*, the golden book of Zakynthos. It was said our great Papos had his name in the *Libro Doro*. Unfortunately the *Libro Doro* was destroyed in a great fire, as I first learned from Nana:

– Oh yes, the great Papos knew how to do everything, Nana would say.
– And he had many holdings, not just our property, *Thia* (aunt) Nana?
– Pretty-well everything you can see in Gerakarion and beyond, Tasouli.
– And did people like the great Papos?
– Oh yes. He was very just and kind.
– And famous too, Thia Nana?
– For certain, Tasouli. Why, he was even in the Libro Doro.
– Oh, the Libro Doro!

– With all the Nobles and Counts and Lords.
– Oh!
– Of Zante and Venetia.
– Too bad the Libro Doro burned Thia Nana.
– Yes, it burned in the great fire.
– I would have liked to have seen the Libro Doro.
– But it is better that it burned, Tasouli!

Nana had a little smile — it was always an attractive smile. She had the perfect teeth of her mother. I think maybe she also cleaned her teeth with charcoal dust.

– But why is it better that it burned, Thia Nana?
– Because now everybody can say their ancestors were in it.
– Like lords of mind, Thia Nana?
– Yes, like lords of the mind, Tasouli.
– But our great Papos was in the Libro Doro for real, is that not right Thia Nana?
– Of course he was, Tasouli.
– But then some Zakynthians would say that their ancestors were in the Libro Doro, but they were not.
– Some do, Tasouli.

Nana's smile was there again. Why was she happy if some people had lied about their ancestors being in the Libro Doro? Surely that would put our great Papos and our family at a disadvantage.

– And how could that be good, Thia Nana? How can it be good if some lie?
– Because everybody would be equal then. We would all have equal rights of our inheritance, of our land. Don't you think so, Tasouli?
– Ahh! Yes, Thia Nana. The burning of the Libro Doro made everybody have ancestors who were Lords!

Nana's interpretation of the burning of the Libro Doro during the great fire, as a god-send for egalitarianism, was not unique or original. I later heard it often, from all kinds of Zakynthians — always with a little smile. It was traditional Zakynthian humor — turning adverse events during the multilayered history of Occupiers of the Island, into something advantageous to the Zakynthians. But for Nana it probably also had special significance. It provided a little ray of hope for her situation, for her very survival which was ever so dependent on the little plots of the agricultural land. Her father had died relatively young, leaving the three daughters unprotected by a male. The first of the three sisters to marry was Marina. She married a man who lived in Gerakarion, close to the little property of Papous Theodoris, Yiayia Ageliki, Nana and Dina and Marina. We will call him 'K'. I cannot remember if K was originally from Gerakarion. While Papous Theodoris was alive the relationship with K was apparently not too bad. But after Papous Theodoris died, which left three unprotected women on the land, things deteriorated. The way Nana and Dina described the situation, it became gradually a state of terror. Initially the threats were mostly verbal abuse but soon they became physical threats. What was behind the threats and abuse seemed to be one thing — the land. Marina had inherited a share of the land which K had control of. But apparently he wanted the rest, and the three sisters seemed easy prey. Then Marina died. She died before I was born, probably from rheumatic fever. With Marina dead, the last of the modulating influence she had on K disappeared. The physical threats and demands by K for the women to yield land or sell to him the little plots became a daily affair.

In the meantime, Dina went on to be qualified as a teacher and started to be away from Zakynthos more and more, having been posted on the mainland. She then met Phoebus, I think in Thessaloniki. Phoebus was already involved in leftist student politics and found in Dina a great political organizer, who was apparently fearless. Initially Phoebus' higher education, the intimidating way he could look and talk to people kept the relatively uneducated agrarian K at bay. But this was only when Phoebus would be visiting in Zakynthos, usually together with Dina. During the Occupation things were bad enough, with the fear of someone squealing to the Gestapo or to their paramilitary Fascist Zakynthian sympathizers. In fact, termination could come either from the right or the left. The Communist-led underground coalition EAM (National Liberation Front) took a hard position towards collaborators. Anyone could be accused of collaboration. An accusation was often enough for execution. It just got worse with the departure of the Germans in 1944 and the ensuing Civil War. Some of the most vicious exterminations by the Stalinists in the Communist resistance came towards the end of the War in December 1945. Hundreds of Internationalist Communists were exterminated in this short period by the Stalinists, including Trotskyites and Archeomarxists.[3] Some had their eyes removed before being extinguished and others were killed for distributing a little oil among starving peasants. While the extermination of the Trotskyites by the Stalinists in the Soviet Union and other Communist countries during that period is well known, the Archeomarxists were few in number. They had split off from the Communist Party and had published a Journal called "The Archives of Marxism", thus the name Archeomarxists (Archive-Marxists). Through this Journal and other publications, speeches, meetings and the like they supposedly provided a more serious theoretical education for the progressive revolutionaries of the time. Some of them seemed to consider themselves to be of a superior moral and educational level, or at least this is the impression that the Occupation Child had been left with. And yet, I later learned that they too were not beyond beating up political opponents. I have not heard of killings by the Archeomarxists them selves but maybe they were not given the opportunity, being so few in number and being prone to be extinguished in any case.

In Zakynthos too there were many instances of atrocities, particularly building up towards the end of the Civil war. There were many examples where brother opposed brother in the Civil War and sometimes brother killed brother. During that period, what was initially Phoebus' protection of Nana and Ageliki, through the respect and fear he generated, might have become a liability. This non-Zakynthian, this foreigner, with all his education and airs — could he be really trusted? Why was he baptized with an ancient Greek pagan name instead of a proper Christian name? How could this be possible? It all just added to the whispering and innuendo of who would be taken away, tortured and terminated. Further, Phoebus was not in Zakynthos very frequently during the Civil War, so revenge could be taken on Nana and her mother during these long absences.

So it became essential for Nana to find a mate, someone she could trust and who could also protect her. She somehow found such an individual from the neighboring village of Trayaki. His name was Tzanetos. He was short of stature and had lost an eye in a hunting accident when he was very young. Tzanetos was very quiet and very considerate. He was also considered to be very tough and not likely to back down in an argument or fight. I think Tzanetos had some property in Trayaki but came to live with Nana in Gerakarion after they got married. He still looked after the property in Trayaki, as they never managed to consolidate the properties. I am not sure how far he had gone in formal schooling, but he was one of the most knowledgeable people I had met. I think he was largely self-taught. He was not encyclopedic and quick like Stelios. Rather, he was systematic and analytical particularly in the history of the Island and of Greece. He was also a very practical and knowledgeable agriculturalist and, in this respect, he had quite a bit to talk about to Phoebus.

What I saw in Tzanetos was quite different from his tough reputation. With me he always had a kind, quiet and gentle, humorous manner. But he was said to be also inflexible and unbendable, particularly when it came to matters of principle. Tzanetos was committed to agrarian equality defined by hard, honest work. He had also become convinced that the opposition to Fascism was only going to be successful by an agrarian form of socialism, where produce, especially olive oil, would bring a fair market price for all. He often talked about this. I am not sure if he was an outright communist, since he hardly used labels, but he was probably considered to be one. On the other hand, he liked to handle disputes especially threats to the property by himself. His small stature and blind eye were no impediment for a fight; for he was known to carry a *souyias*. A *souyias* would generally be translated as a 'pocketknife', like a penknife. But it was said that Tzanetos' *souyias* could really slice up a man. I had never seen this souyias. He kept it out of sight. I had imagined that he kept it handy in his pocket. But, was it big enough, like an agricultural jackknife, to cut small branches off the fruit trees? In that case he could also cut off a man's fingers or even more. Or maybe it was bigger still, like the earliest memory I have of Phoebus and his souyias, which he brought back from the Front. But if Tzanetos' souyias was like Phoebus', during the early part of the War, it could have been more like a sheathed rapier. That would have been made just to kill people and would have no other use. But then, it would be too big to keep in his pocket and it would have to be kept hidden in a drawer, or somewhere. In any case, K. and other enemies of the sisters, with illegitimate interests in their property, had apparently heard of Tzanetos' souyias and did not get too close to him. They afforded him respect of some kind. But nobody I had talked to had ever seen this souyias.

Staying clear of Tzanetos, on the other hand, just increased the innuendo and vindictive political accusations against him. During the post-War oppressive government Regimes, he was apprehended and tortured endlessly. Somehow he handled his torturers and he was not killed. He never talked about it openly. But once I overheard him talk to Phoebus about it. They were sitting outside Nana's kitchen in the little veranda on the wooden benches that were by the window. I was inside the kitchen on a ranch-bed by the open window. I had lain down for a little rest and could hear the conversation, even though they did not talk loudly. I guess Tzanetos could talk to Phoebus (Phivo) about such matters because Phoebus had also been sent to exile by the same type of Regime. However, Phoebus had not been tortured like Tzanetos.

– That kind of physical torture … how did you survive it, Tzanetos? All these months of torture.
– They had their method …
– But how did you survive physically?
– Their method was too simplistic, Phivo.
– Too simplistic? How?
– Each of the levels in their step-wise method was simply designed to increase the physical pain.
– Did they ever get information out of you?
– No, because their method was not properly designed.
– Not properly designed, Tzaneto mou?
– Not properly designed, Phivo. They confused two separate objectives.
– You mean getting information and causing pain?
– Exactly, Phivo. Further, they run into a contradiction.
– A contradiction?
– Yes. Their assumption that more pain would be more likely to yield information has innate problems. In fact, there are three.
– Three innate problems?
– First, a step up in pain causes one to remember less about truth. Particularly at the higher levels of pain.
– And second?
– At the higher levels of torture designed to cause you more pain, the pain you feel actually decreases. It seems to be something physiological that happens to the brain.
– Oh, yes. I've heard of this. This is why the Soviet Stalinists did not use such crude methods. They employed Marxist arguments to get you to admit to an anti-Stalinist position, then "rehabilitated" you and recorded your "confession" before extinguishing you.
– Yes, the pain methods of the rightists are much cruder. If you know this, then you anticipate that the tortures designed to cause more pain can actually lead to feeling less pain. And then, of course, you often pass out in any case.
– And third?
– This is the most important. It depends if the torturer is looking for the truth or not.
– Oh?
– Let's say they are looking for what is advantageous to the Regime; and let's also say that what is advantageous to the Regime is not the truth. The more intelligent torturers could usually distinguish between the two.

– OK, Tzanetos. So, at least some of the torturers start to perceive a contradiction between what is advantageous to the Regime and the truth.

The Archeomarxist was now getting right into his element: Dialectic vs. Torture.

– Yes, my good Phivo. Also, if telling the truth is ingrained in you, it becomes progressively more and more difficult for you to disclose it with increasing levels of pain from torture.
– For reasons one and two.
– Exactly.
– But if you find out that a torturer has some beliefs that are even a little different than those of the Regime, then it becomes easier to disclose his own beliefs back to him. Right?
– Exactly. At least at the lower levels of induced pain, Phivo.
– But why did they finally release you, Tzanetos?
– I gradually convinced them that to learn what they thought was advantageous to the Regime, they would hardly have to torture me at all.
– They bought it?
– My break came when they said that they were just doing their job to wipe out Communism. And I sensed that they actually believed that what was advantageous to the Regime was a separate matter from what was, in fact, the truth. So, they reluctantly conceded that point to me. You know … implicitly they conceded it.
– And why did they release you? Why did they not simply extinguish you?
– For the same reason. They hoped I would provide information advantageous to the Regime when they arrested me again. Even if such information was false. It could be used as another prop for the Regime. If they extinguished me I could no longer be of use. And there would be retaliation in Gerakarion and in Tragaki against their operatives. Almost certainly.
– And what happened the next time they arrested you?
– Similar routine, Phivo.
– Nothing new? No reasons given about the new arrest?
– No. Except they let something slip during the early stages of the interrogation. And before the torture started again.
– What, Tzanetos?
– It had nothing to do with the Regime. It was all local. About the property.
– So, they have people right here.
– Of course. We know who they are.
– But Tzaneto mou, are you not going to do something about it?
– No point. It is the system that needs to change.
– But does it not bother you? To have traitors among neighbors, among the relatives?
– They are actually not traitors, Phivo. They are just operatives for the Regime. They pass information along. Mostly incorrect information. Idle gossip and innuendo.
– Still, to have them among your midst … to tolerate them. Is there not something you can do?
– We still till the same land — we and them; sometimes the same fields. We share the same olive crop. And we divide the profit from the oil according to weight of the sacs of olives that each one of us has contributed. The weights are now recorded correctly. They are gradually learning. So, we've essentially won the chess game. We've won it locally. And they know it.

Tzanetos took out a little aromatic tobacco from a simple pouch and rolled a cigarette.

– Would you like one, Phivo? This tobacco is among the very best quality in the world. Made by the tobacco workers near Kavala. And, did you know that they are still unionized?
– Oh, yes Dina was very active in that movement in Northern Greece. But no thanks to the cigarette. I can't smoke. It makes me sick.
– Too bad you can't smoke. And I know all about Dina's union activities. But you know, Phivo mou, the Regime's senior operatives love that Kavala tobacco. They smoke it incessantly.

He then pulled out his well-used, stained cigarette holder made of old amber, carefully put in the cigarette and gave it a little twist so that the end of the cigarette fitted snugly into the amber. He looked carefully at Phivos with that kindly but analytical, one-eyed manner of his. And he then lit the cigarette and inhaled.

– Say, Phivo, would you like a chess game? I can go and get my chess set. It is the same set that I took with me the second time I was arrested.
– They allowed you to keep it?
– For some reason they did.

Doppia

But for me, in spite of these clouds of darkness, of political oppression, coercion and torture, agrarian life had many ups. Nana knew everything there was to know about the little farm. She knew all about the chickens, the goat, how to make bread in the charcoal-heated outside oven, how to make a delicious meal in a jiffy from the vegetables and olive oil grown on our property. And she loved showing me everything, always with that smile of hers.

Of course, we also had the olive orchard. It started just outside the fenced yard and went a great distance in well-ploughed terraces. The olive orchards belonging to all the neighbors and relatives adjoined each other, their terraces separated by wide paths or by the soil elevations that seemed carved out of the rolling hills of Gerakarion. The first olive tree one came across right after leaving the farmyard was the Doppia. This was a giant tree, with its trunk hollow in the middle, forming a small cave with its roots. It was like a little round tent, maybe two meters in diameter. Doppia means the 'native', the 'local'. And the Doppia had been in that location for hundreds of years. No one knew exactly how old she was. Some people said 300 hundred years, but others said she was much older, maybe 500 or 600 hundred years. Doppia had been hit by lightning within living memory of the oldest Gerakarians. This electricity from the lightning had partially split the hollow which was made up by her roots and sides of her trunk. As a result, it was easy to get inside the little cave that was left. It made a superb hiding place. Likely the best hiding place in the whole of Zakynthos. Maybe, the best in the world. This hollow of old Doppia was like no other tree hollow — this was a cave-like structure where the roots made part of the walls like the arches of a medieval cathedral.

One of my most vivid memories of hiding in the hollow of Doppia had to do with a dog and a priest. The dog's name was Perdiki, named after the *perdikes*, the beautiful and bountiful Zakynthian partridges that Perdiki loved to hunt. The perdikes (used here in the feminine, first person plural), or the perdiki (in the neutral, first person singular), are very perky birds. And everybody knows this. That is why they are called perdikes … perky perdikes they are indeed. It has even become part of the speech. So, if someone was not feeling well and then they perked up, his Mamaka or a friend could say *egines perdiki*, meaning "you've now become as perky as a perdiki". And my adopted dog Perdiki was not only perky but very devoted to the Occupation Child. Perdiki and I became inseparable. I am not sure how old I was when I first met Perdiki but I have a couple of black and white photos from when I was a toddler, supporting myself on a fence made from cane. Perdiki was right there apparently taking a great interest. Now, I am not sure if it was the same Perdiki when the priest came into the picture. And the reason I am not sure is that the priest was six or seven years later. I do not know the Priest's name. The reason was that he was to baptize my first cousin P, who was Nana's first born son and therefore my first cousin. Baptism was pretty well compulsory in Greece then, so it should have been no big deal for me.

Except that for me it did become a huge deal. It was akin to my terror that I would become an orphan if I betrayed my parents' *pro-demotiki* position, during my education at Maraslion. But at least being an orphan under those circumstances in 'Athens then' would have resulted in my being able to eat salami sandwiches in the orphanage. So betrayal of my parents' progressive politics and their resulting extinction or liquidation would have had the upside of the promise of salami sandwiches. There seemed to be no such upside now. If I was seen speaking to the priest, surely this would be a betrayal of my parents' antireligious principles — especially those of the Archeomarxist.

If I refused to speak to the priest then my parents would be labeled as communists and they would be extinguished for sure. After all, even the brilliant strategist Tzanetos just managed to escape being extinguished by his torturers. And this was Zakynthos where everybody squealed and the operatives were right there in the baptismal party. There were no salami sandwiches at the end of this dark tunnel. I tried to explain some of this to Perdiki but all she did was lick my face. The only possible escape was to try to avoid the conflict. I headed straight for the Doppia and hid in her hollow. Perdiki of course thought it was a big game. I breathed very quietly. I thought I could hear the incantations of the baptism from our little family-chapel of Agia Marina, a few hundred meters away on a small hill among the olive groves. Maybe I had been saved. Maybe they had gone ahead with the baptism without me. Agia Marina had been part of my mother's extended family forever. I am not sure how long, for the little chapel had been rebuilt at least once. And now it seemed to me that by isolating the baptismal party inside its walls it was trying to save me. But instead, it was my faithful Perdiki that betrayed me. Tired of being inside Doppia's hollow and her birding instincts coming to the forefront, she started sniffing for perdikes around the Doppia. And she must have caught the scent of some perdikes because Perdiki went crazy. She was running around yelping and even barking, salivating and trying to tell me about the perdikes. And it was Nana, having the ears of a hound dog herself, that came running down the little hill of Agia Marina. With perdiki running around the Doppia, there was little doubt where I was hiding.

    – Tasouli, Tasouli what happened to you? Everybody was looking for you. They waited for a long time before they started.
    – Oh Thia Nana. I did not want to come.
    – You did not want to come to the baptism of your little cousin P?
I had to think quickly.
    – I was afraid, Thia Nana.
    – Afraid Tasouli? What could you possibly be afraid of?

I could no longer stall. I had to choose between the horrid truth — that terrible betrayal of my parents and especially the Archeomarxist no matter how I behaved towards the priest — and an outright fib. But maybe, just maybe there was a middle way. What could I lose by trying?

    – I was afraid of the priest, Thia Nana.
    – But what could scare you about the priest, Tasouli? He is just a normal priest.
Think fast, Tasouli, think fast!
    – It is his beard, Thia Nana. He has such a huge dark beard.

Nana broke out in a silver laugh of relief. She must have suspected much worse … who knows what her little nephew had heard among the conspirators, the operatives, maybe even from his own mother, her very sister. But this was just a child afraid of a big beard of the priest. The world was still alright on this baptismal day.

    – Come on Tasouli. You can still catch the end of the ceremony. I told the priest that I thought I knew where you were. He will extend the blessings and the incantations.
    – Oh Thia Nana. How long can he extend them for?
    – You know these priests Tasouli — they can go on endlessly. And they don't mind. The more blessings the better as far as they are concerned.

Her little encouraging, ironic smile about priests and religion seemed to make everything better. My story about the beard was well received. The priest and the agrarians would be happy enough to have incantations and chants go on forever. After all that is why their *psalters* (cantors) are the ones with the finest village voices. They can continue with the psalms written for the ancient Byzantine melodies endlessly and no one really gets bored.

– OK, Thia Nana. But can I take Perdiki with me?
– Of course Tasouli. Perdiki should not miss the baptism, either.

So Nana heads up to the little church of Agia Marina, with me and Perdiki in tow. Clearly Tasouli has been found and from the smiles on everybody the word is being passed around that Tasouli had hid because he was afraid of the priest's big beard. Apart from some embarrassment, no real damage. My mother and the Archeomarxist were safe. But I still had to be careful. A slip could come at any time. After the baptism was over and attempts to drown little P in the plentiful sacred oil and water in the baptismal cauldron were unsuccessful, everybody had to line up for a commemorative photograph. Now, that black and white photograph still exists. I had a chance to see it again in P's house not long ago. There must be fifteen or twenty people in the picture, all standing, except me. The central part of the photo seems dominated by my mother and the priest. They are standing next to each other, with my mother extending herself to her full height, although she is still one of the shortest people in the picture. She is wearing a sour, superior expression I know very well. Everybody else has a serious expression and hardly anyone is smiling. But to a large extent, that was the fashion of the times. Only fools smiled. Or you might indeed smile if you had fooled someone, and had tricked them out of money or property. Nana, although she is the mother of the child being baptized, seems to be trying to make herself invisible somewhere on the side of the photo. And in the center bottom of the photo, there I am, crouching on the ground tightly holding onto Perdiki who seems intent on trying to escape and chase her perdikes. But I am holding onto Perdiki for dear life. No way am I going to let her go. And I am the only person in the photograph who is not looking straight ahead. My eyes are fixed down on Perdiki. In this way I cannot betray anyone.

A problem with the baptismal story and Perdiki as I have told it was really due to a gap in specific political knowledge about the priest on my part. For my fear of the priest baptizing P was based on the assumption that this priest would be a reactionary. Priests, one would assume, were probably closely allied to the oppressive Regime of the time. The Regime's propaganda was full of the greatness of a Greek Orthodox state with the King, the Church and Katharevousa reigning supreme. And it was inconceivable to me that priests would not have politics in the Greek Church. After all, our school teaching was full of the Greek Revolution of 1821 when the Church and priests played such an important part. Some of these revolutionary priests and monks died horrible deaths for the greater cause.

What schoolchild does not know Athana′sios Dia′kos, the poet-priest who was captured alive after a brilliant but hopeless fight and refused to succumb to the Ottoman rule. He was impaled alive with a skewer, and later roasted slowly over a fire, in a lamb-like fashion. The Ottoman insult was specifically directed towards the Orthodox Christians they had long subjugated and to their Lamb of God. But Diakos wrote a little verse before he died. Nothing noble or religious. Just a simple little couplet about dying on such a beautiful spring day. Diakos' bravery gave great impetus to the Revolution.

I became obsessed with the details of impalement, which I read somewhere, perhaps in an Encyclopedia. I had all kinds of horrific visions of what the impaler looked like:

> his powerful hands would grasp the pole
> would they be hairy, fat, sweaty paws?
> would they be long like sinewy claws?
> and would his eye be full of hate?
> or did he really love to impale?
> or just disinterest in his look?
> that would be the worst of all.

I could not imagine a more horrible way to be extinguished. And it was said that the impaled developed a thirst … a thirst that was never to be quenched and which was beyond all pain. And it was from this thirst that they finally died. I started to live in terror that this would be the method of extinguishing my parents if I accidentally betrayed their political beliefs and they were found out by the Regime. And it was worse still for I could not get out of my mind the children of the Orphanage during the school outing of Maraslion. These were the orphans with the exorbitant privilege of being able to eat salami sandwiches. Extinguishing my parents made the trade-off for salami sandwiches all the more problematic for me.

Of course it was too time-consuming for the Ottomans to impale all of the population in which an uprising took place. Simple slaughter sufficed, like in Chios where it is estimated that 50,000 lives were extinguished and then immortalized in Western world paintings. But for the Church, it was not just priests and monks that were tortured and killed during the Revolution. Many bishops and patriarchs all died for the Revolutionary cause in various manners of martyrdom. In fact, we schoolchildren were taught that this was a main reason why priests were expected to marry, but bishops and patriarchs could not. Namely, leaders of the Church could die for the cause without having a family to worry about. And many of these leaders of Church, no matter what their end, had huge beards. Witness for example, Palaio'n Patro'n Germanos who has been credited with giving the first blessing to the Revolutionary Standard, on March 25, 1821. That is the date that the Revolution is considered to have officially started. As a schoolchild I knew all of this from my compulsory history and religion classes, and I would have seen innumerable pictures of the great religious leaders. But what was striking in those pictures was the size of their beards. It seemed that the more famous the Ethnarch (the leader of the Ethnos, i.e. the country of the race) the bigger his beard. Germanos, for example, is usually pictured with a huge black beard. Now, Germanos was consecrated by Patriarch Gregory Vth, who knew him well from Smyrni. There Gregory was Bishop and Germanos was appointed by him as the Protosyngelos. Gregory was to become the most famous of the Patriarchs of that period. He became Patriarch of Constantinople during a time of great instability and controversy. Part of his fame is based on his being abducted by the Ottoman Turks right after his Easter Sunday service of 1821 in Constantinople, humiliated and hung shortly thereafter. His body was thrown into the Bosporus causing an international incident. By some he is considered to be the last real great Patriarch of Constantinople. He had an immense beard when he was younger but his beard is shown as being white, long but not as thick just before he died.

It turns out, of course, that Gregory Vth was related to the Occupation Child. The relation was through the paternal side from Smyrni, so Tasouli was seven generations down the Gregory Vth family line, and Phoebus was six generations down. But patriarchs did not marry. So, this slightly stretched relation was through Gregory Vth's cousin. That is what is shown, through some rather shifty-looking black lines with arrows pointing sidewise, in the family tree drawn up by Auntie Eleni. This auntie was the oldest surviving female in the Phoebus side of the family in the post-war era. To be precise, Gregory Vth would have been the great, great, great, great, great, great uncle of Tasouli, except he wasn't. He would then have been one degree less great for Phoebus. The shifty lines and arrows pointing to Gregory Vth in the family tree caused much animated discussion and even friction in the extended family in later years. For the leftists considered Gregory Vth as having betrayed the Greek proletariat in Asia Minor to gain favor and power for the Orhodox Church with the Sultan of Constantinople. They claimed that Gregory Vth's political maneuvering could have even indirectly contributed to the destruction of Smyrni by the anti-Sultan, anti-religious revolutionary Kemalist forces. On the other hand, the conservatives and rightists in the family considered Gregory Vth as the true Ethnarch of that period, the leader of the Ethnos … the Nation in its true racial and Christian Orthodox meaning. But how the story of Gregory Vth might have led to the Archeomarxist conversion of a young Phoebus is in itself another story.

One must also remember that the Church also led the cries for revenge and Christianization resulting in the massacres of Muslim Ottomans. In this way Christendom could prevail in the expanding land of liberated Greece. Priests would have been taught all of this history in much greater detail than a schoolchild like me. They would have known all of these bloody events like the back of their hands. Perhaps the atrocities during the Occupation and the Civil War seem minor compared to the bloody history of the Greek Revolution. So I started to wonder what the politics of this Zakynthian priest actually were. I never heard anyone in Gerakarion commenting on this priest's politics. And he seemed to have the approval of Nana and even Tzanetos. He even thought my story of being afraid of his beard was amusing. But he seemed to take it seriously. That worried me somewhat but I am not quite sure why. I never found out about the politics of this baptismal priest. But there was another priest whose politics did become clear.

~

This other priest did not live in Zakynthos. He was near the village of Tolo′, near Nau′plion. Tolo is now a much-commercialized vacation spot, but then it was a picturesque village with fishing and significant agriculture around it. My father had been stationed there for a period, so I got to know the area really well. So well in fact, that I stopped paying attention to where I was going. One day when I was simply exploring what was already a familiar landscape without paying much attention to where I was going, I fell off a cliff near the sea and nearly killed myself. I managed to scramble back up the cliff onto a level field, with only minor injuries. I sat down on the field among the spring flowers to nurse my scrapes. I started thinking what made me fall down the cliff. Was it a total accident or did something else happen? Initially I thought it was just a misstep … but a misstep in such familiar territory? I looked around and then, all of a sudden, it struck me. It was the almost unbelievable beauty of Tolo, in that bright spring morning. From where I sat the flower-covered fields seemed to merge with the azure sea and an almost blue-indigo sky without a break. It was as if earth, sea and heavens had become one, bathed in that bright spring light. I sat transfixed. I never wanted to be anywhere else. I did not want to move. Then I slowly realized that I would have to move. I would finally have to go home. I could not sit in this mesmerizing beauty forever. A conflict started to develop. My conscience told me to go home, where my parents would be expecting me. A stronger pull, an external force of some kind seemed to say: 'stay here, stay here in the endless beauty. Stay here for ever and ever Tasouli'. Then all of a sudden it struck me. I remembered. The instant before I fell down the cliff I was struck by vertigo … the Ilingos had found me. The Ilingos had dominated my orientation. It was not a simple misstep that made me go over the cliff. It was the Ilingos … similar to the Ilingos that I had so badly on the roof in the Bastille waiting for the sunrise in Pagrati. But here in Tolo, the Ilingos did not repel me; it did not make me retract my steps. It was as if the Ilingos knew about the misstep that was about to happen and took me into his arms. The Ilingos welcomed me into the abyss. I could have been killed on the steep cliffs. But I wasn't. Did the Ilingos in some way protect me? I did not remember a single impact on the cliff walls or on the beach below. It was as if I had bounced weightlessly along the yellowish clay soil of the cliff. The boulders made of this clay formed much of the side of the cliff and they seemed to protect me rather than injure me. The Ilingos had been kind to me. It wanted to tell me something. And what it wanted to tell me had something to do with the colors and the continuity of all that I could see around me. But I did not know what it was.

It was in these agricultural fields near Tolo that we met this particular priest. I was with my father and another couple of men, who I think were locals that knew the priest. In any case, the meeting was not totally a coincidence as they went looking for the priest, expecting to find him in the flower-covered fields of Tolo. For it was early spring, around Lent, that most beautiful time of the year. We found the priest wandering around the flower-covered fields, looking apparently far, far away among the scents of the spring herbs and the fresh earth. From a distance he seemed a tall, thin young figure almost floating across the fields with long steps. He did not seem to be heading for anywhere in particular. We finally more or less caught up to him and one of the men that knew him shouted:

– Hello, Father! Beautiful spring day, isn't it?
– All days are beautiful now. It is the Lent.
– Even if it were raining, Father?
The little bit of irony went unheeded.
– Especially if it is raining. We can always use a bit of rain this time of year. It will be good for the lambs.

In truth, our little party had sought out this priest of Tolo to test out his politics. They wanted to probe him and tease him a little about the relationship of his politics to his religion. For it was reputed that he was a leftist perhaps even a communist. It was a risky thing to be openly leftist during that period … even if you were a priest. So the questions from our small group were a little bit teasing and yet full of interest. What did this young priest, with an ethereal visage and only a slight beard, hatless, with his long hair tied at the back, really have to say about politics and religion? Our friends said that he had finished his studies at the Seminary not long ago and that he was originally from Tolo. But no one had seen him for years until he re-surfaced after finishing the Seminary. And it was known that the Seminaries in those years of the Civil War were full of politics … ready to live or die for politics.

– Is the lambing looking good, Father?
– Lent has been good to us.
– Father, we want you to meet Mr. Phoebus. He is an agriculturist. He will be visiting with us here in Tolo for a bit. And this is his son, Tasouli.
– Ah, an agriculturalist! We need one so much here. And, hello Tasouli. Do you like Tolo?
– Very much but I fell off the cliff, over there by the sea.
– Oh, I did too Tasouli, when I was a boy. They say that you are not a true Tolo villager unless you have fallen down that cliff at least once. It is amazing anyone at all is alive in Tolo!
– But I think I got Ilingos near the cliff and that is why I fell off.
– Oh yes, Tasouli. It is the Ilingos that causes most people to fall off the cliff.
– Ohh! I didn't realize that it was that common. I thought I had a particularly bad case of it.
The young priest's serious mien dissolved into a smile:
– Everybody thinks they have a bad case of Ilingos. The Christ included …
– The Christ also?
– Especially the Christ.
And his smile became broader still, before he became serious again.
As the priest seemed to be warming up to the visitors, one of the men that knew the young priest tried broaching the intended conversation topic indirectly:
– Father, pretty well everyone in Tolo would observe Lent, would they not?
– Of course. Why would you even ask?
– Well, Phoebus here, being a visitor and an agriculturist was wondering.
– Wondering what?

My father could no longer restrain himself and decided to cut in. In those days he had a clear, direct and very engaging manner. A little smile would appear in his eyes and it was as if he and the priest were old friends and comrades. He could become so warmly personal, trustworthy and attractive in an instant. Particularly if there was any chance for a little Archeomarxist propaganda:

– I hear you are progressive Father.
– I like to think I am. And you must be too, is that not so Mr. Phoebus?

It struck me that my father and the priest had a similar mannerism, a similar confident, convincing little smile and a familiarity towards each other. Yet they had just met.

– Of course these days it is even more important than ever that we present a united progressive front, Father.
– Very true Mr. Phoebus. Especially for young people and students.
– And is there a progressive movement in the Seminary nowadays, Father?
– Oh, yes, Mr. Phoebus. Much stronger than it would appear. It actually grew during the Civil War. But of course we all have to be careful.
– And what would the progressive students in the Seminary say about following the ritual of

Lent?

Clearly my father was intent in pushing the agenda a little. He was going to find out if this priest really had Archeomarxist sympathies come hell or high water. The others in our party, supposedly also sympathetic, were now carefully listening.

– But there is no contradiction, my dear Mr. Phoebus.
– No contradiction?
– None at all. Just think of the agricultural production in the Mediterranean region. It is the same now as in the Palestine. And it would have been the same in Christ's time. And for thousands of years before.
– Meaning?
– It is very clear. Let's say Lent was not observed and meat was eaten during this time. Would we not have to kill some of the very sheep that would give birth to the lambs? What a disaster that would have been for the whole agricultural region. No, no. It could not have been permitted. It must be prohibited at all costs. And Lent prohibits the eating of meat during this sacred time.
– You are correct, Father. The means of production must be preserved. Especially for agricultural production. Just like Marx says, would you not agree Father?

I could see my father's eyes twinkling. He suspected that he had found a possible convert in a priestly robe.

– Marx was very interested in industrial production that was so important in his time, my dear Phoebus. We are talking here about agricultural production rules set thousands of years before Karl Marx. Perhaps one needs to study what is in the Archives carefully again.

I also watched my father's eyes carefully again, trying to figure out what he was thinking. Could this young priest have even known about the Archive-Marxists … the Archeomarxists? They were such a small, marginal group. But were they infiltrating even Seminaries? Or maybe my father knew more about the priest than he was letting on.

– I am sure you are right, Father. The Archives are the key.
– And the Archives in Christianity are also the key. The Gospel according to St. Luc. And other texts. Some now suppressed.
– Why St. Luc, Father?
– Because he described the events in the order that they occurred. The sequential order in which they occurred. Not like some revisionist-Judaic myth about the genealogy of Christ.
– Revisionist-Judaic myth, father?
– Yes, yes, yes. Like that St. Mathew. All that Judaic propaganda about Christ's genealogy being 'the son of David, the son of Abraham'. What clap-trap. I mean who cares?
– Hmm … I agree, Father, that the historical order … the correct historical order is critical. Not some revisionist position. Marxist analysis depends on the correct sequence of historical events. Both in the development of the industrial society and agricultural society.
– And would you not say that a Christian and an Archeomarxist perspective are similar, at least in the absolute necessity of preserving our agricultural production, my dear Phoebus? I mean … by not slaughtering our animals during Lent.

My father was ready, I am sure, to respond with a more detailed analysis of all the evils of religion, like slaughtering whole human populations. But his friends tugged gently at his sleeve.

– We should be going Phoebus. Remember you said you would be meeting Dina around this time. Goodbye Father. We will see you again soon.

So they all said goodbye to the priest and watched his figure continue its wanderings.

As the thin, priestly figure receded it almost seemed to be mingling with the distant branches of the fruit trees covered with lemon and orange and cherry blossoms.

We never heard any more about this priest. When we visited Tolo again next season I asked around. But I got a few none-too-friendly looks and no one seemed to know or was willing to tell.

He had disappeared from the face of the earth.

It was too bad, because I had other questions I wanted to ask him. Like what did he mean when he said that even the Christ had a bad case of Ilingos?

Perhaps my father knew why he had disappeared.

– Baba, what happened to the priest we met last year?

All I got was a vague look. As if he had forgotten the whole episode.

– You know, Baba ... the young priest that you had the political discussion with ... about Lent and Marxism and religion.

– Who knows.

And he shrugged in a totally disinterested fashion.

Oh well! Maybe I could ask Styppas ... if I could ever get him off the topic of language.

~

Thinking of the daily farm life in Gerakarion, I must explain that chickens lived in the yard along with a goat. The difference in their wanderings was that the goat was usually tied to a rope while the chickens just roamed around free. However, they never wandered very far from the yard, even though they could have. The fencing of the yard was makeshift and the chickens could easily get in and out. Nana was also very good at finding all the eggs that the chickens laid. She knew the right time to find the eggs. I would look and look for the nests but could not find them. I was a failure at finding eggs. One of the reasons that it was difficult to find the eggs in the nests was that there was no chickencoop. So, the chickens would not nest in a chickencoop and in this respect they were unusual chickens. Where they nested at night was even more unusual. When dusk started to descend, the chickens started to test-flap their wings around the yard and cluck. Then, in turn, they would more or less line up in one part of the yard and each would take a big run, flapping its wings as hard as it could. It would briefly become airborne, only to lose height rapidly to land perfectly on a lower branch of a pre-designated tree. This tree was more or less in the center of the farmyard. Each chicken would follow the same procedure until they had all landed on branches of this tree. There they would settle for the night, roosting happily.

– Thia Nana, why are the chickens sleeping on the tree branches?

Nana would smile in her little funny way, which made me think that she found the question amusing but also took it seriously.

– Why, Tasouli, to be safe during the night.

– Safe? Safe from what Thia Nana?

– Oh the weasel, Tasouli. And sometimes the fox comes down too.

– And they would eat the chickens?

– They kill them all. The weasels especially are very destructive.

But I was not that fond of the chickens, in any case. They did not talk to me. Not one of them had ever initiated a conversation. Not like the goat. So, I was not too upset when Nana announced that as a special treat and in honor of our visit and long stay she was going to kill a chicken. She was going to make the famous Zakynthian recipe of the tomato sauce with the chicken in the casserole. Of course everything required in the recipe was from our property — the olive oil, used plentifully, the ripe, non-irrigated tomatoes and the garlic — except for the black pepper and the bay leaves, that is. The Zakynthian casserole was going to be absolutely delicious and I started to salivate. It was still during the time when any kind of meat, including chicken, was uncommon due to the shortages and poverty. So Nana had already picked up a chicken from the yard and called me over to show me how to kill it.

– Come, Tasouli, she said with her usual smile.
– It is not necessary, Thia Nana.

My mother encouraged me. She now was getting into her agrarian-peasant mode.

– Go, Tasouli. See Nana kill the chicken.

But my mother also had a little expression of disgust. The left side of her mouth around her lower lip would curl down in a slightly ugly, disapproving way. It was only too clear to me what that little downward curl really meant: her fear that the killing of the chicken would psychologically damage her little creation! But it was more than that. Time and time again, by word, by expression and gesture my mother wanted me to understand how inferior these agrarians, these poorly educated peasants were to us. Especially compared to her little creation, her little Tasouli over whom she must continually exercise control lest he mistaken his station in life. That is what the little downward curl of her mouth meant in its totality. The only problem was that *I* did not feel that way. I loved my Zakynthian relatives. I was in awe of all the things they could do with the farm animals, the crops and the land itself. Neither I nor members of my Athenian family could do these things. Even worse, the inability of the Athenian side of the family to do farm chores made me less confident in general. Could I do anything at all that involved manual skills, or even childhood sports, properly? So, I went up to Nana to see how she would kill the chicken.

– Ok, Nana. But how are you going to kill her?
– Oh, it is easy. I'll show you.

The chicken that Nana had picked was already happily nestled under her left armpit and against the side of her breast, as happy as it could be. It was literally clucking away in contentment. It was making little movements with its head sidewise and forward, so it would not miss anything going on in this interesting world from its cozy, nestled perch. It obviously paid no attention to the giant, sharp kitchen knife that Nana held in her right hand. In one smooth motion and without the chicken having a single complaint, its head came off. It still did not seem to want to leave the cozy perch, even as blood from its severed neck vessels dripped freely onto the yard soil. Not a drop fell on Nana. The headless chicken was already being plucked by Nana, just as it was leaving her armpit.

And later that evening, that chicken, prepared in an earthen pot with the famous, well-flavored Zakynthian tomato sauce, tasted absolutely heavenly. To us who are used to supermarket mass-produced chickens, it is difficult to describe the taste of these Zakynthian chickens, fending for themselves, pecking all day the rich Zakynthian soil. Somehow the meat of the Zakynthian chicken had a richness and a flavor and, at the same time, a crunchiness or even toughness that one just does not find now, in the North American supermarket. Maybe it is due to the hormones that are now given and the mass production. Maybe because we were still recovering from the Occupation, and with the Civil war still going on, it made any kind of meat seem such a treat. But somehow, I don't think it could just have been the shortages. It somehow must also be the magic of Zakynthos.

It was later that same summer, I think, that another chicken was going to be killed. This time it was going to be cooked in a *tapsi'* (the wide circular, deep, heavy metal baking pan) in our outside clay oven, with fresh potatoes that had just been dug up from the garden. Nana encouraged me to kill this chicken. She probably figured that since I had seen her kill the previous one, I must now have acquired the needed expertise. In fact, I had been practicing Nana's method by trying to get a chicken and have her nestle under my left armpit. I tried my luck in picking up a chicken from the yard. No way! None of the chickens would even let me get a hold of them. After trying to catch one of them a few times they started to run away from me on sight. Finally, after much persistence and chasing, I cornered one and managed to pick her up. She fought me with all her might, feathers flying. No way would she stay under my armpit, let alone nestle there. Finally, I had to let her go and she ran off annoyed and complaining. But I was not giving up. If I could not cut off a chicken's head with Nana's slick method with the long, sharp kitchen knife, surely I could chop off the head of a chicken. I tried to remember. Surely, in my children's books, chickens had their heads chopped off. Or, at least, I had read or heard somewhere that this was how you killed a chicken. So I looked for a hand axe and soon located an old one in the yard shed. I showed it to Nana with pride. She looked at me doubtfully.

– But Tasouli, it is easier with the knife, like I showed you.
– I know, Thia Nana, but the chickens will not settle under my armpit. They want to fight me. It was a bit of a fib since I had only managed to grab one chicken, but Nana looked sympathetically at me.
– They are not used to you yet, Tasouli.
– So, what should I do, Thia Nana.
– You can still use the axe, Tasouli. Some people prefer the axe. I just find the knife easier.
– And where would I chop off the chicken's head, Thia Nana?
– Over here. By the shed. We have a chopping block. See.

It was an evenly sawed off and smoothened block of wood, about two feet high and about a foot wide. I felt the dark, grainy wood and it was very hard.

– Where is the block from, Thia Nana?
– Oh, from the Doppia.
– When the lightning hit her?
– No, Tasouli. Much later. The lightning was a long, long time ago. Nobody is alive that remembers it. But there was a strong storm a few years back and a big branch broke off.
– Oh. So the chopping block must be very hard.
– Of course, Tasouli. Olive wood is very hard. And Doppia's is the hardest. Since Doppia is so old.
– Ok. Thia Nana. I will chop off the chicken's head on the Doppia block.
– Did you want me to get the chicken for you, Tasouli?
– No, Thia Nana. I will get it myself. You can go inside and do your work.
– Be careful with the axe, Tasouli.
– I will Thia Nana. I will be very careful.

Her little smile broke out again. She was not going to embarrass her little nephew. So, I was left to my own devices. I started chasing the chickens again to try to catch one. Surprisingly, it was a lot easier this time. Maybe, it was like Nana said. They were getting used to me. I guess they did not know the reason why I wanted to catch one. They had no clue what was in store for them. I started to wonder if someone knew what was in store for me. The chicken I finally did catch was full of feathers flying everywhere and would not be still.

– Stay still chicken, I told her.
– Why should I stand still? She obviously did not know my name. A good thing too!
– Because I want to chop your neck off.
– Pa, pa, pa, pa. Chop my neck off!
– Yes, you will be nicely done in the clay oven. With fresh garden potatoes, lemon and lots of olive oil.
– Ohhh … nicely done in the clay oven, with potatoes and olive oil, you say!

She must have taken the culinary description to heart, because she stopped going "pa, pa, pa, pa". By that time I had managed to more or less get her down on the Doppia chopping block, trying to hold her down with my left hand, she squirmed even more. I took a good swing with the axe trying to miss my hand. I missed my hand. I also missed her neck. The axe had chopped off her beak mostly. She seemed more surprised than mad. There was no time to lose. I took another mighty swing, again missing my hand. But she moved again and I had managed to chop off only part of her head. It did not slow her down one bit and she continued to fight and try to flap her wings. But by now I was getting my eye and hand adjusted to the task. One more mighty swing … and a clean chop of her neck! I had done it! I had done it! I let her go and she dropped to the ground. I expected the bird to be dead. Instead, she started running around in circles. I figured it wouldn't be long before she dropped, what with all the blood still pouring from her severed neck. No way! She kept running and running. It seemed like she would never stop. I looked at the other chickens around her. They seemed quite disinterested, except when the headless chicken accidentally ran into them, interfering with their pecking the soil and feeding. Then they appeared slightly annoyed. Since there was nothing I could do but watch the headless bird run around and around, I started to wonder what it all meant in the greater scheme of things.

– Did someone really know when their head was going to be chopped off, or of some similar fate? Did the chicken really understand what it meant to have her head chopped off when she went 'pa, pa, pa, pa … '? And was she really happy when she learned that she would be done with potatoes and olive oil in the clay oven — a most tasty dish?

But Nana interrupted my reverie. She had come out of the house.

– Good, Tasouli.

She had already picked up the now bloodless, headless bird and had started to pluck her.

– When are we going to cook her, Thia Nana?
– Later, Tasouli, later. We first have to fire the oven and get it nice and hot.

That was also done in due course, using bits of wood and dry cuttings from pruning the vines. In these clay ovens, the fire was started in the floor of the oven which supported the dome of the oven. There was no underneath chamber for putting the coals and lighting them. One had to wait until the burning wood turned into hot embers. The whole clay oven structure gradually heated from the hot ashes and then the *tapsi* with the chicken and potatoes could be put in. The heat was retained within the clay walls, roof and floor of the oven for hours. But the reward of all this effort was the amazingly beautiful result of even, slow cooking. The little bit of smoke still being emitted from the glowing grape-vine embers provided an additional flavor. The lemons from our lemon trees, the olive oil from our olive trees, the fresh potatoes and a little thyme from the nearby hills, all mingled to perfection, with the chicken. The fact that I had recently murdered her did not seem to bother me. The smell that arose from the outdoor oven attracted some neighbors and relatives who came by, complementing Nana. She was a bit apologetic. She did not want them to think that they had hit it rich or were getting money from Dina and Phoebus. She explained:

– With Dina and Tasouli visiting, we decided to cook a chicken.
– Ohh … they said impressed.
– And Tasouli killed her.

This time Nana's smile was accompanied with a little wink towards the relatives and neighbors. There were six or seven of them. Soon they were sitting on the simple wooden benches in the little outside veranda, which led outside from Nana's house. The *climatariá* (the grape-vine overhead trellis) provided shade. Little sturdy glasses filled with our production of last year's white wine were put out, to treat the visitors. Generally it was the men that drank the wine. The women most often preferred one of the sweet preserves of bitter cherry that Nana had made, or perhaps fresh lemonade from our lemon trees. They would put their wine or lemonade glasses, or tiny plates of the syrupy sweet preserves, on the simple heavy wooden table and sit up very straight and quiet on the wooden benches. They were all very thin, sunburned with these strong, sinewy arms. Some of the men smelled of the sour tang of days of heavy sweat, accumulated while cultivating these Arcadian fields of Zakynthos. Finally, one of the men, who might have been my older agrarian cousin Theodoris, spoke with a serious expression addressing me:

– *Psychou'la mou* (my little soul), you killed the chicken.

This endearing appellation of *psychoula mou* was used all the time by the Zakynthian agrarians. *Psychoula mou* has a little singing lilt to it, accented just a bit on the terminal diminutive (*ou'la*) of the root noun psyche. I am not sure how this Zakynthian affectionate diminutive can be really translated into English, so that the rhythm of the endearment is preserved. Perhaps in American English, a Southern country version of the Zakynthian endearment might come out as something like ' … you li'ttle ol' soul-o'mine'. Problem with English is that it has no real capacity for terminal diminutives of nouns, endearing or not. Except, of course, for the terminal diminutives that can be used with names of persons, like 'Ronnie' and the like. So, this particular Zakynthian musicality of nouns and appellations cannot be readily translated. I don't know how the singing cadences, these endearing diminutives actually arose. How did this language of the Zakynthian peasant which seems ready at any instant to break out into a lyrical cantata come to be? Maybe its origins were during the centuries of the mild and creative, music-filled Venetian occupation. Or maybe it was older than that, dating back to Byzantine times, with all of the psalms and magnificent church music of the Byzantines. But it is unlikely these musical and charming intonations were a product of the unforgiving, later British occupation of the island. These occupiers used a harsher language that matched a cruel and unbending occupation.

– Oh yes, cousin Theodori, I managed to kill the chicken. But only after three tries.
– Three tries it took you, Tasouli mou, psychoula mou?

All the Zakynthian eyes were now smiling — the city child had managed to kill the chicken. A little awkward perhaps, but he was learning.

At that point my mother came to join the agrarian group. She momentarily surveyed them with an eagle eye, these peasants smelling of the earth and the sour sweat of heavy manual labor. Her lower lip curled with disapproval — you never knew about these lowly educated peasants. You could not trust them. All they understood was how to grab a little extra land. They were threatening her and Nana just by having gathered on our property — just because they smelled a chicken being cooked in the outdoor oven. But the agrarian cousins were not easily intimidated by haughty appearances.

– Cousin Dina, psychoula mou, your Tasouli killed the chicken cooking in the oven now, all by himself.

She was not going to be party to any pleasantries. They were just using the pleasantries to put her off her stride.

– He should not have been allowed to use an axe. He could have cut his hand off. You know he is in grade four already. And he will go on in school.

The point was telling. Likely, none of the agrarians sitting on the wooden benches, with the exception of Nana, would have gone past grade three. That was the minimal legal level of education, especially in the countryside, back when most of the visitors had been children. After children had completed three years of school, they were legally allowed to work on the farms full time. That would have been from approximately age nine or ten on. They would have just learned, in these three years of schooling, the basics of how to read, write their names and do some simple arithmetic. But our agrarian relatives were in a good mood by then. They had had their glass or two of the wine and the sweets or the refreshing lemonade. No way were they going to allow the well-known superior snootiness of Cousin Dina interfere with the visitation.

– Oh yes, Cousin Dina, your Tasouli will go far in school. May you live forever!

This was another common polite wish. The glasses were raised again and emptied in one gulp. These peasants were thirsty. After all they had been working hard. And the visit by Dina and Tasouli was a big event for them. The wishes resounded in turn from each of the visitors:

– And may you and your Tasouli live forever, psychoula mou!

It was getting a bit repetitive, but by then another round of our wine was being gulped down. By and by, the women were also permitting themselves to have a little glass of wine too. After all, they figured, they worked just as hard as the men ... and even looked after the men ... and gave birth and brought up their children. So, why not have a little drink, just like the men on such an occasion? And no one in Gerakarion is likely to have added preservatives to the wine. Certainly Nana wouldn't. It was well known that it was the chemical preservatives that could make one dizzy. Never the wine itself, of course! Why they took it in communion all the time. So, no fear that the women would get dizzy and behave improperly, or something. No fear of that at all.

– And where is Phoebus, Cousin Dina? Could he not come to see us all, psychoula mou?
– He has been very busy in Athens, Cousin Maroula.
– Ahh ... Good health to him too. May he live forever, our good Dina.

Still, another little round of the wine went down. And there were no polite refusals for another round of sweet preserves, either. You could tell from their now relaxed expressions that this had been a most excellent visit for them. Finally, the well-wishing, after every round, was starting to become a bit thin. And you had to wish your hosts well with every round. More importantly, the cousins had now had their fill of wine and the preserves. There was a momentary, thoughtful silence.

– We must go now and let you enjoy the chicken Tasouli killed.
– They don't teach students how to kill a little chicken in the schools in Athens, Cousin Dina, do they, psychoula mou?

I didn't think my mother liked the little joke by the way she twisted her mouth and did not respond. These Zakynthian peasants never missed a chance for a bit of irony if they thought someone was being superior. After all, they had had pretty good training in the matter of superiority. All their conquerors over the ages thought they were superior to them. Except, perhaps, the Venetians. And the Venetian Aristocrats no doubt thought they were vastly superior to either Zakynthian or Venetian peasants.

– We too must go, Cousin Dina. Goodbye Nana.
– Us too, Cousin Dina. You'll all come by and visit us soon, won't you, psychoula mou?

With the visiting relatives and neighbors gone, the great moment of serving up the chicken cooked in the oven was finally approaching. Nana would serve the chicken and the potatoes and the sauce in the kitchen and bring out the plates to the veranda, under the climataria'. It was a little different way of doing it than Yiayia Sophia, where the serving platter was put on the table and the serving was directly visible to everybody. Nana would ask everybody what they wanted first, and then come back with plates that contained their preference. Yiayia Sophia seemed to just know what everybody wanted and then would basically tell them what they wanted as she was serving them. I could not figure out which was the more democratic system and which was the more psychologically astute — the best system to make one feel really good about getting exactly what they wanted on their plate. Maybe it had something to do with the long history of both civilizations: The Zakynthian and the Smyrnean civilizations. Or was it just the habits of my Yiayia Sophia and my Aunt Nana? But I was also confused about the names of these civilizations. Why were they both called Ionian? They were virtually at opposite ends of ancient Hellenism. Zakynthos, of course, was the most Southern of the Ionian Islands, in the most western part of Greece. Smyrni was the center of the Ionian civilization, far in the East, in Asia Minor.

Yiayia Sophia and Nana knew each other well. They both seemed to have a great deal of affection and admiration for each other and the manner in which they cooked. Yet, Yiayia Sophia had nothing good to say about the cooking of housewives in mainland Greece, including Peloponisos, but she talked with great reverence about everything Zakynthian. Nana had come many times and stayed in the Bastille and in Rafina. She greatly admired Yiayia Sophia's Smyrneika soujoukakia. Yiayia Sophia had never been to Zakynthos, as far as I know. But she had been to Kerkyra (Corfu), the most northern and richest of the Ionian Islands, a very long time ago. Curiously, that Ionian connection through Kerkyra might have been instrumental in molding the relationship between Yiayia Sophia and her husband, my paternal grandfather, Anastassios, the great man of Smyrna. It could also help explain many a quirk of the great Agriculturalist-Archeomarxist, my father, Phoebus. More curiously still, it would shed light on the relationship that developed between Yiayia Sophia and my Joujoukos. Yes, I am talking about how events of nearly a generation before, on the island of Kerkyra, led to Joujoukos becoming the great resistance hero during the German Occupation in Pagrati.

Now the chicken and the potatoes from the clay oven were being served by Nana. Her commentary was simple, almost laconic. It was just a sentence here and a sentence there — about the quality of this year's oil crop that was used; about the crop of freshly dug potatoes; about the lemons from her favorite lemon tree; about the thyme from an excursion to the Zakynthian mountains a month or so ago. Each of these sentences seemed to accompany each plate that was brought in from the kitchen. And each plate contained pieces of well done, unbelievably tender and tasty chicken and potatoes to suit your heart's innermost desire. It was to die for. I am sure the chicken would have agreed. In fact, she had said so, just before I finally managed to properly chop her head off at the neck.

Now, the goat in our yard was a very different matter than the chickens. I took a special liking to the goat immediately and befriended her. I liked her so much that Nana named her 'Tassia' in my honor. This made me feel that I had a special understanding with the goat. Perhaps it was more of a sense of attachment, like she was mine. Nana would milk her expertly every day. I asked to milk the goat also.

– Here, Tasouli, here is how you do it.

She would pull down, seemingly without effort, on the teats of Tassia's udder and the rich milk would shoot down, splashing into the metal pot. Nana moved over a bit so I could try milking. I closed my hand around Tassia's teat, with a bit of trepidation. The teat was nice and warm and a lot firmer than I had thought. I pulled down, trying to imitate Nana. Nothing much happened.

– But Thia Nana, the milk does not come out when I pull.
– You have to pull harder, Tasouli. Harder and faster.
– And Tassia does not mind?
– No, she likes to be milked. It is her time.
– Oh … it's her time.

I again closed my hand around the teat and pulled down as hard as I could, trying to repeat the motion quickly. Maybe I squeezed out a few drops, but the white milk did not come out splashing, no matter how hard I tried. Nana just laughed and continued with the milking. I was despondent. I would never be able to milk Tassia. I was a dismal failure. But Tassia still liked me. I could tell. I could tell because she would stand deadly still when I tried to milk her. While with Nana she showed disinterest during milking, mostly concentrating on grazing and chewing. And even after my failed attempts at milking her, I could tell by the way she held her head and never moved away when I petted her. That was the main thing. Tassia still liked me.

My failure to milk Tassia started to really bother me on the day after the visit by the Cousins, followed by the feasting on the most delicious chicken, which I had killed. I had very mixed feelings: I had killed and loved eating a being that I did not care about, and I cared about a being that I had no intention of eating. Farm life was complicated. I needed to go to my hiding place and sort it all out. So, I retreated to the hollow of the Doppia. It was cool and airy there. The aromas of the Zakynthian countryside permeated in. The only slight problem was that everyone knew that this was my favorite hiding place. I had told them so. Plus everyone knew from my previous somewhat embarrassing escapade from the priest. On the other hand, because I told them Nana had even given me an old *kourelou* and a pillow, so I could nap inside the cave of the old Doppia. Burdened with my dilemma about the farm animals and with a rather full stomach, from eating what was left of the chicken and potatoes for the second day, I retired. Lying on the *kourelou* and the pillow, the cool breeze blew through openings in the above-ground roots of old Doppia. I fell asleep in a jiffy, with my last thought being about Tassia.

~

– Tassia, sorry. Sorry, I could not milk you.
– It's OK.
She'd make an emphatic upward movement with her head while chewing her cud.
– Nana is very good at milking you.
– She is used to it.
– Are you ever afraid, Tassia?
– What of?
– I thought so. You are never afraid.
– …
– Yesterday, I thought I would be afraid but I wasn't.
– Oh?
She looked at me with curiosity out of a brown eye. She was now chewing her cud with a lot of interest.
– Yes, Tassia. I fell into a deep pit.
– Oh.
– Yes, I had gone on an excursion. Up the hills.
– So, what happened?
– I thought I was stepping on dry grass, but it was a pit. The sides were of smooth stone. It looked old.
– It could have been a grave.
– A grave, Tassia?
– Yup, a Mycenaean grave. There are plenty of them in Zankynthos. In the hills.
– But how do you know this, Tassia.
– My mother fell into one of these grave pits. She had real trouble getting out. But she managed in the end.
– Yes. I had trouble getting out too. They are deep and narrow and not very long.
– That is why my mother had trouble getting out. It was too short for her to take a running jump or even a step-jump. Like us goats have to do.
– I was able to reach the top, so I scrambled up. But I scraped my knees.
– You were lucky.
– But why were these graves made like that, Tassia?
– They were cut into hard rock. Chiseled into the granite.
– You know a lot, Tassia. But why are they so short? They are deep enough. But not long enough for a human to lie at the bottom.

134

– How do I know? Maybe the Mycenaeans were very short. Or maybe they were buried in a sitting position.

– Or maybe it was not people they buried. Maybe it was goats, Tassia.

– Don't be rude.

– Sorry, Tassia. I did not mean to be rude. I thought maybe there were goat gods in those times.

– Of course there were.

– Then maybe they made graves for them.

– Naah. They just milked the goats and ate them. And used the skins a lot.

– What did they use the skins for?

– Everything. Clothing, wine and water containers and shields.

– Shields too!

– Yes. Especially in the revolt of the Zakynthians in Mycenaean times against King Odysseus.

– Who won?

– The Zakynthians. They got their freedom from Odysseus.

– I would never allow anyone to eat you or use your skin, Tassia.

– Don't waste your time.

– No, it is true Tassia. I love you. I love you a lot.

– Falling in love with a goat is a waste of time.

– But you are beautiful. And you know ancient history.

– All goats in Zakynthos do.

– I will always love you, Tassia.

– Never mind. I want to ask you something. Had you fallen into a grave before?

– Why would you even ask, Tassia?

– Just the way you behave. Like, you took it in stride.

– You are a very smart goat, Tassia. As a matter of fact, I had.

– Oh?

– Yes. I fell into my grandfather's grave.

– Which grandfather?

– Papous Anastassios. The father of my father.

– How did you manage that?

– I didn't mean to, Tassia. Yiayia Sophia, his widow, would regularly take me to the Nea Smyrni cemetery to attend to the grave. One day I stepped on the soil of the grave and the whole thing collapsed.

– Did you see his corpse or his bones?

– No. Just a big hole.

– Were you frightened?

– No. Just surprised.

– Was Yiayia Sophia upset?

– No. She didn't even seem too surprised. But my mother, Dina, was really upset when I told her.

– Afraid her little boy would be scarred for life, I guess.

– Don't make fun of my mother, Tassia.

– Sorry Tasouli.

– You called me Tasouli …

– So?

– You must like me too, Tassia. Otherwise you would not call me Tasouli.

– Oh, I like you alright, Tasouli. I just don't think you should get to like me too much.

– Why Tassia?

– Never mind. Aren't there any human females you like?

– My mother of course, and Nana …

– I don't mean them. Anyone that is not in the family?

– Not really … unless you count Pamela.

– Who is Pamela?

– She lives in Canada. She knows all about marbles and gutters, blood alleys and Lords of the mind.
– Hmm. How did you get to be friendly with this … this Pamela, Tasouli?
– I was actually looking for Styppas. But it was very cold in Canada, so she allowed me to crawl into bed with her.
– Blaahh! She did, did she?
– Yes, she is nice.
– I bet she is.
– … Tassia, did you ever fall in a grave.
– Naah. I was very careful after my mother's near escape. Especially around old wells.
– Old wells?
– Yes. Deep abandoned wells were used as graves for the sick in ancient times.
– The sick?
– Sick mostly from goat disease. It would last for years and then they would die.
– Goat disease, Tassia?
– Goat herdsmen got it mostly. High fever for months. And then it would come back again. And again. Until they died.
– And they threw them into the deep, abandoned wells?
– Probably after they died. Children and infants too.
– Do goats still get it?
– Naah. We don't get it very often now. We even get inspected by the veterinarian. Our milk is safe.
– Nana still boils it.
– I know.
– I don't like your milk too much after it has been boiled, Tassia.
– You'll get used to it, Tasouli.

Dina

It was all about a relationship. The relationship between Dina and Nana. And what their parents did or did not do for each of the girls. It was also all about education. Whoever did the best in school would go on. This poor agrarian family of Papous Theodoris could not afford all of the girls going on. Yet, going on in education was the ticket … the ticket to get out of Gerakarion. Dina got the ticket. Marina must have been out of contention then, having married K. So, it was really between Dina and Nana. Dina was the more confident one, always putting herself in front of the class. But Nana was a very good student also. Dina was also the oldest, so she had first bragging rights or at least Nana would always have to catch up to Dina. We have no documentation as to what their marks actually were but Dina always captured the center, the interest. Her teachers in the Chora apparently thought that she should go on. So the critical decision was made. Dina would go on to higher education and be allowed to leave Gerakarion. Nana, whose education was pretty good for the time and a valuable qualification for a decent marriage, would stay and mind the property. Of course with Dina meeting Phoebus who was even of a higher status and living in the Athenian Capital and all of that, made Nana feel she had been disadvantaged. She was disadvantaged for life — having to live and struggle among the peasants, to even fight for her rights of the land. Dina coming to visit from time to time and lording it over all likely did not help matters. But I must say that during the Occupation and the dark days of the post-war years, I never heard Nana complain once. It was later on, after we had moved to Canada, when according to Dina, Nana's resentment really started to surface. It was no wonder. Most post-war Zakynthians and Greeks alike thought that Canada was the land of milk and honey. Of course the reality was very different, but at least Canada did not have the oppressive political regimes of Greece or the horrid, prolonged Civil War whose consequences no one really escaped.

The other thing about Dina getting the nod to go on was that she would always find a way to manage as a teacher, or for that matter in any situation. She also had the lip to deal with any obnoxious student. Of course she was not very tall, if height were a consideration for commanding respect from students. She might manage to stretch out to a full height of maybe five feet, as she did with the tall German Officers during the days of the Occupation in Pyrgos, but her actual height was likely well under that. Dina liked to say she reached five feet when we were in Canada; she may have rounded out a couple of centimeters from the metric system to achieve that lofty five footer. But she was quick to point out that height was never a constraint for great leaders, particularly those that intimidated their populations. Napoleon was a virtual midget (his para-conjugal bed is still in the Versailles) and Hitler did not exactly tower over his General Staff. Zakynthians were generally short in any case.

Legendary among the inhabitants of Gerakarion was a real shorty who everybody was afraid of. This was the mythical Koronios. I say 'mythical' because I certainly never met him and neither did I ever meet anyone who had actually met him. But many a Zakynthian told me that Koronios was no taller than my mother. He was always ready for a fight — just like Dina. And Koronios was always ready to settle a score — again just like Dina. But there were also differences. Koronios always wore a most ferocious expression. He was always armed to the teeth. The armaments he wore were ready for battle — he bristled with pistols, knives, long guns and crisscrossing belts for all his bullets and gunpowder pouches. When Koronios walked into a room, apparently all conversation would cease. People would immediately run over themselves to offer him a sweet or a drink — anything he wanted. But Koronios was very sparse in what he would accept. And if he took a sweet or a little brandy, his ferocious expression would never leave him. Some of the relatives in Gerakarion said his Spartan behavior in accepting treats from neighbors and relatives were part of his persona … after all he had to maintain appearances. I never determined when Koronios lived. Somehow I thought he was a figure from the late 19th or early 20th Century. Once during the afternoon, sitting in the veranda after a few little glasses of local wine and my mother holding center stage, a Zakynthian relative whispered in my ear:

– Psychoula mou Tasouli … your mother … she's a real Koronios! I could detect definite admiration in his voice, but with a twinge of irony.
– Yes, Uncle. She is.

I disregarded the irony and briefly basked in the admiration of having my mother considered in such distinguished company. But I had never even seen a picture of Koronios and I wondered what he really looked like. Especially, what were all these arms of his? Were they all fancy like I had seen in myriads of illustrations of the Revolutionary heroes of the 1800s? Or were they more like the guns of the Insurgents and the English prisoners in the Bastille, in Pagrati?

All of these considerations and the images of the old Revolutionary heroes started to whirl around in my head. The conversation had changed to how distant relations were doing and I didn't even know many of them. I started to get bored. Soon enough I left the company as I was also getting a little sleepy. My mother would normally see me getting sleepy and send me off or even take me to my assigned little bed. But on this occasion she never said anything about my afternoon nap. She was busy holding forth about the injustices of some people wanting more property than really belonged to them. I wandered off to the yard and no one seemed to pay any attention to me. But then my eye caught Nana's as I started to cross the yard. I think she knew what I was up to. I was heading for my hiding place … I had decided that I would have my nap in the hollow of my beloved Doppia. As I lay down on my kourelou, laid on the ground of the hollow, I could feel the slight rustling of the Doppia green and silver olive-tree leaves that seemed to bring both coolness and warmth. I always thought that the foliage of the olive trees was the most amazing of all foliages because of its subtle changes. From a distance the olive trees usually look a silver-green color. Yet the color seems to change depending on the weather and the color of the sky, whether there are great clouds on the horizon and the time of day, the season. From close up you could see that the leaves were, on one side, that characteristic glistening slightly off-green. On the other side they had that silver shade — like an old pewter but more dispersive of the light somehow. When I lay down on the kourelou in my little nest, I could watch the leaves of the Doppia which seemed to be sorting out the warm summer breezes. I felt protected against all the evils among the roots and the trunk of her hollow. It was not long before the sounds of conversation coming from the yard started to intermingle with the light rustling of the leaves of the old olive tree, and then all sound receded into a deep quiet as Morpheus called. I was only mildly surprised to see an unusual image of my mother.

~

– Mamaka, Mamaka what are you doing dressed up like Koronios?
– It is to frighten all these ignorant peasants that want our land.
– But you haven't really turned into Koronios?
– If they get me angry enough, I will!
– But these big curled mustaches?
– I just stuck them on.
She started un-sticking them so I could make out her face now.
– And all the guns and pistols?
– Oh, they are real enough. She started demonstrating them one by one.
– Look at this pair of beautiful Brascia percussion pistols.
– Why are there two of them?
– For dueling of course.
– Who would you duel with?
– Anyone that challenges our property.
– Would you not be afraid of being killed, Mamaka?
– Of course not, Tasouli. I would have the clear advantage.
– How so, Mamaka?
– Because they are my pistols.
– And how is that the advantage?
– Only one is loaded. I would give them the other.
– Could they not check and see if it is loaded?
– Not if you get them really red hot and angry first. Insult them and challenge them right on the spot and these Zakynthian peasants would be ready to fight like cocks — at the drop of a hat.
– But you wouldn't kill them, would you Mamaka?
– Naah … just wound them. And quickly take their pistol away.
– The empty one that you gave them … right?
– Right. And word would quickly spread they could not even get a shot away against me.
– That is a good trick Mamaka.
– And look Tasouli … this fine Italian Beretta pistol. And look at this 18th Century flintlock brass baby. She pulled each out of her leather belt and let me handle them.
– Ohh … it is beautifully engraved, Mamaka.
– And if I really wanted to frighten one of them, I would tell them I will kill them with this Scottish pirate flintlock. See it is also beautifully engraved with the hangings of the pirates and skulls and crossbones.
This one she pulled out of the back of her belt where it was hidden amid the folds of her skirt.
– Why would the Scottish pirate flintlock frighten them so much?
– Because they are ignorant. And they still remember that the English Occupiers would hang whole families up in the Fortress if they just suspected that any of them had anything to do with pirates. Or just to hang them — as a lesson to others.
– Ohh … you are like a real Koronios, Mamaka!
– *Ame'* (like "for sure" but intonated full of pride)!

At that moment I saw a figure standing in the shadows of the great roots of the Doppia which were sticking up like giant wrinkled fingers. The figure intoned:

– *Ame'* what?

I recognized him in a flash. *Styppas had appeared from nowhere.* He must have come into the Doppia hollow just at that instant, so he had not heard any of the previous conversation.

– Oh Styppas, you surprised me. My mother was just saying that she is like a real Koronios with all the guns and an attitude to match.
– Who in the world are you talking to, Tasouli?

My mother seemed to be genuinely puzzled. Yet Styppas was standing right there, in front of her, big as life.

– Styppas of course, Mamaka. Can't you see him? He has come to visit me.
– There is no one here, Tasouli, except me, your Mamaka. The sun must have affected you, Tasouli. After your nap in the shade of the Doppia come in the house. Sleeping under the olive tree is light. It does not give you strange dreams. Not like sleeping under the sycamore tree whose shade is heavy, and you should not sleep under it. I will make some nice chamomile tea for you when you come to the house.
– But Mamaka I was already taking my nap.
– The chamomile tea will clear your head.
– Ok, Mamaka. I will come to the house and drink the chamomile tea after my nap. I tried to explain to my mother that Styppas would most often come and visit me after I was asleep, but to no avail. She shrugged and left.
– She thinks she is like Koronios, does she, Tasouli?
– Oh yes, Styppas, and some of the relatives and neighbors think there is a real resemblance.
– Yeah … they are right … totally different from her mother, Yiayia Angeliki.
– Speaking of Yiayia Angeliki, I wanted to ask you a question …
– What's that?
– Styppas, people in Zankynthos say that Yiayia Angeliki had perfect teeth when she died because she used charcoal all her life to clean them. Could that be true?
– Which people?
– Nana and some cousins and my mother too.
– Hmph. There are no clinical studies showing this.
– What are clinical studies?
– Like doing a comparison between charcoal and toothpaste.
– Can't you do that yourself, Styppas? You know everything.
– No. It would take hundreds of people, and many, many years.
– So?
– And millions of dollars.
– But it would be worth it. No cavities!
– It wouldn't be profitable for the toothpaste industry.
– But the dentists? They are always telling us how to avoid cavities.
– If charcoal really worked, they could go out of business too.
– … but could charcoal work?
– Yep, it might.
– How so?
– We used to use it in the Lab.
– In the Lab?
– Yes, in our chemistry Lab. To remove impurities from substances.
– Ohhh … impurities! This sounds important!
– Yes, deactivated charcoal adsorbs impurities.
– What is 'adsorbs'?
– Like stick to the surface of the charcoal.
– Ohhh … you do know everything, Styppas.
– I didn't visit you to discuss toothpaste and charcoal, Tasouli!

139

– But how would Yiayia Angeliki know all about charcoal and impurities, Styppas?
– She wouldn't, likely.
– She only finished grade three, I've heard.
– Experience. She would know from long experience.
– Experience from trying charcoal herself?
– Mostly from what she would have heard, Tasouli.
– From what she would have been told … by her parents … word of mouth?
– Word of mouth for generations, Tasouli.
– For many, many generations … just word of mouth?
– The only way. In feudal times most could not read, Tasouli.
– And before? In Byzantine times, Styppas?
– Probably the same.
– And before? In ancient Greek times, Styppas?
– Probably still the same.
– … So, what did you want to discuss with me?
– That very same topic.
– Charcoal, Styppas?
– No, no, no. Word of mouth — in antiquity.
– Ohhh …
– Don't you remember how you used to rile about the 'caterpillars' in English writing and how you wanted to simplify phonetic Greek by having symbols for just four vowels?
– Of course, Styppas. How could I forget? And I am still very interested in all of this. And also in becoming pedantic. It is just that the big events in Zakynthos overtook me … you know the baptism and the priest, and having to kill the chicken, and falling in love with Tassia … I've been preoccupied.
– I know. But I found someone who has really studied language and the beginning of writing in Greek and all of that.
– Where did you find him, Styppas?
– In Canada. Well, I didn't actually find him. I found his books. He died a few years back.
– Stelios would know all about him. Especially if he is dead and gone for a while. And if he was famous at all.
– No, Stelios could not know about him.
– How come, Styppas? Stelios knows everything. Like you do.
– Never mind. His name is Eric Havelock. He was a professor of Classics. At the University of Toronto.
– Oh, I've heard of Toronto. It is like Montreal, but not as famous.
– It all depends who you talk to. But this man Havelock had a theory about how writing came about. Ancient Greek writing that is.
– And how do you know about his theory?
– Because he wrote many books and articles over many, many years.
– And did you read these?
– I read mostly a book of his called *The Muse Learns to Write*. He wrote it towards the end of his life and it puts together a lot of what he had to say and most of his writings over decades. I just read it a few days ago. And that is why I came to find you and tell you about it.
– That's a nice, catchy title for that book, Styppas, but I wouldn't think that a Muse would have to learn how to write. Not if she was a real Muse … So, how did the Greek writing come about?
– He thinks it was the ancient Greeks who first invented the symbols for the pure consonants. Before then the consonants were considered to be 'aphona', like having no sound.
– Like no sound by themselves, Styppas?
– Something like that. Yet consonants do have a sound by themselves. I guess it is just that their sound is not like a voice that can carry, like for the vowels.
– Oh, Styppas — I know! That is why they are called *syn-phona* (Greek equivalent of consonants). It's like accompanying a vowel sound.

140

– Exactly, Tasouli. So for the first time in history the Ancients could make visual representations for both consonants and vowels. And keep a record. Like putting the sound of the language in storage.

– So other languages before could not do that?

– Apparently not. Like Phoenician and other Semitic languages.

– Oh, yes, Styppas. Stelios has mentioned all these older languages. He remembered the names of a whole lot of them, but I don't. So, was Homer written like that?

– No, the epics of Homer would not have been 'written' to start with. It was probably not until Hesiod's time that this new Greek writing was discovered.

– So the grave I fell into, Styppas — up in the hills, which Tassia said was Mycenaean, would that be older?

– Sure quite a bit older. And the Mycyneans probably would not have had Greek writing.

– Tassia did not say that, Styppas.

– She is goat. What could she know!

– She knows a lot, Styppas. And don't forget — I love her.

– Gives new meaning to 'love is blind'.

– If you keep insulting Tassia, I won't talk to you anymore, Styppas.

– OK, Tasouli. I will not say anything bad about your Tassia.

– OK, Styppas. In that case, you can keep going on about your Havelock.

– Equating a bleating Zakynthian goat to a brilliant professor of Classics! Oh well ... So, Havelock thinks that with the older forms of writing like in Hebrew and Sumerian and Babylonian, one could not 'hear' the full richness of those languages by looking at the written texts — like from what these peoples had chiseled on tablets and stones.

– Bravo Styppas — these were the other languages Stelios had mentioned! Now I remember their names! But exactly what do you mean that one would not be able to 'hear' the full language from those scripts?

– Because they condensed and they economized with their scripts creating symbols, which were not really phonetic. So their symbols were good for ritual and record but not too good for the flexibility and mobility of literature created by the spoken word.

– Like the *librettos* of the Zakynthian Cantades, Styppas?

– Exactly. You could never write Zakynthian *librettos* in ancient Hebrew or Sumerian or Babylonian script. Much of the color and emotion and the musicality of the language in the *libretto* would be lost.

– But you say that the writing of those older languages would be OK for rituals and magical incantations?

– For sure, Tasouli. But not for poems of the imagination, not for the color and emotion of language — not really.

– So if the Ancient Greeks did not have their writing at the time of Homer, how did these poems survive to the time that their writing was invented?

– That is the central issue. Havelock thinks it was all by creating an oral tradition of everything they wanted to preserve — like all their big epics — in verse. It is much easier to memorize verse and pass the memorized verse from one generation to the next. They even had specially trained memorizers in each generation.

– Oh for sure, Styppas. Nana says that a lot of the verses in the Zakynthian cantades have never been written. Some people just remember lots and lots of the verses — and the music that goes with it. Tzanetos likes to go and listen to them in the cafés.

– In the cafés?

– In the cafés and the clubs at night. Nana also said that many of these memorizers sing the cantades without music. She says that the memorizers had not gone very far in school and they are mostly comrades of Tzanetos.

– Hmm. You seem to know it all. What is the point of telling you how language developed in antiquity if these Zakynthians still behave like primitives? Maybe you should have asked your Tassia to tell you all about language instead of me telling you.

141

– Please Styppas, do not tease me about Tassia.

– I am not making fun of your goat.

– I am glad, Styppas. Because don't you think that if Tassia knew about things Mycenaean she would also know about the Homeric poems?

– How so?

– The Zakynthian goats remember forever. They remember sounds they learned from their mothers and fathers. Goat generation upon goat generation. That is why they bleat so. Why else would they bleat, Styppas?

– I can't think of any other reason!

– But goats can't do everything. Even Tassia can't read, Styppas.

– I am so surprised!

– You are?

– Listen Tasouli. Forget about the bloody goats and Tassia. Just for a minute! Concentrate on what I am saying. In Mycenaean times the poems of Homer would only be recited. Probably to music. Recited to rhythm and music and over and over again. It was the only way to retain a rich and colorful history of the race. To store it in memory.

– I am concentrating, Styppas! Music for poems was before writing?

– Certainly before Greek phonetic writing, Tasouli. That is why the Homer and even Hesiod generally appeal to the Muses at the beginning of their poems.

– Oh … the Muses … the Muses!

– And the Muses were the daughters of Zeus and Mnemosyne, Tasouli.

– Mnemosyne?

– You know … like Mneme. Like we still say *mneme* in Modern Greek for memory. But Mnemosyne would be more like remembrance or recall.

– Did your friend Havelock say all of this?

– He was not my friend. I hardly knew him. But he does say this kind of stuff in his book.

– What else does he say, Styppas?

– Quite a lot. Most importantly he thinks that Hesiod's poems would be the earliest when Greek poetry was actually composed with the alphabet in mind. And written down too.

– Oh … Hesiod! Stelios considered him even more important than Homer.

– Of course he would, Tasouli.

– Why do you say this?

– Because Stelios is an Engineer. And Engineers are all about writing … symbols and formulas and all of that.

– I guess so … And when does this Havelock friend … sorry I mean professor type … say that Greek writing was first really used?

– He thinks not much before 700 BC. But then later Plato seems to have used the written text as his main way of transmitting ideas. He was very influential. And very rigid.

– Oh, I know, Styppas. And very boring too. It is the only time I fell asleep listening to Stelios. When he starts talking about Plato and does not stop. I didn't mean to fall asleep, Styppas, but my eyes just closed.

– Don't worry about it, Tasouli. It also happens to me.

– And what, do you think, your Havelock admired most? Verse remembered just by speech … and rhythm, or what was written?

– I think verse and speech.

– So, he thought that speech in verse was superior to writing in texts?

– More or less, Tasouli. What are you getting at?

– Well then Tassia, who remembers what her mother taught her by bleating … and her mother taught her … all the way back to the Mycenaeans, must be superior.

– Superior to whom?

– To people who write.

– You are really getting me mad, Tasouli.

– Sorry.

– You are not at all sorry. You become pedantic just to insult me.

– Do I have to be pedantic just to insult you, Styppas?

– Ahhhhhhhh … !

– But Styppas, why are you shouting? Could I really insult you without being pedantic, like you taught me to be?

– I never taught you to be pedantic. You were born pedantic!

– Thank you Styppas. That is even better. Isn't it?

– Shut up … shut up … shut up … you little twerp!

I had never seen Styppas so mad. His face became all distorted and very, very ugly. Green spit was coming out of the sides of his mouth. He seemed to grow hair everywhere. He started to scream:

– I try to teach you everything and all you do is turn it around. Just to your own advantage. Now it is to show that your ridiculous girlfriend of a goat is superior to me … You are worthless! You are evil! I should extinguish you! I should terminate you!

Oh my God — this was horrible! Styppas is going to extinguish me. Just like the torturers could have done to Tzanetos! A cold terror broke over me. My heart started to race. It was up in my throat. I started to scream.

– Mamaka, Mamaka, Mamaka … come quickly … come quickly! Styppas wants to extinguish me. He wants to terminate me.

Fortunately, my Mamaka ran to the Doppia in a flash.

– Why are you shouting, Tasouli? Are you having a nightmare? I told you. You should have come for your chamomile tea.

– Styppas is very angry with me. Very angry. So angry he wants to extinguish me … to terminate me.

– What nonsense Tasouli. There is no Styppas here. And why are you imagining there is someone with our family name who is trying to terminate you? This is horrible. Tell your mama who has really frightened you. It is one of these … these operatives. I know who they are. The same ones who gave the information about Tzanetos. So he could be tortured. And terminated. I will go and fix them in one second flat. These peasants need to be taught a lesson.

– No Mamaka, no. Styppas is not bad. He just got very angry. Because it came out that Tassia was superior to him. It just worked out that way. Because I am learning to be pedantic.

– Your mother really has it in for your relatives who she thinks are operatives for the Regime and squealers. She really does, Tasouli.

– You don't sound as mad now, Styppas.

– I am starting to calm down.

– I am so glad. I was afraid you would terminate me, for sure.

– Who in the world are you talking to again, Tasouli? Is it that Styppas? You can tell your Mamaka what is really bothering you. Come, tell me. I am your mother. You must tell me everything. You cannot keep secrets from your mother.

Now my mother's face was starting to turn ugly. Not as ugly as Styppas' had turned. But that accusatory, like, 'why are you lying to me' ugly face she would often put on.

– I told you, Mamaka. It is just Styppas.

– Wow, your mother is right into the psychology, Tasouli! Like something else must be … ha, ha, ha … bothering you.

– Yes, Styppas. She is always figuring out what must be bothering me. Even if nothing is.

– I am telling you, Tasouli. It is not natural to talk like that to someone that I can't hear or see. It's not natural to not tell your mother what is bothering you.

– Yes, Mamaka. But Styppas always answers back and has good answers.

– Is that so? So, why can't I hear him then?

– I don't know. I don't know why you can't hear him, Mamaka.

– OK, Tasouli. We will go and have the chamomile tea. And you will get away from that imaginary Styppas of yours. We are going now.

Anastassiades

I woke up and looked around the Doppia hollow. My mother was gone. She must have just been in my dream. The conversation from the yard had ceased. The relations must have left and also gone for their little siestas. I looked for Styppas. He was still around but had climbed up onto the higher parts of the roots of the hollow. He seemed to also be taking a siesta in a little shelf that was formed by the twisted roots and the inside of the tree-trunk making up the roof of the hollow. I think his little bed may have been made decades or generations ago, by one of the lightning bolts that had hit the Doppia. I did not want to disturb him from his rest. So I headed back, across the yard, and through the back door into the kitchen. My mother and Nana were still sitting there talking in a quiet, conspiratorial manner, with their elbows planted on the plain wooden kitchen table.

– Mamaka I came for the chamomile tea.
– Nana, he wants his chamomile tea.
– It is the middle of rest time Dina.
– But Mamaka told me that I should have it, Thia Nana.
– OK Dina? OK. I'll make it for you Tasouli.

Nana was always willing and physically quick in all kinds of chores. My mother was not. She would always consider what was advantageous and analyze every movement. Nana had already added the water to the dry, aromatic flowers and the chamomile tea was quickly made on the little gaziera.

– Thanks Thia Nana. This is very nice chamomile tea.
– Oh, yes Tasouli. I gathered it up in the hills. Just the other day. Up where the agrarians are still finding antiquities they say.
– There was lots of chamomile by the Mycenaean grave. Where I fell in.
– What? My little boy fell into a Mycenaean grave? And I did not even know about it? He could have been psychologically damaged for life. This is totally unacceptable. Don't you think so Nana?
– Don't worry Mamaka. I was not hurt. And I was not afraid. And I told Tassia.
– You told a goat but not your mother? Your own mother … your mother that suckled you!
– But Mamaka I was talking to Tassia about 'being afraid'. Because her own mother fell into a Mycenaean grave. And I said I was not afraid.
– You were having these kinds of conversations with a goat and not telling your own mother?
– But the goat … I mean Tassia does not get as agitated and ready to fight, not like you do Mamaka.
– Of course not, it is just a goat. A dumb animal. She doesn't have farm property to protect. And other worries. What else did this goat ask you?
– She asked if there were any human females that I liked.
– Pa, pa, pa, pa … and what did you say?
– I said that I liked you and Nana …
– I should say so. And who else?
– Well, Pamela.
– Pamela? Pamela? Who is this Pamela?
– She lives with Styppas. In Canada. Where it is very cold.
– I know it is very cold in Canada. How did you get to be friendly with this Pamela?
– Funny you should ask me, Mamaka. Tassia asked me the same question.
– 'That so.
– Yes, and I told Tassia how I was looking for Styppas, but because it was so cold Pamela took me into bed with her.
– What will I hear next! She took you into bed with her! First the goat, and then this Pamela.
– No Mamaka. The other way. I met Pamela before Tassia.
– This is awful. Don't you agree Nana?
– Oh, Dina … it's just his imagination. The boy just has an active imagination.

144

– But what if he catches something? Who will then be to blame … ? You can't but warn him. Imagination will lead to other things. You know very well what I mean. It is awful … some of them are diseased. My little son …

– Don't worry Mamaka. Tassia said that nowadays the Zakynthos goats get checked by the Veterinarian. So, I won't catch the goat disease.

– Goat disease! Catch goat disease! May St. Dionysos protect us! And this Pamela … who says you can't catch something from this Pamela.

– Why are you calling on St. Dionysos, the patron saint of Zakynthos to protect us Mamaka? I thought you were not religious.

– I am only evoking the patron saint because we are in Zakynthos, of course.

– And Mamaka what could I catch from Pamela … you mean like catching worms from the little girl, which were hanging out of her pippi … in Pagrati … when she would come to play with me in the hallway of the Bastille. Could I catch worms like that, Mamaka?

– Or worse. Who knows! There is not a moment to lose. I must find this Styppas and give him a piece of my mind. Lives with this Pamela in Canada you say … come along … come along now. So I find myself being dragged by the hand back to the hollow of the Doppia in pursuit of Styppas. I had not even finished the nice cup of chamomile tea Nana had prepared for me.

– What could be worse than the worms, Mamaka?

– Never mind. Why can I not see Styppas? Has he disappeared? Where is he now?

We look into the Doppia hollow, my Mamaka and I. Styppas is hard to see. He seems to have become smaller. But he was still nestled in the little shelf made by the roots towards the roof of the hollow olive trunk. Where one of the lightning bolts had struck.

– Ah, you've come back Tasouli. With your Mama.

– Yes, Styppas. My Mamaka wanted to talk to you.

– What about?

– Pamela, she says.

My mother is now getting anxious as well as agitated. Her voice has risen by a decibel:

– What did he say? What did he say? Tell your Mamaka everything that Styppas said.

– He only asked what you wanted to talk to him about Mamaka. And I said Pamela.

– Of course it is Pamela. What else would I want to talk to him about? How come he knows this Pamela? How did he meet her? And how come she took my little boy into her bed? In Canada no less!

– Oh your mother fusses too much, Tasouli. Tell her I've known Pamela a long, long time. I met her over a dead body. And Pamela took you to her bed because it was too cold.

– I have already told her that Pamela took me to her bed because it was too cold, Styppas. I will tell her the rest.

So I transmit to my mother the rest of what Styppas said.

– I don't like you just repeating what Styppas said, Tasouli. I can't see his expression and I do not like it one bit. And what is this about a dead body? He and this Pamela were up to no good. Were they studying to be morticians or something?

I look at Styppas. He is just shaking his head in disbelief.

– No Mamaka. They were not studying to be morticians.

– It is very ghoulish. How is it possible for normal people to just meet over a dead body? Are there vampires in Canada?

– Oh what an imagination your mother has Tasouli! Is that where you get it from? Tell her no, there are no vampires in Canada. She was a nurse and I was a Resident in Medicine, in training. An old man died … was expected to, and Pamela just called me to pronounce him dead. And tell her, no — there are no vampires in Canada.

Anastassiades

So, I tell my mother again all that Styppas said. It is too bad she cannot see or hear Styppas, for having to transmit everything he says is starting to get a bit tedious.

– Ash, a nurse and a doctor! That is different then. Still how can normal people start a romance over a dead body? There is something strange here …
– It is not strange Mamaka. Just Styppas and I having a conversation.
– We'll see! But I have to run back to the house now. I can hear those no-good second Cousins visiting again. They could be plotting about our property. But I will be back … and you must tell me everything this Styppas of yours has said. Word for word. Do you hear?
– Yes, Mamaka. I will tell you everything. When you return.

Styppas waits for a minute or so, as if to collect his thoughts. His voice is now calm and happy and he has a little smile on his face:

– OK, Tasouli. Then I'll tell you exactly how it all started. It was the middle of a late autumn night in Montreal. In a Veteran's Hospital — and it's like three o'clock in the morning. I get called by this nurse with a nice, reassuring English accent, all apologetic about having to call me and wake me up. That was unusual in the first place … I mean this kind of comfortable politeness and such a nice accent. Most nurses in the big Teaching Hospitals, where I trained, would breathlessly screech at you when they called in the middle of the night. So, I toddle over to her ward and notice she is even nicer looking than her voice suggests. I like her walk in particular. Especially from behind. So, as she is walking towards the corpse, she turns around half apologetic, half smiling, half ironic and she says something like: "So sorry to have disturbed you doctor, but nurses cannot tell if someone is dead."

I have to think quickly. I don't want to say something cheesy like: 'Oh, of course nurses can tell if someone is dead.'

So, I say nothing. I follow her over to this guy in a hospital bed who is as dead as a mackerel in Saskatchewan. I notice that he has a chest that looks like a barrel — typical of emphysema … he had probably smoked like a chimney since he was a child. He was a World War I veteran and his chart said he was poisoned by pineapple gas. It appears that anyone who breathed in pineapple gas, which was admittedly not good for the lungs, got automatically compensated by the Veterans Affairs Ministry. No matter how heavily he had smoked. It seemed to me that just about all World War One veterans in that Montreal hospital that had emphysema had been poisoned by pineapple gas. I am explaining all of this to the politely attentive, neat and attractive English nurse, while trying to figure out a strategy to approach her.

Then I have an idea. I listen to the dead guy's chest, which is of course as silent as the grave. I turn to English nurse, who by now has got a bit closer, and tell her I cannot hear any heart sounds. However, we have to be a little cautious because huge emphysematous barrel chests often do not conduct heart sounds well. She seems to accept it. It is actually true, except of course in the case of dead people, who have no heart sounds to conduct. So, I look as thoughtful as I can and say to her:

– In your opinion, Miss H … is this patient dead?
Unhesitant green-blue, reassuring eyes respond:

– Oh, yes. Quite dead, Doctor.

Did I read her right? Maybe I should probe a little more. So I say:

– We wouldn't want to sign him off as dead and then he sits up in the morgue on us — would we now?

Again, the same unhesitating, now smiling eyes, the reassuring voice:

– No, we would not, Doctor. And he will not. The papers are filled in and ready for you to sign.

Hmm … efficient as well. So, I settle down to check and sign the already filled-in forms. All is correct. The final diagnosis is not 'pineapple gas poisoning' but 'end stage emphysema; *cor pulmonale'*. I asked how she got the diagnosis. She says:

– From the chart and from rounds.

And she was again apologetic.

– Sorry again to have to call you in the middle of the night. Do you think you might like a cup of tea?

I try to contain myself while pretending to pay attention to double checking the boring death forms, while she is preparing the tea. No tea bags in those days, at least mostly. But then she looks very upset …

– I am so terribly sorry.

I had no idea what she was talking about. She pointed to the floating tea leaves with her face all reddening. I now knew I had a clear opening. So I asked her out for breakfast. She agreed. And then:

– Will you knock me up in the morning, then?

I smile to myself about her use of the British idiom. She obviously does not know what the expression means in North American slang. I assure her that I will knock her up in the morning.

– What does 'knock her up' mean in North American slang, Styppas?
– Never mind.
– Styppas, this is a really good story. You did a lot better with Pamela than I did with Tassia. On the other hand, even though I was a failure in trying to milk Tassia she still liked me.
– Stop comparing that goat with Pamela! Do you hear!

Styppas was starting to shout. He was getting mad again. But at least he was not growing hair everywhere … at least not yet. I knew that my Mother had gone to the house but I whispered in any case:

– Styppas do not shout.

But then, by coincidence, my mother had just appeared again at the opening of Doppia. Obviously she had made short work of the second Cousins and sent them packing.

– What are you whispering? You should not have secrets from your mother. I gave birth to you. You cannot have secrets from your own flesh and blood. She is again getting agitated and intimidating.
– No, Mamaka. I am not keeping any secrets. I will tell you the story Styppas just told me about how he met Pamela.

And I do, leaving out the more gushy stuff. My mother seems again impressed.

– Oh, that's interesting. So this Pamela of this Styppas of yours, Tasouli, seems to be an independent woman. She seems to have pride in her work.

Anastassiades

My mother was now making a 180 degree turn about Pamela. No more cross-examination about how I ended up in her bed. That was progress! But then Styppas says something strange:

– She would have to come around in any case. She would have had no choice.

I did not want to get my mother started up again by her hearing me ask Styppas what he really meant by that remark. Even if I whispered the question she would know I was saying something to him. So I say nothing. But I could see Styppas was starting to get a bit restless. He had come down from his perch and now looked his normal size.

– Actually, Tasouli, I did not come down to Zakynthos just to get involved in discussions about your goat, your mother and Pamela. Not that I have anything against discussing these women … I mean females. But I want to continue our discussion about language. About the change from orality to literacy in ancient Greece … you know from speech to being able to write down everything you want to say. And how Socrates is related to all of this and why he was tried.
– Wow Styppas … Socrates, and why he was tried! That was another big topic for Uncle Stelios.

But my mother starts getting combative again as soon as she hears me mention Socrates in conjunction with Stelios:

– Don't you dare think that your Uncle Stelios knows more about the trial of Socrates than your father and I do, Tasouli. Why Phoebus and I have had continual discussions about this topic. Phoebus from the Archeomarxist perspective and I as a teacher and social behaviorist.
– Yes Mamaka. But Styppas has been reading a book about this and he has lots to say about language and the trial of Socrates. But since you can't hear him you should let me listen to him. Then I will tell you everything he has said. Everything Mamaka.
– Now you are being my very own child, Tasouli mou. You listen to what Styppas has to say and then you tell it all to me. Word for word. Do not forget anything. In any case, I have to go to discuss something urgent with Nana. About the property. We will have to go to the Chora and see our lawyer.
– Oh, a lawyer, Mamaka.
– Our cousin. He is the best lawyer in Zakynthos. So we have to plan all of this. You come directly to the house after you have rested properly here in the Doppia.

So, my mother stomps off again. This time to talk to Nana about serious property matters and she will not be rushing back. No more interruptions for a while!

– Well done, Tasouli. We can now discuss the important topic I came to talk to you about in peace and quiet.
– OK, but how did you get interested in this topic, Styppas? The change from spoken to written Greek.
– It was because of you, Tasouli.
– Me? Do you mean the hated caterpillars in English?
– Yes. And you trying to cut down the total number of Greek letters to make a phonetic language that would be simpler.
– True. But this was only because I hated the Greek Grammar and all its rules, Styppas. And all the problems with the *Katharevousa*.
– Nevertheless, when I came across this theory by Havelock on why Socrates was tried, I had to come and tell you. Because it was all about language.
– And what exactly is his theory, Styppas?
– Well, first of all he thinks that the change in education from just oral learning to learning by written text happened over a pretty short period of time. So, until the latter half of the fifth century BC, Havelock says there were no real complete texts in law, in history, in literature or in

any discipline. Only very contracted writing forms existed. And these writing forms had existed for thousands of years before.

– So like in Homer. One had to learn literature and history by reciting in verse or poem form.

– Yes, but not just poems or songs like the Zakynthian Cantades singers learn. Learning only by reciting applied to everything there was to learn.

– So did everybody learn like that, Styppas?

– No, not all. This kind of oral learning was not open to everyone. It was mostly members of the older men in Aristocratic families who knew by heart everything of historical and cultural value.

– And then they passed it on to their children?

– They passed it on to the young men and adolescent boys in their families by teaching them to recite all that knowledge as poems, in rhythm.

– So, the girls were left out from learning all of this, Styppas?

– That is what Havelock thinks. At least for the richer Athenian families. Like the more powerful aristocrats of the time. All that there was to know would be passed down among the males by recitation. So he says that this would also favor homosexual bonding.

– Oh, is that the same as homophilic, like we say in Greek, Styppas?

– Hmm. In English they use the term homosexual not homophilic. But I guess homophilic is a better word to explain how knowledge was passed on then. For it means that one is more friendly and likely favors people of the same sex. Homosexual is more like having sex with people of the same sex.

– Yuk. Mama would not be happy about me discussing this. On the other hand Stelios would not mind. Like in Cavafis. He says some of his best poems are homophilic.

– I know what Stelios says about Cavafis, Tasouli. But let's not stray too far from the topic. Getting back to Havelock, he says that oral tradition favors the knower while writing favors what is known.

– You mean writing favors anyone that can read what is recorded in writing, Styppas? That is pretty obvious.

– But Socrates wrote nothing down, at least as far as we know. He was an oralist … he thought oral communication was much superior to writing.

– So what did he do that was so wrong? You say that oral communication was the tradition then. Why would he have to drink the hemlock?

– Havelock thinks Socrates used spoken language to break the power of the Aristocratic families of Athens. They all depended on oral memorization to retain control over knowledge.

– And how did Socrates do this, Styppas?

– He did this by argument developed by questioning. But his method was mostly by using what they call the dialectic.

– Oh, Styppas, I know about the dialectic. My father is always talking about it. It is the favorite of the Archeomarxists. You are not a true Archeomarxist if you do not use the dialectic. But still, why the hemlock?

– Well, Havelock thinks that the dialectic taught by Socrates was appealing to the male youth from the Aristocratic families of Athens. So, they started to feel that they no longer needed to get all their knowledge from what was passed on to them through memorization of the spoken verses by the elders in the family. They could start to analyze things for themselves …

– So?

– So, the accusation was that Socrates was corrupting the minds of youth by teaching them how to use spoken language in a different way.

– And was Socrates against the Aristocratic families, Styppas.

– That was the paradox. He was, it is said, from such a family himself. And he was conservative. He wanted to retain oral teaching, not to replace it with the new phonetic writing. This now also became very powerful with the invention of symbols for the complete consonants. But he wanted to examine conventions and to apply new standards to behavior.

– So, would he have been against the hated caterpillars and for simplifying Greek by using fewer vowels, Styppas?

– Probably he would ask you why you would want to use writing in the first place. That is if you can speak well. Then he would demonstrate that writing is inferior to speech or force you to admit this through questioning.

– So, Socrates would try to show that my question was invalid in the first place?

– Something like that.

– I don't think I like Socrates too much, Styppas. I worked hard in simplifying the Greek vowels and using fewer letters in writing.

– Lots of people did not like Socrates.

– I can see why the Aristocratic Athenians would not like their children … sorry, their sons I mean to learn these language tricks taught by Socrates.

– It would likely become even worse than that for them, Tasouli. Spoken knowledge — the education of the time, was concentrated in the wealthy Aristocrats. These kinds of families would likely gradually lose power and influence too if they lost the spoken knowledge, the history of their tribe. They could not reliably transmit all there was to know about themselves, and where they came from to their boys if the boys were influenced by the dialectic nonsense. Maybe they felt that Socrates really corrupted the Aristocratic boys by teaching them the dialectic.

– Enough reason for him to have to drink the hemlock, Styppas!

– Reason enough.

– But Styppas, there is something I don't understand. What happened to the Muse?

– The Muse learned how to write the new phonetic alphabet, but because it was so phonetic she could still be a Muse. But such a Muse could only be Greek. For Greek was the only language then where the writing could transmit the sounds and emotion of speech.

– But that is not what I mean, Styppas.

– What then do you mean?

– Was the Muse not called a Muse because she had something to do with music?

– Likely.

– But then, Styppas, the Muse was before the Ancient Greek writing with the 24 letters of the alphabet.

– So?

– So, if she was before the writing she must have something to do with teaching the poems, like Homer.

– Right. Havelock says something like that.

– But then, Styppas, she must have known how to put music or at least rhythm to the epic poems.

– So?

– So, if she could put words to music and music to words, she must have had a language of her own much before the invention of the Greek 24-letter writing.

– So?

– So Styppas, does even the dialectic argument not have a sequence, a pattern?

– I guess it does.

– So, maybe Socrates was tried because he did not honor the Muse. Even though he said speech was superior to writing.

– Hm. Never heard that before.

– But it is worse still for Socrates, Styppas.

– Why?

– Because he was contradicting himself.

– Socrates would never contradict himself.

– But Styppas, would you not agree that the Muse must have had a system, a designation for the music, the rhythm of the poems.

– That's obvious.

– So, there must have been some symbols for the notes even if they were not written.

– Symbols for unwritten notes?

– Like a sequence of fingers of one hand plucking a string.

– That is probably so, Tasouli.

– So, is not some kind of sequence, written or not, like a form of writing? Like concrete symbols made with one's hand.

– I suppose.

– Then, Styppas, would you not agree that Socrates, by rejecting writing in favor of the sounds of speech, was adopting another kind of writing, of a more ancient designation?

– I suppose, Tasouli. But you are starting to wear me down. And you are becoming annoyingly pedantic again.

– Thanks Styppas. You have paid me that complement before. I am just trying to improve being pedantic.

– Unbelievable! Hurry up with your argument! What's your case against Socrates?

– It is this, Styppas: Socrates was really tried for both abandonment and a contradiction. He abandoned one of the oldest goddesses, the Muse, in favor of the dialectic. That would have been bad enough for the conservative ancient Greeks. Is that not so?

– Hmm. I never heard of that either.

– But then, worse still he failed to acknowledge that the Goddess he abandoned was still hidden in the dialectic he taught. So he lied by omission.

– And exactly what else do you have against Socrates, Tasouli?

– That he falsely taught a contradiction — he favored speech over concrete symbols in writing. Yet speech was tied into the concrete symbols of rhythm and music. We already agreed that music had concrete symbols back then, right Styppas?

– That is an absolutely fantastically baseless accusation against Socrates. And you know it! You are just saying these things to irritate me.

– Sorry, Styppas. But this contradiction might have been his worst crime of all. Because the Aristocratic families, including his very own family, based everything of value that they knew and taught on the rhythm and music of oral language.

– So you think he should have been convicted and executed?

– Doubly.

– Doubly?

– Yes, Styppas. Twice over.

Styppas said nothing. I could understand him being annoyed at me. He had spent so much time researching the transition of oral to written Greek on my behalf, and I went and wrecked it all in the end. But I could see that he was more than annoyed. He was getting very angry again, his face becoming ugly and distorted. He was again growing hair everywhere. He started to shout and scream even louder than before, gesticulating with his index finger as if he was going to extinguish me right there and then:

– First, you try to prove that your goaty girl friend is superior to me … then you start comparing your relationship with the cursed goat to that between Pamela and me. And now with your bloody pedantic arguments you want to execute Socrates twice!

I became afraid that he would extinguish me this time for real.

I ran out of the Doppia hollow as fast as I could into the yard. The chickens looked peaceful, pecking away. It was a relief. And Tassia, dear Tassia, gave me a welcoming, all-knowing glance. I found my Mama and Nana still talking to each other about the property and what they would say to the famous lawyer-cousin of theirs. I told my Mamaka that Styppas and I were discussing the trial of Socrates but omitting the details about how much work Styppas had put into reading Havelock and how mad he got with me. My Mamaka was very impressed. She said to me in a very affectionate voice:

– You know, since Phoebus and I often discuss Socrates, your daddy will be very pleased that you are also taking an interest, Tasouli.

– That is good, Mamaka.
– This man Styppas that you have these discussions with, I wonder how come he has the same name as us. He is not a known relative, is he?
– I don't think so Mamaka.

I felt all warm and cozy now. My Mamaka was all happy and approving. I would also win the approval of my father. Maybe the fight with Styppas was all worth it. But I really did not want to be extinguished. Especially, if it was going to be by impalement.

Urinals are bad

Away from Zakynthos, away from Gerakarion, away from Nana, the chickens, the wise but goaty darling Tassia and the Doppia, life in Pagrati and the Bastille carried on. But it had started to take a dark turn of its own. It seemed to start inconsequentially enough with my mother's usual worries about the horrible things that could befall her little treasure.

I had just finished another school day at Pagrati Elementary School and I had wandered into the Alsos in Pagrati without going home first. These rough gang-kids were hanging around, looking threatening. It was probably the same bunch that used to chase me when I would have to cross the Alsos every day, when I started going to the Maraslion Academy, a year or so later. I should have gone pee before I left the Pagrati School, but I was in a rush to explore the Alsos and not get home too late, and I did not. Things became more urgent by the time I reached the Alsos and I wanted to go pee very badly. But I did not dare pee in the bushes of the Alsos, in case the rough kids saw me in a vulnerable position. So I made short work of Alsos exploration and ran towards the main Platea of Pagrati, Platea Plastira, where I knew were some underground urinals. I barely held on until I got to Platea Plastira. I ran down the old marble stairs which were slippery and wet from the cold winter rain, into the darkened, subterranean, smelly urinals. And there I finally peed to my heart's content.

One small problem was that urinals were a little high for me, as they had no children's urinals in those days. So, I tried standing on my tippy-toes to get my pippi past the porcelain lip of the urinal, but still I could barely reach. I wanted to go so badly that the urine just shot out with a big force. And this led me to a most important discovery. For I found that if I pointed my pippi slightly up, the urine shot right over the lip of the urinal as well as the part of the urinal with the drain holes. It would then forcefully hit the back of the inside of the urinal which was also made of the heavy white porcelain. Almost instantaneously I discovered that if I manipulated the position of my pippi I could change the trajectory of the stream. It was a great revelation.

In truth, I sort of knew that one could do something like this from limited experiments in the Bastille. But I was not allowed to experiment too much in the Bastille, as my Mamaka made me sit down on the toilet before I peed. She said it was in case I also wanted to do *kaka*. And when I objected and said I did not want to do *kaka*, she would say that she did not want urine all over the toilet seat. And, of course, there were no urinals in the Bastille. In Zakynthos and in Pyrgos, I could pee anywhere in the countryside and as a result I never had to go really badly. So, my amazement of discovering that I could stand a bit back from the urinal and the urine stream would curve right into the urinal was understandable. It was exactly like a *sydrivani*. A *sydrivani* is like a fountain, except they are usually located in important City squares, like in Syndagma or Omonia. Of course there were not many *sydrivania* which were operational during the Occupation or even after the War because of the water shortages. But I must admit that I did notice that I had a little problem. For as the force of my sydrivani diminished, and as I could not reach the urinal, it caused the last part of my pee to fall on the old, stained ceramic floor tiles. But no one seemed to notice. In any case, these tiles looked like they had been there since antiquity and they seemed to absorb endless amounts of spilled-over urine. That is why the whole of these public toilets smelled so strong.

As I walked from the Pagrati urinals towards the Bastille, I started to think that if I had not been afraid of the tough kids in the Alsos, I might have not made this important discovery. I would have simply peed in the bushes of the Alsos. So, there would have been no sydrivani. At least not a really good one like I was able to make in the underground urinals. It is amazing how adversity and fear of the tough kids had led to my discovery. But thinking of my pippi and the excellent and most satisfying sydrivani I was able to make, I also started to think about the little girl that used to come and visit in the dark hallway in the Bastille, I mean the little girl with the worms sticking out of her pippi. It was too bad that my mother had not allowed her to visit again. I could have showed her how to make a sydrivani. She would have been impressed. Oh well …

When I got home I started to relate my adventures and discoveries to my Mamaka. I was rather proud of the fact that I had managed to evade the rough kids and on top I was able to use the public urinals and make my discovery. It certainly gave me a feeling of accomplishment … a feeling of being grown up. But my feeling of accomplishment and adulthood lasted but a few moments. My mother's disapproving turn of her lower lip and the sour expression on her face both started to appear before I had got past the first few sentences of my narration of how I got down into the Pagrati urinals.

— You must never do that again.
— But why, Mama?
— Urinals are bad. They are very bad.

I was being scolded for having done something bad. I did not know why, but I could tell it was having an unpleasant effect on me. My voice would become higher, apologetic and I could feel tears starting to swell in my eyes. In circumstances like this I would revert to the affectionate diminutive for my Mamaka. It was automatic, but maybe I thought it would placate her. The more she scolded me, the higher my voice became and the more affectionate diminutives I was prone to use to respond to her.

– Why Mamaka?
Making her Mamaka, little Mummy, might help make everything alright again.
– Just because.
– Because what, Mamaka?
– Bad people go to the urinals.
– But I did not see any bad people.
– Who did you see then?
– Just the old lady that cleans and begs. She looked like she lived there. She was going in and out of a dirty little room all the time.
– And who else?
– Just a few men peeing.
– Aha! Men you say?
– Of course, Mamaka. These urinals are for men.
– You don't have to tell me who the urinals are for! And what were these men wearing?
– Overcoats and raincoats, Mamaka.
– Aha! Overcoats and raincoats. Just as I thought.
– Of course, Mamaka mou. It is the middle of winter.

Maybe by calling her *Mamaka mou* my Mamaka, my little Mummy, would help me get out of this very bad thing I had done.

– Overcoats and raincoats are very suspicious in men.
– But Mamaka mou, just about all men in Athens wear overcoats and raincoats in winter. It is different from Zakynthos — there they wear patched up jackets and country clothes.
– I know what they wear in Zakynthos.
– But Daddy and Stelios and Thales and Yianis all have raincoats or overcoats for the winter.
– Your father and uncles do not end up in underground urinals.
– But where do they go when they have to pee, Mamaka mou?

153

– They plan their day, of course. So they don't use public urinals.
– So, men that use the public urinals do not plan their day?

The look she gave me made feel like a worm. The increasing curl of her lip and the ever more souring expression on her face said it to me ever so clearly. Only someone very bad and very, very inferior would ask a question like that.

– Of course not.
– But why, Mamaka mou?
– Why? Because men who do not plan their day are inferior, of course.

I should have stopped. *I should have stopped right there.* But I did not seem to be able to. Something seemed to drive me to find out why urinals were bad.

– But if daddy and my uncles wear overcoats and raincoats, does this mean that they are very suspicious, Mamaka mou?
– Don't be silly. It is only men that go down to the public urinals wearing the overcoats and raincoats who are suspicious.

I could see I was getting myself more and more entangled. What I had done was not only bad, not only horribly inferior, but suspicious on top. And yet … I could not stop. Maybe going on to a petting-affectionate diminutive combined with the possessive appellation of my Mamaka might help a little to get me out of this terrible mess. I would try the *Mammakoula mou* appellation. Retreat from the topic of urinals-are-bad seemed now impossible.

– But if daddy and my uncles had to go pee very badly one day … like really had to go, *Mammakoula mou* … would they be inferior?

What a blunder! What had come over me? Implying there could be circumstances that my family could ever be inferior … I was really in for it now.

– Of course, not. How could you possibly think that, Tasouli? Our family is not like the others. It is superior.
– … oh of course, Mamaka. We are superior. Then, why should I not go to the public urinals if I am superior in any case?

Once again! Saying things I did not mean to say. This had come out sounding all wrong.

– Because very bad things can happen to a little boy in the public urinals.
– Even though I am superior, Mammakoula mou?
– Especially if you are superior!
– But what could happen to me, Mamaka?
– Unspeakable things.
– What unspeakable things, Mamaka.
– I will not tell you.
– Please Mamaka.
– No.
– Mamaka mou, please tell me.
– No. You are too small.
– Oh, please, please, please Mamaka mou. I am not too small. Please Mammakoula mou … pleaeeeeese.

My Mama was conspiratorially looking around. Her face had a terrible expression on it. Finally she turned around to me and whispered.

– You must not tell anyone.

– No Mamaka mou. I never will.

– These bad men in raincoats … down where the public urinals are …

– What Mamaka, what?

– They might show you their pippis.

– But why would they do this, Mamaka?

– It is too terrible. You must immediately run away.

– But I did not run away when the little girl showed me her pippi, Mamma. You know … the little girl with the worms.

– It is not the same.

– Oh, I know, Mamma. Men in raincoats would not have little worms coming out of their pippis.

– Of course not. Where did you ever get that idea?

– But why would their pippis be so bad that I would have to immediately run away Mamma? Would they have longer worms coming out? And other critters, Mamaka? Maybe even scorpions? Like the one you killed, on the dammaki wall, in Rafina.

I could see she was thinking carefully. Her eyes took a funny, but half-satisfied expression.

– OK. You understand then why you must not go down to the public urinals. And why you must not speak to suspicious men in raincoats.

– But Mamaka, they did not speak to me.

– That is good.

– I tried to speak to them.

– You did? You tried to speak to men in the public urinals … with raincoats …

– Yes, I tried to tell them about the kids in the Alsos and how I escaped from them.

– And what did these men using the urinals do? What did they say to you?

– Nothing. They did not look interested. They just kept on peeing.

– Thank God!

– Sorry, Mamaka. I did not know they might have worms and scorpions coming out of their pippis. I should have looked more carefully. And I should have asked them.

– You should have done nothing of the kind.

My mother's look changed. She now looked disgusted but did not say anything. I think she was tired or something. She often seemed more tired recently. If she was in her usual feisty mood, she would have shot down to the Platea of Pagrati and down into the men's urinals in flash. Then she'd be giving a piece of her mind to the old lady taking care of the toilets and any men in long raincoats that happened to be around.

This was not a good time for my mother. Perhaps it was because my father was away. He had been away for a long time it seemed, and would be away longer still. He had gone to America. But before he left he had said that he would have to go for a very important reason. He would go to study for a year or so, at the very important Agricultural University. It was called Rutgers in a place called New Jersey in the United States. He had got a very important scholarship called a 'Fulbright' that was given by the Americans for people to go study in the United States after the War. And he would do a Master's degree in Agriculture studying with very famous and important people. It was for the future. Our future, he said. I could not remember what year it was that my father had left for America. But I do know that it was a period that my mother was not feeling well. As I say she was not her usual self. Maybe that is why I associate the episode of the 'urinals are bad' with her not feeling well. It was just so uncharacteristic of her to not have taken the fight right to the doorstep of the old lady in the urinals. My mother would have oodles to say to the old lady about having parked herself in the damp, dark men's toilet beneath the Platea of Pagrati, and allowing young boys from better families to use the urinals along with the usual riff-raff. After all, my mother had not hesitated to take on the teachers of Pagrati Elementary School about searching kids' heads for fleas and insisting that my hair would be kept long. She started the head-flea fight even though short hair and flea searches were public health regulations. This was hardly the case for children from superior families going down into the urinals.

I think others had also noticed the change in my mother's behavior. Stelios seemed to generally avoid her and not say much to her. Thales would still try to make his little jokes, but when she would repeatedly not answer, he would finally look discouraged. But the most unexpected reaction was from Yiayia Sophia. I figured she would know what was wrong with my mother, so I asked her.

– Yiayia, what is wrong with Mama?
– She knows what is wrong.
– But she sometimes cries, Yiayia.
– She should manage her affairs better.
– How do you mean, Yiayia?
– It is not for me to tell you. Ask her.
– But I have, Yiayia. She will not say or she cries.
– Women should not permit these things to happen to them.
– Which things, Yiayia?
– …

Stelios would also avoid the topic when I would ask him. Thales would just give me a little encouraging smile and tell me she would soon be her old self or change the conversation. So, my last resort was Kyra Maria.

– Kyra Maria, why is my Mama like that. Yiayia will not tell me.
– Oh, she is just depressed Tasouli.
– 'Depressed'? How do you know that Kyra Maria?
– I know because I have seen it often enough. The nuns often get depression.
– Ohh! What do they do then?
– They generally pray more?
– And does praying more make them better.
– No. Usually they get worse.
– And what do they do then?
– They are told to pray less.
– And does that make them better?
– Usually.
– So, less praying is good for depression, Kyra Maria?
– No.
– But praying more then made nuns more depressed?
– No.
– Then what does praying have to do with depression in the nuns, Kyra Maria?
– Not much, likely.
– Then why do they pray more and then less, if they got depressed?
– The psychiatrist said they should.
– Ahh, the psychiatrist, Kyra Maria! Was he religious?
– Absolutely not. The nuns would never hire a religious psychiatrist. You never know what crazy ideas he might have.
– So, why did he tell the depressed nuns to pray more and then pray less?
– To change their daily routine, of course. He always said that was the best thing for depression.
– But why is my Mamaka depressed?
– Because Mr. Phivos left for America.
– But he did it for our future, Kyra Maria.
– For women the future is mostly now Tasouli.

This is as far as I got in finding out what was upsetting my mother. Which wasn't really very far. But actually, the words that Kyra Maria used, like my mother being 'depressed' or having 'depression' helped a lot. I tried out the words on both Stelios and Thales on different occasions. Their eyes immediately brightened up and they each agreed that this was what was wrong with her. She was depressed. So, my conversations with Stelios and Thales became just about normal again. We had determined what was wrong with my mother. And this made it better for everybody. For everybody that is, except for my mother. And also for Yiayia Sophia, who stayed glum throughout that period. She remained convinced that whatever was going on with mother was somehow her own fault.

I have tried to tie the period of my father's absence with other events that I remember then. This is a bit difficult because my father not being home in the Bastille did not seem to have impacted me much. At least it did not impact me in a way that I can remember clearly.

But I do remember a book that made a great impact on me. It is a magnificent book and likely the most favorite book of the Occupation Child. It is called *The Peacock* (*To Παγώνι* or, in Latin phonetic characters, *To Payoni = To Päyoni*). *To Payoni* is made up of 22 exquisite original pictorial woodcuts in color, by John Kefalinos. There is a catchy little epigram for each of the pictorial woodcuts, by Zacharia Papandoniou. These numbered epigrams are also woodcuts but are on the left-hand page while the pictorial woodcuts take up the whole of each right-hand page. The epigrams, many of which are animals talking, and the pictorial woodcuts together tell the story of the proud but self-centered *Payoni*.

Each of the woodcuts shows another animal in their work or function and some commentary by the animal. In some of the woodcuts the Payoni makes snotty little comments to different animals about his superiority. Finally, each of the other animals will have nothing to do with the proud and superior Payoni and will not even talk to him. So in the very last woodcut, the proud Payoni is left all by himself. Night has now set in and the dark-blue sky is illuminated by a single star. The Payoni has roosted on the one remaining branch of a partially sawed-off evergreen. His head is now hanging down on his chest. He is no longer strutting with his head high being all superior. The other animals which the woodcuts portrayed in bright, almost white Athenian sunlight have now disappeared. Behind the lonely Payoni is the ironwork of a cage, but it is not clear if the Payoni is inside the cage or outside. The dark ironwork creates an image of imprisonment of the Payoni. In the National Garden, in the center of Athens where I would often walk by myself or with my parents, there was such a Payoni. It would go to roost in an iron cage and there was an evergreen with a sawed-off branch where the Payoni perched. And once I watched this Payoni when it was starting to get dark. The National Gardens closed at sunset and anyone lingering was asked to leave by the guards. The dusk had set.

I am not sure why this last woodcut was my favorite of all the woodcuts in the Payoni book. Maybe my memory of the Payoni of the last woodcut has been superimposed onto the Payonia, the peacocks, in the National Gardens. They were real enough. They really existed then and they still exist. Perhaps it was because of the real Payoni that I had seen during the setting dusk in the National Gardens. But I think there is another reason. It has to do with the colors of the last woodcut. The blues, the deep purples and the greens, in particular. But these were not the bright blues and azures of 'the color of freedom'. The colors of the last woodcut were more subdued, like what one might get with pastels. Yet they were not pastels. Somehow the effect had been created by the ink layers of the woodcut. I have seen many fine woodcuts in exhibitions in Museums in Europe and North America, but to this day the clarity and precision of the setting of the Payoni woodcuts seems extraordinary to my eye. Yet, the Payoni book was printed in Athens in 1942 and 1943, it says, during the height of the Occupation. How did they get such beautiful dyes, such quality of paper for the woodcuts? Were these materials obtained before the Occupation, that were left over, or were they still being produced in occupied Greece? Who knows if repression and darkness brings out such brilliant and careful work? I remember that some years after I was given the Payoni I got a set of pastel crayons. I think that then I tried hard to emulate the blues and the greens and subdued azure variations of that last woodcut in the Payoni.

Now, the very first woodcut of the Payoni is the title and the names of the artists. This title-page woodcut, like the pictorial woodcuts is on the right hand page. The facing page, on the left, is blank. But this blank page contains a different kind of epigram. It is done in extremely careful, draftsmanship-style handwriting and, if one looks really carefully, there are thin, almost imperceptible drafting straight-edge lines to guide the handwriting. It is just the dedication of the Paγoni to a child. It says:

"To our precious Tasouli
His Yiayia, his Mama, his Stelios and his Nonós
New year's Day 1947"

On initial reading it is benign enough. What could be more normal for the times? My Grandmother, my Mother, my Uncle Stelios and my Uncle Thales (also my Nonos, my godfather) likely had all pitched in together to get me what must have been an expensive but glorious present. In those days, Christmas had not become the commercial holiday it is today and presents were not usually given on Christmas Eve among family members. A nice present would be reserved for New Year's Day. This was the major holiday. Traditional New Year's Day carols would be sung by children who would go from house-to-house, musically accompanying themselves on triangles. It was Agios Vasilis (St. Basil) that brought the presents: exactly as prescribed by ancient Christian tradition. St Basil, the sanctified Emperor, Basil the Great, was born in Caesaria in Cappadocia. This was the famous seat of Hellenic and early Christian civilization of Asia Minor. Later I found out about Santa Claus. I did not understand the idea of Santa Claus. Who could possibly want to get a present from that ridiculous, red-faced fictional character and his silly red-nosed reindeer from the North, in any case? It was totally illogical. Christ was born in Bethlehem, not in some frozen northern tundra full of snow! It hardly ever snows in Bethlehem. And presents were brought to the baby Christ by the Kings — that is what Agios Vasilis literally means — a saint named after the King. Everybody knows this. And, we children were certain that Agios Vasilis would come trudging along, across the mountains and deserts of Asia Minor, carrying presents all the way from Caesaria.

But New Year's Day also had an additional special significance for our family. For my father was born on New Year's Day … the first day of January. Not only that, but because his name was Phoebus, an ancient Greek name, he had to be given by law a Christian name. So he got the name of the Saint celebrated on January 1. This was none other than St. Basil of Caesaria, the bearer of presents to children. So, his Christian name is, in fact, Basil. That means that his birthday and his name's day were both on New Year's Day and both would be celebrated together. And name's day celebrations are at least as big as and usually bigger than birthdays in Greece. Everybody with the same first (Christian) name would celebrate on the same day. A big deal would be made among relatives and friends with the same first name visiting and wishing each other well and maybe bringing little presents and sweets, on their common name's day. But there was also another coincidence. That same day as my father's birthday and name's day is the feast of the circumcision of Christ. It is the first occasion on which the blood of the Christ is spilled and a feast of great significance to Orthodox and Lutheran believers. My father, in later years, made a very big thing of celebrating his birthday and name's day. I had not heard him saying anything about the feast of the circumcision coincidence. Of course he was supposed to be an Atheist Archeomarxist yet he was willing to celebrate the feast of St. Basil, his name day, with great ceremony and gusto. These coincidences all falling on New Year's Day 1947 built up to a very puzzling situation which I must now explain.

After the carols and the presents, the traditional New Year's meal would be served. This would be followed at the end with the New Year's pie, made according to an ancient Smyrnian recipe by Yiayia Sophia and Kyra Maria. The pie would be baked with a valuable coin inside. There would be much discussion and merriment as to who might get the slice of the pie that contained the coin. Whoever got the coin would not only be much richer but would have excellent luck for the rest of year. I think they tried to jig the pie cutting so I would be more likely to get the coin, but I did not get it every year. I did that New Year's Day of 1947. After the pie was eaten what few presents there were would be distributed. So, for New Year's Day 1947 I had got a very nice present. The Pαyoni was the kind of book which I would be expected to keep forever. And, as it turned out, I have kept it.

The Pαyoni had a very nice dedication written for me in the blank page after the heavy cover. But the Pαyoni dedication made questions form in my mind. Slowly, ever so slowly and vaguely at first, but then more clearly as the questions seemed to arise. And then a certain uncomfortable feeling began to overtake me. It is the feeling of familiarity of something that made me uncomfortable, something that made me feel bad that I had totally forgotten. I think I remember that I had asked something about my father and the dedication of the beautiful Pαyoni. But everybody looked as if I should not have asked. I had done something that was bad, but I did not really know why it was bad. Just like going to the Pagrati urinals. And then I started to remember a certain secrecy creeping in about how the Pαyoni was obtained. I can't remember if I asked that question or someone else did. But it was the same kind of deadening response. This topic needed to be avoided also. And I recall a certain distance that my beautiful Pαyoni created. I cannot remember the exact questions that I wanted to know the answers to, but they were mostly around the dedication ... the absence of my father's name. I think I wanted to know many things. But I could only ask the questions of myself ... silently, as I wandered around the dark rooms of Bastille in that cold winter's day. Bastille was cold that day as only the back room, facing the little garden with the high walls was heated with the open *magali*, using a bit of charcoal. The shutters had been pulled in some of the rooms in an attempt to keep some of cold winds of Pagrati out.

But there was a puzzling question in my mind. For some reason, I did not want to ask it from any of the family members in the Bastille:

– Who actually wrote the dedication?

It was almost impossible to recognize the handwriting, because of the careful, draftsmanship-like characters. But I suspect it was that of Uncle Stelios. After all he was the Civil Engineer and knew all about how to write in draftsmanship style on plans for buildings and bridges and the like.

Then there was the question: "who had found and bought *The Pαyoni*?"

It must have been Stelios again. He was most likely to have had connections with the artists and artisans of the day.

– But then, if he found and bought the book should his name not be last or maybe first?

That would have been customary.

– And why was my grandmother's name first?
– Should my parents' names not have been first in a combined, big present like this?

On the other hand Yiayia Sophia was the undisputed matriarch. Maybe she had also opened her little black purse and taken out a golden pound — yes ... golden pounds were still legal tender. These were pure gold coins produced in Cyprus, even after the British golden pound had disappeared from circulation. A Cypriot golden pound would have bought the fine Pαyoni and one would have got plenty of change back.

– Would that have justified her name being first?
Then here is the biggest question of all:

– Why was my father's name not in the dedication?
Of course, I had already said that my father had gone to America after the War.

– But is it not odd that his name would have been left out of such an important dedication to their precious Tasouli?

Especially, since Phoebus was away in far-off America.

159

– And how could it be that my father's was left out from the Pαyoni which was dedicated to me on the very day that both his birthday and his name's day were always celebrated?

And of course it would have been St. Basil, who my father celebrated and was named after, that would have carried my fine Pαyoni in a bag over his back, across the deserts of Cappadocea. By that accounting my father's name should have been first. Certainly not left out.

– So, why was his name left out?
– Yes, why indeed? Could there be other stranger reasons why his name does not appear on the dedication?
– Did they all agree to leave his name out?
After all, this was supposedly a very tight-knit family.
– Were these so called 'reasons' actually accusations against him?

That evening, the evening of New Year's Day 1947, I went to bed with all kinds of foreboding. The voices of my Yiayia, my mother, my Uncle Stelios and my Nonos — my Uncle Thales, were all ringing in my head. They were talking about my father. They were all criticizing him. They were against him. Even my mother was not defending him. I thought I heard her say to someone that it was because he had left for distant America that I had ended up going to the urinals. His absence must have upset me. That is why I had forgotten to go pee before I left school that day and I finally ended up in the underground urinals of Platea Plastira in Pagrati. I was suddenly startled from my sleep with the nightmarish accusation of being abandoned by my own father and being driven to the urinals. But the startle must have really woken me up. I could now think clearly — not in the fog of dreams of a disturbed sleep. So, I figured that I was imagining, I had dreamed perhaps, all of the accusations against my father.

Then I noticed my mother. She was lying in her bed, the big double-bed, with the varnished bed board with the decorative squares. It was very close to mine, in the front bedroom of the Bastille. In fact, it was my mother's and father's bed, except that he was in America and she was in Pagrati. I knew there was something wrong with her. Her breathing was not that of a sleeping person. It was much more irregular. I knew she was not sleeping. And it was much too early for her to be sleeping in any case. I think she was pretending to be sleeping. But then, so was I. For by almost completely closing my eyelids and looking through my eyelashes, I could see her eyes. Her eyes were closed but her eyelids were fluttering. I knew she was not asleep. Just pretending. I would use the same trick myself when I was pretending to be asleep, but my mother seemed to always know. I really did not know what the 'depression', that Kyra Maria had said was the problem with my mother, actually was. But I had also known instinctively that whatever was wrong with my mother was somehow related to my father being away. Kyra Maria had confirmed it. But the bigger mystery was why other family members were turning against my father? Why was my father cut out of being mentioned in the dedication, in the epigram of my glorious Pαyoni?

I started to fall asleep for real with these thoughts in mind, when I heard talking coming from the living room, next to our bedroom. I looked at my mother's bed and she was gone. I listened carefully. The voices were coming through the door made with opaque glass which connected our bedroom with the living room. That door was generally locked and one accessed our bedroom through a regular wooden door that opened into the Bastille corridor. I got up and went to the door with the opaque glass to hear who was talking in the living room. It was Yiayia Sophia and my mother. They were talking in low, subdued voices and I could not hear clearly what they were saying. But I could hear my mother's voice better than Yiayia Sophia's. At least I could hear my mother addressing my Yiayia sometimes as Mamma and sometimes as Sophia. The latter was the familiar appellation, which would not be used in front of others. Also, they were both using the singular to address each other. That was a little unusual too. Yiayia Sophia was of course entitled to address the younger woman in the singular, but my mother would normally address Yiayia Sophia in the plural. Certainly that was the case if we had company, but also when only other family members were present. Even if it was just me, my mother and Yiayia Sophia, my mother would use the plural to speak to Yiayia Sophia. It was just good manners. And of course, I would always use the plural to speak to my Yiayia, but generally I used the singular to address my Mamaka.

There was a nice *kourelou* on the floor by the opaque door and I sat down there, near the door. The voices could now be heard more clearly as they conducted through the crack between the lower part of the door and the floor. I went back to my bed and got my pillow. I thought that my Mama's and my Yiayia's voices would put me to sleep. Like a lullaby. But by lying down near the crack of the door, on my pillow, their voices came through more clearly still. I found that I could not go to sleep now. They were talking about my father. It was not at all like a lullaby.

– He has always been like that, Dina.

– I never thought he would leave me like that, Sophia.

– Once he gets something in his head nothing will stop him.

– But how could he not understand my condition?

– He just sees ahead what he wants to see. You know that, Dina.

– He keeps saying it is for our future. As if that excuses everything.

– It excuses nothing. And this thing about the future …

– What about it, Mamma?

– It is really what he wants to do.

– I've never tried to stop him from what he wants to do. You know that Sophia. I've always been by his side.

– Oh, I know my good Dina. But it has got nothing to do with you …

– … I just wish he was more considerate. In my condition, now …

– He has to have the competition …

– You know, Sophia, I have not slept for days … endless nights … forebodings … nightmares …

– I know, Dina, believe me … I know.

– But why America now? He could have waited … a year or two. America is not going to float away.

– He made up his mind. He was going to do it now. You know Stelios got that big government contract about a year ago.

– Yes, right after that he said he got that scholarship to study in America. The Fulbright.

– These Americans and their money … they control us all, Dina.

– He could have waited, Sophia. They told him he could have.

– He could not have waited, Dina. Not after Stelios got the big contract.

– What does Stelios have to do with me?

– Nothing, of course. But he could not let his brother be more important.

– He would cover it all up, Sophia. With his Rutgers and his Master's and his Archeomarxism. But of course he was doing it all for our future. Ha, ha … for a while I tried to believe him …

– But you know … he believed it, Dina. He was always like that.

– And during the War … when he was up in the Front … in the snows of Albania … when I didn't know if I would ever see him again … and during the Occupation and the years before, when they were hunting them … to kill them like animals … we were so close and believed in the same, the very same … does all of that mean nothing?

– I had three sons in the Front, Dina. I could have lost them all.

– And I have lost my very self. Everything I was, or I thought I was, I have lost.

– But you have Tasouli. You have Tasouli, Dina.

– Oh it is for our and Tasouli's future, our and Tasouli's future he would say, Mamma. Just another pawn, another debating point to win the game.

– And does Tasouli tell you anything about his father being away?

– He has said nothing. As if he hasn't noticed. But then he goes to the Pagrati urinals.

– But that was just once, Dina. He just had to go pee very badly.

– I don't know. I don't know, Sophia. Maybe he was looking for men. Maybe to find his father there. Who knows where his imagination takes him. I cannot sleep. All these things never leave my mind. I don't think I will ever sleep again.

I did not like to hear all of that stuff. My mother and Yiayia Sophia could go on talking forever. They were criticizing my father. He had said that he left for America for our future. What could be more important? Could they not just leave it at that? I took my pillow from the kourelou and put it back on my little bed. I wanted to sleep. But I couldn't. I started to become afraid that I was catching my mother's insomnia. I hoped I wouldn't catch her depression also. Then I would never sleep again. I stayed with my eyes open for a while listening to the now distant voices of my mother and my Yiayia. But fortunately my beautiful Ραγoni was on the little bedside table. I started to look at it by the dim light illuminated through the glazed glass door from the living room. Soon I started to drift off thinking about all this conflict. If only Styppas was here, he would be able to figure it out. But Styppas was probably still mad as a raging bull after the Doppia episode in Zakynthos. He might try to extinguish me … by impalement no less! Nevertheless it was worth the risk. No one else could help me out of this horrid mess. I had to find him. I would try to be on my best behavior with Styppas. I would try not to be too pedantic, although it was he who told me that I should become pedantic and that is how the problem between me and Styppas started. I should try to find him … unless of course he appeared on his own. Gradually I grew tired of all this thinking, while watching my mother through my nearly closed eyes and pretending to be asleep. Finally I fell asleep for real.

~

It did not take me long to find Styppas this time. I found him straightaway in Kingston. It was morning and he was having tea with Pamela. But they were not having tea in the kitchen or the dining room. Not at all. I found them upstairs in the bedroom. They did not see me come in and, I guess, I had not made myself too visible yet. So I had the opportunity to look around and observe them for a while. I don't know why I had not seen before all the paintings hanging around on the walls. They were all reproductions of Impressionists, mostly in nice, decorative frames. Stelios had taught me all about the Impressionists, so I knew their names and recognized their styles. These were all portraits or figures by Renoir I think. There was a huge naked lady behind Pamela wiping herself with a towel beside some kind of rural stream in the French bucolic countryside. I remembered the naked ladies Tougias used to paint in Plaka, but his were much more angular than this really rounded out French lady. I figured if the naked lady in her huge frame ever fell it could do serious damage to Pamela or the bed board of the humongous-sized bed. Then there was the portrait of the young man, with a little beard with wistful but very spooky eyes. I carefully moved along the wall to avoid his spooky look but his eyes just followed me. Right across from the spooky-eyed Rodin there were two sisters sitting together in a garden bench. They were surrounded by vegetation in beautiful spring colors and not at all spooky. But on the other wall, across from the naked lady, there was another young girl who had a look in her eyes that made me think she was from outer space or something. She was enough to give nightmares to anyone sleeping in that room.

Pamela had been sitting up in bed with her pillows all nicely fluffed behind her back against the bed board. Styppas was sitting in a comfy leather armchair across from her with his legs crossed. They both had these strange mugs of tea resting comfortably on their laps. Styppas' mug was the stranger of the two. It was tall and shaped like an urn. But instead of being decorated by some ancient motif, it had these ridiculous cats, standing on their haunches and stupidly smiling and licking their chops. There were three of these felines, one colored in blinding yellow, one in a nauseating bright green and one with an equally unworldly, bright red hue. Pamela's tea mug was also kind of weird in its own way. It had a white background with thick sea-blue circular, parallel stripes so it looked almost like the Greek national flag. It also had a big chip on the lip. Why she drank her tea out of a chipped cup like that was a mystery to me. They were unceasingly talking about something that was in the morning paper and seemed to be totally involved in some kind of major discussion. Styppas was doing most of the talking and gesticulating mostly with his left hand since he was holding the stupid cat mug with his right. But Pamela was talking nearly as much, coming up with point after point to support her position. I had no idea why their discussion was so vigorous first thing in the morning, while they were still in their bedclothes and having their morning tea. Particularly since they seemed to be saying more or less the same thing.

I must say though, it was a bit unfair that they would be sitting so nice and relaxed, endlessly discussing, while I was having all these problems. Nevertheless, I tried to be as polite as I could. I used my sweetest Tasouli voice — the one that I frequently employed when my Mama got mad at me and I would address her as my *Mamakoula*. Unfortunately, in these circumstances, my voice would always come out high pitched and whiny:

– Good morning, Styppas.

Styppas, startled on hearing my voice, just growled at me. My unexpected appearance had not put him in a very good mood. But at least he took a sip of his tea from the nauseating feline urn. But Pamela, who initially was startled even more, was very cheerful.

– Good morning, Tasouli. What are you doing here so early in the morning?
– Oh good morning Pamela. Another disaster has befallen me! I think it is worse than when I lost my marbles.

She looked at me with a little smile. She made a slight downward movement of her head, to convey a mixture of encouragement and emphasis:

– Each new disaster just seems worse than the previous one, Tasouli. Is that not so Styppas?

Styppas just growled again. But at least there was no green spit coming out of his mouth and he was not growing hair out of funny places in his body. Also, I noticed he took two sips of tea this time, which I interpreted to be a good sign. Pamela, in the meantime, was either unperturbed or being very brave with Styppas.

– We should hear what disaster befell Tasouli this time, don't you think so Styppas?

Styppas growled for a third time, but now I thought that I had detected a tone of consent in his growl. Still, I thought it was a bit chancy to speak to him directly, so I thought I would continue to address Pamela mostly:

– My mother has become very depressed, Pamela.
– Oh! That is not good, Tasouli. Do you know what has made her depressed?
– I am not sure, Pamela. I think it might have something to do with my father. He left for furthest America, you know.

Styppas gave me a strange side glance, but at least he did not growl. Pamela was all sympathetic:

– That could do it Tasouli. Maybe she just misses him.
– But, Pamela, he had said that he did it for our future.
– Hmm. For women the future can be now.
– That is strange you should say this, Pamela. Kyra Maria said the same thing.
– Kyra Maria must be a wise woman, Tasouli. But was there anything else that was strange?
– Oh yes, Pamela. I got as a New Year's Day present, the beautiful Pαyoni book with all the woodcuts … and it had this dedication …
– And … ?

I could see from the side of my eye that suddenly Styppas was paying attention to what I was saying. But I thought it best if I continued to address Pamela:

– Well, this dedication in the Pαyoni had first Yiayia Sophia, then my mother, then Stelios and then Thales.
– So?

Anastassiades

– Well … my father's name was missing …

I thought Styppas had been struck by a thunderbolt!! The stupid cat mug nearly flew out of his hand as he jumped up gesticulating and shouting:

– Missing? Missing? You mean they left it out!
– That is what it seems like, Styppas.

Pamela looked slightly uncomfortable:

– I have to go to the bathroom. You can discuss this among yourselves.

So, Pamela heads off to the bathroom. She took a gaudily illustrated magazine with a big crossword puzzle with her. She did not intend to return soon. Finally I had Styppas' full attention. Here was my chance to find out what really happened to my father. Why the rest of the family had turned against him. But I had to be careful not to enrage Styppas. So, I put on again my best sweetie *Mamakoula* voice, high pitch and all:

– But why would they have left my father's name out, Styppas?
– It was Stelios. Stelios! He was behind it.
– But why, Styppas? Why?
– Long standing conflict between Phoebus and Stelios.
– But why, Styppas?
– Stelios was favored by their father, your grandfather, Tasouli.
– How was he favored, Styppas?
– It is a very long story. But just before Stelios went to university, their father agreed to buy very special Engineering books for Stelios.
– What kind of Engineering books, Styppas?
– All the construction standards and specifications and the like for Civil Engineering.
– Why couldn't Stelios buy them himself?
– Stelios did not have any money then. He was just starting University. He had been admitted to the Polytechnion in Athens. The most prestigious University Faculty in Greece. So he insisted that he needed these books and his father bought them for him.
– But did he really need them, Styppas?
– That is the big question. They were terribly expensive and most students would not own them. They could use the library copy or other less expensive books, I suppose.
– So, how did my grandfather get the money? He was not well-to-do after the Great Catastrophe.
– He certainly was not. But they had been given an extra land allotment in Nea Smyrni somehow. So your grandfather sold the allotment to buy these expensive books for Stelios.
– My father would have resented this later on.
– Resented it! He talked about it continuously in later years. The property that was sold could have been developed into apartments, he'd say. And everybody in the family would have been well off.
– Oh … I can see why my father would not have liked that, Styppas.
– He most certainly did not, Tasouli. But it got worse. Much worse.
– How is that?
– The first day Stelios took these very expensive books to the University they were stolen.
– That must have enraged my father Phoebus. Is that right, Styppas?
– You can say that again! Phoebus, being a couple of years younger than your Uncle Stelios, still did not have his University path cut out for him.
– So, my father finally went to the Faculty of Agriculture in Salonica, which was much, much less prestigious than studying to be an Engineer in the Polytechnion in Athens.
– Exactly, Tasouli. And then Stelios went on to set up his own civil engineering company and

164

now they are getting some very big contracts from the government.

– Oh, I know that Styppas. There are many manual workers in Stelios' company digging the great water tunnels in Northern Greece. They will bring water from everywhere to Greece.

– Yes, it is a very big project; Stelios has made and is still making a lot of money from it.

– I know Styppas. And Stelios likes to entertain all the workers. He had them all for a big dinner and party in the Bastille not that long ago.

– Yes. He likes that kind of thing. And he can afford it.

– While my father's means are much less. Working for an Agricultural company. Importing the fertilizer 'Chilean Nitrate'. Down in Syndagma.

– And Phoebus resents Stelios' business success.

– I think so, Styppas. Although he does not talk to me about it. But does this mean that Stelios could have bought the brilliant Pαyoni himself? I mean, without Yiayia Sophia having to go to her little black pouch and pull out the golden pound?

– Of course, Tasouli. He could easily afford it. No problem.

– But Phoebus wanted to become an agriculturalist, is that not so Styppas?

– Yes and no, Tasouli. It is rather complicated. You have to understand the prehistory of your family.

– Oh … Styppas … the prehistory! But why did Yiayia Sophia and the rest agree to exclude my father from the dedication of the beautiful Pαyoni?

– Yiayia Sophia blamed him for being the cause of your mother's depression. And your mother probably the same. And Thales likely just went along. In any case, Stelios had probably already made the draftsman-like dedication of the beautiful Pαyoni before he showed it to the rest. Who knows exactly how it happened!

– But my father was well-intentioned. He went to study in America for our future he said.

– And for political reasons.

– Ohh! Always the Archeomarxist politics, Styppas!

– And to be as important as Stelios. Perhaps, even more important.

– Ohh … still is it not strange that Yiayia Sophia would have sided with one son over another? Would she not have asked Stelios that Phoebus' name be included in the dedication, Styppas? Particularly since it was dedicated on New Year's Day — both the birthday and the name day of her second son. She could not have forgotten that?

– No, it is impossible she had forgotten that.

– So, why then?

– Resentment and punishment. Resentment and punishment, Tasouli.

– But such a special day … such a special day … Styppas. Even the important Christian observance of the circumcision of Christ fell on that day. I know that they were not religious, except perhaps Yiayia Sophia a little, but …

– I am sure that the spilling of the first blood of Christ did not escape their attention, either, Tasouli. Especially Yiayia Sophia. And Stelios also.

– But to what purpose, Styppas? To what purpose?

– What better way to punish an Archeomarxist than to ignore him on the day that first blood is spilled!

– I don't know about big hate between brothers, Styppas. I never had a brother.

– Best not to know, Tasouli.

– Best not to know, what?

– If you had a brother.

– What do you mean, Styppas?

– Never mind.

– No, I want to know, Styppas.

– Look, Tasouli. Just pretend Giannakis was your brother. At times you hated him, right? Like in Pyrgos when you split your head.

– Oh, he made me hate him totally, Styppas. And that was the first time that I spilled my own blood. By dropping the giant rock on my head … while trying to squash Giannakis.

165

– So, brothers could hate each other like that and still be close.

– I understand it now, Styppas. Just like me and Giannakis. Except Giannakis was not my brother. And he was not even favored over me by my father or had expensive engineering books bought for him that he lost. But still, isn't it odd that Yiayia Sophia would want to punish her second son so much? She said she did not favor one son over the others.

– Maybe it had something to do with your mother.

– Oh?

– You know … her depression and things, Tasouli. And how she reacted when you told her that you had been down into the Pagrati urinals.

– But what connection could there possibly be with my mother's depression and her behavior about the urinals,

with Yiayia Sophia wanting to punish my father?

– Oh … Tasouli. I should not be telling such things.

– No Styppas … please tell me. Pleeease …

I could hear my voice getting high pitched and whiny again. I was not even doing it on purpose this time.

– Ok, Tasouli. I can't tell you everything. You are too young. But I will give you a clue. OK?

– OK, Styppas. Just the clue then.

– Joujoukos.

– Joujoukos?

– Yes, Joujoukos, Tasouli.

– But how can my Joujoukos have anything to do with Yiayia Sophia wanting to punish her second son, even if it was because of my mother's depression.

– I said it would just be a clue, Tasouli.

– But my Joujoukos was an important revolutionary hero during the Occupation … that wouldn't have anything to do with it, Styppas? Does it have anything to do … like being all tangled up in politics?

– I said, and we agreed, I would just give you one clue, Tasouli. But I can tell you, it had nothing to do with Joujoukos' revolutionary politics during the Occupation.

– I didn't think so, Styppas. Too bad you won't tell me. But it is fair enough. We agreed that you would just give me a clue.

– You've become so reasonable, Tasouli. You are not being pedantic.

– I haven't given up becoming pedantic, Styppas. But you haven't been talking or arguing about language, either.

– True, Tasouli. We have had a much nicer conversation about family and their camouflaged conflicts.

– Language just has much bigger arguments and fights, Styppas.

– But we must not give up on language, Tasouli. There are important issues still to be resolved there …

– I feel a lot better now, Styppas. So, I think I will go back to the Bastille and sleep there. I think I will sleep well.

– Good bye, Tasouli. Sweet dreams.

– Oh, thank you, Styppas. Say hello to Pamela … when she comes out of the bathroom with the giant crossword puzzle in that sleazy magazine of hers.

– It is called 'The Globe', Tasouli. And it is pretty sleazy.

The Corruptors

Later in the '40s Thales had started up a clinic in Central Athens. I don't remember the exact location but it was not too far from Maraslion. In any case, I could walk there from Pagrati or could take a tram. So sometimes I would go there just by myself or with my parents. Thales must have finished his training then in Otolaryngology, because this was a private clinic in which he also did surgery, such as tonsillectomies and the like. It was common in Athens then to have private medical clinics of this type. I think most of the surgery he did was in-and-out cases but he also had a half a dozen beds or so for overnight stay. Thales, as always, was full of confidence about the success of his enterprise, and I think he may have got some investors to put up some money for the startup of his clinic.

For a long time I think that I had sore throats on and off. It seems a fairly trivial matter now but this was still in the pre-antibiotic period, and people were terrified about getting rheumatic fever from a streptococcal throat infection. This could develop into rheumatic heart disease from which people could die. In our own family, my mother's sister Marina had died supposedly from rheumatic fever and so had Rikos, the great friend and cousin of Thales. But at the time of the 'Corruptors' Rikos was very much alive and in full throttle of his socializing and joking, his ultra-fashionable dressing. He was much as we found him, after he had come out of his glum teenage years in Steptonakis' store. In any case, my mother's anxieties would be exacerbated each time I got a sore throat. So, when Thales qualified in Otolaryngology and started up his clinic she would run to him, with me in tow, to his clinic. I remember some of their conversations.

– I cannot take any responsibility about this any longer, Dina.
Thales was unusually stern. There was no question in his mind about what needed to be done.
– But can we not wait a little, Thales. His sore throats usually subside. Having his tonsils out is such a big step.
– Come and I will show you, Dina.
I was made to sit in the big surgical chair with all kinds of metal handles for adjusting position and some kind of opening clamp was stuck in my mouth to keep it open, and a bright light was aimed at my throat.
– See his tonsils. They are red and inflamed and enlarged! There could even be some pus there.
– But they often look like that when my Tasouli gets a sore throat.
– I tell you, Dina, I cannot take responsibility if he gets rheumatic fever.
– Don't say that, Thales. I will not let my own child get rheumatic fever.
– You can't prevent it. The only way to prevent it is to have his tonsils out.

My mother looked horrified, but I knew I was in for it. I was going to be subjected to having my tonsils taken out. A tonsillectomy had been ordered by Thales. Of course he was going to do it himself, and I had unshakable confidence and love for my favorite uncle. Except that he looked a little worried. I suppose things could go wrong with a tonsillectomy, like a lot of bleeding, they said. But they did have those beds in the clinic which were generally unoccupied.

So, the day came for my tonsillectomy with much anxiety from my mother and a supervisory silence from my father. I was made to sit in the same operating chair, except the clamp to keep my mouth open was put in much more tightly, and so extended that my jaws hurt me. It was quite unpleasant. Particularly, since I could not swallow my saliva. Then things got much worse. Thales prepared some syringes with immensely long, thin needles, which he proceeded to stick into the back of my throat in order to freeze it. It was one of the worst sensations in my life. The needles hurt a lot more than I expected and the bitter almost burning taste of the anesthetic was awful. I could swallow it and I just kept gagging. More awful still was that I could not spit out anything because of the opening clamp. I made a valiant effort to get rid of the clamp and spit out the vile taste but they restrained me. I think there was a big nurse standing by who was as strong as a bull and took no nonsense. I started to whimper and had tears in my eyes, but no one paid any attention to me. It was also unbelievable that my most favorite uncle was paying no attention to my distress. He was busy preparing all kinds of long scissors and tweezers with which he started to remove my tonsils. I started to bleed and he looked very worried. If the taste of the local anesthetic was vile, the mixture of blood and anesthetic was absolutely nauseating. In any case, the surgery seemed to go on and on. I think he had some trouble getting all of my tonsils out. Finally, it was done and I was rushed off to one of those beds with all kinds of packing in my throat, which felt even worse. I can't remember if I stayed in that bed for a few hours or overnight. Everybody's anxiety about me made things worse.

However, my survival of the tonsillectomy seemed to have somehow elevated my status with Thales, from the child nephew to something slightly up the scale from child to adult. And this elevation of my stature, I think, is the reason the trouble really started.

Thales' clinic was on one of the higher floors of a fairly old Athens building and one had to take these wide old wooden stairs to get to the clinic. I don't remember an elevator but perhaps there was one — multilevel buildings generally had elevators in downtown Athens. But there was another set of stairs from the clinic that went up. These stairs were much smaller and hidden away. You would not know they were there unless you knew what part of the clinic to go to. After my tonsillectomy and the gradual elevation of my status, I was casually invited to go up those stairs. They led up to the very top floor of the old building and there, almost separate from the clinic it seemed, was a room with glass on its roof like a little studio. I think some of the panels could be opened like skylights. Perhaps it was used as an atelier by an artist in years past. It would have been ideal for that. I think there was a tiny kitchen with a small stove and a little bathroom that were off the studio room. The studio room had a table in the middle and a sofa, which one could sleep on. Maybe Thales slept there on occasion if he had a sick patient staying in the clinic overnight. I remember going up there when it was raining in the winter. It seemed magical when the winter rain would hit the old glass roof; it was all framed in by a copper frame that had turned green with time. All kinds of patterns would form on the old glass panes from the rain. I could watch these patterns forever. If I sat on the sofa, I could see the roofs of taller buildings. And if I stood on a chair I could make out, between the taller buildings, many of the red-tiled roofs which still existed then. Clothes lines with washing seemed to connect some of the taller buildings and there were people moving in and out of balconies. Swallows and other birds often nested there unbothered by the people. And if I was lucky, I might catch a glimpse of a Joujoukos-like cat ruling his domain. I was soon transported into another place, the magical surroundings of old Athens' rooftops.

Thales was then married to the beauteous Ourania, his classmate, who by then had either qualified or was studying to qualify in Pathology. And Thales, Ourania and Rikos made up an inseparable trio. Their personalities were similar and, to some extent, so was the way they dressed as well as their behavior. Any time I visited my Uncle Thales in his clinic after hours, I knew I would find the three of them in the little studio room. As soon as I went up those narrow wooden stairs and opened the door I would enter a different world. A world that was totally different from the intellectual and straight-laced world of the Bastille, which was so full of serious cultural and secretive political discussions. Here in the studio-room hideaway merriment ruled. I could hear their laughter from the stairs. Rikos' laugh had the highest pitch and a care-free wildness about it, that made it resonate the most and almost seemed to dominate the others. Thales' laughter came through as a counter point to Rikos' hilarious, loud jokes, a little lower in pitch and always ever-reassuring. Ourania did not have a high pitched laugh, even though she was a woman, and her laughing voice was often the most ironical. It seemed to incite Rikos to tell even more outrageous jokes.

I would usually find the three of them sitting around the little table playing cards. They were dressed immaculately. Rikos would be in one of these white silk tailored suits and matching tie, the ultimate dandy and ladies' man. Thales would look really handsome in a casual shirt. Ourania would be dressed in a fashionable slinky black dress with a showy décolleté which accentuated her blue eyes and her black hair, all nicely cut and combed back. I had no idea why they were all dressed-to-kill like that. They never seemed be in any hurry to go out. I had formed the impression that in order to have a really good time you really had to dress up as an adult. All three smoked cigarettes incessantly. The whole little studio apartment was filled with a dense bluish smoke. It took a little while for me to get used to it, and did not bother me after a while. The excitement the three of them generated made me feel unbelievably good. I felt exhilarated for no clear reason. For I did not really understand their jokes which, I think had to do mostly with sex and outrageous stories of people they knew. Some of the words they used in their jokes were also not familiar to me. I think they were slang or off-color expressions or their own vocabulary. They projected a sense of superiority over the rest of the world. Not the kind that my mother tried to convey to me that had to do with education and status, but rather because they told the best jokes, dressed the best, had the best time and knew the newest best fads in society. They did not seem to drink much, but in the middle of the table was a bottle of Scotch whiskey. Scotch would have been unusual in Greece at the time. It was part of their avant-guard image, as it was foreign. They just took tiny little sips from small glasses in between cigarettes. I didn't understand their card game either. It was not for money, but each hand seemed to generate an immense amount of merriment. All I knew was that I wanted to be like them. I figured that if I could learn their card game, perhaps I could be as happy as they were.

As soon as I would step inside the room they would welcome me with smiles, loud greetings and amusing comments. Thales would usually break out in a big smile.

– Ah, Tasouli. You've come to visit us. Well done.
– Oh, Uncle Thales, I walked through the National Garden and down to Syndagma to visit my father at his work, but they said he had gone out. So, I thought I would come here. Rikos' loud infectious laugh resonated.
– Maybe he went gambling!
– Oh, no, Uncle Rikos. My father does not gamble. He does not even play cards. He is an Archeomarxist, remember?
– Who can forget it! Ourania, with the sarcastic little turn in her humor, cut in.
– He certainly will not let us inferior souls forget it! But Thales was always the great compromiser and pacifier.
– Tasouli, these are just little jokes. Rikos and Ourania admire Phoebus.
– I know, Uncle Thales. But Uncle Stelios also says my dad has superior morality. There were peals of laughter from everyone now. Rikos, behaved as if it was the funniest thing he had ever heard.
– Is that right, Tasouli, even Stelios says that Phoebus has superior morality!

There were lots of giggles and laughter now. Even Thales could not keep a straight face and I saw him give a little wink to Ourania and Rikos. More cigarettes were lit up and there were sips of the Scotch from the little glasses. Somehow my comment about what Uncle Stelios had said about my father seemed to greatly elevate my status. They were all smiling and complementing me. Thales was the first to do so.

– Tasouli is an excellent reporter about everything that goes on in the Bastille.
– Thanks, Uncle Thales. Rikos was roaring with laughter again.
– Tasouli, you must not tell him about smoking and cards and whisky here. And Ourania, half joking, half challenging, always ironic:
– And certainly do not tell him that there is a den of vice here!

More giggles and laughter and meaningful looks to each other would follow, among the cigarette puffs taken theatrically and the playing cards held high and thrown down on the table with gusto and showmanship.

In spite of my elation and enjoyment of the joking conversation, I felt a bit dubious about my loyalties. I knew that my father was very strict about what was permitted and what was not, but telling jokes and laughing and smoking certainly did not seem bad. I convinced myself that my father would not be upset if he found out what the trio was up to. But I was worried because I had a propensity to talk too much, as I wanted to tell everybody about everything. So, I kept quiet in the Bastille about exactly what I did during my visits to Thales and his clinic. Even when my father asked me what I had done after I had gone to his office and not found him, I simply said I had gone up to Uncle Thales and visited him for a while. My father seemed to be pleased.

And back in the Bastille when my father saw Thales return later that evening he proudly said:

– Tasouli said that he came to visit you in the clinic, after he could not find me in the office.

Thales merely encouraged this little conspiracy of misinformation,

169

– Yes, Phoebus. He walked all through Athens by himself. He is getting to be grown up. We had a really nice time together.

My father's eyes twinkled with pleasure and he smiled approvingly at me.
But then, one day, my luck changed.
I had again gone to visit my father in his office in Syndagma and again he was away. Again I was greeted warmly by his colleagues. I think it was Andoniades, his closest colleague that would pay the most attention to me. He was likely at the same level at work as my father. My father's office was in the company that imported natural fertilizer for the peasants, as I have mentioned. The fertilizer company, 'Chilean Nitrate', was established and owned by a very important man, Chrisos Evelpides. He was from an old wealthy family and I believe he had served as Minister of Agriculture in one of the pre-war Governments. I understood that in spite of his wealth and patrician origins he held generally liberal views. He and his wife lived in an old luxurious apartment facing the National Garden, right next to the old palace and the parliament buildings. It was exactly across Syndagma square, where the offices of 'Chilean Nitrate' were located. Mrs. Evelpides was an excellent violinist and they held birthday parties for children in their luxurious apartment, at a time when birthday parties of this type were unknown in Greece. It was during one of these birthday parties that I ate the little salami sandwiches and I thought I had entered fifth heaven. The Evelpides had no children of their own. When they held these birthday parties for children, the children all dressed up in nice frilly clothes and behaved very properly. Mrs. Evelpides would sometimes play the violin. They seemed to regard these children at their birthday parties as wondrous beings, created primarily to exist and behave just right. I did not particularly like the birthday parties. Except for the little salami sandwiches, that is. So, when I visited the offices of 'Chilean Nitrate', Andoniades was always the friendliest.

– Ah Tasouli, your dad has again stepped out. Sit down in that nice chair. He will not be long.
– That is OK, Mr. Andoniades. I just came for the outing — through Zapion and the National Gardens.
– Oh, that is a good walk from Pagrati! Can we bring up a sweet for you while you are waiting, Tasouli?

This was a common practice then. There were lots of sweets and coffee shops very near most downtown offices. When anyone wanted a coffee, which was more often than not, somehow the 'boy' from a local coffee shop would appear. The service provided the Greek coffee boiled in tiny individual little coffee pots with the desired amounts of the coffee powder and sugar. All the variations between coffee strength and sweetness seemed possible. The 'boy' would bring the coffee made according to the exact specification in the little heavy, white porcelain coffee cups sitting on matching tiny coffee saucers and the statutory glass of Athenian cold water. Coffees and waters all sat on a solid metal tray with a wide lip, which he carried suspended from three chains attached to the tray. Who exactly had called the 'boy' and how he had the coffee made so quickly was always a mystery to me. Sweets, usually in the form of fruit preserves, would also be ordered and brought up on occasion.

– Oh, no, thanks very much, I do not want a sweet right now.

I really did not feel like sitting in the big, somewhat stuffy office, full of endless bookshelves all piled up with old, dusty papers and books. It was all about agricultural practices and ordering and accounts of fertilizers and the like. The people that worked with my father were all nice enough to me, but they all seemed preoccupied with their dusty papers and old typewriters.

– I can take you downstairs for a proper pastry, if you like Tasouli.

I had to think quickly. I liked Mr. Antoniades alright, but I would much rather explore this part of Athens by myself. So, I said the very first thing that came to my mind.

– That's OK, Mr. Antoniades. I think I will go and visit my Uncle Thales at the clinic.

I only said this as an excuse not to be stuck with having to have a long polite conversation. I didn't usually turn down an offer of a pastry treat.

– Alright, Tasouli. I will tell your dad when I see him.

So, I left and went on with my wanderings. But now the idea of visiting my Uncle Thales was embedded in my brain. I knew there was a good chance I would find Thales, Ourania and Rikos, the inseparable Three Musketeers, in the little apartment above the clinic joking and smoking and drinking the whisky. Their jokes and edgy conversation would be a thousand times more exciting than sitting with nice, polite Antoniades in a pastry shop waiting for my father!

I wound my way to Thales' clinic. I rang the doorbell when I got up to the floor where his clinic was and was met by the immense gruffy nurse who had helped hold me down when I was having my tonsils extracted. I was as polite as I could be.

– Is my Uncle Thales here? I would like to see him, please.

She gave me a disapproving look, looked up to the sky as if to say 'what is the world coming to' and pointed with her head upstairs all without saying one word.

I scrambled up the stairs all excited that I would find the trio having again the time of their life. I was not disappointed. As soon as I opened the door, Rikos' voice shrieked in excitement:

– Tasouli, Tasouli! You came at the best possible instant … what an unbelievably funny story Thales was telling …

They were all roaring with laughter. Thales was looking at me with tears in his eyes from laughing so much.

– When your mother … Dina … thought you were bitten by a scorpion in Rafina … and I had to tell her that story that you must have got immunized by all the bee stings you got in Pyrgos … Ourania, who was also almost in tears, finished off the story:

– And the night before Thales and I had seen this Journal article about people getting sensitized to wasp stings …
– But, but, Auntie Ourania, what is so funny about this? Thales said to my mother that he had seen a recent article in a Medical Journal.
– Tasouli, Tasouli! They were getting terrible reactions from other types of bites …
– Ohh, Auntie Ourania … you mean if you were first bitten by one kind of insect you could get bad reactions from other kinds … like the opposite of what Uncle Thales told my mother?
– Bravo Tasouli! Bravo, bravo Tasouli … you got it.

Their merriment had no bounds. How I wished I could be like them … to laugh so easily and so much about all kinds of events, all types of people. Even about what might have been a serious event … like my scorpion bite. I did understand that they were making fun of my mother and my father too, and I felt a little uncomfortable about that. But Thales and Rikos started imitating my mother about the scorpion episode and her running to the neighbors so full of anxiety, thinking something horrid would happen to her little son … even when I was so well. Somehow, I found myself laughing with them. But my merriment was cut suddenly in mid-stride.

The door had flown open.

Anastassiades

The laughing Trio froze,
Faces now motionless
Budding from fancy clothes.

Birds plumed so colorful
Rendered stock-still by fear
The snake has now found them
Feathers cannot protect them.

Somehow the image of these two snakes, dark and gray, swerving and trying to stand up on their tails in our bathtub had flashed through my mind. It had happened in Pyrgos and I had totally forgotten about it until that instant. We had been away for some time and when we returned my mother found them in the deep, cast iron, white enameled bath tub in our little country house. My father regarded them with analytical curiosity. But my mother said they looked poisonous to her. They could be asps. Like the asp that Cleopatra presented her famous breast to. And it was presented in a manner that the asp had to bite it. In this way ended both Cleopatra's life and the glorious reign of the Ptolemy dynasty. Every schoolchild knew that story. And my father loved it. He loved it, even though no one has ever accused the Ptolemies of being Archeomarxists. It was about the principle and sacrifice above all. So my mother ran out and got one of the local farm-hands. He confirmed that they were asps. They might have got in through the drain pipe to the bathtub. He took them out on a long stick with a little noose and killed them. I felt ambivalent about these asps. On the one hand, I was afraid of them but, on the other hand, I admired them. They had a single purpose to all their movements: to get out of the deep bathtub. In their own way they were beautiful.

In that instant that the door of the rooftop den had flown open and my father was standing there, something strange happened. His terrible look and momentary silence froze Thales, Ourania and Rikos. But as I looked from my father to the trio, their fancy clothes — their fashionable dress changed into colorful plumage. Maybe I transposed them to the dreamy colors in the woodcuts of the plumage of the glorious Payoni. Or maybe I saw them wearing feather coverings of other beautiful birds. I can't remember with certainty. But I do remember one thing clearly.

It was right after that instant that the storm erupted.

I had never heard such invective from my father. Screaming at the top of his voice about the treacherous behavior of the trio, about how they did not deserve to be called human beings let alone progressives and revolutionaries. How they were worse than the Fascists. They were betrayers of principles and of decent human interactions. How they were harbingers of corruption, responsible for all of the counter-revolutionary sleaze, vice and dishonesty that Society would ever face.

The diatribe seemed to gradually revive the trio from their paralyzed state. Thales was the first to gradually mount a defense. Of course, he knew his brother best. He had heard this kind of attack before. Probably many times. He tried a bit of his infectious humor. It was to no avail. Ourania tried her ironic remarks. She was met with an even bigger attack and a stare of accusations against her of unspeakable things. Rikos tried to appeal to friendship among cousins. He was dismissed as a piece of lightweight, dilettante garbage.

Finally, the trio started to get over their shock. They lit up new cigarettes. It was clear that they would try to disregard my father. So Rikos shuffled the cards and started to deal them out for another game. Ourania even offered my father a drink of scotch to calm him down, she said. I think she knew he did not like, or could not tolerate, strong drinks.

That did it! My father grabbed me by the hand and he pulled me out of the den of vice, storming down the stairs and out into the street.

– But, Baba, why were you so mad?

He gave me that look, which made me feel like an ignorant insect and said nothing. But, as usual, I could not keep my mouth shut.

– But Baba, they were just having a good time. They were telling many funny jokes.

Again I got the frozen look. And again, of course, my anxiety I think, made me continue.

– And Baba, they were just smoking. And playing a very funny card game. Although I did not understand their card game, *Babaka*.

I could see my father softening a little. I knew that soon he would start to speak to me again. After all I had called him in the affectionate diminutive *Babaka*.

– The things they were doing are all despicable things the *petits bourgeois* do. They cannot call themselves progressives. They cannot be on the side of the proletariat with this unacceptable *petit-bourgeois* behavior.
– But Babaka, they were so nice to me. And they were having such a good time.
– That is exactly the point, Tasouli. They were corrupting you.
– Corrupting me, Babaka?
– Yes, corrupting you.
– But why would they be corrupting me, Babaka?
– Because they are corruptors.

Corruptors sounded really serious. I did not want to have to face another diatribe on behalf of the proletariat. So, I stepped up the charm offensive by resorting to the possessive affectionate diminutive to address my father in a voice that became higher pitched and whiney:

– Corruptors, *Babaka mou*?
– Yes, corruptors. Corruptors of the worst kind.

1950 — 1951

Entrance Exams

During my sixth and last year in Maraslion, it was decided that I should sit the exams to enter a prestigious Gymnasium (high school in North American parlance or Grammar School in Britain). The name of this Gymnasium was Varvakion Model School. It was chosen after endless discussions and consultations in the family and among the relatives. The educationalists, including of course the rabbits, were brought into full force. Varvakion it was to be! I am not sure if all children at the time were expected to sit these types of exams. After all I was just eleven. But in my case at least, I was not really given an option. Preparations for these important exams were started and a special preparatory teacher was hired to work with me after school. I don't remember very much about this teacher. I don't think she was too intrusive. Certainly she had nothing to do with the hated caterpillars, since English was not taught in primary school and would not be part of the exams set by the prestigious Varvakion Gymnasium. Also, I had to see her just a couple of times a week for an hour or so when she tested me. She seemed to think I was doing well enough. I guess what was taught at Maraslion fitted with what was expected at the great Varvakion.

Now, there was a big problem with all of this. My father had decided that we would all go to Canada for at least a year, so I would likely end up in a Canadian school for grade seven. He had obtained a one year post at the National Research Council in Ottawa for some kind of agricultural research project. He must have caught the bug when he went to Rutgers in the United States, to do a Master's degree. That of course was the year that he was punished by my mother coming down with depression and by everybody, it seemed, by leaving out his name from the dedication in the beautiful Payoni. The latter punishment far exceeded the first, at least in my mind. Nevertheless, I was told that I had to sit the great Varvakion exams, in case we came back after a year or so, and this was the time to do them. That logic made me feel slightly better about taking the exams and possibly failing them, but only slightly. My anxiety about having to take these horridly demanding exams just kept increasing.

After all, only a small proportion of students that took the Varvakion exams actually scored high enough to get in. The number seventy seems to stick in my mind. That is, seventy out of the hundreds of kids that took these cursed and inscrutable exams. You had to be on the list of the first seventy to get in. If I did not make the list, I would be a failure in my father's eyes and likely also my mother's and the rest of the family. I would surely be judged to be inferior. I would have betrayed them. Even if I could learn to enjoy myself like Rikos and his friends, I would be regarded at least as inferior as he was by my father.

The night before the exams at the Varvakion, I had trouble falling asleep. I did not think I was actually prepared. The preparatory teacher had not tested me on things I did not know. Only on things I already knew. Something was wrong.

But it was not long before the ironic yet reassuring voice of Styppas cut into my restless anxiety.

– Ah. Tasouli, you are tossing and turning.
– Oh, I am glad you are here, Styppas. These exams in Varvakion tomorrow— they will surely test me on things I do not know.
– How do you know that?
– What is the point of testing me on things I know? If every child was tested only on things he knew, how could they choose just seventy out of all those taking the exam?
– They don't know what you know or don't know.
– But they will soon find out, Styppas. And then they will keep testing me over and over again on things I don't know.
– First, your fears are unfounded. It is just your obsessive and pedantic attitude. And you are already starting to irritate me.

– And what is second, Styppas?

– Second … oh, yes … you know, you are not the only one. Just about every child in Greece has to climb this long ladder. If it was intended for him to become an academic citizen, that is.

– Ohh, I know, Styppas. But what is really at the end of the long ladder?

– The great guillotine of course!

– The great guillotine?

– The great guillotine that sharply divides white collar from blue collar.

– And when will the great guillotine fall on me?

– Not for a long time. Not until the end of the Gymnasium, namely grade twelve.

– I suppose that is good, Styppas. I mean that the great guillotine will not fall on me for a long time. But then tomorrow, the little guillotine will fall.

– But you did not have to prepare for the little guillotine like you would have had to for the great guillotine. You only had a preparatory teacher who just tested you on a few things you already knew. This would have been very different if you were preparing for the great guillotine.

– Oh, I've heard about the preparations for the great guillotine. My cousin Theodore Zed in Nea Smyrni is already preparing for the great guillotine. That is all he does. That is, when he is not telling strange jokes about girls.

– You can't even imagine what preparing for the great guillotine is like, Tasouli. For several years before the great guillotine falls parents who had hoped that their children would become white collar academic citizens, spent all their attention, and often all their savings, in the preparation.

– You frighten me, Styppas.

– Oh, yes! It is expensive to send a child to a preparatory school for the great guillotine. Working class women, without means often have to do endless menial jobs as domestics for richer families in order to earn a few drachmas. They even starve themselves so their little treasures can go to preparatory school.

– Don't say these things to me, Styppas. You worry me more before I have to stand before the little guillotine tomorrow.

– You need to know all of this, Tasouli. So you can understand why you must not fail your parents at the little guillotine tomorrow. These preparatory schools are all private and many of them are very expensive. Not like the free education in ordinary public schools. Then, finally, finally after the years of preparatory schools, your time would come to be tested by the great guillotine.

– Ohhhhhh … I don't feel well, Styppas.

– You will feel worse in the future.

– But maybe things will change in the future. Don't you think so Styppas?

– Not a chance! Things will get worse.

– But we will go away. We will go to Canada. We will escape thinking about the great guillotine.

– Wherever you are, the great guillotine will follow you. And it will get worse here. When the time of the great guillotine comes every year, everything will seem to stop. Wars, natural disasters will hardly even make the papers. It will all be about the great guillotine exams. They will be the national exams, after all. The identical exam will be taken everywhere in the country. Great secrecy and intrigue will surround the setting of the great guillotine exams, which try to find out what you don't know.

– Pleeeease, Styppas! Don't tell me anymore. I will not be able to sleep. Ever again.

– The only thing which will be important will be to slave at the after-class preparatory schools. You will be paying less and less attention to the gymnasium lessons. In the preparatory school you will only be prepared for the fall of the great guillotine. You will not need to pay attention to anything interesting that the teachers teach in the gymnasium. Only the great guillotine and the great guillotine alone is what is important.

– But that is horrible, Styppas. Look at all the interesting stuff we learn at Maraslion. Like History. All about the French Revolution and Napoleon Bonaparte and the Greek Revolution. And the Industrial Revolution. And …

– Ha! History! That will not count for much when the great guillotine falls. Being able to solve any type of mathematical problem — that will count!

– But I like History, Styppas. I like it a lot.

– And difficult grammar. And Katharevousa. And Ancient Greek. They will all count.

– But Styppas, whose head will the great guillotine cut off?

– Why, the heads of the inferior ones of course.

– And who are the inferior, Styppas?

– The ones who will not make it to University, of course.

– And what will become of them?

– They will be condemned to being lowly, of course. Like manual workers. You know, blue collar workers.

– Like those that go the urinals in Pagrati, Styppas?

– That's them.

– And the guillotine will not cut the heads off the superior ones.

– Of course not. For they will go to University.

– But that will be hard for them, Styppas. I mean once they reach University. They will have dozens and dozens of little guillotines that they will then have to face. With all the difficult courses they will have to pass, I mean.

– Noooo!

– No … , Styppas?

– Of course not. Once you survive the great guillotine and you get into University, it is easy-street then.

– You don't face little guillotines anymore?

– Naah! You could fail a hundred times all the courses and nothing ever happens. Once you have survived the great guillotine you have become an Academic Citizen. No one can do anything to you.

– But you would have to work, Styppas. Wouldn't you? To make a living, I mean. So you could eat. And maybe even have the occasional salami sandwich.

– Naah! Your parents would pay for you, for as long as you are in University.

– And how long would that be, Styppas?

– Uh, for years and years and years. For as long as you want. You don't really have to pass any exams for the courses they teach. You can keep failing them time after time and no one minds. You are an Academic Citizen after all.

– And what do Academic Citizens do, all that time in the University, Styppas?

– Ehh! … drink coffee at the outside cafes, smoke a lot, talk endlessly to other students, wear nice clothes, play cards and tavli, tell jokes about girls …

– I know, Styppas! Like Uncle Rikos. He was in University forever doing all those things you described.

– Exactly.

– And is this how he learned to have so much fun with Thales and Ourania and to become such a good Corruptor?

– Exactly.

I awoke to face the day and the little guillotine of the Varvakion entrance exams. The alternative course of missing the exams, as explained by Styppas, would be a blue collar existence and passing a lot of time in the urinals of Pagrati. Of course if I was chopped off by the little guillotine today, it would not automatically mean that it would be Pagrati urinals for me, but it would be a step in that direction. And I already knew the dread my mother would have had if I even thought about a blue collar existence and the urinals. But I still had not figured out what was really wrong with the urinals. Faced with the little guillotine, I started to think of them in their subterranean location as an abode one could escape to. Maybe, I could go there after the little guillotine. Maybe the men frequenting them and the old woman cleaning them would speak to me or at least acknowledge my existence. But I knew that if my mother found out I would be toast. None of our family had ended up like that — peeing in the Pagrati urinals. They were all superior. Except for my Zakynthian relatives, all of whom were peasants after all and often peed in the fields. But they never seemed to be considered in my future. Nobody ever asked me. But if they had, I would have told them that the Doppia and the other olive trees, the lemon and orange trees, the vines, the chickens and the wise, protective Tassia were all big pluses for a career on the farm. But I would never have been allowed to be a peasant.

So, I showed up somewhat anxious for the first day of my exams. The long discussion with Styppas during the night, about the educational guillotines and my future, had made me bleary-eyed and I was not feeling too bright. To make matters worse, my mother announced that she would accompany me to the Varvakion exams. I objected.

– But Mamaka it is not necessary. I can go to the Exams by myself.
– What kind of a mother do you think I am? Not to be there when my child is taking such important exams!
– But Mamaka, these are all day exams. You can't wait for me.
– Oh, yes I can. What if one of these examiners is not fair to my child? Or other children try to get an advantage?
– But Mamaka, the exams can go on for more than one day.
– I told you. What kind of a mother do you take me for? It does not matter how many days the exams take. I will take you there and back.
– But why there and back, Mamaka? I know how to get back.
– Unthinkable! Who knows what could happen walking back after these exams. You could be traumatized and taken advantage of.

She had now put on the big sour expression on her face. She was not going to let me out of her sight for this really important beheading. Any post-beheading reprieve in the urinals was also out of the question.

These cursed exams were quite comprehensive and I think they stretched out for a couple of days. They were both written and oral. The written part was the longest and was first, I think. It included all types of math questions. I ploughed through them without having any clear idea whether I had got the answers right. Then there were long answer questions in history and religion and geography and I can't remember what else. Something that mildly surprised me was that the questions were set in *Demotic* Greek rather than *Katharevousa*. I assumed that I would be permitted to answer in Demotic. But I did not have time to ponder that issue as I needed all the allotted time to finish the questions.

Finally, I was done with the written part and started on the orals. The orals were much more intimidating. There were many examiners sitting more or less next to each other on a very long desk in a large, old hall with great windows. These were the Varvakion professors, no doubt. High School or Gymnasium teachers were all called professors, while the term 'teachers' was reserved for primary school teachers. The great hall had large windows situated behind the professors. These professors all looked similar. If I ran across one of them in the street, I don't think I could tell which one it might be. First, they were all middle-aged men with serious expressions, all dressed with well-worn jackets and ties. Second, I think nearly all of them had little beards and wore wire-rimmed glasses. They seemed to work more or less in pairs, even though they examined on different topics. I noticed they would often nod to each other. Each student would stand in front of this row of examiners and would move from his right to the left. I was surprised that there were more math questions that one had to solve on the blackboard. If you got stuck, an examiner might give you a clue or ask a question. With some of these math problems, even though I had not finished the solution, I was again surprised to have the examiners tell me to move along. I was not sure if that was a good thing or a bad thing. Then I moved away from the math section to language and arts topics. I was under the impression that I was managing well the questions in geography, ancient history and the like. Then suddenly they threw a real surprise at me.

– Would you prefer to be examined in history or religion?

The examining professor who asked that question looked much like all the others. I looked at him carefully. I thought I could detect a little smile in his eyes behind his wire-rimmed glasses. In a flash I knew that I was in very dangerous territory. He was not talking about ancient Greek and Roman history. I had already done that. No, he was talking about modern history. I would have to discuss the French Revolution and Napoleon, the Greek Revolution and its various leaders and their politics and perhaps even the Russian Revolution. I loved modern history. I disliked religion, with all the Councils and their heretics, the dogmas of the Orthodox and Catholic Churches, the controversy whether it was the Father or the Son that propagated the Holy Spirit and the like. It was endless memorization. But could I trust this professor? Could I trust any of them? If I chose history, one slip could expose my family's politics. The professor could then ask me if my father felt the same way. Anything in modern history I could be asked could expose his Archeomarxist politics. He could then be arrested, exiled, tortured and even extinguished. Maybe other members of my family would follow. I would have betrayed them all.

– Religion, Sir.

The little smile behind the glasses seemed to disappear.

– Religion?
– Yes, Sir. Religion.
– Are you sure? Don't you find history more interesting?

What a horrible dilemma. I was so tempted to say 'history'! Modern history, which I really liked and my family talked about all the time. Why was I putting myself in this situation? I looked again at the professor. He seemed animated and even a little excited. He now had a definite smile, through which he was slightly showing some rather strangely malformed, nicotine-stained teeth. I took it as encouragement to tell the truth about how much more I liked history over religion. But I couldn't.

– I am sure, Sir. Religion.

He gave me a strange look. The smile had totally disappeared from his face. His expression of animation had gone. His voice seemed bored.

– Very well, then. Religion.

This was the last station of the oral exams. I was finally finished. I had no idea how I had done overall. My mother was sitting waiting for me with a superior smile. I wanted to pee. There were bathrooms with boys' urinals in Varvakion, but when I indicated that I wanted to go she put on the sour expression and said there would be a better place outside for me to go. There was a big eucalyptus tree outside and she indicated I could pee there. I did while she stood guard.

I soon forgot about the Varvakion exams. The goings on in Bastille and the streets in Pagrati totally preoccupied me. Also, my parents were running around getting important visas for different destinations in Europe. It was all part of our going to Canada for a year. We would visit different European capitals and meet important people. But a couple of weeks later my father came in all excited and proud-looking. The results of the entry exams for Varvakion had been posted. I was accepted! In fact, I had done quite well. I think my parents said I came in 17th or something of the 70 children that were accepted. All my conflicts and worries about not betraying my parents by choosing to be examined in Religion rather than History had dissipated. I had made the right decision. I had easily got in without chancing being examined in History. I briefly debated with myself whether I should tell them what really happened, and that if I had chosen History I might have done better still. But I decided against it. I said nothing. Instead I bathed in the glory of approval from my parents and the Bastille family and their friends.

That night I went to bed early. I felt so happy and warm that I just wanted to go to sleep in my own little bed and have sweet dreams about my success. For everybody said what a superior boy I was. There was no fear now that anyone could ever consider me inferior. No chance at all!

But as I was falling asleep, I wondered if Styppas knew of my success. Probably he did. He seemed to know everything about me. But it might be best to tell him in any case. Just to be sure. In this way my great success would be complete. Also, my success in the Varvakion exams would likely help patch up the episode in the Doppia in Zakynthos when he got so mad at me because I wanted to execute Socrates twice. Of course executing Socrates even once, let alone twice, was a serious matter. And I knew that, to some extent, it was my fault he got so mad. After all, I had irritated him at the start by suggesting that goaty Tassia knew more than him and that my goat was superior to his Pamela. And I had never given him any credit for finding out that the real reason why Socrates was executed had to do with language, and him explaining it all to me according to the research of Havelock. That must have really riled him, since our relationship had evolved all around language, from the very start. And he had gone to a lot of trouble to understand how the beginning of written language led to the execution of Socrates, so he could explain all to me. On the other hand, I thought that he had gone a bit far by threatening to extinguish me. By impalement no less! No, that was a bit extreme, for sure. And I wanted to have a nice relationship with Styppas — like we used to have in the past. So, here was my opportunity to fix it all up. This would be an additional success for me. And everything would be truly perfect in my life.

So I set off to find Styppas. It was not difficult for he was in his usual hiding place in Kingston. It was dark outside. He was sitting in a big leather chair in the living room reading a book by a lamp. The lamp was the only light and it provided just enough light to read under a yellow-orange cloth lampshade, on a little wooden stand. He looked agitated and was reading the book intensely. He did not see me come in the dark living room. I squinted to see the book he was reading. It was "The Muse Learns to Write" by Havelock. It was the same book that had caused all the trouble in Zakynthos when I was hiding in the hollow of the Doppia. Immediately I sensed that this was not going to be a good outcome. But I was still optimistic. I would tell Styppas about my success at the Varvakion. Surely he would not be angry at that. So I tried to think of a nice opening to the conversation. It would be best if I did not mention the book. The wooden reading lamp looked kind of interesting and old, so I tried that.

– Hello Styppas. That is a nice lamp for reading.
He startled. He looked angry. I could tell it was a bad start.
– What's that to you?
– Oh, nothing Styppas. I was just commenting on the lamp.
He seemed to soften momentarily. His face did not look as tight.
– I made it myself.
– It looks old.
– Well it is.
– Styppas, I came to tell you some very good news.
– What's that?
– I got in at Varvakion … I passed the exams …
– I know all that crap.
– But how did you know Styppas? And why are you calling it crap?
– Because you are full of crap.
– Me? Full of crap, Styppas?

I could tell that I was in big trouble from Styppas' tone of voice. And he had never used an expression like that before, even when he got really mad and was growing hair everywhere. Right now he was not growing hair but he would not answer me. He pretended I did not exist. He was just silent. It was awful. I just waited and waited in silence. He knew I was getting more and more uncomfortable. Finally, I could not stand it anymore. So, I said nervously, my voice becoming higher and more pathetic:

– I did well in all subjects I think, Styppas. Even religion.

I guess that must have been the wrong thing to have said. Styppas exploded. He started shouting. Hair was now growing out of the middle of his forehead:

– You idiot! You absolute idiot!
– Why an idiot, Styppas?
– Do you think your parents picked Varvakion without knowing who the teachers were?
– Who were the teachers, Styppas?
– Progressives, of course. Democratic progressives. What is the matter with you — couldn't you tell, you idiot!
– How, Styppas? How was I supposed to tell?
– By their appearance of course, stupid! By their appearance!
– But how by their appearance, Styppas?
– They all had little beards and wire-rimmed glasses of course. And wore worn jackets and ties. And sat in a row, so no one appeared more superior from the rest. What more do you want?
– Ohhh!
– Ohhh! Ohhh! That's all you can say: Ohhh!
– But Styppas, I was afraid. I was afraid I would betray my parents. I didn't know they were progressives.
– You certainly managed to betray them! You idiot! I should extinguish you once and for all.

Cold sweat was now running over me. Styppas was growing hair everywhere and some green spittle was coming out of the corner of his mouth. I tried to speak, but only a high pitched squeaky voice came out:

– But how did I betray them, Styppas?
– What the hell is the matter with you? By choosing to be examined in religion rather than history, the teachers thought that your family was religious and only pretending to be progressive, so that you could get in. What could be a worse betrayal than that!

All I could do now was squeak. I could not form sentences.

– Ohhh!

I think Styppas meant the part about extinguishing me. Betrayal like that was very bad. And choosing religion to be examined in had made things worse. I now remembered how I got a little carried away during the exam on religion and related to the professor examining me the story of Athanasios Diakos. And how he was impaled by the Turks at the beginning of the revolution. The professor reminded me that this was history and I was being examined in religion, but I retorted that Diakos was a religious leader as well. The professor had looked rather peculiarly at me and had not said anything. I had obviously mixed up the two topics and in the process betrayed my parents. I knew it now. This was it! Styppas would extinguish me by impalement. Just like Diakos. I tried to explain how I got mixed up to Styppas, but all that would come out was my pitiful high sound:

– Ohhh!
– Stop your ohhhing! With your behavior you deserve to be extinguished not once but twice. Just like you wanted Socrates to be executed twice. Just in case you have forgotten!
– Ohhh!
– Everybody is now ridiculing your parents about how you chose to be examined in religion, when they are supposed to be progressives.

– Ohhh!
– Worse still, the gossip and ridicule has spread around Athens, and bad tongues are whispering that they used a child to cover their radical Archeomarxist tracks.
– Ohhh! Ohhh!
– This places them in serious risk for their lives. The Stalinists were waiting for something like that. They can now bring charges against them for high immorality and would have justification in ordering that they be abducted, secretly tried and then extinguished.
– Ohhh! Ohhh! Ohhh!
– Stop your ohhhing!

I could barely see clearly now. Styppas seemed to be in a haze. Hair had grown out everywhere and a big wad of sticky green stuff was coming out of his mouth, sticking to his mustaches. It was the worse I had seen him. Somehow his awful sight revived my voice slightly. It was still pretty squeaky:

– How would my parents be extinguished now, Styppas? How would the Stalinists do it?
– The guillotine of course! Had you not heard? In their last congress they adopted the guillotine for the execution of traitors — just like Robespierre in the French Revolution. It all was directed against the Archeomarxists.

I ran as fast as I could to try to find Pamela. There she was calm as anything, having a cup of tea and looking outside at her garden.

– Pamela, Pamela you have to save me. Styppas is going to extinguish me.
– He is not going to do that.
– Yes he is. By impalement, like Athanasios Diakos.
– This is just your imagination, Tasouli. Come and see the beautiful magnolia tree in the garden. Look, it has flowered!
– Ohhh! Ohhh!
– Don't you think magnolia is even lovelier than the willow tree?
– Nobody can save me now … Ohhh! Ohhh! Ohhh! Ohhh! Ohh …

I sat up sweating. I was back safe in the Bastille. In Pagrati. Away from Styppas' lair in Kingston, where he had been transformed into a merciless monster.
But it was still dark. No one was stirring in the Bastille. I could hear my parents' regular breathing. They had not been abducted by the Stalinists. At least not yet. I closed my eyes and started to drift off.

Impaled I am now suspended
By willow and magnolia trees
No pain just thirst thirst thirst
Endless endless is the thirst
And Ilingos
The distant mountain
Slowly slowly spins
But does not fall
Like I will
Yet I cannot fall
Impaled
And Ilingos

The light reflects

Off the lagoon
Willow tree twisting
And twists twists
Branches swaying
Around me move
Round and round
They'll make me fall
Yet I cannot fall
Impaled

And Ilingos
Vertigo spinning down me
Down into abyss of gray
Disrupted only by the thirst
Thirst that's untouched
Unchanged

And hope for pain
For blinding rushing pain
To take me out of the abyss
To take the thirst away
The ripping pain
Of the gut
The flashing lights
Of the traverse
And then recover
Consciousness
To hear the impaler say
"He seized"
"The bugger seized on us"
A voice that's Styppas-like

And pain now
My older pal
Who came so long ago
Has left
He's left forever gone

But now they will take me
Take me to another place
Near the distant mountain
Up to a hill that's timbered
And standing there waiting
On fresh-cut planks of pine
Smiling smiling smiling
A Styppas-like smile
Is now my Executioner
For me to be beheaded

His guillotine all shining
Like an asp it coils
It strikes and strikes against me
But it cannot behead me
A branch of the magnolia tree
Like a willow stretches
around my chest
And near my neck sticks out
And turns and twists
Against the steel
As if it was wind that bent it

But the guillotine is striking
Still striking over all again
And the willow branch
Is breaking it's falling away

Yet in the cracks
Within the branch
White petals now sprout
And sprout and sprout

Anastassiades

And spread athwart
The guillotine's entwined
It can no longer coil up
And like an Asp attack me
Its blade is now quiet
And it has lost its shine

And white petals coalesce
Flowers they're turning into
White, white Magnolias
They're blossoms with no color
And I wish they would become
Anemones dreamt so purple
And blue and red and yellow
And I could dream and dream
And dream anemones of Pyrgos

But white, white
death-white Magnolias
Is all that's budding out
White blooms the willow
And not a drop of color
Then I hear raindrops fall
Yet it's blinding sunshine
But I can see the rain form
Blood red in heat white

Now I know my own blood
From my neck is oozing
And dripping down, down
On the Magnolia blooms
It streaks their petals white
Fine lines of red, blood red
Are spreading through
The dead, dead white

Then the branch of the willow
With which I am now joined
Now turns to a Magnolia tree
And grows and grows outside
And I am within the tree itself
Watching its blossoms fade

And dropping from the Magnolia
Red-streaked the petals white
Spinning squall they turn, turn
Turn and now I twist with them
And I spin and spin in Ilingos
The vertigo never leaves me

For within the petal streaks
Red arteries now pulsate
A beat that's so familiar

It's my own pulse I hear

~

– Tasouli, Tasouli! Wake up!
– Ooooh!
– Why were you hitting yourself?
– I was not Mamaka.
– Yes you were. On your neck.
– The guillotine, Mamaka.
– The guillotine? What guillotine? You were having a bad dream. A nightmare.
– Yes, Mamaka. The guillotine. And then the Magnolia.
– Don't be silly. It was probably the scorpion bite.
– The scorpion bite, Mother?
– Yes. You were hitting at the scorpion that bit you on the earlobe. Remember in the Dammaki. In Rafina. That was your dream.
– OK, Mamaka. It was the scorpion bite then.
– Of course. I would know. I am your mother. But we cannot waste time. Tomorrow we will be flying to Rome. To start our very important trip through Europe.

It was often like that. My mother knew better than me what caused my dreams. It was the scorpion bite on my ear that made me think I was being struck by the guillotine. I did not even tell her about the impalement. She would have really freaked out. Or how the willow branch turned into the Magnolia. I would never have heard the end of that. In any case, there was no point in arguing. We were preparing for the great trip to Europe and then we would be going to Canada. I knew it was real since the past few weeks had been a flurry of running to embassies to get visas, to exchange money and to do all the other important preparations.

Europe then

Rome

We departed from Athens on July 11, 1950. I know the date because it is in my mother's passport, on which I was added. Both her photograph and mine are there well-preserved in black and white. The entry stamp is for the Rome airport. So we must have flown from the old Athens airport to Rome. A Visa for Italy (as well as for the other European countries we visited) is duly stamped and paid for. I have no recollection of the departure or arrival of this trip, but another airplane trip, the first I had ever taken, is embedded in my mind. It is strange that I would have no recollection of the flight from Athens to Rome itself, yet clearly remember that I was thinking about this earlier airplane trip.

This other airplane trip must have been about two years earlier from Athens to the island of

Crete. I remember the airplane had a noisy propeller and we went through a lot of clouds and came down in rain. In Crete we went to Chania, an old and important city on the island. Chania was an agricultural and commercial center. Perhaps we went there because of my father's agricultural business with the Chilean nitrate fertilizer. What I remember most about that first trip with an airplane was that we visited an antiquity. It was near Chania, I believe, but it might have been Knossos which is some distance away. My mother made it seem as if it was the most important antiquity in the world and we were the most important people ever to visit it. But my impression was exactly the opposite. It was a miserable site with a bunch of stone walls, many of which were to the height of my knees, partially excavated. No palaces or goddesses anywhere, as my mother kept saying, dominated this incredibly great excavation. Instead it was rain. Rain, light drizzling rain, coming down continually. And it was penetrating to the bone. I could not understand how something so incredibly important could be so incredibly miserable.

Perhaps, it was the drizzle which has somehow connected the flight to Rome with my very first flight to Chania. For when we arrived in Rome, I think there was drizzle as well. That is the only explanation that I have, about connecting a previous memory as the only recollection that I have of the flight to Rome. I should remember that flight, leaving Greece, and yet I do not.

Rome had many impressive buildings, all old and very heavy looking. We climbed up to a great piazza on higher ground, where one had a great view of the city. The piazza was laid with marble tiles and formed this immense lookout surrounded by a low decorative wall that you could lean on and made up of urn-like small columns. I have an old photograph of my mother and myself leaning on the wall. It must have been taken by my father. I remember wondering why such a giant piazza would be nearly deserted. In Athens, or anywhere in Greece, it would have been full of people, talking, reading their newspapers, playing *tavli*, or at least playing with their *koboloi*, and crowded outdoor cafes surrounding the piazza would have abounded. In Rome fountains were everywhere, sprouting water from weird parts of the anatomy of all kinds of massive sculptured figures. Nothing like that in Athens, where water was always in short supply and would not be wasted sprouting out of strange sculptures.

I do not recall the Italians as being either particularly friendly or hostile. They were just going about their business in a rather self-absorbed manner. They did not look with interest or curiosity at us, and I do not remember any of them trying to start up a conversation. They all seemed a bit depressed to me. Perhaps it was after their defeat in the war, and the come-down from the expectations built up by Mussolini and the Italian Fascists that they would again have a great Roman Empire, extending into Greece, Asia Minor and North Africa. Perhaps it was just that they were trying to make a living under difficult post-war conditions. But they were certainly not like the friendly, gregarious Italian prisoners-of-war, behind the German barbed wire in Pyrgos, who would beg me over to show me pictures of their children and give me candy.

One day during our stay in Rome was devoted to a special visit. We were going to visit the great Maria Montessori. She was of course the leader of the important educationalist friends of my parents, the rabbits. We took trams and buses to distant neighborhoods of Rome, where there were massive old stone houses, each one with great iron doors and marble or stone stairs to climb. Then we had to go by foot through eerily quiet streets lined with these stone houses. Only the occasional passerby could be seen and my parents would stop them and ask for directions to the house of the great educationalist. Finally we found the house. We climbed the immense stone stairway and rang the bell of this huge decorative, massive iron door. No one responded. They rang many times and still no one. Finally, we started to go down the stairs when my mother went up again for one last try. Surprisingly someone answered. She was a small Italian, middle-aged to older Italian woman who seemed generally annoyed and was gesticulating, indicating that we were not to go in. We surmised she must have been a housekeeper or something like that. My parents were not easily dissuaded. They pulled out letter after letter from the rabbits and other educational notables, presumably introducing us to the great signora Montessori. I wondered what language the letters were in. But it was to no avail. The little Italian woman had absolutely no interest in the letters, in any language. Her gesticulations became more and more rapid, indicating simultaneously with one hand we could not go in and with the other that her mistress was not in. Finally, my parents gave up and we left.

Surprisingly, they did not seem upset or disappointed with the dismal failure of our long trek into the distant, forbidding Roman neighborhoods. Quite the opposite. They were laughing and obviously pleased with the adventure. After all, they were the only ones, possibly in the whole of Greece, which had ever visited the great signora Montessori's home. Better still, they were one up on the rabbits. By the time we got back to the hotel that we were staying in, I was pooped. But my parents' merriment and endless discussion went on into the night.

From Rome we went to Florence by train. I do not remember much of Florence, other than my mother loved it, and went on and on about how much she loved it for years to come in Canada. She had bought a lace placemat for a coffee table, since Florence was so famous for its lace. She said that all the Zakynthians knew how prized Florentine lace was, so it was an indisputable fact. I do not remember what happened to the famous lace placemat. But I do remember a gaudily painted hand-fan made of straw, with 'Firenze' in bright yellow letters over a purple background. Actually, the hand fan came in handy during the hot Montreal summers and survived for many decades in the Dinion.

Lausanne

On July 18, 1950 (dated on my mother's passport) we crossed by train into Switzerland. Our destination was Lausanne. I remember the polite but very careful, Swiss uniformed train conductors checking our passports. I only have a vague recollection of the trip, but a clear memory of the large, well-organized train station in Lausanne. How clean, yet ever so busy it all seemed! As soon as we got off the train there was a familiarity about this station.

And a promise.
A promise of excitement.
A promise of travel far away.
A promise of freedom.

Had I seen the Lausanne train station before? Maybe in a periodical? But I do not recall. As I stood on the platform, trains kept coming in and out. People poured in and out, but somehow all orderly. The trains were all on time. Famous destinations, like Geneva and Zurich, were being announced. It seemed that all one had to do was get on the train to go to these magical places. There was no fear on people's faces. They travelled effortlessly, as if it was completely ordinary. As if they had always done it. I could have stayed there and watched for the rest of my life.

Finally my parents came to get me. We were going to get a taxi to our Hotel, 'The Lord Byron'. Or maybe it was the hotel where the Lord once stayed. In any case, the Lord sat on a beautiful and magnificent site. It was near the lakeshore of Lake Geneva (Lac Léman). I had never seen a lake like this. The water was a bright, reflecting blue. It had a calming influence. It was different from the azure-blue seas of the Aegean or the almost green-blue of the Ionian waters around Zakynthos. These seas always created a feeling of excitement and pleasure in me, especially if I saw them again after an absence. The absence could be only a night or even a few hours and this feeling would invariably overtake me. It would usually last for a few minutes and then I would become used to the colors and reflections of these Mediterranean seas. But here, the great lake was surrounded by distant mountains on one side. And immaculate gardens on the grounds of the hotel along the coast framed the other side. Perhaps, it was this enclosure of the water by the mountains and the regulated gardens that gave Lake Geneva this calming influence, yet depriving it of the excitement of the Greek seas.

The hotel room we had was magnificent. I think my mother had negotiated endlessly with the man at the desk and we had ended up with a suite on the ground floor. There was a lovely glass enclosed veranda-like extension facing the gardens and Lake Geneva. And there was a living room space, all with nice furniture made of polished wood and beautiful chairs with decorative padding depicting mountain scenes and gods and goddesses. We certainly never had anything like that in the Bastille. I might have seen chairs like that in the Evelpides' luxurious apartment near the National

Gardens in Athens, but of course my father's boss was wealthy from old money, while we were poor. In later years, I've often wondered how my parents could have afforded that trip, let alone the imposing hotel of Lord Byron.

However, the pièce-de-résistance of the Lord Byron suite (or so my mother called it) was the bathroom. It was made from some kind of polished marble, with a huge bath that had immense brass faucets. When I tried them, huge amounts of water poured out. The water could be adjusted to any temperature! This was amazing to me, being used to the Bastille or Rafina, where water had first to be boiled in the gaziera and carried to the bath and then used very sparingly and carefully so you did not burn yourself. But it was the amount of water that came out of these brass spouts that made the biggest impression on me. I had never seen so much water running out of a spout. Even the Roman fountains did not have as much water, or so it seemed. Running water was so limited in Greece. Often there was no running water, especially during the Occupation. When it did run, it came out of small, old brass or iron faucets and the stream was not strong. But it tasted OK and was safe to drink. Except for Rafina where even though the water was safe to drink, it tasted very brackish. And, of course, except for Zakynthos where there was no running water at all. But there, the water from our spring was safe to drink and tasted the best of all. The water here at the Lord Byron in Lausanne had almost a sparking quality. I thought the taste of it would be out of this world, but it was not. The Zakynthos water from our spring and the Athens water tasted at least as good. But I was usually very thirsty then. Especially in the summer.

Finally I thought I should try to take a bath at the Lord. My mother was smiling a smile of great encouragement and pride. I had never taken a bath before with enough water to cover my body. The massive amounts of water ran into the giant marble bath and soon covered me. And then the water kept pouring out and pouring out. No one knocked on the door to tell us to stop wasting water. The water never became colder or hotter from what I had adjusted it to. I could not believe my eyes or the luxurious feeling that all of this clear warm water created. I lounged and practically floated in the giant marble tub. And there were immense thick white cotton towels to wipe myself with. Each of these towels must have been five times the size of what we had in Bastille and even bigger compared to the scrawny little towels in Rafina. After my bath I tried the bed. I lay down among luxurious fluffy pillows and covered myself with a strange light but layered covering. My mother, in great excitement and pride, said it was a *duvet*. I had never heard or seen of a duvet before, but it felt immensely comfortable and soporific. I was asleep in a jiffy.

~

Surely Styppas and maybe even Pamela would like to know about The Lord Byron and the light blue color of Lake Geneva and the giant marble bath with the immense spouts and endless water. But in my dream now, Styppas was still going to be pretty grumpy and ready to start sprouting hair if I irritated him anymore. After all I had ended up being impaled and guillotined because of him, if not by him. And I was barely saved by the willow and the magnolia tree. Yet I had to tell Styppas. He would get over the big misunderstanding over my condemning Socrates to death, twice. But he was still smarting from me trying to protect my parents by choosing religion over history in the Varvakion entrance exams, and ending up making it really tough for them. Right now I had to put all of this out of my mind and concentrate on how to find him. I knew how to go from the Bastille in Pagrati to Kingston, but I had no idea how one gets from The Lord Byron in Lausanne to Kingston. So, I figured I might as well go up to the Lausanne train station and see what I could find. Maybe, if from there I travelled to Geneva, everybody would know how to get to Kingston.

So, I made my way to the Lausanne railway station in light drizzle and a descending mist. I wandered over the glistening cobblestones of narrow nearly deserted byways. Finally there was a wider street heading downhill and to the right was the *piazza* of the grand old station. I wandered through the station out to the platforms to check the trains. I noticed that I was protected from the light rain by a giant roof. It covered the platform, but not the track itself. I looked up at this elaborate roof. If I could climb up on it I would be able to see everything. But it did not seem possible to scamper up the steep station walls.

189

Then I remembered that the last time when I travelled to find Styppas in Kingston, I had ended up on the ceiling of his bedroom. It seemed easy then and I could remember exactly how I did it. So, I gave it a go and found myself on the roof of the platform. Once up there, I started to worry that I might get the Ilingos. But then I discovered that I did not mind being high up. The height of the perch did not frighten me or wake me up, like you do after a nightmare. It was an excellent observation post and I could see all that was going on without being noticed. So, I climbed a little higher still, above the track for trains heading west towards Geneva. It was a safe perch, among the iron and glass latticework and trellises. I would not be disturbed by the station master up here or told to go home. Except, that is, for the dozens and dozens of annoying pigeons who were fluttering about.

– Go away, pigeon. Go away.
– Coo … coo … coo
– Stop your silly cooing.
– Coo … coo … coo
They would never stop.

In spite of the pigeons, I could see that the train station was not nearly as busy as when we first came into Lausanne. Only the occasional train would come in or leave now, and there were very few people on the platforms. It was almost dark by then. It was getting late for Lausanne — it might have been after nine, although I could not see the Swiss clock on the platform from my perch. I started to think how different the Lausanneians were from the Athenians. In Lausanne most people were not out at this time and might have even gone to bed, but in Athens they would just be getting ready to go out.

Right underneath me a train came in and there was a brief flurry of a few people disembarking and getting on. The announcing system made me jump, as the speakers were close to my lofty perch. It said something about the train going to Geneva. I could see three figures, two of which were embracing and kissing the third. I figured that the third figure, which was that of a man, was going to get on the train. Indeed after a few more waves he got on the train which in a few minutes departed for Geneva. I was debating whether I should also get onto that train. Then the remaining two figures, still standing on the platform, caught my attention. It looked like they were crying. I slid silently down an old iron drain pipe from the latticework of the platform roof to the cement of the platform. The two figures were waving to the third, inside the train, and in a minute or two the train departed. As it disappeared into the night the figures turned around. They were about half way down the platform but I could now make out their faces in the dim light. I could not believe my eyes. I shouted to them, waving as hard as I could.

– *Styppas, Styppas! Pamela! It is me … It's me … Tasouli!*

They both looked towards me blankly making me think I had made a terrible mistake. But an instant later they were running towards me also shouting:

– Tasouli, Tasouli … what are you doing in Lausanne?
– I am here with my parents, of course. For our big European adventure before we go to Canada.

Styppas immediately nodded:

– Of course you are, Tasouli. And you are staying in the big Hotel your mother likes to call "The Lord Byron". With the giant marble bath and tons of running water out of the massive brass taps — all at the right temperature.
– How did you know Styppas … Oh, I forgot … you know everything.

Then I noticed that Pamela wiped a tear from her eye and she looked as if she was crying. Even Styppas looked a bit sniffy.

– Pamela, why are you crying?

– It is Fion … he came to see us in Lausanne for a couple of days. And now he is leaving. To go back to London.

– But who is Fion?

Pamela wiped off another tear and seemed not to hear my question. Styppas had his arm around hers and his voice was unusually soft.

– He has no way of knowing, Pamela. He has never seen the children.

– That's right Styppas … he has only visited us in Kingston when the children were away.

Pamela had now composed herself:

– Tasouli, … Fion is one of our children.

– Ohh! But why were you crying then Pamela? And even Styppas looked like he was crying.

– Because … because … I don't really know Tasouli. It was like Fion was leaving home … to go far, far away … to travel by train into the darkness … into the misty darkness and the drizzle …

I thought I shouldn't ask Pamela any more questions. She was becoming too emotional. And also, now that Styppas was definitely being nicer to me, it was a real opportunity to fix things between us. So I turned to him:

– But Styppas, I am a little confused. What are you and Pamela doing here in Lausanne?

– We are just here for a conference, Tasouli. Just for a few days.

– Ohh, a conference! And where are you staying, Styppas? You are not staying at The Lord Byron by any chance? Is that how you knew about the great marble bath and the giant brass taps and the water just at the right temperature?

– No, Tasouli. We are not staying at The Lord Byron. But I knew about the marble bath and the giant brass taps of the Lord.

– But where are you staying Styppas?

– It is called the Mövenpick Hotel, very near the port, in Ouchy. It is quite a new and modern Hotel.

– Hmm … that is strange, Styppas. My father is always talking about Ouchy and my mother loves modern hotels and yet neither of them mentioned the Mövenpick.

– They could not have known it.

– If you say so, Styppas. Although it is a little strange. And why did Pamela say that it was like Fion leaving home? That is a little strange also, isn't it?

– Not as strange as it seems, Tasouli. Fion lived and worked in Lausanne for a few years. We often visited him and stayed in his spacious apartment, overlooking Lake Geneva. Very near here. As you come out from the station it is up the hill to the left for a couple of blocks.

– That is convenient. But it must have been expensive.

– Naah … his company paid for it all. And a maid included.

– Ohh, that's sweet, Styppas. But still, why did Pamela get so emotional and was even crying?

– It was like an old black and white movie … the mist … the train leaving the station … the familiarity of the station … isn't that right, Pamela?

– Of course, Styppas. And I often cry at old black and white movies, Tasouli. Like 'Casablanca'.

– I don't remember 'Casablanca' playing in the Cineac, or in the outdoor movie houses. And it is a bit much for Pamela to start crying … just because Fion's departure reminded her of an old black and white movie. I mean, it wasn't really like leaving home — isn't that right Styppas?

– But you know, Tasouli, Lausanne has always seemed very familiar to me. Like it was also my home.

– But why would that be, Styppas? That seems even stranger.

– Maybe it is because I visited and stayed in Lausanne many years ago. At the Lord Byron.

Anastassiades

– Ohhh! … so, that's how you knew about the marble bath and the endless water, Styppas.

– That's how Tasouli.

– And were you very small then, Styppas?

– Your age, Tasouli.

– My age?

– Exactly your age.

– That's a big coincidence, Styppas!

– A very big coincidence.

– But, Pamela, it still doesn't explain you feeling that Fion was leaving home. I mean, you weren't also in Lausanne as a child? Were you Pamela?

– So …

– So, were you?

– No, not really, I wasn't. But don't you remember?

– Remember what, Pamela?

– That marbles and gutters
blood alleys
and Lords of the mind
in London of old
in Mitcham of mine
is that still the same?

– Oh yes Pamela,
for if something at all
is forever the same
in London of then
and Athens of now
I'll be looking for you
as I freely wander
on my cobbled paths

– And also on the cobbled
paths of Lausanne, Tasouli?

– Oh yes, for on these paths
and rooftop trellises
I freely now also wander

Paris

According to the passport we arrived in Brussels on July 24 and in the Netherlands on July 31. This was all by train. But I hardly remember anything at all about Brussels and the Netherlands. I have only the vaguest recollection of huge, stone, stuffy-looking buildings in Brussels with lots of space and some kind of gardens around them. I think my mother kept saying how important they all were.

Our passport was stamped for entry into France on August 2. Again, I don't remember much about the train trip, but I do remember a few things about Paris. I was impressed by the Louvre and its endless galleries, lavishly decorated rooms and paintings and sculptures. I remember setting meeting points with my father, like famous sculptures or entrances, where we would meet if we got lost. Of course, this was much before the new immense underground entrance to the Louvre was constructed. One had to enter from a relatively less imposing entrance in one of the wings of the old palace. But there were other similar exits and entrances and it was easy to get mixed up. I think we made several lengthy visits to the Louvre, and as I got to know my way around, was less likely to get lost. But I did get lost in any case and had to ask for instructions to particular meeting points. I don't remember the French being either particularly rude or particularly polite when I asked for instructions. I suppose the guards at the Louvre were used to being asked lots of questions all the time. At that time most Europeans spoke only their own language and my comprehension of French was none too great. Nevertheless, I managed to follow their instructions. I discovered that I could improve my French by asking different guards the same question — like where was the Venus de Milo or where the Victory of Samothrace was located. The Victory of Samothrace dominated a whole large hall at the top of a giant marble staircase in a huge alcove. It was one of the most striking parts of the Louvre. More importantly still, all the guards seemed very pleased to tell me where to find *La Victoire*. I relayed this finding about the guards of the Louvre to my parents with great certainty and enthusiasm. From then on we agreed to always meet at the famous *La Victoire* in the Louvre when we got lost.

During the visit to Paris there was an episode of great secrecy and conspiracy. It was centered on one man, steeped in myth, intrigue and fear that he might be betrayed. When he was talked about, the adults would talk in hushed, reverent tones. He was a great revolutionary, and the reactionary police forces all through Europe were looking for him. He was now in Paris. He lived in hiding there, although his main base of operations was Algeria, which was then still the most important French colony. I should not reveal his name even more than sixty years later, as I am narrating this story. Who knows if the descendants of the same reactionary forces are still on the lookout for him? After all, he was instrumental in ultimately delivering the most stinging blow to European imperialism since the War and the Occupation. And strangely, his efforts were brought to fruition finally by the most famous imperialist French leader, none other than Charles de Gaulle. Of course I am talking about the Algerian War of Independence which ultimately brought the French Fourth Republic to its knees. De Gaulle had to finally cede to the revolutionaries, and Algeria gained its independence from France.

But none of that had happened by 1950. The fermenting revolutionary politics of Algeria would not break out into outright uprising and war with France for a few more years. Yet, this international revolutionary must have already started his activities. Why else would my parents talk in such hushed tones about this individual? The seeds must have been sown. The conspiracy of the peasants and revolutionaries was being constructed. I figured that is why this secrecy was necessary.

Since I cannot reveal the name of this man, I will use the code name by which he was known. But even that carries danger, so I will call him by a name which only sounds like his code name. I will call him Sparrow.

Sparrow's here Sparrow's there
That's the Sparrow everywhere.
Sparrow in all of France is sought
Just a slip and Sparrow's caught.
Sparrow flutters, Sparrow picks
Sparrow the Fourth Republic tricks
Sparrow's in a black cloak disguise
Sparrow will something else devise.

My parents said that we were supposed to meet the Sparrow one evening. But how would I even recognize him? Perhaps he would have a different disguise than a black cloak. Perhaps mask as a woman or a very old man. And what about the risk of betraying him? Then surely my parents would end up in some dark French prison. I imagined that they would even have opened parts of the real Bastille for these kinds of cases. We should have never named our house in Pagrati 'Bastille'. When my parents would go to prison, it would serve us right for playing with fate like this. They would stay in prison until they died. I would then be an orphan in France! And probably the French don't even give salami sandwiches to their orphans. I must keep totally silent and warn my parents about all kinds of traps that they may not see. They seemed to be laughing and joking a lot. I did not like this. Obviously they were not aware of the danger. The police and secret agents were themselves wearing all kinds of disguises. I would have to be particularly careful about what conversations I would have with my parents in front of the guards at the Louvre. After all, the guards were agents of the French state. And in police-like uniforms, no less. If I asked for directions too many times about the *Victoire* they would get suspicious for sure. I could see myself asking Styppas:

– Styppas, what do you think about me asking the guards at the Louvre about where the *Victoire* is? Just to practice my French …
– Are you crazy? Which *Victoire*?
– Which *Victoire*? Why, the Victory of Samothrace of course.
– Ha, ha, ha … Victory of Samothrace …
– Why are you ha, ha, ha-ing, Styppas?
– And you don't think they would understand the code?
– Which code, Styppas?
– The Victory of Samothrace is of course code for the victory in Algeria.
– Victory in Algeria, Styppas?
– Are you dull, Tasouli?
– No …
– The victory of the revolutionaries over the French colonialists, of course!
– Of course, Styppas. I am not dull.
– Ha, ha, ha …

But in reality, I had not asked Styppas. In order to do this I would need to find him first. And I did not know if he was still in Lausanne moping with Pamela about that Fion of theirs in the train station, or if they had finally toddled off to Kingston. I had just imagined I had asked him. And I had no intention of asking him. I did not want him to get mad at me again for betraying my parents because of my stupidity. And he would start sprouting hair everywhere and green spittle would be coming out of his mouth. Just like he did when I told him that I had chosen religion over history in the entrance exams for Varvakion.

My parents had arranged to meet the Sparrow on a well-known street corner in Paris and then we would go to eat in a French restaurant. When we arrived at the appointed street corner I did not see anyone that looked like the Sparrow. But then I heard them talking excitedly and laughing. I looked again. No black cloak, no other disguise, not even standing in the shadows. Right in the middle of a broad sidewalk was a tall ordinary looking man with an affable smile and a resounding voice.

– Tasouli, Tasouli you have grown so much since I last saw you!
– …

– You are practically a man, and strong and smart as well.
– …

I was taken aback. Surely this could not be the legendary Sparrow. The terror of the Fourth Republic. And if he was not wearing his black cloak where was his other disguise? But his manner was so friendly and personable that I was immediately won over. And my parents were not using his code name or even his second name, which was kind of code as well among close circles. It was everybody by their first names like the best of friends and relations. At once, the Sparrow reminded me so much of my Uncle Thalis. The same openness, the same 'everything is OK' attitude, the same ability to make you feel good with a sentence or two.

But then a certain feeling of discomfort started to creep in. It had something to do with this familiarity and approachable manner of the much revered Sparrow. And all of a sudden I knew why I felt uncomfortable. After the fiasco of 'the Corruptors' my most favorite Uncle Thalis was a persona non-grata with my father. Surely, he would not fail to detect the similarity between the Sparrow and Thalis. And then if he saw me being friendly with the Sparrow it could become 'the Corruptors' all over again. But the Sparrow was obviously not deterred by my gloomy thoughts.

– Tasouli, why don't we go to a Chinese restaurant?
– I have never been to a Chinese restaurant.
– You have never been, Tasouli? Well we must correct this.
– I don't think we have any in Athens, do we daddy?
But my father was just benignly smiling. He was glad to be in the elevated company of the famous Sparrow with my mother, and me having a conversation with the Sparrow.
– We can have swallows' nest soup, Tasouli. It is delicious.
– Swallows' nest soup?
– Oh, yes. The swallows use their saliva to make the nests. And the Chinese love to make soup from it.
I thought it was all a joke, as the Sparrow was laughing and encouraging me to laugh with him. Which I easily did. Swallows' nest soup seemed very amusing.
– How do the Chinese make the soup, Mr. Sparrow?
– Oh don't call me Sparrow, Tasouli. Call me by my first name.

The Sparrow had burst out laughing again. He thought it was amusing that I was calling him by his secret code name. I looked around suspiciously to see who was following us. I had inadvertently revealed Sparrow's code name and now they also knew his first name. The streets were full of reactionary spies and informers. How could the Sparrow be so casual and laughing so much? But maybe I had been lucky and got away with it and no one had heard me. Probably the best policy from now on was not to use a name at all when I was speaking to the Sparrow.

Soon enough we were in this large Chinese restaurant. It was brightly lit and had large windows and daylight was still coming in as it was summertime in Paris. We all sat around a big table and the Sparrow ordered. After a while, I asked him if he had ordered the swallows' nest soup.

– Of course, Tasouli. It will be here in a second.

The Sparrow had hardly finished his sentence when the swallows' nest soup arrived. There was huge merriment from the Sparrow about the quick arrival and perfect timing of the soup. I was served a bowl with an actual bird's nest in the soup. I tasted the soup and it was indeed delicious, but with a taste that was neither fish nor meat. Then I asked whether I could eat the actual bird's nest. There was a look of horror from my mother, but the Sparrow again thought this was most amusing and encouraged me to taste it. So, I took a few twigs from the nest and started to chew on them. I made a general announcement:

– They are crunchy and also tasty.
– Of course they are, of course they are, Tasouli! Of course they are!
– But how do they get all the swallows' nests?
– The swallows nest up on high cliffs in the thousands and thousands. And the Chinese climb those cliffs to collect the nests. It is amazing, Tasouli, isn't it? Do you like the soup?
– Oh, yes, it is most delicious.
– But you know, Tasouli, birds' nest soup is also made in parts of Indochina.
– Oh … Indochina! That is very exotic.
– Very exotic, Tasouli. And the French must be careful not to fall into that soup …

The Sparrow laughed more quietly this time. But he was having a really good time. Just like the Corruptors used to do. The Sparrow was laughing — the same kind of laugh and amusement over little things that Thalis and Rikos and Ourania used to laugh about in their small studio with the skylights. My mother's face had turned from horror to acceptance and my father was broadly smiling. His response to the Sparrow's amusement and laughter was so different than his reaction to the Corruptors. I needn't have worried that he would detect the similarity in the laughter of the Sparrow to that of Thalis and his co-conspirators. It now seemed like it was OK for Archeomarxists and revolutionaries to laugh and have a good time. It occurred to me that it all seemed a bit contradictory but I soon put that thought aside. I continued to enjoy my swallows' nest soup and all the amusing commentary.

A few years later I started to learn about the war of liberation in French Indochina, which culminated in the final defeat of the fabled French army at Dien-Bien Phu in 1954. Certainly the Dien-Bien Phu French fortification was isolated from its guarding birds (i.e. the French air force), by the Viet Cong like a bird's nest before it ended up in the soup. The American involvement in Viet Nam would then begin. Was the Sparrow, the great international revolutionary, involved also in the French demise in Indochina? Is that what he meant about a bird's nest and the French being in the soup in Indochina? I never found out. Also, I never tasted swallows' nest soup again. It seems to have gone out of fashion. I must try to taste it again — to see if it still tastes as good as it did then, during that Paris summer evening with the humorous Sparrow.

London

We continued our train journey from Paris and crossed the English Channel by ferry from Calais to Dover on the 8th of August. Then on to London by English train. I remember the Charring Cross Station. How exciting and busy it was. So many Englishmen dressed in dark suits all serious and rushing about, with newspapers tucked under their arms! Quite a few were carrying long black umbrellas even though there was bright sunshine that one could see through the roof and platforms. That was pretty strange. Others were wearing funny hats. I recognized them immediately as bowler hats from the description and pen drawings of my cloth-bound British booklets for learning English. I somehow had it my mind from those booklets that Lords often wore bowler hats, as well as top hats. So I started to think that all those who wore bowler hats were Lords. How else could one explain the strange phenomenon of men wearing hats in bright summer weather? In Athens men would never wear hats unless it was raining or really wintery weather. Unless, of course, they were older and then a few might wear straw hats in hot summer weather, which used to be the fashion a long time ago. But here in the Charring Cross Station just about all the Englishmen also wore dark suits in summertime whether or not they wore a bowler hat. And these dark suits were just like those the Lords wore in the drawings of my booklets, except that sometimes the drawings also showed them wearing tails. So I figured that, most likely, they were all Lords but some had left their bowler hats at home because of the bright August weather.

So, I started to wander through the Lordly crowd rushing mostly towards the platforms, gaping at their dress and behavior. I soon lost myself in the movement and smells of the crowd. They smelled of pipe or cigarette tobacco and some nice kind of mustiness. Soon I would find out that much of London smelled like that. It reminded me a bit of the smell of the English prisoners in the Bastille. And they all seemed tall and purposeful. They were all in a rush. One Lord brushed by another Lord.

All of a sudden, I accidentally ran into one of the Lords. I was not looking where I was going. I looked up at him and he said, barely glancing at me:

– Sorry.

I have no idea why he said 'sorry'. I tried to explain in my squeaky voice and limited English that I was studying the English Lords and that is why I ran into him. He quickly smiled and rushed off, saying again:

– Sorry.

I had barely managed to get my orientation when I ran into another Lord:

– Sorry.

This time I did put a few words together to explain my predicament, but the second 'sorry' Lord had disappeared. And immediately I ran into a third:

– Sorry.

By now I had practiced my explanation in English, as I tried to get out of the crowd going on the platform. There was a chorus of 'sorry', 'sorry', 'sorry', 'sorry' … No one was paying the slightest attention to my explanation. So, I tried the 'sorry' myself:

– Sorry.
– Sorry.

I kept repeating my squeaky 'sorry', 'sorry' and it seemed to bring smiles on the faces of some Lords. Lots more 'sorry' emanated back from them.

And then an amazing thing happened. I stopped bumping into the Lords. A kind of path seemed to open through the crowd of Lords, even though I was going generally the wrong way, in the opposite direction, away from the train platform. That is, as long as I kept saying 'sorry'. I had never seen anything like it. Obviously, 'sorry' was a secret form of communication among the English Lords, which I had accidentally discovered. Maybe something like the flocks of geese I had read about in my childhood books. Or something like the radar that the British used against the Germans during the War. Stelios had said that the Germans never quite figured out the radar. How could they, if it was like hundreds of 'sorry' coming from different directions and yet communicating with each other? Very advanced, I thought.

And the people in London were so different from Athens. In the Omonia underground station in Athens if a boy my size started to get in the way of passengers he would be told off in no uncertain terms. Of course, no one would smile at a strange child. The child might even be threatened with getting a good *carpaziá*. A *carpazia* is a slap to the back of the neck with the open hand. If expertly administered it numbs one and can send tingles down your spine. Children that collected a lot of *carpazias* were definitely inferior. They were called sometimes by other children as 'carpazo-collectors'. And often the adults would threaten them by telling them they would 'eat' a carpazia or two. In which case, they could be called 'carpazo-eaters' (*carpazo-phagae*, in alliterated Greek). They were usually poorer, lower class kids who had perpetually stunned expressions. I remember debating with myself whether they became stunned 'carpazo-eaters' from eating so many carpazias, or whether they were stunned in the first place and that is why they ate so many carpazias. I considered discussing this dilemma with Styppas, but his endless theorizing would be sure to disrupt my study of the Lords in Charring Cross. So, I decided against it.

Looking at all the superior Lords, I could see myself becoming a carpazo-eater if I was not careful. That would have been a terrible fate for me here in Charring Cross. But fortunately I had discovered the secret communication of the Lords. Saying "sorry" repeatedly had allowed me to get out of their midst safely.

In any case, I did not get the feeling that the Lords of Charring Cross Station knew anything about the carpazia. Saying 'sorry' seemed to suffice for them even though it was me who had got in their way. Yet I must say that I thought it was a very unusual way for adults to treat a mere child. Particularly if they were Lords.

Soon, after I got out of the crowd of Lords, I saw my parents waiting for me in a pre-arranged spot in the great Charring Cross Station. They had superior smiles on their faces, and were looking important. I ran to them to tell them about my discovery of how the English Lords communicated by saying 'sorry' all the time.

Anastassiades

My mother looked dubious:

– I had looked it up in the dictionary before we left, Tasouli. 'Sorry' means they are sad.
– But why would all these Lords be sad, Mamaka?
– Perhaps because they are all going home.
– Going home, Mamaka? Why would that make them sad?
– Because they are going to their wives.
– And why would going to their wives make them sad?
– Because they are English wives.
– What about English wives, Mamaka?
– English wives don't know how to deal with their husbands.
– Ohh!
– Yes, they are too rigid psychologically — not like the Greek wives.
– Ohh, Mamaka, psychologically!

In the meantime my father was standing there with his superior smile. He then spoke in a very authoritative voice:

– What my little Dina says is very important. She has studied psychology and she knows all about family relations.
– Of course, Babaka.
– But I also looked up 'sorry' in the very important Oxford dictionary before we left. Tzanetakis has a copy, you know.
– Oh yes, Uncle Tzanetakis, Babaka!

George Tzanetakis, the most senior cousin of my father, was more English than the English. As a young man he had entered the Greek Air Force, the most dashing and newest of the Greek armed forces, having trained as an officer in Britain. His impeccable British accent, his deep authoritative voice, his tall dark good looks, and when dressed in a dazzling white Air Force uniform, had all the girls swooning. During the War he served in North Africa where his Unit made important contributions against the Rommel army. After the end of the War he took part in an uprising against one of the reactionary Greek governments and was either imprisoned or exiled for a period. He then worked as a senior mechanical Engineer in a Greek firm, Markotsis, which made small engines famous for their reliability and longevity. The fact that my father had looked up 'sorry' in Tzanetakis' Oxford dictionary gave immense weight to his opinion. My Babas would have certainly discussed the meaning of the word with his great cousin.

– And what did the important Oxford dictionary say, Babaka?
– That something could be in a 'sorry state'.
– But what would be in a sorry state, Babaka?
– The upper classes thought that England was in a 'sorry state'.
– Ohh! That sounds very serious.
– They were against the Labour Government and that is why they kept repeating 'sorry'.
– As in a "sorry state", Babaka?
– Exactly. They emphasize the word 'sorry' so you didn't hear the 'state'.

So, it was political commentary I was overhearing. It had nothing to do with a secret system of communication of the Lords.
So, that was that.

But having my theory about 'sorry' dismissed did not dampen my enthusiasm of exploring around Charring Cross and the adjoining Trafalgar Square. I discovered many more interesting and important things. The National Gallery, on top of Trafalgar Square, was not as humongous as the

Louvre but it had every type of painting imaginable and everyone went in and out freely. And the English guards were not nearly as grumpy as the French. And the fountains on the square had lots of children playing around them. They were not as ornate or impressive as the fountains of Rome or Paris but somehow they seemed more open and accessible.

Of course the most impressive thing about Trafalgar Square was the pigeons. Hundreds of them it seemed. Some of them even on the top of Nelson's column and on the backs and heads of the great bronze lions. They were all around your feet. If you kicked at them, they would take a few quick steps to get away from the kick and be right back. They all expected to be fed, it seemed. This was very different than the pigeons in the squares of Athens, who would run for their lives if you got too close to them. Of course Athenian pigeons had good cause to run for their lives. During the Occupation and the great hunger, catching a pigeon or two could make all the difference between starving or not.

But I could not see the Lords of Charring Cross chasing pigeons. They were too busy saying 'sorry' to each other.

For whatever reason.

~

In London, we stayed in a hotel-pension near Marble Arch. I am not sure of the district that the hotel-pension was in but it was walking distance for me to the Marble Arch itself and the Speakers' Corner. It might have been in the Mayfair or Marylebone districts. But this was no ordinary hotel-pension. It had a beautiful dining room, which was more like a great solarium, facing a very deep garden enclosed by old brick and stone walls. This immense garden had an unreal quality to it. I had never seen anything like it. Not even in Lausanne. It had these cultivated lawns with shades of green I had never even dreamt about. I don't think I had seen a cultivated grass lawn in Greece. No one in their right mind would waste water to keep grass green and then cut it. And certainly not walk on it. But here people walked on this grass. And they walked on it freely.

And then I walked on it
And it was so short and manicured
And felt like a thick, thick carpet
And everywhere roses were planted
And in the sunny London afternoon
The light seemed to take a golden hue
Reflecting off these magic lawns

Perhaps it was an August Sunday I remember
For in deck chairs well-dressed people sat
Who seemed to come from the neighborhood
And there were girls in frilly white dresses
And children played a game I had never seen
Hitting a wooden ball with a wooden mallet
Which rolled through little wire arches
That seemed like gates built in the lawn
Connected to the different hues of green

And the children seemed connected
Connected to the green grass
Connected to the shades of green
Connected to each rose bush
Connected to their strange game

And it was so all other worldly

Anastassiades

For no child was shouting
And none of them competing
And when amongst them I crept
None looked peculiarly at me
And no one asked me to join them
Yet no one seemed to exclude me

It was as if I had been there before
And was in the game already
The wooden mallet passed to me
I tried hitting the wooden ball
Aiming it through the wire arch
And when I missed no one laughed
A little girl then wanted the mallet
I passed it on to her
And the ball she hit
Went through the arch
And she never even smiled
Again she hit the ball quietly
Still through another gate
And never looked superior
But just passed on the mallet
To someone else to take a turn

And nothing that was of myself
Seemed to have ever happened
Yet as the time wore on and on
I couldn't tell how long I'd been
On the green imaginary grass
In that early evening light
That seemed to have no start
And now slowly faded
Just like the game played

Then after the sun had set
And the Pension-Hotel
Quieted and darkened
I thought 'was it really me?'
With my hapless mallet
But no people were now left
None to ask about the game
None even at a table eating
Or playing cards or checkers

Now that the darkness came
Why had my day ended so?
What was one supposed to do?
Now that daylight was gone
Perhaps I had dreamt all this
Perhaps it never happened

~

But then, next morning I found myself again. For I saw a cat, a beautiful black cat, all slinky and self-assured with her tail up in the air.

This cat was outside on the sidewalk of the cobblestone street outside our hotel-pension. The street was very quiet. There were many trees, oaks perhaps I think. There were no automobiles and just the occasional pedestrian. There was no noise or conversations from the old houses or their gardens that lined the street. I followed the cat quietly on the sidewalk to see where she would go. Of course cats know all the good places to go in quiet streets. She was sure to lead me to adventure in these leafy deserted streets of London.

And sure enough, this cat purposefully and full of concentration started to cross the street. She saw me following her across the street and quickened her pace. I did not want to make her nervous, as she would never then take me to her secret places. So, I backtracked to the sidewalk, and pretended to walk slowly down there looking for my own secret places. The cat slowed her pace on the opposite sidewalk and seemed unconcerned as she explored her cattish places. I decided that this was a superior cat, for surely she knew she was being watched but was hiding it. Maybe it was her way of showing me her secret places but pretending she wasn't.

Just as I was thinking what to do next without spooking the cat, a couple started to walk towards me on my side of the sidewalk. They were the only people on the street, except me of course. They were walking very slowly but they soon caught up with me. The reason for this was that I had stopped walking on my sidewalk because the cat had stopped on hers. When the couple approached I saw that they were elderly. They were also very English. The man was slightly stooped and smoked a pipe and wore a woolen jacket and had a nice tie on, even though it was summer. He looked very much like some of the black pen drawings of English gentlemen in my English language school books. The woman was a little more stooped and also wore woolen clothes and sandals with woolen socks. She had her arm in the arm of the man. So if he was a gentleman, she must have been a lady. Maybe he was supporting her as she walked, or maybe it was the other way around. They slowed down as they approached me, although they were going pretty slowly in any case. I could smell the aromatic pipe tobacco and by now the familiar smell of the English emanating from the gentleman. But the lady also smelled of a familiar flowery smell, in addition to the English smell. I recognized it from Zakynthos. It was the smell of lavender.

When the couple were about to pass me on the sidewalk I thought the man said 'Sorry'. If that was the case, he must have been a Lord. This was higher than just a gentleman. So, I figured I had to respond in a Lordly manner and mumbled 'sorry' in response. Except my 'sorry' came out squeaky as usual. So, I thought I should follow it up with an explanatory statement, as to why I was stopped in the middle of the sidewalk.

– I was following the cat.

The couple stopped completely. The gentleman put his hands behind his back and held one hand with the other hand. I had never seen anyone do this before. He bent forward a little and looked at me with great attention and curiosity. His lady did something similar, except she did not put her hands behind her back. In Greece you would never see adults behaving like this towards a child. No adult would ever pay this much attention to a child just because he said he was following a cat. Never! At the most you might see a smile or hear a dismissive comment.

– But the cat crossed the road.
– Mmmm.

This was something else I had never heard before. It was a very peculiar sound with the lips held tight and the head moving forward a little. Both the gentleman and the lady seemed to make a similar sound more or less. The gentleman would make the sound first and then the lady would usually follow. Usually, but not always, that is. The lady's sounds were similar but slightly shorter and quieter than the gentleman. And they seem to vary more in length. And they had a lower pitch than the gentleman's 'mmmms'. No Greeks that I knew had ever made these types of sounds, certainly not with those little head movements. And I had never seen this behavior in Rome, or in Lausanne or in Paris. But these unusual sounds had an encouraging quality. So, I continued.

– Of course this is a black cat.
– Mmmm.
– Mmm.
– And black cats can bring bad luck if you see them crossing in front of you.
– Mmmm!
– I read this in my book for learning English.
– Mmmm?
– Mm?
– And the book had this black ink drawing of a black cat crossing the road in front of someone.
– Mmmm.
– But my mother says that a black cat crossing the road is good luck.
– Mmmm?
– Mmm?
– Yes. Because my mother says that only smart black cats can cross the road.
– Mmmm!
– Mm?
– Oh yes. For a black cat to cross the road safely she must be smart.
– Mmmm?
– Mmm!
– Oh yes. Because if she is not smart, she could be run over by a car. Or spooked by people and be afraid to cross.
– Mmmm.
– Mmm.
– Oh yes. And this is a very smart cat.
– Mmmm?
– Mmm?
– Most certainly a very superior cat.
– Mmmm?
– I know because she was going to her most secret hiding place.
– Mmmm.
– And when she heard me following her on the opposite sidewalk, she stopped.
– Mmmm.
– Mmm!
– But I stopped following her and then she went on to her secret hiding place.
– Mmm!
– Yes, but then she went behind the fence over there, and I lost her.
– Mmmm.
– Mmm.
– So she is very smart and very superior.
– Mmmm.
– Mmm.
– Probably the smartest and most superior cat in London.
– Mmmm?
– Mmm!
– So, she will bring us the best luck in London!
– Mmmm.
– Mmm!!

The English elderly couple was standing very still throughout this conversation. Finally, after I had finished telling them why this particular black cat would bring us good luck by crossing the road, they stopped making their 'mmm' sounds. They said a few sentences to me again very carefully and rather slowly, but I couldn't understand a word they were saying. So, I started saying:

– Mmmm, Mmm …

They seemed to be pleased. Then they went on their way, arm-in-arm, talking to each other. But they kept looking back at me as they walked down the sidewalk.

Since the cat was gone and I could not find any particularly interesting places to explore on that road, I returned to the pension-hotel. There I explained my adventure and the beliefs about good luck and bad luck when black cats cross in front of people or cross roads, to my parents. My mother said I must be making good progress in English if I was able to explain all of that to an elderly English couple. So, I didn't tell her that I hadn't understood a word of what the English couple had said to me after I had finished talking to them. But I did say that I thought the English paid a lot more attention to children than adults did in Greece. This was a clear mistake. Immediately my father reminded me how much attention my uncles paid to me over the years, and all the things they taught me in the Bastille. Of course, that is not what I had meant at all. I was talking about strangers in the street, not my relatives in the Bastille. But I thought it was best to keep quiet rather than start an argument.

So instead, I said that I would like to go to the Marble Arch and the Speakers' Corner where I had not yet been. My father said this was an extremely important excursion for one would see firsthand the fabled freedom of speech in politics in England. We would go there in the afternoon. My mother immediately arranged for me to have a rest after lunch, to which I objected vigorously since I was not at all tired. As usual, I lost the argument.

~

The walk to Marble Arch and Speakers' Corner was quite short from the pension-hotel. Marble Arch was nice, but hardly impressive, especially compared to the marble arches I had seen in Rome and Paris. But Speakers' Corner was something I had never seen. There were all these people gathered around listening to an odd-looking man, with a lot of unruly hair, lambasting the government. Other times, when I went back again, equally odd-looking people were sticking it to the church or God or poodles. Somehow the listening crowd was disorderly and at the same time orderly.

The police showed no intent in arresting the speaker, and while everyone was paying attention to what he was saying, no one was really paying attention. Certainly, the police was not paying much attention to what he was saying. And the police did not seem interested in arresting the speaker in spite of all the bad, even outrageous things he was saying. When I say 'police' this was nothing like the Greek police, all coming out of dark, old police vans with cages for locking up people, ready to beat up crowds and demonstrators. In fact there was just one policeman, standing near the Speakers' Corner crowd. He was taller than just about everyone and just stood there with a little smile on his face. I had never ever seen a policeman smile. That would have been impossible in Greece. Or in Rome. Or in Paris. Or even in Lausanne. Even more amazing was that the policeman seemed to be chatting with people in the crowd. Initially I thought he was chatting with friends of his. Perhaps other police in plain clothes, planted to take notes on the gathered agitators and anarchists. But as I watched his strange behavior, I was not sure he was chatting with his friends. Surely, the English police would have to be the stupidest in the world if a policeman in uniform was giving away his own police spies by openly chatting with them. And this policeman must have been a bit simple. He was not even taking notes on the anarchists and agitators. He didn't even wear a pistol. I had never seen that before. Can you imagine — a policeman without a pistol! And as if his rather well-kept uniform was not odd enough, his pointed helmet was stranger still. Fortunately I had seen drawings of this type of hat worn by policemen in my cloth-bound English study books. There in the black pen drawings, their silly hats were always flying off when they were chasing a thief.

But this policeman was not chasing thieves or pickpockets in Speakers' Corner and Marble Arch.

Anastassiades

He was not taking notes on agitators and anarchists. He was not even conspiring with his friends to infiltrate the radicals and the supporters of anti-government speakers. And no matter how the speaker, standing up on a little platform ranted on, how much his hair flew in the London air, how he shouted and gesticulated, the policeman just continued on with his little smile. The speaker would continually respond to comments someone or other made from the audience. It was as if the speaker was more of a sideshow rather than the real reason all these people had gathered in Speakers' Corner. But the speaker was unperturbed and he went on and on as if he was arguing mostly with himself.

– This Government will pay for it …
– Don't say no … they will pay for their sins …
– I tell you … do not laugh … do not deny it …
– Clement Attlee promises … Promises he couldn't keep …

Now he is teetering … almost a minority[4] …

– The British people are tired of Attlee's socialism … I'm in the poorhouse now … God does not listen … you say yes he does … then why did he make Attlee break his promises?
– You say he didn't … then why is he God? … I say there is no God … you say that's a bloody poor excuse … Attlee couldn't have done it by himself … I tell you he had help …
– Yes he did … from the industrialists and the capitalists … Mr. Stalin said so … Capitalism rules all countries except the Soviet Union … yes he did … just the other day, it was Pravda, in the Guardian[5] … in all the countries encircling the Soviet Union … and socialism could only be in one country for now … so socialism in other countries is not possible … so, I'm condemned to stay in the poorhouse … and God is not going to help me … that's for sure … and neither is Mr. Attlee … and neither is Mr. Stalin … not in England, he's not …

I sat down on the grass. I could no longer see the Speaker very well from where I was sitting but I could still hear him going on and on. My mind must have wandered off or maybe I had dozed off because the Speaker was now on a somewhat different tack … in fact, he seemed to be saying something different from what he was saying before, and Attlee and Stalin and God and the poorhouse were all sort of mixed up. Also, his voice seemed louder.

– Atlee has brought socialism to Britain …
– And the NHS … they will not go back now …
– Fascism will never prevail in Britain … and neither will Stalinism … Britain has strong and advanced agricultural practices …

Then I noticed something odd. The speaker had converted from English to Greek. And he was going on in stentorian tones.

– We must see the English agricultural organization …
– We will go to a farm tomorrow, Tasouli … We will see advanced farming practices, Tasouli …

How could the Speaker know my name? How did he know to call me Tasouli? Then as I concentrated as hard as I could, I solved the mystery. The Speaker was Styppas! He was standing over me and sounded just like the Speaker before. Except he was speaking in Greek rather than English. I must have fallen asleep on the grass.

– Styppas, I didn't realize it was you. I thought it was the Speaker.
– Why are you calling me by our last name, Tasouli?

I gathered my wits and concentrated harder still. I focused my eyes. It was not Styppas at all who was speaking … it was my father.

– Ah … Babaka! Sorry. I must have fallen asleep listening to the Speaker. When did you come?
– Just now. Your mother sent me.
– Why did she do that?
– She said that there are crazy people in Speakers' Corner and you were not to be by yourself.
– Ohh, but I am fine. I just fell asleep on the grass.
– But you thought I was this Styppas of yours?
– Who told you about Styppas, Babaka?
– Your mother, our Dinaki — our little Dina, of course.
– Ohh …
– You know we do not keep any secrets, Tasouli. Our Dinaki told me about you talking to this Styppas in Zakynthos.
– In the Doppia.
– When you had the important discussion about Socrates, Tasouli.

I had forgotten that my mother had said she would tell my father about the episode with Styppas. It was strange that my father never mentioned it until now. Of course, I had never told my mother that there was this horrible fight over Socrates and I was afraid that Styppas would extinguish me. By impalement no less! So, I was a bit shaken. Maybe my father had found out in some other way. Maybe I had talked in my sleep and revealed my nightmare of impalement. Maybe he knew about the nightmare and he was just baiting me, in that sarcastic manner of his. I had to stay very calm and hope this was not the case.

– That's right, Babaka. It was a very important discussion about Socrates.

My father put on that proud, superior little smile under his mustaches. There was a feeling of relief that ran through me — likely he did not know about the nightmare of impalement. Or, so I hoped. Maybe he was just trying to put me off guard.

– Of course, Tasouli. We will discuss it further sometime.
– Of course, Babaka.
– But for now we need to go back to the hotel-pension so we can prepare for our important excursion to the English farm tomorrow.
– The one with the advanced farming practices, Babaka.
– Exactly.

I had dodged another bullet. Advanced English farming practices had saved me.

~

The next day we travelled to the English farm. We went by bus, travelling into the English countryside. I don't know how my father had come in contact with our farmer host who was going to show us the advanced English practices. But I remember him clearly. He was dressed in a waistcoat and tall farming boots, with a pleasant red face and bald head, and smoked a pipe that smelled nice. He was similar to what I remembered from the black pen drawings in my English language books showing a gentleman farmer. I recognized the similarity at once and decided he must be a gentleman and therefore superior. But he never said 'sorry', which I found a bit odd. He acknowledged my presence and greeted me but he certainly did not go overboard to talk to me. So, I liked him but kept my distance a little. This detail about keeping my distance a little is worth narrating, as it played an important part in my sexual development — in an unexpected manner.
The fields of the gentleman farmer were not too impressive. Of course, compared to Greek farming areas there was a lot more green grass. But by then I was used to the green, green grass of the hotel-pension where girls in white dresses played the odd game of croquet, and the great

expanses of green grass around Speakers' Corner and Regent's Park. Also, I had expected to see many cows grazing but there were very few. But the gentleman farmer was keen to show us the advanced milking practices it seemed and he was going to take us into the barn. So, my expectations increased as I thought we were going to see many cows and automated milking. But there was only one cow in the barn. It is true the gentleman farmer and some farm hands showed us the automated milking machine and clear plastic tubes for the milk to be collected into vats. But I had seen automated milking before in Greece. By then my father had assumed a very important expression under his mustaches and he was asking questions in a very important tone of voice. So, I assumed that the solitary cow must be a very important cow.

Next, the gentleman farmer and the farm hands showed us how the milk coming out of the tubes was processed. They said that the milk was not pasteurized and was sold directly as fresh milk. And people would drink the non-pasteurized milk and be willing to pay a little more for it. This was more interesting because in Greece at that time we would boil all milk, whether it was pasteurized or not, as we did not trust the pasteurization. The cows would be checked for tuberculosis and other diseases. But so were they in Zakynthos and the agrarian relatives would always be talking about when they were last checked by the veterinarian. So, I figured that the way the milk was collected by the gentleman farmer and his farm hands must have very special vats, maybe of shining metal, to collect the milk. But they were rather ordinary milk cans and the way that they washed them, which they showed us, was also by very ordinary hand-washing. By then my mother was very much into the conversation and greatly admiring the advanced milking operation and my father was deferring to her in his usual way.

I found myself getting more and more bored of the advanced milking practices and wandered off. Not too far from the barn there was kind of a shabby fence made up of wire and sticks stuck in the wire. Some of the sticks appeared to serve no particular purpose as they did not support the fence. They were just stuck there. One particular stick caught my attention. It stood out from all of the other sticks because it was painted red. It was also a bit tapered, so the top of it was about an inch in diameter and the bottom was about half an inch. It was made of some very hard wood and looked very sturdy. But the most interesting feature of this stick was its height. It came to a little more than my middle in height, so it would make an excellent walking stick. The only problem with it was that it was a little bent, so it had a gentle curve from top to bottom.

I looked to see if anyone was watching me, but they were all in the barn. I gave an upward tug to the stick and after a couple of twists it came free from the grass and mud, and I was able to pull it out of the fence. It seemed to make absolutely no difference to the fence. It could have come out by itself and no one would have known the difference. I went back to the barn, now armed with my new walking stick. The gentleman farmer looked at me. I said to him:

– Can I have this stick, please?
– Where did you find it?
– It was just lying by the fence.
– Just lying by the fence?
– Yes, over there.

I could tell that the gentleman farmer was not pleased. Perhaps he knew I had pulled it out of his fence. But by then my mother was beaming about the accomplishment of her little boy. The gentleman farmer did not smile and did not say anything. But he nodded.

I figured that the stick was mine.

That very evening back at the hotel-pension I started to work with my little penknife on the stick. The wood was harder than I had even imagined. So carving any décor or molding on it was very difficult. But on the other hand, because of the hardness, it was also difficult to do much damage to it. Over the next year or two, my stick became my inseparable companion. Any chance I got, I would add to the décor. I took it to all trips in the woods and my rod always accompanied me on any of my adventures. It came in immensely handy for fending off undesirable fauna or flora and real or imaginary opponents.

The 'Canberra'

On the 29th August, 1950 we embarked on a passenger ship in Southampton bound for Montreal. This was a regular line service to cross the Atlantic Ocean. The name of the ship was 'Canberra'. To me it seemed like a very large ship. But I was not surprised because I knew it had to cross a very large ocean.

I was very excited as soon as I got on board. There were huge areas to explore. As soon as the ship sailed I started my explorations. There were many decks and types of passengers. Over the first couple of days I made myself familiar with all the decks and I even got up on the bridge briefly, before I was told to get off. Although I started to get a little bored with some of the decks, there was one spot that I found where I never got bored. This was down on a lower deck, where there were no passenger cabins, and it was on the tip of the bow. There were huge chains and ropes there for the anchors, and it was open to the sea and the elements. The chains were taut, as they held the anchors in place, and disappeared into black holes in the hull. The immensely thick hemp ropes were more interesting still. They were secured through great studs and could be pulled tight by immense machines when the boat was docked. They were left on the hull, uncovered, in great coils forming nest-like arrangements.

I could hold onto the heavy iron parapet of the top of the prow and I could lean a little over the front of the prow, so my head was the most forward object of the great boat. Strangely enough, no one told me off for doing this. I was partially hidden from sight and maybe this is why. On one occasion one or two of the deckhands looked at me, but said nothing. I noticed that there were some pretty rough-looking types and perhaps it was not in their character to warn kids. Or maybe they thought that if the waves came over the bow and covered me or even washed me overboard, it would have served me right. But the waves were mostly not very large. The prow was going up and down through the crests of the waves, but I had seen as big waves on the Greek ferries of the Aegean Sea.

No one else ever came to the very front of the bow. The rough deckhands that occasionally worked there soon lost interest in me. I thought that the bow was visible from the Captain's bridge, because I could see the front of the bridge, but this did not bother me. For all practical purposes it became my hiding place on the Canberra. I did not tell my parents about it. When they would ask me where I was, I would respond:

– Just exploring.

My parents seemed happy enough with the explanation and had little smiles on their faces.

But as we moved further into the open Atlantic Ocean, some days the wind would come up and the sea would really rise. The waves would come crashing over the prow and I could not avoid getting wet. A few times great waves would come crashing over me and I would have to hold onto the heavy iron parapet for dear life. Yet still no one came to tell me to get off the prow. I figured they must have thought it was safe, or the rules of the sea were such so that every person was assumed to have enough sense to protect himself against the raging sea. This latter thought gave me a great sense of excitement. I imagined that I was a seafaring adventurer in the open sea, crossing the mighty Atlantic. The more I got into that sense, that mindset, the stronger and more confident I felt. There would be no wave big enough to take me into the deep dark sea. I would dominate the prow of my great ship and meet the high waves head on and always go through them. I was invulnerable.
But then a rhythmical Voice seemed to rise out of the dark blue sea:

– Down and up
Down and up
Down and down
Up and down
Toss you up
Toss you down
Toss you in
Till you drown

Anastassiades

Toss you high
N'er come down
Up you stay
Crashing down
Crashing down
Falling far
Falling down
Up you stay
Then fall down
Falling down
Crashing down
Falling down
Falling down
Spinning down
Spiral down
Down n' drown …

I couldn't see anyone around. I looked carefully. No one! I thought I was imagining this rhythmical chanting from the sea. Maybe it was coming from my own head. Maybe it was just induced by the rolling sea. So, I experimented and blocked my ears with my hands. The chanting nearly disappeared. I unblocked my ears. Clearly as anything:

– Falling down
Falling down
Crashing down
Crashing
Falling
Falling
Falling
Spiraling
Spiraling
Down
Down
Down
…

The sound became more and more mournful and frightened. I looked around again. No one. It had to be someone. It could not be the sea itself. Or could it? I had heard stories of the sea speaking to stranded seafarers as they went slowly crazy from lack of food and water. But I was well-fed and watered. In fact the food they served us from the Mess was plentiful and good, and you could eat as much as you wanted.

Then, all of a sudden, I thought I located where the Voice was coming from. It was from inside one of the great rope coils on the hull of the prow. I approached the great coil slowly and carefully. You never know what could spring out at you! I cautiously leaned over the rope that made the top of the coil and looked inside the coil. I had to look twice for I thought I saw a figure lying there. Momentarily I thought I recognized it. *I shouted as loudly as I could:*

– Styppas! Styppas! Is that you?
– …
– Styppas! What are you doing inside the rope coils?
– …
– Styppas — can you not hear me?
– …
– Wake up Styppas! Wake up!

– Ohhhh … , Ohhh … Tasouli …

– What is the matter Styppas? You look terrible!

– Oh Tasouli. I must have fallen asleep.

– But what are you doing here, on the Canberra, Styppas?

– I followed you and your parents, Tasouli. I hid here among the coils, as I am really a stowaway.

– Ah, no ticket?

– I usually get along fine without one. But you can't tell with these ocean liners. The Purser is pretty picky on the Canberra.

– Styppas, you are starting to look better. There is some color flowing back in your face.

– I am starting to feel better. I was having this most awful nightmare.

– You were moaning and crying out all about falling and crashing.

– I was?

– Yes, it was rhythmical. Like the movement of the Canberra through the waves.

– … Maybe that induced it. It is the most awful nightmare.

– Nightmares are awful, Styppas.

– This one is particularly bad. When it comes …

~

A couple of days passed. I tried to forget about Styppas and his nightmares in the rope coils and I started being nice to my parents. They had said that they would approach the Captain and other important people. That was usually a prelude to put me on show. Now they were both smiling superior smiles:

– Mamaka, Babaka did you speak to the Captain?

– Oh yes, Tasouli!

– What about Mamaka?

– Very important news, Tasouli.

– Ohh?

– Oh, yes. The Captain has invited you to sit at his table.

– Oh?

– Oh, yes, yes. For your birthday. On September 6. Just a few days from now.

– How many days before we arrive, will that be Mamaka?

– Just a couple, Tasouli. Just a couple.

So, I figured that this would be the highlight of the trip — sitting at the Captain's table for dinner on my birthday! I imagined all kinds of wonderful foods and desserts and celebrations. And how brilliant the Captain and his officers would look, dressed in white uniforms and eating politely at the Captain's table! We would be in the mighty St. Lawrence River by then, in calm green waters with marvelous views on each side. I could hardly wait.

But there was still Styppas. I wondered if he was still inside the coils of the great ropes in the bow. He must have overcome his nightmares, since the sea was not as high now and the waves were just cresting. He had probably found an empty cabin and a proper bed or at least a bunk to lie in. *But, as I approached the prow I heard the unmistakable sounds:*

– Falling down
Crashing down
Falling down
Falling down
Spinning down
Spiral down

Styppas was still there. He was still having his falling nightmare, even though the waves were much smaller. I looked over the coiled ropes and there he was. He seemed in a trance as he repeated the falling limerick over and over again. He must have been there for several days, while I was daydreaming about sitting at the Captain's table on my birthday. He looked awful. He also smelled badly. I thought carefully. This was an opportunity of sorts. I could leave him here and not tell anybody. Then he would probably die. This would rid me of my fears of him, especially when he went into rages and grew hair all over and threatened to extinguish me. Especially fearful for me was being extinguished by impalement with his hairy hands. Also, if I told my parents and they came and found him they would know that he was not imaginary and there would be endless trouble. Particularly from my mother — I would never hear the end of it. On the other hand, if my mother came to look for Styppas and couldn't find him, she would start all her psychological talk. Maybe she would even send me to a psychiatrist. That could be really dangerous and I could never fabricate my way out of that mess. I thought of telling the rough deckhands that were still hanging around the bow. But then, if they found him they would lock him up in the hole, since he was a stowaway. This would really enrage him and he would extinguish me by impalement for sure. On the other hand, if they weren't able to find him they were sure to report me to my parents and the Captain. So, we would be back to me being sent to the psychiatrist and, and worse still, the Captain would not want me at the Captain's table.

While I was pondering all these bad choices, I noticed that the rhythmic limerick sounds of falling were no longer coming from Styppas' coil. I stuck my head over the coil and he saw me at once. He looked worse still. I saw that the reason he smelled badly is that he must have been vomiting for a few days. I knew that I should not do anything since all the choices of doing something led to really bad outcomes for me. So, I just froze there. *Then I heard my own voice coming out all high-pitched and squeaky and barely audible:*

– Styppas …
– …
– Styppas … can you not hear me?
– …
– Styppas?
– …
– Styppas … do you want something?
– …
– Do you want anything?
– … get …
– Get what?
– … get …
– Styppas, you are growing hair again …
– … get …
– And producing green spittle …
– … get …
– … What, Styppas?
– … get …

I knew that I had to get away. Styppas was going to go into a great rage in spite of being weak. I ran as fast as I could into our cabin and pulled down the latch of the door. Fortunately neither my mother nor my father were there. I lay down, on my upper bunk bed, and covered my head with the pillow. I had to think and also I did not want to be seen. I was afraid Styppas would regain his strength and come after me all full of hair and green spittle. I had to find out what he wanted me to do. What did he mean by repeating 'get'? What was I supposed to get? I kept repeating:

– Get? Get? What am I supposed to get? Get what?
– … ?

Then just as I was drifting off, there was this familiar, reassuring Voice:

– He wants you to get Pamela, of course, Tasouli.

– Pamela, to get Pamela?

– And here I am!

– Pamela? Pamela! How did you get here?

– It wasn't difficult. One of the fishing boats off the Gaspé took me. They signaled the Canberra for me to get on and pick up Styppas.

– But Styppas is a stowaway, Pamela. They would put him in the deep, black hole where they put stowaways.

– No he isn't a stowaway, Tasouli! He has a perfectly valid ticket. First class, in fact.

– But he said he was, Pamela.

– Oh, he just said that he was a stowaway. You know, to bring attention to himself.

– I know, Pamela. He certainly does this by growing hair all over and his mouth foaming with green spittle!

– That is for your benefit Tasouli. No one else sees all the hair and the spittle. Except for me, occasionally, that is.

– Oh! Just you and I have seen the hair and the spittle then! But, still Pamela, I still don't understand. How come he happened to be on the Canberra?

– It wasn't by chance, Tasouli. Don't you remember when we all met up in Lausanne? We to see Fion off, and you with your parents.

– Of course, I remember, Pamela. How could I forget!

– Well, then he decided to follow you around your European trip.

– I never saw him, Pamela. One would have thought he might have said something.

– You know how he manages to become invisible when he is in a good mood.

– Oh, I know, alright. Because no one else sees him. Unless he wants to be seen. But how did you know to come and pick him up, Pamela?

– The deckhands reported to the First Mate that he was moaning and groaning. The First Mate told the Captain. Then a nice Officer called me at home on the wireless.

– On the wireless! And then you managed to find a fishing boat off the Gaspé?

– That is a bit of a longer story.

– OK.

– It has to do with goats.

– It sounds like a longer story, Pamela.

– Styppas and I took a holiday in the Gaspé a few years back. And on the northern coast, in the Gaspésie — off which we are now, there are many goat herders.

– So?

– So, we visited some of them to taste their goat cheese.

– So?

– So, they told us to taste the goat cheese with the tip of the tongue against the palate and that they all belonged to the goat-herders' Union, which had very strict rules.

– So?

– So, Styppas said they were all Quebec sovereignists.[6]

– What is a sovereignist, Pamela? And why, did Styppas say they were all Quebec sovereignists?

– Because they all had tiny, perfectly groomed beards and wire-rimmed glasses.

– Ohh! Just like my examining professors at Varvakion.

– Exactly. And they all spoke perfect French-Canadian. And they got very angry if you chewed and swallowed their tiny samples of goat cheese without first melting it with the tip of your tongue against your palate.

– Ohh! It is complicated to be a sovereignist. But what does all this have to do with the fishing boat that will bring you to the Canberra, Pamela?

– Styppas tired of being made to taste goat cheese with the tip of the tongue against the palate and we drove off to the coast to find some fish.

– Ah! Fishermen! I think I am starting to see now.
– Yes. We found a harbor with a small fishing fleet and bought some lobsters and crabs off them. And we became friendly with the fishermen.
– And you did not have to taste the lobsters and crabs with the tip of the tongue against the palate?
– Not at all, Tasouli.
– And the fishermen did not wear wire-rimmed glasses and little beards?
– Not one of them, Tasouli.
– Ah, so they were not sovereignists! But how did you find the fishermen again now, Pamela.
– I have my ways.
– And how did you convince them to take you to the Canberra?
– They remembered us buying the lobsters and crabs.
– But when did the nice Officer from the Canberra call you on the wireless?
– Just this morning.
– Just this morning! But how could you have got here so fast?
– I have my ways.

~

The great day that I would sit at the Captain's table finally arrived. I was very excited and full of happy anticipation. It would be a perfect celebration for my birthday. After all, my parents were in a very good mood all smiling their superior smiles and telling everybody how their little treasure was going to sit at the Captain's table for his birthday. More importantly still, Styppas was gone from the boat which was now in very calm waters of the St. Lawrence. And Styppas was unlikely to come back since he had been taken home by Pamela. So, there was virtually no chance I would be extinguished on my birthday.

The Captain and his crew ate early. I found this a little unusual since I was used to important celebrations taking place late in the evening, when we would go out in Greece. But my parents knew about the early dinner time and they were continuing to be full of smiles. So I figured it was alright. The early dinner would not dampen the brilliance of the celebration. I did not want to be embarrassed, so I told my parents that I would meet them at the Captain's table since I had something important to do.

At the appointed time I went looking for the Captain's table and the brilliant uniforms. I couldn't find it. Someone showed me where it was, in the general dining room. I thought it was a bit strange that I had not noticed it before. Then I realized that the reason I had not noticed it was that it looked just like all the other tables. Except, maybe a little longer. My parents were already sitting down. But there were no brilliant uniforms. Ah … the Captain and his Crew hadn't arrived, I thought. Perhaps there would be a procession. Like a military parade. Perhaps there would be music playing to accompany the entry of the Captain and his Crew. But nothing like that was happening. I wasn't too keen to sit with my parents and their superior smiles, so I asked someone where the Captain was. This person, who looked like he had just come up from the engine room pointed with a disinterested movement of his head. He had pointed towards the end of the long, rough wooden table. So, I found a seat near that end of the table where the Captain was supposed to be sitting, diagonally across from my parents. They kept giving me proud, encouraging smiles, which could have been embarrassing. After all, I would be sitting closer to the Captain — all on my own initiative! Fortunately no one seemed to be paying any attention to them or to me.

The meal was pretty ordinary. It was good, but so was the ship's food every day. No one was bothering to speak to me but, on the other hand, neither was anyone telling me not to sit where I was sitting. Most people sitting at the table were wolfing down their food. I could see that after a while of feeding themselves they started to become more talkative. So, I was emboldened and I asked the person sitting next to me:

– Who is the Captain?

– Down at the very end — on this side.
– Ohh — he does not put his uniform on?
– Not until we get into Port.
– Ahh … tomorrow.
– Ahmm!

I tried to take a good look at the Captain sitting at the end of the table. He looked very much like the other men sitting at the table. He was dressed in ordinary working clothes — not even a jacket. And he was unshaven and a bit shabby and rough-looking. So running out of conversation, I played my big card. I turned again to the person who had told me who the Captain was:

– It is my birthday.
– Ahmm?
– My birthday, it's today!
– Ahmm.

So, I figured that was it. No one particularly cared that it was my birthday. But then I saw the shabby Captain look at me and he seemed to raise a table glass in my direction. Somehow, it was communicated to him that it was me who was the birthday boy. Likely by the person sitting next to me. But I have no idea how. These naval hands had fast and secret ways of communicating, no doubt!

As the dinner meal was getting to the end, a cake arrived. It was a very plain-looking cake that looked more like brown bread. I can't remember if it had a candle or not. But it certainly did not have twelve candles. I assumed it was for my birthday, but I was not sure. It might have been just the pudding dessert and it was on an immense baking pan. The cake was being passed around the table and people were cutting off pieces for their plates right off the baking pan. I cut off a small piece. It was nice and warm but it tasted as plain as it looked. Then I noticed the Captain. He had taken two big pieces and was devouring the first piece with giant-size bites. He looked at me and gave me a little crooked smile. Then he rubbed his belly while chewing and looking at me. He smiled again his little crooked smile. My parents had even bigger smiles than usual.

So, that was my much anticipated birthday celebration at the Captain's table on the Canberra. Much anticipated events were starting to take a certain pattern in my life. Like the Occupation goose, that was inedible although we were so hungry. But at least for my birthday, I did not have the conflict of having to have the pet goose killed in order to eat her. Or like after my great success after the Varvakion entrance exams, when I told Styppas, with so much pride, and he turned the whole thing around as a betrayal to my parents. But for my birthday, everyone seemed happy enough at the end — from the grumpy Captain to my parents, to all the people around the table. And Styppas had gone home and could not, and did not, turn anything around. Not while he was under Pamela's watchful eye. Certainly, I was not extinguished on my birthday by impalement, or by any other method. So, I decided that it was a pretty good day for me overall. And we were now far into the calm Canadian waters of the St. Lawrence.

Rupert Street

We arrived in Montreal on September 7, 1950. From there we went to Ottawa, where my father's job was at the National Research Council. I don't remember how we got from Montreal to Ottawa or how we ended up renting a house in Ottawa. I think someone had recommended the family that owned the house. It was on Rupert Street. 16 Rupert Street. It was in a neighborhood now called the Glebe, although I don't recall that name being used much then. The Glebe is an older district now, fashionable and expensive. I wouldn't have considered the Glebe fashionable or expensive then, and the houses were certainly not new. It seemed more or a less a working-people neighborhood but not a poor district either. Not too different from Pagrati, except the houses were mostly from red brick while in Pagrati there would have been more stone and cement. Soon I got to know all the streets and their short cuts around Fifth Avenue, the large street to which Rupert Street connected. And Fifth Avenue connected to Bank Street, which was the main commercial street. In fact, Rupert Street was a small street coming off Fifth Avenue. It was not a through street, so it formed a little enclave of its own. This gave it a sense of enclosure and safety. It was my center of operations. Whatever my adventures were and no matter how badly I got lost, I remember the huge sense of relief when I found myself in a familiar part of Bank Street. Then on to the right part of Fifth Avenue. 16 Rupert Street would not be far now.

16 Rupert Street was an old three-storey red brick house. It was owned by a family called the MacPhersons, from which we rented the back part of the second floor. Our lodgings were quite comfortable. There was a small kitchen on the second floor and I think a couple of bedrooms and sitting room space. But what I loved most about the second floor of 16 Rupert was a spacious glass-enclosed veranda at the back of the house facing the little garden. This veranda extended past the house, a construction that was common in Ottawa and can be still found today in houses. This veranda was meant mostly for use when the weather was warm. It projected out past the third floor, so it gave a great feeling of openness and space. I loved to sit out there and occupy myself with little chores, such as carving my walking stick which I had abducted from the British progressive farm with the unpasteurized milk. Of course it was too cold to sit out there in the Ottawa winter, where outside temperatures dropped down to -20° or -30° Fahrenheit, as the veranda was not heated. But I would still go in the veranda to marvel at the giant icicles hanging from our rooftop and the roofs of the neighboring houses.

Mrs. MacPherson

The somewhat eccentric matriarch of 16 Rupert Street was Mrs. Dorothy MacPherson. She was British (Welsh, I think actually) and sounded a bit BBCish, but I can't remember for sure if she had worked for the BBC. Here in Ottawa she worked for the National Film Board. Mrs. MacPherson had some very odd habits, or so my mother and father thought. One of her oddest habits was how she made salads. My parents thought it was the most amusing thing they had seen and they would laugh and joke endlessly about it.

– Can you imagine, Phivaki,[7] she uses a wooden bowl to make the salad!
– Yes, my Dinaki. It is unbelievable!
– Not even the poorest peasant in Zakynthos uses a wooden bowl nowadays, Phivaki.
– Everyone has at least a glazed pottery bowl for salads.
– Not even my mother who lived in the mud hut with soil for the floor would eat out of wooden bowls, Phivaki.
– She told me once, that there were peasants in Zakynthos in her mother's time still eating out of wooden bowls. Meaning they were that poor.
– Yes. And she does not wash it after use, Phivaki. One is only allowed to wipe the wooden salad bowl!

So, the merriment would continue, with the stories about Mrs. MacPherson. How she was so, so BBC. And how she threw her husband out in England and took her children, Andrew and Jay to Canada. But my mother and father also admired Mrs. MacPherson because of her independence and resourcefulness. Also, I liked Mrs. MacPherson. Even though I didn't understand all of what she said, we seemed to communicate pretty well. I don't think she understood much of what I said either. But she was totally un-phased and would go on and on as if the conversation was perfectly comprehensible to both parties. I think talking in funny accents and associating with somewhat odd people was very much her milieu. I don't think her attitude towards my conversations with her had much to do with the fact that I was a child, since she carried on in the same manner, often off the subject, when adults would talk to her, including her own children. This seemed to cause a bit of consternation among adults and there were often a few looks and sighs of exasperation.

But I felt very comfortable with Mrs. MacPherson and her off-kilter conversations, which were mostly carried out in the kitchen on the first floor of 16 Rupert Street. I remember the repetitive rhythm in her speech, which I found reassuring. And I remember thinking that it was better to hold a conversation with someone like her, where neither of us would fully understand what the other was saying, rather than with someone who would tell me that they didn't understand exactly what I was saying. I think I was also comfortable with Mrs. MacPherson's repetitive English ramblings because of this reassuring quality in their tone and speaking rhythms. Through her speech she had created a world in which things seemed alright at 16 Rupert Street in the MacPherson household. Somehow her disorder seemed to me the order that must have always existed there.

Andrew

But my favorite and the person I admired most at the MacPhersons, was Andrew MacPherson. I think Andrew was probably an older teenager at that time. I don't recall his exact age but I knew he was a few years older than me. He was tall and lanky with a little smile most of the time. Andrew always joked around with me and showed me many tricks and told me many stories about Canada and the strange people he knew. His little smile would take on a mischievous or even a wicked quality if he was about to show me a trick or tell a funny story about someone. His room was up on the third floor of the house facing towards Rupert Street.

Once I walked into Andrew's room and he was lying on his bed. It was early evening and the room was lit with a single light bulb hanging from the ceiling with a long electric cord. There must have been a little bit of a breeze through the window because the light bulb was slightly swinging. Andrew had a glimmer in his eye, so I knew something was up. He asked if I knew how to turn off the light without getting out of bed. Once I assured him that I didn't, he grabbed an air pistol that was near his bed and shot off the bulb. He just fired once. He thought it was the funniest thing and laughed and laughed. I was really impressed.

This air pistol could be loaded one pellet at a time. A heavy lead pellet shaped like a small chess pawn would be inserted in the back of the muzzle. One did this by pulling back hard on a black steel lever that was hinged to the back of the muzzle until it made a reassuring click when the chamber was loaded. The air pistol was then ready to use. The pistol itself was heavy and shiny black and somehow looked like a real gun. For some reason I started to become very attached to that gun. I had never handled a gun freely before and I would borrow it from Andrew on every possible occasion. Ultimately I inherited Andrew's air pistol, but it might not have been until a few years later when we no longer lived with the MacPhersons. After I acquired the air pistol, I used it to shoot at squirrels in our back yard, although I think I generally missed. But I got pretty good at shooting bull-frogs sitting still on lily leaves in ponds. I found out it was easy to pull off the long legs of the bull-frogs, skin them and fry them on a camp fire. This, in turn, impressed my friends. And that gave me a great feeling. That was because, contrary to Greek kids, these Canadian kids clearly admired my exploits with Andrew's air gun and moreover they were not reluctant to say so.

The gun must have been very well made because I kept it for decades and decades after Andrew gave it to me. It would always make that same reassuring click when I loaded the chamber with air by pulling hard on the strong, black lever.

Being able to borrow and play with Andrew's air gun any time I wanted might have had something to do with the beginning of this feeling of freedom I started to have soon after we arrived in Canada. Any time I asked Andrew if I could borrow his air gun he would give me a slightly disinterested little look, like 'why are you even bothering to ask me?' And since I had asked Andrew, I felt that it was not necessary to ask my parents. So I figured that I was free to play with the gun at any time without permission. It was a kind of boldness, a rising confidence. Perhaps it was related to the gun, or perhaps related also to all of the other events that started to happen soon after we arrived. In any case, I don't remember this feeling of freedom when we lived in Greece. There freedom was a word, a glorious concept, that one day would be achieved after much struggle, deprivation and death. But it never came. Not really. Not like the freedom to play with Andrew's gun.

Andrew certainly kept 16 Rupert Street stirred up. He would often disappear in the wilds, without apparently telling anyone and a few days later would appear with game he had shot. The game was not what one usually thinks of a hunter bringing back home. One day he appeared with a huge porcupine and demanded that his mother cook it. There was no way Mrs. MacPherson would touch the spiny creature. The animal also smelled badly. Maybe it had even been trapped first, and lay around for days. Or maybe he had shot it after it had been trapped, and left for who knows how long before he decided to bring it in. It was one of the few times I saw Mrs. MacPherson being very firm and even angry as she made Andrew take the smelly beast out of the kitchen. I am not sure if he disposed of it by dumping it back into the woods or if he gave it to one of his friends.

Another time Andrew came in waving about a groundhog he had shot. The groundhog was not as repulsive as the porcupine to Mrs. MacPherson. And, the groundhog did not smell as bad as the porcupine. So, some discussion actually ensued as to whether it should be cooked. I felt sorry for the groundhog and named it 'the poor groundhog'. Everybody thought that calling it 'the poor groundhog' was very amusing and the name caught on. Andrew insisted that the poor groundhog should be cooked in the oven and that it would be delicious, even if it wasn't skinned or gutted. That was a big strategic mistake because Mrs. Macpherson really put her foot down. There was no way she would allow the beastie to be cooked with its skin and guts in her oven!

So, beastie was put out of the back door in the garden by the garbage.

I saw that Andrew was quite miffed to have the poor groundhog so unceremoniously treated. It was at this point, when I had an idea. Little did I know that it would become a *cause célèbre* at 16 Rupert Street. So, I said to Andrew:

– I think I should bury the poor groundhog.
– If you wish.
– I can bury him in the garden.
– Mm …
– There by the corner.
– Mmm …
– Then everyone will see where he is buried.

I could see Andrew's eyes light up all of a sudden. He was no longer miffed about his ground hog being put out by the garbage.

– And, Andrew, we will have a little ceremony.
– For him to go to the happy hunting grounds!
– The happy hunting grounds?
– That's the Indian lore.
– The Indian lore, Andrew?
– That is where all animals killed by hunting go.
– So, poor groundhog will be happy?
– Most certainly!

This was all very magical to me. I had never seen or even heard of the animals Andrew brought in. There were certainly no porcupines in Greece, or even in Europe, I think. There we had the little hedgehog who was a fraction the size of a porcupine and brownish with little quills and rather retiring. And I certainly did not see hedgehogs often. I might have seen one or two in Zakynthos or Pyrgos. I think sitting on a fence. The groundhog was also an animal I was not familiar with. Certainly nothing resembled their large size that I could think of.

And the happy hunting grounds! That was very strange. I could imagine this dream-like place where animals and ancient native hunters were running about. I tried to force myself to make these happy hunting grounds a pleasant place to dream about. I tried to visualize the happy hunting grounds before I went to sleep, thinking that this might help. But each time a disturbing thought seemed to come into my mind or even my dream; how was it possible that the shot porcupine and the groundhog could actually be happy, if they were shot? And even if they went to the happy hunting grounds before they were shot, surely their fate was to be hunted and likely killed. The place was called 'hunting grounds' after all, happy or not. So, I figured that maybe it was the magical Indian hunters who went to that place and who then happily hunted ever after. That at least would make more sense.

I asked Andrew about my dilemma.

– Andrew, would the poor groundhog be happy in the happy hunting grounds?
– Certainly!
– But he was shot before he went. He could not be too happy about that.
– Mmm.
– Maybe it is the Indian hunters in the happy hunting grounds who are happy. Is that so, Andrew?
– Yes … that's why they are called happy hunting grounds.
– But can the animals be happy if they are being hunted and killed, Andrew?
– It is a cycle … the Indians think everything is a cycle.
– You mean they would become alive again after being killed in the happy hunting grounds.
– Something like that.

Andrew sounded a bit vague about this kind of cycle. He seemed to confirm that it was the hunters who were happy, although he did not sound too certain about this either. But then, where did this leave my poor groundhog who we had buried with such honours and ceremonies? It was all a bit of a disappointment for me. Until then I thought Andrew knew everything about animals in the wild woods of Canada and what happened to them in the happy, happy hunting grounds.[8]

Jay

Andrew McPherson had a sister, Jay. She was an older teenager. But Jay was very different than Andrew. She was thin and shadowy and wandered about the house. She would not say much and I could not tell if she liked me or not. Because she did not say much, I figured that she probably did not like me very much. But as I watched her in her wanderings she seemed to come out of shadows and then fade again into darkened rooms. She was in her own world. So, I started to figure that it wasn't that she did not like me. She was simply self-absorbed.

At times Jay would say things about Greek myths. She seemed to assume that I would know what she was talking about. But this was not the case. Most of the time I really did not follow what she was talking about, but I had a general idea about the myths. So, I would make a comment or two. That seemed to animate her and even excite her. But when I could not keep up the conversation about the particular myth she was talking about, she seemed to lose interest. She would then withdraw again and go off on her own.

Andrew did not seem to be particularly fond of his sister. He was dismissive of her peculiar ways and would even make fun of her. But he never said anything that was bad about her. Andrew liked to make fun of people in a kind of humorous way. Of course, Andrew was my friend and I felt that I had to agree with him on how one regarded Jay.

But my parents had a different attitude towards Jay. Probably because of the Greek myths they elevated Jay to great intellectual heights. Her peculiarities and silences proved to them that she was a great intellectual. They also would engage her in conversations, more than I did, about the myths and talk to her much more than they talked to Andrew.

So, as usual, I ended up in conflict. My friend, Andrew, seemed to make fun of Jay's peculiarities while my parents admired them. I did not want to tell Andrew that my parents admired Jay, or to my parents that Andrew was making fun of his sister. Finally, I decided that the best policy was to agree both with Andrew and with my parents, while not saying very much to either. But this policy soon backfired, as I started to feel badly since by not saying much to either, it was as if I was lying to both. But then I reasoned that I would feel worse still if I told both Andrew and my parents what the other was saying about Jay. Surely then, both Andrew and my parents would think that I was telling them what the other was saying about Jay because I was taking the opposite side. Then they would both be upset with me. This reasoning actually made me feel much better. I figured that I had made another important discovery: one inner conflict is better than two, at least if it involves other people.

I never tried to explain to Jay this conflict I had of how Andrew and my parents perceived her. I imagined that if I had done, she would just be dismissive of her brother, with something like:

– Oh, Andrew is always like that.

But Jay also had other things on her mind. She had met and become infatuated with Robert Graves, the eminent scholar of poetry and Greek myths. So, Jay Macpherson ended up in Majorca chasing after Robert Graves and his myths. Unsurprisingly Andrew had lots of ironic and amusing commentary about his sister's perambulations.

Of course my parents turned out to be right. Jay soon became famous after the publication of her books of poems, notably 'The Boatman' for which she got the Governor General's Award. The Greek myths that she talked so much about soon became the focal point of her life.

Geoffrey

A few months after we arrived at the MacPhersons another tenant came. He was very English. His name was Geoffrey Hatterslay-Smith. Tall with a muscular build, his hair flying out on the sides and back, he spoke mostly with a pipe in his mouth. The tobacco he smoked smelled very nice to me. Later I learned that the tobacco was called 'Three Nuns — none nicer'. Also, I learned that the Three Nuns could be kept moist in the leather pouch by adding a small slice of potato. Geoffrey told me that English Lords would knock out one of their side teeth so they could talk without taking the pipe out of their mouth. He certainly often spoke with his pipe in his mouth but I could not tell if he had actually knocked out a tooth. Both Andrew and Geoffrey would just laugh whenever I would ask for confirmation of that peculiar habit, so I was not sure if I could believe the story.

Many of the stories and comments Geoffrey told me had to do with English aristocracy and the Lords. It was as if he came out of the pages of my English books in Greece about the Lords. Initially I did not think that his stories were all that funny, but Geoffrey seemed to relish telling them as if he personally knew all the peculiar habits of the Lords. Each story brought out something about the behavior or a custom of the Lords. Yet each story had something in it that would teach me something or test my knowledge about the aristocracy. Soon, I started to think that Geoffrey was much more like a Lord than any of the Lords of Charring Cross who, after all, mostly just said 'sorry'.

A typical Geoffrey story, which sticks in my mind, was about a titled family with two young sons and an ancient butler, James. The story goes that the two boys were playing at the top of a winding staircase. All of a sudden, the older brother slips and comes crashing down on the stone-paved courtyard of the family castle. The ancient butler hobbles over to see if the boy has been hurt. The younger brother calls to the butler from the top of the staircase:

– How is he, James?
– Dead m'Lord.

To get the joke, one would have to know that it is only the eldest son who can be addressed as 'Lord'. Also, for the right kind of effect the ancient butler must give a deadpan, toothless, matter-of-fact response.

Geoffrey had mastered all of the intonations and facial expressions of his Lordly characters to a 'T'. And the fact that Andrew, who was often around, would provide an appreciative giggle after Geoffrey's stories confirmed for me that the story was, indeed, funny.

I was not sure if Geoffrey came from a Lordly family but he had gone to Oxford from where he ultimately obtained a doctorate. In fact, he was a glaciologist. He was in Canada to study the ice in the high North. Geoffrey led expeditions to the ice of Ellesmere Island and had endless stories to tell. In this way he was kindred to Andrew who wanted to study the animals of the North. I am not sure who recommended the MacPhersons to Geoffrey, or for that matter who recommended them to us. Maybe Andrew came across Geoffrey and asked him to come and stay at 16 Rupert. These things just happened and there was a kind of normality about them. It never occurred to me that events could have unfolded in any other way. But we did have influence over one event that turned out to be important in peoples' lives.

One day Geoffrey announced that he was going to go for a trip to England. He had to go to Oxford, so my parents mentioned that my Aunt Maria (Litsa) was in Oxford doing post-graduate work in genetics there. That is the same Litsa from the days of the Bastille, who was the cousin of mother's from Zakynthos.

When Geoffrey returned from his trip, he was obviously much taken with Maria. But he did not talk about her in terms of whether he liked her or not. Rather, he went into the Lordly mode and kept relating with great importance and Englishness her origin from a great family in Zakynthos. They must have been Zakynthian Lords, named in the *Libro Doro*, with fine property on the island. Obviously Maria had forgot to apprise him of the situation of the Libro Doro, which originally may have contained the names and families of the old titled Zakynthians, but with the burning of the Libro Doro in the great fire, all Zakynthians now claimed their ancestors were listed in the great golden book of titles. And of course, Maria was studying very important genetics from a very important professor.

But my parents had also received correspondence from Maria before Geoffrey had returned to Rupert Street and she must have been more explicit, since they were giggling and laughing and making all kinds of insinuations. I figured that the long and short of all of this intelligence was that Geoffrey liked Maria and vice versa. But I was not sure. When I asked Andrew about it, he would just put on his mischievous smile and would not say anything.

Unfortunately, I could not find Styppas to ask him to explain to me what was really going on between Maria and Geoffrey. He was always very good at this sort of thing. But Styppas was nowhere to be found. I looked and looked for him everywhere. I looked for him behind all the curtains of 16 Rupert Street and under the sofas and in all the rooms, and where the poor groundhog was buried and all around the neighborhood. I asked many neighbors and no one had seen him — nobody even seemed to know him. He had vanished from the face of earth. In fact, I had not seen Styppas since the boat, since the Canberra, when he had become seasick among the ropes. He had disappeared since we had landed in Canada. And even though I was curious as to what had happened to him, the peculiar thing was that I had not really missed him.

Hopewell

I started school in Canada in September 1950. I had completed grade six in Athens at the Maraslion, so I could enter grade seven in Ottawa. The closest school was called Hopewell. It was an old school in a nice red brick building. I could walk to it from Rupert Street in about half an hour by crossing the Rideau Canal at Bank Street.

Of course, I was wearing short pants as all Greek children of my age. When I first went to the school I noticed that all other boys were wearing long pants. Gradually, I became aware of something quite peculiar related to my short pants. In Greece, if a boy had such a big difference in attire from other boys, he would certainly be made fun of. At Hopewell nobody made fun of me. In fact, nobody even seemed to notice or look peculiarly at me. The situation became even stranger as the weather started to get colder. My mother, I suppose, assumed that short pants were in order for her darling little boy, even as the temperatures started to hover around freezing. But, still no comments or funny looks or giggling from my classmates. This was my first clue that something was very different at Hopewell from my schools in Greece. As the temperatures got colder still, even my mother figured that I should have long pants, so they bought my first pair of long pants. They were made from good wool, my parents said, and they certainly kept my knees from freezing. But still there were no comments from anyone in school about my major change in attire!

The second clue about the difference in Hopewell and my Greek schools had to do with my English. I knew I was not very advanced in English and my own speech sounded different to my ear from that of the other children and adults. But I was well prepared to face my fate in this respect. I knew that I would be the Frank of Hopewell. I am talking, of course, about the Frank who was the only foreign kid in Maraslion. The same Frank who accidentally had split my head, and who felt so badly about it. Here at Hopewell, I was the only foreign kid in my class. There were no others. So, I had resigned myself that I would certainly be the 'Frank of Hopewell' and be treated as such by the other children.

But for some strange reason, I never did become the Frank of Hopewell. First, with respect to English it is true that I had trouble with spelling. The word 'spelling' does not even exist in Greek, since the language is phonetic. A schoolchild might be simply asked 'how do you write' a vowel sound in a word, since there can be more than one written representation of a vowel sound (mostly derived from Ancient Greek). The child would respond by indicating the vowel letter or letters that make that single vowel sound in that word. But the child would never be asked to identify all of the letters making up a word, because each of the consonants has a unique and unambiguous sound. So 'spelling' whole words seemed a very strange concept to me. In fact, children being asked to spell out words at Hopewell simply reinforced my opinion that English was a defective language, which had to be corrected so it became phonetic. I can't remember if I told the teachers this, but I think there might have been some discussion between the teachers and my parents as to whether I should be kept back a grade so I could learn how to spell. This apparently did not get very far because I was well ahead in math compared to the kids in my class at Hopewell, and I would ace the math tests without having to study. So, they couldn't very well keep me back because of the spelling, if my math level was at least one grade, or possibly two, ahead of the rest of the class. Plus, I was probably a little ahead in English grammar which was heavily emphasized in my Greek books for English learners. And again, for whatever reason, the kids in the class never made fun of me because I was not too good at spelling. Instead they seemed to admire my math ability. How totally different from poor Frank at the Maraslion, who spoke very good but heavily French-accented Greek and was continually teased about it!

I don't know

Except for the mysterious 'spelling', I found school at Hopewell relatively easy compared to the Greek schools. Much of this was due to the attitudes of the teachers. When the teachers at Hopewell would ask a question of the whole class and no one put up their hand, or someone gave the wrong answer, they would then ask individual students. This was more or less as it was in Maraslion. But then, amazingly to me, not only did the Hopewell teachers tolerate an 'I don't know' answer, but if a student had guessed and gave the wrong answer, they would actually say:

– If you don't know, just say so.

This would never have happened in Maraslion where the teachers would not accept an 'I don't know' answer, and would cajole and force the student to come up with something that made at least some sense. If all else failed, the student would then be made to stand up and be humiliated in front of the class with simpler questions and comments matched by the teacher. It was, of course, worse in Pagrati Elementary School, where an 'I don't know' answer could earn you a beating with a ruler in the palms of your hands or your legs.

When I first heard a Hopewell teacher saying 'If you don't know, just say so', I thought that this was a trick. Surely, the plan of the teacher was to make a list of all the students that said 'I don't know' and keep them back after class. Then she would make these students write out the correct answer a few hundred times and give them additional exercises. But this never happened. At the end of the class, the Hopewell students who said 'I don't know' would leave unscathed and never be asked to do detention. Just like everybody else.

So, I started to think that Hopewell was easy street. And I liked it. I liked it a lot. The system did not have built-in anxiety and fear induced by the Greek school system. One did not have to worry about being identified as inferior in every class. You could simply say the magical words 'I don't know' and no one seemed to think worse of you.

Also, some of the classes in Hopewell were ridiculously easy. I think they may have been called 'citizenship classes' or something like that. They consisted of girls and boys doing dances and singing and playing music of other, mostly European, countries. They generally were dressed up in native costumes from these countries and I remember little girls in Ukrainian dresses dancing about. And you got marks just for being there and watching. I don't remember ever having been asked a single question about the geography or language of these countries, like the population or geography of Ukraine, or even having to participate in the songs or dances. Yet, I always got a good mark. As far as I could see, so did everybody else. Louis St. Laurent was then the Prime Minister of Canada and I remember something being said at the start of these classes about the Prime Minister, and how good it was to have all these cultures and for everybody to attend. But as far as I remember, they never took attendance.

Shop

Probably the class at Hopewell that had the biggest impact on me was the industrial arts shop. I had never done anything like this in Greece. Also, none of my extended family knew much about working with their hands. As a result I had never made anything in a shop although I always tried to carve and shape wood and other materials. Hopewell had a large and very well-equipped shop for woodwork, metalwork and pottery. More important still, the teachers were excellent. They had a simple way of showing you how to design the article and work the tools. They somehow transmitted the expectation that you would be able to carry out the task as if it was quite normal. I made all kinds of articles. They included an excellent wooden lamp stand, a very nicely rounded small wooden frame for a round picture, a small bookcase from a superior kind of wood, an ashtray from a copper sheet with an engraved maple leaf, a fine decorative iron poker and all kinds of pottery, which I also glazed and fired in the shop kiln. My parents were amazed but I don't think that they believed I had made these things with my own hands. But I didn't care. The work in the shop gave me a kind of confidence boost that I had not experienced before. And I was marked very fairly on what I had actually made. The teacher would explain how the numerical value of the mark tied into the finished article. This gave a special meaning to getting a mark — for an article I could keep forever. It was very different from getting a mark for a math or English test, where the test question that you got the mark for would be soon forgotten. When I brought these articles home, I would look at them and look at them, not believing I had actually made them with my own hands.

Rough kid

The work at the shop was certainly a new experience for me, but it was my relationship with other kids that amazed me. I had certainly expected to be the odd kid out, the outlier in the schoolyard and sport. In fact, I expected to be bullied and pushed around as would be normal for Greek children, in any case, and a little more since I was a foreign kid. But I did not notice anything like that. In the schoolyard, marbles were popular, although they played different games from what I was used to in Greece. When I joined in the games, there seemed to be a general tolerance to me, but I was not too enthralled with the unfamiliar games they played.

There was a rough-looking kid who did kind-of try to bully me a bit. He would give me a shove and say some things, which I did not completely understand but which I interpreted as being derogatory. Since I expected this kind of behavior, which would have been normal for Greek kids, I just gave him a little shove back. But I didn't say anything back because I hadn't really understood what he had said in the first place. To my amazement, instead of him trying to beat me up for the shove I gave him, he seemed to want to play marbles with me. Wanting to play marbles with someone who had just shoved you would be unheard of among Greek boys. At every recess after that, that boy would seek me out, and we would end up playing marbles or some kind of game. And on a couple of occasions he really surprised me.

Once in the gym there was a supervised game that we played. It was a everyone-for-himself type of game. The idea was that you would hold one foot up with your hand and then hop around on the other foot, trying to knock down the other boys who were also hopping around on one foot. Each boy would try to knock down other boys generally by shoving them. If both of your feet had to touch the ground, even for a moment, you were disqualified. Last boy left standing would win. It was fascinating. The strongest boys did well knocking others off their one-footed perch by hopping towards them and giving them a good shove. The rough-looking kid was doing very well in the melee. It seemed the game was made for him. He was about the right size, strong and good at shoving. Soon, he had knocked most of the other kids off. I had knocked a few kids off also, as I too was suited to this game. But as I was fascinated by the way the rough kid attacked and succeeded, I stood on the side-line watching him. The gym teacher signaled a couple of times that I was to hop in the middle of the battles and not stand on the side lines, but I disregarded his instructions. My attention was focused on the technique of the rough kid. In a few instants, it seemed, the rough kid knocked over the last couple of boys remaining in the competition. The gym teacher signaled to me more emphatically that I was to enter battle. So, having studied the rough kid and thinking that I had picked out a weakness, I took a mighty one-legged hopping run at him and hit him as low and as hard as I could. He went flying, while I managed to keep my one-footed balance!

As he got back on his feet and was catching his breath, he looked admiringly at me:

– Good strategy, Tassos!

I could not believe my ears. Here, I had basically cheated by staying out of the thick of the competition until he had knocked most people out, and yet he was congratulating me? I was surprised that such a rough-looking kid even knew the word 'strategy'; let alone how to use it correctly in this context. If he was a Greek school-boy, he would have been shouting and complaining to the gym teacher that I had cheated and should have been disqualified. And so would a lot of other kids that had been knocked off. And then I would have been ostracized at recess by most boys that had been knocked off. But none of this happened. I had no idea why it was like this in Canada, but I liked it. I liked it a lot!

And it carried on like this in Hopewell. One day in class I was sitting more or less in the back and generally fooling around and talking during the lesson, which annoyed the teacher. But I had taken care that I would only fool around and talk when she was not looking in my direction. She was obviously getting quite annoyed, as she wasn't sure who was talking.

– Who is talking? Who is talking? Put your hand up!

There was a terrible moment of silence. I was trying to become invisible behind my desk.

– Whoever was talking put your hand up, or you will stay back after class!

I felt horrible. I had not put my hand up when I should have and now matters had become worse. I tried to put my hand up, but it had become too heavy. I could not lift it, it seemed. The silence continued for another small eternity. And then it happened. My rough classmate, who initially bullied me, stuck his hand up.

– It was me.

He had spoken in an almost sub-audible voice, which made his guilt even more convincing. The horrible feeling I had for not admitting my guilt had turned into an even more horrible guilt, something akin to terror. I was sure other children, especially ones near me must have noticed. All my ability to function and follow the lesson now disappeared. I did not hear another word that the teacher said. All I could think of was for the class to finish, so I could apologize to my ex-bully. My protector, now it seemed. Finally, this eternity also passed and the class was finished. I ran up to him.

– It was me who was talking. It was *me*!

He just looked at me a little blankly. At least I had now confessed to him. But I still did not understand why he did it.

– Why did you put your hand up, when it was me who was talking? It was me who was talking!

He just shrugged.

– They got it in for me in any case!

And that was the end of it. That was all he said. And at recess, none of the other kids seemed to be fussed about it.

This would never have happened in a Greek school. It's unimaginable. Never in a thousand years! But it did happen in Hopewell! It happened in Canada, in Canada then.

Volleyball

The other thing I liked at Hopewell was sports. I had never done really well in sports in the Greek schools I attended. There the main team sport was football (soccer). It was not really organized and more like a pick-up game where children just entered a game at any time. The strongest and most aggressive children totally dominated. They dominated both in choosing the positions of their liking but also in kicking children, who were not their friends or who they did not like, out of the game. Here at Hopewell, the sport teams were much more organized. In Hopewell I chose the volleyball team, since I had played a little volleyball, mostly in the streets of Rafina. I was not too good at it and I could not jump high enough to spike the ball or block spikes from the opponents. Nevertheless, I liked the game and when I said this to the Hopewell coach, it was good enough to get me into the team. That again was very surprising to me and unlikely to have happened in Greece. Moreover, most of my teammates were much taller than I and physically bigger also.

So, we practiced during physical education classes and were taught how to retrieve the ball, set it up and hit it over the net. As the year progressed, we learned that we were going to go into a big inter-school volleyball tournament. I think it was schools of the greater Ottawa area, or something like that. There was great anticipation and excitement about this tournament.

Now, just before the tournament, something happened that turned out to be very important in my life. It was a total accident. I had registered for after-school activities at the Museum of Natural History, which was relatively close to where we lived. I loved that museum. I spent hours looking at the wonderful exhibits of stuffed animals, prehistoric animal skeletons, plants, and American Indians and how they lived. But I loved the beautiful rock exhibits and the fossils more than anything. So, when I found out that there were excursions that we could go to search for fossils, I joined. My parents were very proud, I think. A favorite location to search for fossils was in 'Hog's Back' just outside of Ottawa, off the Rideau River. I was fascinated by the name 'Hog's Back' particularly when I found out what a hog was. I imagined this funny looking hog with rocky spines in his back, much like the area that we explored for fossils. I would tell almost everyone I met that I was going to 'Hog's Back' and watch their reactions. But only Andrew seemed to really get the joke and laugh with me. And, in turn, I would take to Andrew my best fossil finds and he would usually know what they were. Or, he could mostly give them a name or at least say what they likely were. A lot were fossils of spiny fish. Gradually, I built up a little collection of my favorite fossils, which I kept in a cardboard shoe box.

I, like other children who had joined the fossils excursions, had been provided with a small hammer with an edge on one side. This edge allowed one to remove sections of the slate and uncover fossils. Sometimes one had to hammer at the slate to do this. And this was what led to the whole problem. Accidentally, a small piece of slate flew away and hit my open eye. There was immediate pain and I could not see too well out of that eye. They took me to the hospital and there they said it was not serious and I would recover without permanent damage. However they put a white bandage over my wounded eye. I was not to remove the bandage for a couple of weeks.

As luck would have it, my eye was injured just before we were to go to the big tournament. I showed up at practice to tell my teammates what had happened and that I could not play in the tournament. To my great surprise they did not agree. They were all saying more or less the same thing.

    – You must play, Tassos.
    – But I can't play, I can only see out of one eye.
    – That's OK, Tassos. You can still play.
    – But it is our big chance. You don't want someone who is half blind.
    – Oh, come on Tassos. It is only a game.
    – Only a game! It is our big tournament. We have been practicing all season.
    – You are our mascot, Tassos.
    – How is that?
    – You will bring us good luck! You have to play.

It was amazing. This, of all things, would never have happened in a school in Greece. There, even if I had asked to play they would have made fun of me and called me names such as 'blind man' and 'cripple' and the like. And the tournament would have been taken very seriously, with a lot of jockeying around for positions on the team and hyperboles being shouted about how good they were and how lousy the other teams. Certainly no one ever would have said that the big tournament was 'only a game'. No kid would have encouraged another kid with an injury to play in the tournament. And certainly no kid what have told a crippled-up classmate that he would be the team 'mascot', or that the crippled kid would 'bring them good luck'.

So, more from shock and not knowing what else to do in view of their persistence, I agreed to play. Of course I was expecting the worse. I would be an embarrassment to the team, since I was not a very good player and rather short for volleyball in any case. But the enthusiasm of the teammates, because I had agreed to play in spite of the injury overrode everything else. For a while, I forgot all my fears and reservations and I was swept into the excitement of the tournament.

The tournament was set up so that the undefeated team would win the championship. At the start of the tournament we seemed to be winning our games fairly easily against the couple of other schools we played against. I am not sure if this was just by chance, or whether the coaches had pre-arranged it from seeing the various teams practice. I assumed that defeated teams also played each other, as there were multiple teams playing simultaneously in the large gym where the tournament was held. As the tournament progressed the games became more difficult, but we managed to get through. During those games, I tried my best and saved a few balls and set up other kids on the front to spike the ball over the net. I did not think I was playing particularly well, which I attributed to the injury. But strangely, my bandaged eye gave me more confidence as the tournament progressed. After all, nobody could really criticize me if I missed a ball here and there if I was playing with just one eye!

Ultimately, and almost before I knew it, there was now only one other unbeaten team in the tournament. I had been keeping my eye on them as they played other teams, which they seemed to beat easily. This other unbeaten team looked to be easily the best team in the tournament. By far! To me they were a class above all of the other teams, including us. What distinguished them most of all, were two ferocious spikes that they had. My teammates knew all about these spikes, who were apparently Korean and were twin brothers. It was rumored that they may have been brought in specially and accepted into that school because of their volleyball prowess. Now bringing in oriental imports was very unusual. I do not even remember seeing oriental kids in Hopewell. I think the Korean brothers were the only oriental kids I saw in the whole tournament. And these Korean spikes certainly caught your eye. They were not particularly tall but they seemed to be able to jump a mile high to spike the ball. They had an unbelievable intensity and ferocity about them as they spiked and did all kinds of tricks and fakes. Their team must also have been coached well as they were continually fed nice set-ups by the rest of their team. I certainly could not imagine that these ferocious Korean spikes would tolerate having a cripple like me on their team. They were after perfection. They certainly seemed to me to be at a professional level, although I had never seen professional volleyball. I had no doubt that they would make mincemeat out of us and my own one-eyed weaknesses would be horribly exposed. However, I figured there was one good thing about the overwhelming superiority of the team with the Korean spikes. They would beat us so badly that my teammates could not blame our defeat on me. They would not have second thoughts about wanting me to play in spite of my injury, after I had warned them that I should not play. So, with this reasoning and my resignation to defeat by a much superior team made me feel very calm.

So, the final game came. Hopewell, who took cripples on because they considered them mascots, against a really serious team with ferocious Korean spike imports. No match! It would be like going to my own execution. But because I felt calm and resigned I was not at all nervous. The game started much as expected with the team with the Korean spikes taking it to us. They were winning about two or three points for every one we managed to win. So, we had got behind. Since, we all rotated through the different positions I figured that their strongest position would be when they had both of the Korean brothers as spikes on the front line. Luck would have it that both brothers were on the front line when it became my turn to serve. All I could think of was to try to get the ball over the heads of the spikes and as far as I could into the back of the court. It was then that I noticed a kid in their back line, diagonally across from me who did not appear to be paying much attention. Maybe he was not paying too much attention because the ferocious spikes were in the front line. So I hit my pitiful underhand serve quite high, to keep the ball away from the spikes, to that kid. That may have confused the kid in the back row who had missed my serve and we won the point. In all fairness, most kids served underhand, except of course for the Korean spikes who knew how to smash the ball with an overhead hit. A few other kids had also mastered the overhead serve, but not nearly as well as the Koreans. In any case we had got one point on my serve.

Then it happened! Somehow my vision narrowed so all I could see was that one kid on the back row. I tried to understand him. Why had he missed my high underhand serve, and how exactly had he missed it? I got ready to serve again. I noticed that my one-eyed vision had now turned into an advantage. I was not distracted by other movement on my blind side. Also, my otherwise weak underhand serve when it was hit high seemed to be effective. The kid in the back line missed again. Another point! And then another and another. The kid next to him tried to back him up, but they got tangled up with the high serve and we got another point. And I kept hitting it like that, piling up points. I could see that the Korean spikes on the front row had a look of disappointment and almost resignation on their faces. From being behind we were now just a few points from victory. Unfortunately, that thought distracted me and I over hit my next underhand high serve, and his teammates all shouted to let it go and one or two actually restrained him from trying to get the ball. Another kid from their team picked up the serve, and my long and glorious run was over. The service went to the other side and our opponents, with their Korean spikes back in operation again, started to make a sizeable comeback.

Then it happened again! Somehow my teammates on the front row started to block the ferocious Korean spikes. I don't know how they did it. These were tall, biggish, affable kids on our team, who I had never seen jump up and block like that. But what was even more extraordinary is that they were going up to block in a coordinated fashion, as if they formed a wall. The formation of the wall during their jumps, to block the ferocious spikes, was absolute poetry in motion. All I could do was look at them in amazement. A feeling of incredible pride overcame me. I had never imagined that this kind of cooperative athleticism could shield one from such a ferocious attack. And I was part of their team! I watched this back and forth of wonderfully attacking spikes being defended time and time again by my teammates who, until then, I did not even know could defend us like that. Unfortunately, my admiration and pride overcame me as I watched, and my feet became rooted to the floor and I missed a couple of easy balls. It did not matter in the end. All the free points I had gained on my service and the extraordinary cooperative defensive effort of my teammates were enough for us to win the game. We were now the volleyball champions for intermediate schools in all of Ottawa and Region! We had our picture taken and were given a cup.

I felt elated beyond words. I had never won anything in sports in real competition. And this was much more than I could have ever imagined. My teammates were very happy, of course. But I did not see amongst them the wild jubilation that I would have expected if this was a school team in Greece. And then something else happened which was totally outside my experience. The champion team was supposed to play the second team for a 'consolation game'. By then I was expecting the magic to happen again. I kept telling my teammates that we can beat them again. In Greece that was the way you would show your real superiority. The opponent had not only to be beaten but also humbled. Is that not what happened to German occupiers! At the end, they did not only retreat from Greece, but they would have been humiliated and humbled by the Resistance during their retreat, at every conceivable opportunity. After all that was the joy of victory. This was what made all the sacrifices, executions, tortures to finally overthrow Fascism worthwhile.

But the magic did not happen a second time. My service only got me a couple of points and the spikes dominated our defense and defeated us in the 'consolation game'. I really felt badly about that. I did not think we tried hard enough. I told that to my teammates. To my surprise they just laughed happily. I couldn't understand it.

– Why are you laughing? We lost the 'consolation game' to them.
– But that is good, Tassos.
– How can it be good?
A couple of them were still smiling.
– Oh, they won't feel so badly about losing the championship.

How incredible, I thought. How can they be like that about an enemy team? But my teammates remained very happy. They seemed to easily socialize with kids from other schools. I stayed close to a few of my own teammates, until it was time to get back on our school bus and go home.

I really did not understand the attitudes of my classmates. On the other hand, I had never won anything in competition until now either. And I knew that my school, my classmates, the people at 16 Rupert and life in general in Canada made me feel good. Nearly always. And that was not the case in schools and family in Greece, where an undercurrent of intensity and anxiety was always percolating. And this anxiety was related to politics, education, or language but, above all, competition to prove one's self superior to others.

Decision maker

During that time there were intense discussions among my father and my mother whether we should stay in Canada or return to Greece. My father had a good job in Greece as an agriculturist in the company that imported Chilean nitrate. The job remained open for him but there was correspondence back and forth about when he would return. Ultimately they decided to stay at least another year and he got a job to work in the stockroom of the Department of Agricultural Chemistry at McDonald College of McGill University, just outside of Montreal. His plan was to start as a mature graduate student for a PhD. In this way he would become superior to his brothers and relatives in Greece. But they always made me appear as the center of their decisions. Their conversations, in my presence at least, invariably ran the same way:

– Fivaki, Fivaki you should write to Evelpides to make sure your job is retained at Chilean Nitrate.
– Whatever Tasouli wants, Dinaki.
– And Tasouli is doing so well in school, Fivaki.
– Tasouli, you must make this important decision.
– I like the school Babaka.

– See Dinaki — Tasouli favors staying in Canada.
– I didn't say that Babaka, Mamaka. But I like it here.
– See Fivaki — he would like to stay, but does not want to say it outright in case we want to go back.
– Whatever Tasouli wants, Dinaki.
– Of course, Fivaki.
– But I really don't mind.

So, more or less the same conversation would go around and around, time and time again. Endless procrastination was a kind of decision-making. And this pattern of discussion was certainly not limited to whether we stay in Canada or return to Greece. One day my mother and father approached me in a very hush-hush manner:

– Tasouli, your mother and I have a very important matter to discuss with you.
– Yes, Tasouli, your father is correct.
– What is it Mamaka, Babaka?

They would look at each other in a very meaningful and secretive way. I thought they expected me to be embarrassed from the way they looked and the tone of their voice. But they were mistaken. For now they were speaking to the conqueror of the ferocious Korean spikes ... the volleyball champion of Ottawa and District intermediate schools.

– Well, Tasouli, you know we did not make a brother or sister for you in Greece.
– What your Babaka means is that circumstances were very difficult in Greece during the war.

It was on the tip of my tongue to ask them 'what about after the war?', when my father left for America and my mother went into a big depressive funk. But I thought I better stay on the straight and narrow.

– Of course I know that I don't have a brother or a sister.
– What your Babaka is saying is that circumstances are better now ...
– But Dinaki, we should let Tasouli decide.
– What do you think Tasouli?
– I would very much like a brother or a sister.
– See Fivaki. Tasouli would like us to have a child.
– Of course, Dinaki, Tasouli is the one who will make the decision.
– But we have very little money for a child. Tasouli should know this, Fivaki.
– But Mamaka, Babaka, I know all of that. I could go and work. I can deliver papers before school. And there is a shop on Fifth Avenue that needs help.
– Po, po, Fivaki ... to have our child deliver papers and work in a shop ...
– He is just saying this, Dinaki, because he wants a brother or a sister. Don't you understand what a child you have here?
– But Babaka, Mamaka, other kids deliver papers or work after school.
– You are not 'other kids', Tasouli.
– Dinaki, we must let Tasouli make the decision.
– But I've already said I want a brother or a sister.
– Can you imagine, Fivaki, he is saying that he would even go out and work during school.
– The decision should be only Tasouli's.
– Of course, Fivaki.
– But ...

I could hear my own voice becoming tired as it became higher and higher. What was the point of continuing to repeat myself?

These conversations with my parents would often occur at weekends. This particular weekend, when I went to bed I started to think whether we would stay in Canada, or whether my mother was going to have a baby. I had turned on my wooden lamp that I had made before I fell asleep. It now had a little cloth lamp-shade which produced a soft, calming yellow light. I could see in my room the other artifacts I had made in the shop at Hopewell. Seeing these artifacts, made with my own hands, in this lamplight gave me a sense of accomplishment and of confidence. I thought of 16 Rupert Street and the reassuring, familiar people that lived there, my classmates, and the great volleyball victory. I was in a good frame of mind. I had never before made professional-looking artifacts or won in sport. Canada had shown me how to achieve all of that. I knew then that we would stay in Canada. *I had started to fall asleep when I heard a distant Voice that I had almost forgotten.*

Styppas Returns

– So, Tasouli, your parents are putting the decision of having a brother or sister on your shoulders.

– Styppas, Styppas, is that you?

– Of course it is me. Who do you think it is?

– But what happened to you, Styppas? All this time?

– I was around, alright. After that terrible time I had on the Canberra.

– Among the rope coils — moaning and groaning. That was the last I saw of you.

– I said, I was around. You were just too preoccupied to notice me.

– It is true. Hopewell has kept me very busy.

– Don't fib to me Tasouli! It is not that you were just too busy.

– It is true, Styppas. All these new and exciting things — a shop in the school where I made real things … winning in the volleyball tournament … and classmates who protected me and never made fun of me …

– Made fun of you like Frank, in Maraslion?

– Not at all like Frank, Styppas.

– But now that you have a problem about whether your mother should have a baby, you start looking for me …

– It is not true, Styppas. I was not looking for you. You found me!

– If you weren't looking for me, Tasouli, you must admit it is strange that you see me again in your dream right after your parents wanted you to make the decision of whether your mother should get pregnant.

– Pregnant? My father would make my mother pregnant … Disgusting. I don't really want to think about it.

– Of course not, Tasouli. But no matter …

– No matter what?

– It doesn't matter, because they really don't mean it. It is just for show.

– But how do you know that, Styppas?

– I tell you it is all a big show. They have no intention of your mother having a baby.

– But how do you know, Styppas?

– How do I know? Of course I know. It is even in my story.

– Story, what story?

– The story I will be writing, Tasouli.

– But what story will you be writing, Styppas?

– My story about you, of course.

– You never told me you would be writing a story about me, Styppas.

– Well, I will be!

– But that is not fair, Styppas. I have been telling my own story.

– And I will be writing the story of Tasouli.

– So, others can read it?

– Of course.

– And even read it from one generation to the next, Styppas?

– Possibly.

– But why would you do that, Styppas, when you knew I was telling it?

– Because a written story stays forever. But telling a story is only momentary.

– Oh, ohh, ohhh … but don't you remember the terrible fight we had about Socrates?

– How can I forget it!

– But it was you, Styppas, who first brought up the argument that Socrates taught that orality was superior to writing.

– And you got me livid by arguing that Socrates should have drunk the hemlock not once but twice, because he was for oral communication … an absolute and rigid oralist!

– I did not understand why you got so livid then, Styppas.

– It was the absurdity of your argument, Tasouli.

– Oh, thanks Styppas for telling me my argument had absurdity.

– You are starting up again, Tasouli … you better be careful!

– And you are starting to get very mad again, Styppas. I can see a little green spittle starting to form in your mouth. It makes me very afraid.

– You should be. With the insults you threw at me then, even before we really started the Socrates argument.

– And what insults were these, Styppas?

– Don't you remember? When you said that your goaty girlfriend was superior to me. And worse still, when you then started comparing your relationship with the idiotic goat to that between Pamela and me?

– I have a vague recollection, Styppas.

– That is the problem with just telling a story. At best, you only have vague recollections of what you actually said.

– Still, Styppas. It was me who started to tell the story. It is my story!

– The other thing, Tasouli, is that I see your story a little differently.

– Of course you do, Styppas. I am Tasouli and you are Styppas.

– Don't start getting pedantic again, Tasouli. You have not done this for a long time!

– I'm glad you think I am pedantic again, Styppas. You have not complimented me like this for a long time. But if I was there at the beginning, I was there at the beginning.

– But I was there at the beginning too, Tasouli.

– That is not possible Styppas. Both you and I could not have been at the same beginning if your beginning is different than my beginning.

– Let's just say that the way I tell the beginning of the story is different than the way you have told it, Tasouli.

– Of course it would be a different beginning, Styppas! I am Tasouli and you are Styppas. And if I am Tasouli and if you are Styppas my beginning would be different, so would your start.

– … And you are getting repetitive as well as pedantic.

– Thank you, Styppas. You are now paying me two compliments instead of one. So, I suppose I better listen to what you are planning to write in your beginning … I mean your start.

– … Condescending as well!

– … Ohhh, thanks Styppas … three compliments now!

– Listen carefully, Tasouli. You will NOT be listening to my beginning. Or my middle or my end!

– But why is that, Styppas?

– Just because.

– Because what, Styppas?

– Because, I am not going to tell it you or read it to you.

– That is OK, Styppas. I can read it myself after you write it.

– No, you will not!

– But why not, Styppas?

– Because I am going to lock it up.

– But where will you lock it up, Styppas.

– In a secret place, where you will never be able to find it.

– But I know all the secret places at 16 Rupert Street.

– It will not be in 16 Rupert Street.

– But I know all the secret places in the neighborhood, Styppas. And in Hopewell. And even in the museum and in Hog's Back.

– It will not be anywhere like that.

– Then where, Styppas?

– I will lock it away in time.

– When in time, Styppas?

– Just a little ahead of now.
– Then I can just read it tomorrow.
– No, you will not, Tasouli.
– Why not?
– Because it will be permanently locked, just a little ahead of now.
– So, I could not even read the start of your story, Styppas.
– Especially not the start, Tasouli.
– Why not?
– Because if you try to read even the beginning of the start, you will not be able to. Because it would always be locked just a little ahead of now.
– I am already starting to get tired, just trying to think of how I would catch up even to the start, Styppas.
– Of course you are, Tasouli. Soon you will be totally asleep.
– Oh, Styppas. Just one more thing before I fall totally asleep.
– What is that?
– How will you write the story, Styppas?
– I suppose I can tell you that. I will write it in the evenings, by the light of a little wooden lamp, with a lamp shade that gives a calming, yellow light.
– Oh … just like the one we have here in my room now, Styppas?
– Exactly.
– Oh, I suppose then that it is OK, Styppas. You can write the start of your story if you want to …

Styppas' Start

My father, Phoebus, was born in Smyrna in 1911 and died in Montreal in 2009. My mother, who was born in Zakynthos, had died some 25 years previously. For as long as I remember, Dina did most of the talking and Phoebus seemed to be in the background. After her death, my father gradually changed. He created a new mien, a novel character. He started to wander about in an unkempt, long, white beard and hair, and wore a black suit that looked as if it had never seen a cleaner's. In the winter he wore a black fur hat. In the summer a black, wide rimmed Bordelino which had also never seen the cleaner's. He liked to be called the *Papous* (Grandfather), although I often still called him *Babá* (Dad). He would always be figuring out how to start endless, important-sounding philosophical arguments that he spouted in a loud overpowering voice. He had created a mausoleum out of their little house, with the walls and ceilings covered in photographs of my mother. The mausoleum, surrounded by a large totally overgrown garden on the Montreal Lakeshore, was the *Dineum*. All of philosophy emanated from Dina and the Dineum. He was not at all like that before she died.
– Dina is the important Great Saint and I am the little saint.
He would intone the words like an old wizard.
– But, Baba, you are not even religious. You used to claim you were an atheist.
– We worship in the Epicurean garden of Dina, in order to cultivate the civilizing, internationalist principles of Smyrna.
His index finger would wag with every syllable.
– But no one will come to the garden. It is so overgrown that the town will fine you.
– Dina wishes to demonstrate the failure of capitalism through natural ecology!
– But she is dead. And when she was alive she used to keep the garden so nice and neat.
– Her spirit is the guiding light of humanism and natural ecology.
– And as the little saint, you intend to demonstrate that to the capitalists?
– Um, um, um …
And his eyes would twinkle.

We had a small memorial for Phoebus at MacDonald College, outside of Montreal, where he had lived and worked for decades. We had it at the Faculty Club of McDonald College, on the shore of the St. Lawrence River. It was early spring, with snow on the ground, but the weather suddenly warmed up and the sun came out. We were all able to go out, but some of the older guests still kept on their winter overcoats. Our boys, Fion and Philip were there. Fion, the humorist in his amusing easy-going style, told a story of a Christmas family trip where the car had gone off an icy highway in northern New York State. Phoebus was delighted with the near disaster and had run off in the blinding snowstorm to find help. He returned with a New York state trooper who swore that he thought it was Father Christmas that had come to get him.

Philip, the more laconic of the two, demurred from telling a story, but a few colleagues and a former students had a few reminiscences that they shared. I talked a bit about Phoebus' early years, from what I had been told and read. After, the boys came up to me. Fion was often the first to introduce a social topic.

– Dad, I never knew any of that stuff. It is really interesting.
– You mean that with all the incessant conversations about every subject on earth, he never talked to you about his early years?
– No, Papous never said anything.
– But Fion, with all your History background, I would have thought it would have been a major topic of conversation.
– No. Never.
Philip nodded in agreement. And then he added laconically,
– Write up your own experience.
– You mean in case I pop off soon … ?
– Yup.
– Thanks a lot!
I tried to think back. I was sure I had told them wartime stories from when I was a child.
– But you must both remember some of the wartime stories I told you.
– No.
– Nope.

Then a few other people approached me, mostly elderly colleagues of my father. It turned out that Phoebus had never said much to them either about the 1920s, tumultuous as it was, let alone any recounting of his own childhood.

Later that evening sitting in a little Lakeshore motel, I was alone with Pamela. There was a light, cool misty drizzle outside. It was typical Montreal weather for this time of year. The silence and familiarity of the light rain created a comfort … an expectation. Pamela poured us each a little glass of scotch. It was Teacher's bottled in Glasgow. Pamela's mother, Mary, would drink Teacher's — on rare occasions when she could afford it.

Mary was brought to London by her mother, as a child. They came to London to escape from the deep poverty of Glasgow. Born also in 1911, the same year as my father, she had died just over a decade before him in London. As she got old, Mary gradually become more and more senile and then broke her hip. She was in a nursing home then and was taken to a London hospital where the hip was pinned without trouble. But then, while recovering, she became lucid again. Lucid enough to refuse to eat. She told her caregivers that they were wasting their money. The English were being wasteful feeding an old Scottish woman who had no future. She told them so.

– It was no good.
– No good for the English to be wasteful.
The Londoners finally agreed. They stopped trying to feed her.

Pamela had a sip of the Teacher's and was gradually coming into her element. The quiet rain and the little motel room had created a home for her … a little nest. I could see that she now felt confident, maybe even a little magical. Perhaps she could answer the question that still puzzled me.

– Why do you think my father never said anything about his early years to Fion and Phil?
– He wouldn't.
– So, why?
– He would never say anything personal. You'd say 'it's raining out' and he would go into a big dissertation.

We stayed for a few days in the little Lakeshore motel, near my father's house, during the memorial. We could not stay at his house, 'the Dineum'. It was unlivable. It had been broken into a few times, while he was in the hospital, and it looked like it had not been cleaned in years. There were cockroaches everywhere, including in a pot of vegetables rotting on the electric stove, which had only a couple of working elements. He refused to change anything since Dina died. The pot with the cockroaches and vegetables was his main source of nutrition. He would simply add more vegetables and rice and never wash it. He would laugh and call it his *pot-au-feu* that never came off the element. He would laugh more when the cockroaches in the *pot-au-feu* were pointed out to him, and he would say that they were a good source of animal protein. Just the right amount of animal protein, it seemed! After all he had out-survived all of his relatives on that diet, and was almost never sick and strong as a bull. He took no pills, even if they were prescribed, and had never been in a hospital in Canada. This, his first admission to a hospital was also his last at the age of ninety-eight.

The house contained books, books, books and the endless photographs mostly of the Great Saint, which we tried to sort out. I started to consider how I could write a narrative of what I recalled as a young child during the Occupation, the Civil War and the still difficult times of the late 1940s. I thought that I could try to provide a narrative from a young child's point of view. From Tasouli's point of view, the Occupation of Greece was delayed by the failed invasion of Mussolini's forces. So the German army did not occupy Athens until the spring of 1941, which was later than the rest of Europe. That meant that what he says were his earliest memories would have been even before the Occupation, which would have started when he was not yet three. So, how could I recount the narrative for a child that was so young at the beginning of this central event?

I thought I would talk it over with Amandina, the beauteous one, big sister of the boys. She would have ideas — she always did. Amandina was then living in Greece. She did not come to the memorial as she had recently given birth to Saphia. This was Saphia with the big, inquisitive, engaging, azure eyes. These were the same inquisitive eyes that her great-grandfather unmasked as he sat up briefly, shortly before he died.

So, I rang up Amandina in Athens. It was a crackly overseas line.

– How can I do the narrative, Amandina?
– Just jot down episodes, as they come to you.
She was without hesitation, full of confidence.
– But I am not sure if Tasouli would have complete memories of the episodes; he was so young.
– Just write them down and the rest will come.

But then, there is the problem with the desire to know one's own 'prehistory'. What I had heard from my father could color my own childhood memories. This would not have been a problem for Fion and Philip. My father had never told them about his childhood. Or at least they had forgotten what he had told them and apparently also what I had told them. That was not the case with me. I recall ever so clearly how Phoebus would have no hesitation to get into endless discussions about the causes of the destruction of Smyrna. It was always the same thing.

– It was the Allies that were the root cause of the destruction.

Anastassiades

That was his constant cant.

– But what about Attaturk Kemal and Turkish nationalism, Baba?

My question would set him off each and every time. He would get progressively more excited and start to shout. The index finger would wag.

– They were unimportant. It was British Imperialism that betrayed Smyrna.
– But, Baba, everybody knows that the British were the strongest supporters of the Greeks in Asia Minor.
– Nonsense! They were mortally afraid of the internationalist culture of Smyrna. The remnants of the Ionian Civilization still posed a threat to British Imperialism. Smyrna had to be destroyed!

At about that point, he would usually start screeching at the top of his voice. I felt a little badly I made him screech, but only a little.

And then there was his relationship with Pamela ... Pamela, the Englishwoman whose major fault was that she wanted to be nice. In simple ways.

– Would you like a cup of tea, Papous?

Silence. He would put his head down to his chest, impervious to anything other than his own dark train of thoughts. No one else existed.

– Did you hear me, Papous?

Silence. Head down. All other inferior beings are unimportant.

– Papous, do you or do you not want a cup of tea?

The response would finally come in the anticipated dissertation about how the English dominated, conspired and undermined the Ionian, internationalist culture of Asia Minor. It would always lead to the destruction of Smyrna. And the delivery would always start as a monologue in stentorian tones and end up in shouting accusations against the English: the Great Power then, and then the great betrayers. It was the Imperialist English that cajoled and encouraged the Greeks to undertake the campaign against Kemal's revolutionary forces. It was the same English that never helped when it came down to it.
One might think that the anti-English tirades were covertly directed against his very English daughter-in-law, Pamela. Yet, at the very end, dying, and unable to speak now but still with a clear mind, it was Pamela's fingers he grasped unto. Ever so tightly.
He would not let go.

Something else was curious. In relating all of these upheavals my father never mentioned once how he felt as a child. Even the startling monthly Journal which he, his brothers, cousins and friends wrote and distributed as young teenagers between 1923 and 1930, the *Micri' Academia* (The Small Academy), provided only glimpses of their family relationships. I turned to Pamela, the woman of the English race.

– You know, Pamela, my father told me endless stories about his father who was a very great man in Smyrna.
– Of course he would.
– But it is curious.
– What is?
– That he avoided talking about his mother, Sophia.

Pamela looked at me thinking, but had no good explanation.

The light, cool rain continued to fall outside the little Motel during that weekend. There was nothing else to do but think. Think back, a long time ago. And it was there that we started to discuss the problem concerning Tasouli.

– You know Pamela, Tasouli is a child and I am telling his story.
– He is growing up though.
– But I couldn't tell him.
– Tell him what?
– All the bad things that would happen to his childhood heroes.
– Neither should you tell him.
– But I told him that I would be writing his story, Pamela.
– And what did he say?
– That it was his story.
– He is right about that!
– And that oral narration is far superior to writing. And he has these ideas about Socrates and how he had to drink the hemlock because he betrayed orality.
– Mmm … so how did you get out of it?
– By telling him I had hidden the writing — in a place where he would never find it.
– Tasouli did not believe this, did he Styppas?
– I said my story was locked away in time.
– Locked in time?
– Permanently — just a little ahead of his time.
– And did he believe that?
– Gradually he seemed to accept it. But he was falling asleep when he did …
– Well, you didn't lie.
– No, I suppose not.
– So, what did you hide from him?
– Oh, you know. What happened to Thales and Ourania and Rikos.
– Ah … 'The Corruptors'. Or don't you want to tell me what bad ends you are hiding from him?
– No, I can tell you, Pamela. It is not only the Corruptors but the death of his own mother and father.
– That would really upset him, Styppas. At his age.
– I don't know. I think he probably suspects who I am. Yet he is lucky, Pamela. He would not have seen in his future the ends that I have.
– Let him stay like that. What endings are you referring to?
– The endings of his childhood heroes. But you don't really want to hear my endings of his heroes … do you?
– What else is there to do — and the rain on the roof … I could stay here forever, Styppas.
– The rain will continue they say.
– For how long?
– For days they say.
– Go ahead then …

I could see her little smile of happiness and anticipation at the prospect of being isolated and protected from the world by the endless Montreal spring rain.

– Styppas, shall we pour a little scotch for your story?

Styppas' Ends

The Corruptors Revisited

– Unfortunately, Tasouli's much beloved and admired Corruptors and their progeny came to unexpected ends. Pamela, maybe you remember how Rikos died suddenly in bed, dressed in silk, surprising everyone.

– Mmm …

– So with the most dynamic and outrageous member of the trio gone, irreparable damage was done to their magical world of adventures and good times.

– Too bad for Tasouli. Just as well you did not tell him.

– But I must first tell you the story of Sofoula.

– Another bad end?

– Not initially. After Thales and Ourania got married and left the Bastille, they had a daughter, Sofia, named of course after Yiayia Sofia. Little Sofia was called Sofoula, the affectionate diminutive, which also distinguished her from our grandmother. Sofoula was born in 1948, I think, so she would have been ten years younger than Tasouli. She was blond with big blue eyes but had to wear big glasses and she was cross-eyed. She hardly ever cried. She was a very nice little girl and Tasouli liked her a lot.

– She sounds English.

– Tasouli's mother had said he should be jealous. All older children in a family are jealous of the younger ones she said. His mother had made this pronouncement with great authority and knowledge.

– She would of course!

– But Tasouli was never jealous of Sofoula. He even tried to think of ways he could be jealous of Sofoula, but he could not come up with any. This was because she sat around mostly quietly and never did anything to attract attention.

– A really nice little girl. Are you sure she wasn't English?

– Don't be funny Pamela … one day Sofoula got very sick. Then, she attracted a lot of attention. But by then, Thales, Ourania and Sofoula were not living in the Bastille, so still Tasouli could not become jealous of her, but I think that he felt that he should have been.

– His dear Mommy must have finally got to him.

– Then something very important happened. Sofoula was given a magical substance for those days. It was called penicillin and it had only recently appeared in Greece. Thales was totally focused on how to get the penicillin, which was in very short supply, and how many units to give her. It was a few hundred or thousand units. Because penicillin was so precious, Sofoula's urine had to be collected and the urine given to a Lab from which penicillin could be isolated again, so it could be given back to her less expensively, or to someone else.

– I don't remember having to do this in England during the war.

– Of course not, Pamela. Penicillin was discovered in England and supplies were more readily available there. But the point is that even the attention Sofoula received with the urine collections did not make Tasouli jealous. Even when she was very sick with a high fever, she never cried, never objected or even while she might have been wondering why all her urine was being collected.

– So, what happened to her after the illness?

– Sofoula recovered and grew up. Tasouli used to see her from time to time when he took trips to Greece many years later and they were always very friendly. She remained very good humored in a quiet way. Sofoula married a nice man, who was an author and a broadcaster, and they had a daughter.

– And then?

– Then Sofoula got sick from a lymphoma and went to Europe and the United States for treatments.

– That must have been hard.

– Phoebus was very anxious and was always talking about sending money to Sofoula from Canada.

– Typical!

– But she died in any case at a fairly young age. I imagined her to have retained her pleasant, non-complaining personality to the end. But, in fact, I don't know. Tasouli did not see her when she was sick.

– So, what happened to the Corruptors?

– Sofoula's father, Tasouli's favorite Uncle Thales, died before Sofoula. He contracted hepatitis B from a poorly sterilized needle used on him for a blood test. We were in Canada then. My father was continually very anxious about Thales and the medical news of his health came to Canada, mostly by letter. Thales worsened gradually and developed cirrhosis. He became very yellow and then his belly swelled. He started to have bleeding from his stomach and he finally died.

– So, Papous never went to visit his brother.

– He always avoided the topic of going, Pamela. Thales' blow-by-blow description of his demise, came through letters from Stelios, Yianis and Yiayia Sophia, and the occasional long distance call. It became the dominant anxiety in our family for the several years that his illness lasted.

– Did Papous call often?

– Not really. Whether to make one of these long distance telephone calls, which were admittedly expensive, was discussed endlessly with argumentative justifications and a high degree of stress with each of the arguments, for or against. Most of the time the phone calls would be postponed. The few times a call was made not much information was garnered or the connection or the line was bad. My father behaved as if it was his fault that he could not save his brother.

– So what did he do?

– Money had to be sent on every possible occasion, even though we were quite poor during that period. I did not think Thales really needed the money, what with both him and Ourania being physicians. I tried to say this to my parents. But my father insisted that all the Greeks thought we were very rich, since we had come to Canada and expected the money to be sent. He was often extremely angry about this and would screech and shout accusatory statements: he was just an agriculturalist, eking out a living, first as an older graduate student and then a poorly paid lecturer at McDonald College, while they were successful entrepreneur doctors and engineers in Greece. But the money and lots of long letters were always sent.

– So, what happened finally?

– My father never made a trip to see his dying brother, Pamela. He always said it was too expensive and his work was too important to leave.

Cigarette

– Styppas, all this is starting to depress me. I think I'll have a cigarette.

– And a drop more scotch?

– If you pour it … or would you like me to?

– Quite a few years after Thales died, Ourania also died. And speaking of cigarettes, she, like the rest of the trio, smoked a lot. After Thales was gone she smoked incessantly. Finally, she contracted lung cancer and died from that.

– Oh, I remember her smoking alright, Styppas.

– We last saw her before she got sick.

– She was a rotter.

– Just because she didn't offer you a cigarette?

– You automatically offer people, if you are smoking a cigarette.

– But the poor woman is dead!

– I bet Thales would have offered a cigarette.

– Too bad you never met him, Pamela. He would have offered to everyone.

– In any case, the height of the good times of the Corruptors had ended. I am glad Tasouli would not have known.

– Yes Pamela. The Corruptors were extinguished. But before they were, I was able to enter part of their magical lives, that so enthralled Tasouli, one more time.

– Oh, how?

– I visited Greece when I was still a young man and Thales and Ourania were still alive. Ourania's nick-name, really a pet name, was 'Rània'.

– How cute.

– You don't have to be sarcastic. Everybody who knew her well and liked her called her Rania.

– I never called her Rania.

– There was a sophisticated and fashionable sound to Rania. And her looks suited the sound of Rania to a 'T'. Rania had jet-black hair.

– Dyed, I bet!

– And she had these unusual blue-green, rather beautiful eyes. She also had a slim, curvaceous figure, which she was not shy to show off in slick black dresses, usually with a large *décolleté*.

– A real vamp!

– And she would often smoke her cigarettes from a long, silver holder.

– A vamp alright!

– Before I left for Greece for that visit I thought I would bring a present to Thales. But I did not know what would be an unusual present from Canada, something that would have a North American flavor. I was not sure what would impress Thales but it would have to be something he liked. By then years had elapsed but in my mind Greece was still the Greece of the Occupation Child. I finally settled on music and, figuring that jazz would still be foreign to Greeks, I bought Thales a Dave Brubeck record.

– Good choice.

– Brubeck was just becoming popular in Canada. The record was an LP made of bright red, semi-transparent plastic. I was sure that Thales would think this was a strange gift. But to my surprise, he knew all about the top American jazz artists and even said he admired Brubeck and how much he wanted to have a record of his.

– He knew all about American music?

– He certainly knew how to make his nephew feel good.

– Thales was a nice man.

– But you never knew him.

– Just from your description, Styppas.

– So during that visit, Thales and Rania and I became very friendly.

– An inseparable trio again?

– I saw them frequently and we started to go out together. I had a real desire to go to see the *Bouzoukia*.

– I remember the *Bouzoukia*.

– It is difficult to explain what the Bouzoukia really meant then. They had grown out of the sweat, labor, heartbreak and loves of the Greek working class. And after the dictatorship they became intertwined with the freedom fight.

– How very romantic for the three of you.

– It was the beauty of the Greek seaside and its beaches and ports that made the Bouzoukia played in these seaside open air clubs, seem so magical to me.

– And the company, no doubt!

– Don't make fun of me, Pamela.

– Sorry.

– I bet — 'sorry from Surrey' Pamela.

– Please tell me.

– OK, I wanted to tell you that within the Bouzoukia there lives another genre of music, the Rebetica.

– Rebetica?

– The origins of the Rebetica have faded. But their sad, chanting character, seem like mixtures of Byzantine chants and Anatolian-Turkish pain and sweetness. Mostly sung by men.

– Very manly!

– You are doing it again, Pamela … I am just trying to say that the origins of the Rebetica are probably from Constantinople and above all Smyrna.

– I'm sure you did not have to explain all of that to Thales and your darling Rania.

– Of course not. But the Rebetica were undergoing a revival then. So it was fashionable to go to the increasingly sophisticated seaside clubs to listen to the artists of the day.

– And Thales and Rania knew them all.

– Of course. So, the trio of now Thales and Rania and a younger Styppas started to go out to the Bouzoukia.

– How young a Styppas?

– Young enough.

– Really romantic — the clubs by the seaside in the warm summer evenings.

– It is only Thales and Rania and the incredible feeling of beauty and lightness of the Bouzoukia clubs that I remember clearly now.

– Lucky you.

– Thales, with his endless encouraging humor that always made me feel good. And Rania with her looks and flirtatiousness which excited me, on the one hand, but made me feel uncomfortable, on the other.

– At least something made you feel uncomfortable.

– So, one evening in one of those outdoor, seaside clubs, I made a smart-Aleck comment that had a sexual context to Rania.

– And I bet she loved it.

– I wasn't too sure.

– Oh … ?

– Before I could react she put out her lit cigarette on the back of my uncovered elbow. It hurt like hell. And it even sizzled before it went out.

– Didn't you draw back your elbow in pain?

– No. I did not want to show that she had hurt me.

– Infatuation with the Rania vamp!

– The scar is still here.

– I wondered how you had got that scar …

– Something to remember her by.

– You are just trying to irritate me, Styppas.

– No, it was you smoking a cigarette with so much passion that reminded me.

– You will force me to light another one!

– But speaking of cigarettes, Pamela, do you remember how you, taking out a cigarette, tamed that tough gang in New York?

– In Central Park, in Manhattan.

– And it started to rain, just like it is raining now, and we sought shelter under the roof of what must have been a bandstand. It was circular and kind of elevated with a wooden, decorative railing, all painted green. I remember it well.

– Yes and this gang of rough young men came up also seeking shelter from the heavy rain. They were a little distance from us on the wooden bandstand.

– They kept looking at us.

– And then another gang came. Do you remember, Pamela?

– This lot stood right next to us.

– Yes and I was starting to get even more nervous with that second gang at close quarters. There was hardly anybody else around because of the rain. I was starting to think what could I do if they started to rob us or attack us? They probably had knives or worse.

– Yes they were certainly a real New York gang.

– And that is why I was amazed to see you take out your cigarette package and offer cigarettes to the gang members.

– But some of them took a cigarette and lit up.

– I think you did something to them with your eyes, Pamela. A little smile perhaps?

Anastassiades

– It was the normal thing to do to offer a cigarette to others. Especially with all of us caught in the rain together under the shelter.
– But now there were two gangs and they looked different. You did not offer the first gang a cigarette.
– They were on the other side of the bandstand.
– And I don't know if you remember, but this weird thing then happened. Some of closer gang members moved nearer still to us, ever so casually, as if to enjoy their cigarette more. But they had, in effect, gradually surrounded us.
– Oh yes, I clearly remember that, Styppas.
– I had no idea what was going on. I started to get worried. No one said a word. In either gang. It was total silence. Just the sound of the rain on the shelter roof. I was starting to get a little afraid.
– They certainly weren't a talkative bunch.
– But then, something peculiar happened to me. I'm not sure if I have told you before Pamela.
– Go on.
– My fear went. I felt protected. Being surrounded like that …
– I remember that. I felt the same.
– I thought it was just me.
– It was as if the second gang was protecting us … no one was to touch us.
– And then the rain stopped, Styppas.
– And the first gang left, without giving us a glance.
– And then the second gang, our gang, left.
– But as they were leaving one or two gave us a little glance but not a word, Pamela.
– It wasn't necessary to say anything.
– No. The rain had stopped there. But it is still raining here …
– You can carry on then …

Phoebus

– Do you remember, Pamela, a couple of weeks ago when my father was getting close to death, I brought him an anthology of Greek poetry from which I wanted to read to him?
– You looked for the poetry books at the Dineum?
– I knew his favorite poet had become Ko′stas Va′rnalis. Varnalis gradually became politicized and wrote about the destruction of Smyrni and against fascism.
– But did your father not like Cavafis?
– I did not think that the relatively apolitical Cavafis was a favorite of his.
– Oh …
– Yet, when he was too weak to talk and I gave him several choices, he signaled with his hand that it was 'Waiting for the Barbarians' by Cavafis that he wanted to hear. I read to him the poem several times before he seemed satisfied.
– Yes, he wanted you to go on forever, Styppas.
– I thought it was my last chance to ask him a question I always wanted to, about that period.
– What was that?
– I never got up the courage to ask him about the thief in Pyrgos, Pamela.
– The thief they caught in Pyrgos Vassilissis.
– Yes, the one that stole a little of the food supplies from the stores for his family to eat, who were starving. He was tied up to a tree and beaten continually with the rope by the farm hands. And the thief was totally silent, never uttered a sound with all the rope-beating. And my father, the important agriculturalist and their supervisor did not tell them to stop …
– But he wouldn't, Styppas.
– Why do you say that?
– 'cause he never would.

Phoebus' letters

– But, you know Pamela, Phoebus' letters show a different side of him.
– What letters?
– The wartime letters he wrote to Dina.
– I didn't know these letters existed.
– Oh, he mentioned them often enough.
– I would just tune out, Styppas.
– The War started later in Greece than in Britain.
– I know …
– By the spring of 1939, Italian armed forces had occupied Albania, in preparation for invading Greece and in October of 1940 they invaded.
– How far did they get?
– The Greek army counterattacked through the steep mountains and deep snows of Epirus and Albania, forcing the Italians to retreat.
– Oh, the brave Greeks!
– Don't be cheeky, Pamela. By April 1941 the German offensive on Greece unfolded and the Greek Army in Epirus surrendered to the Germans.
– What's so great about that?
– Pride mostly. They never surrendered to the invading Italians.
– Can I take a look at the letters please, Styppas?
– Here you go, Pamela. It is just a sampling.
– Just a sampling?
– Yes, these are just nineteen letters I picked in random from over sixty that I found.
– I don't think I want to read the lot now.
– Then just read a couple, Pamela.
– OK, let's see.
– Here are just a couple.
– Where did you find them, Styppas.
– Just in an old shopping bag in the shambles of Phoebus' house, 'the Dineum'.

~

Athens 3 August 1939

My beloved Dina

Up to today I have not received any letter from you except for your telegram in which you wrote to me that you arrived. I still have not managed to leave. However, it is likely that Saturday, the day after tomorrow, I will leave. I will go first to Thessaloniki, where I will get the glasses of my father and after that I will go directly to Alexandroupolis. At the address of Nicolaou Petala Alexandroupolis, you can send to me one letter because I will remain there only for 10 days. But you must send it to me as soon as you receive my letter and you should mail it, if possible, from the Chora so I'll have time to receive it.

Although it [has been] just one week since I left you both, you can't imagine how much I have missed you. I am thinking of how difficult it will be for me if I go in the army and we will perhaps stay for so many months separated. Because I have got my salary without as yet receiving any money for this training period, I have sent you by the post-office 800 drachmas. So that I will not send to you money twice [so] close together I will delay a little mailing to you the money again. However, if necessary you can write to me in Alexandroupolis, from where it will be possible to mail to you. I expect that the child will be showing a difference even from one day to the next. With the separation I understood more that I have loved him a lot. However, I find more difficult the separation from you. On the other hand, this loneliness that developed again when you left is an excellent demonstration of our bond.

I have told Chrysoula about your lessons. This past January she had a job in hand. An American woman wanted her child to learn Greek and assigned Chrysoula to find a teacher for her. She was offering 2,000 drachmas a month but with a commitment every morning she thought. Finally, since she could not find anyone she herself knew, so she recommended a friend of Eli. Even for this year she might be able to do something but it will be after October. It would be great luck if we could ensure a little work for you so you could come.

I kiss you very sweetly my beloved Dinoula
With love

Your Phoebus

Kiss for me sweetly the little one. Greetings to Nana and to your mother.

Thesalonki 28 of August 1939

My beloved Dina

Unfortunately or fortunately I did not receive your first letter that you sent to Alexandroupolis because it seems, in the meantime, I had left. So your second letter hit me like a stroke. Some of your phrases make me greatly worry since I don't know what you wrote in your first letter. What was the diagnosis of the first doctor? Has the child been sick continually since the first day you arrived in Zakynthos?

My worry is so great that I thought that I should stop my excursion and to come immediately to Zakynthos, but the second thought stopped the first. What will I be able to do for the boy? Besides, I have arranged to be in Lamia on Sunday to visit the farm of an employee of the Bank of Greece. It is not so easy to bring the man there and then not to go myself. But as soon as you get my letter, write to me in Athens at once to the address of the house — a letter with all the news of the child.

You cannot appreciate something unless you are deprived from it. Only now do I understand the great weakness I have for the child. The same thing is happening, and not for the first time, for my great love for you. Our separation for the month seems to tie us together more than five years of living together. Is this what happens perhaps to everybody? If not it means that I am a peculiar psychological phenomenon. If it does happen, then no calmness can ever occur in the psychology of the human being. Can one say that this phenomenon is another view of boredom? Perhaps. But it is not possible to verify this positively because boredom is always demanding new horizons. And rarely does it ask to return to the old ones.

I greet you and kiss you very sweetly both you and our child,
Your Phoebus.
Greetings to Nana and your mother.

~

– These are nice letters, Styppas.[2]
– They are all like that. Don't you think he intellectualizes a bit too much?
– Mm … not really. I'll have to read the rest of them.
– I have left them here for you, Pamela.
– He comes across as a different person.
– These two that you read are after he was conscripted but before he went to the front.
– Does he seem changed in the later letters?
– I think so, Pamela. Once the fighting started the letters became shorter.
– They would have been also more heavily censored.

– And the fighting would have become more and more intense in the mountains …

Falling

– Styppas, Styppas wake up!

– Who …

– It is me Tasouli. You were shouting in your sleep.

– Where am I?

– Here in Kingston, in your bed.

– What are you doing here?

– I came to find you. From 16 Rupert Street in Ottawa.

– But why did you want to find me now, Tasouli?

– To talk about the story you have written about me, of course. Which you said you have hidden away in time.

– What about it?

– It is not fair to have it locked away where I can never reach it. It is my story.

– But I wrote it from observing you, from watching you all the time.

– Were you observing me when I was both awake and asleep, Styppas?

– Why do you ask?

– Because, I can do all these things when I am asleep which I can't do when I am awake.

– Like finding me in faraway places?

– Or you finding me when I am asleep.

– But this time you found me when I was asleep, Tasouli.

– It is true, Styppas. I heard you shouting when I was asleep.

– You heard me shouting in your sleep even though you were so far away?

– Yes, of course. The distance does not matter — I even found you when I was asleep in Pagrati.

– What matters then?

– Just that you want or need to find the other person, Styppas.

– So, why did you want to find me this time?

– I told you. I wanted to talk to you about you hiding my story. Then I heard you shouting in your sleep. And then I knew you had your nightmare. So, I came over.

– You knew I had my nightmare?

– Of course, Styppas. I used to have a nightmare that would wake me up shouting. Just like your nightmare.

– It is a terrible nightmare. I had it nearly all the time when I was on the Canberra.

– I know, Styppas. When you were lying among the ropes.

– But I've had it for a very long time, Tasouli.

– I know.

– You seem to know everything, Tasouli. You used to say that I knew everything.

– That is because I am growing up, Styppas. But tell me about your nightmare. Tell me exactly what it is like.

– Why do you want to know?

– Because I have two nightmares. The falling nightmare and the murder nightmare. If your nightmare is like my murder nightmare, I don't want to talk about it. It is too horrible. But if it is like my falling nightmare then I can talk about it.

– I used to have a murder nightmare, but it is long gone. But the falling nightmare keeps coming back. It was the falling nightmare, during our trip on the Canberra.

– You were certainly groaning and shouting. So, what was it like, Styppas?

– You know, Tasouli. One is often in another dream and all of a sudden you start falling. There is a horrible feeling of vertigo, dizziness and an awful sensation one is going to crash and be killed at any second. Other times the other dream seems to drive you to a situation where you might start falling, like one approaches a cliff or the edge of a high building. And there is the absolute terror as one is about to crash. And usually one wakes up terrified just at the instant of the crash.

– Oh I know, Styppas. But I no longer have them. I have cured myself.

– You have cured yourself? How is that possible?

– It is not that difficult, Styppas. I have discovered a method that works.

– What method? Tell me. What method?

– I am not sure that I should tell you, Styppas.

– And why, not? You shouldn't play games with me on this, Tasouli. It is not a good idea.

– Why Styppas? Are you going to have green spittle come in your mouth and you will try to terrify me, and I will become afraid that you will impale me? Well, it is not going to work, Styppas. I have grown up now and I am not as afraid of being impaled or extinguished. That worked pretty well when I was in the Bastille in Pagrati, but it does not work too well at 16 Rupert Street in Ottawa. But I will tell you what. I will make a deal with you.

– A deal, a deal? Where did you learn about deals, Tasouli? You never knew about deals before.

– At my school, Hopewell. The kids there often talk about deals.

– I should have guessed! Ok, what is your 'deal'?

– Just that I want to see your story that you have written. I want to see what you wrote about me. I don't understand why you said you locked it up in time.

– I was afraid that this was going to be your deal, Tasouli. I suppose that the best thing now would be to explain to you why I locked up your story in time.

– OK, explain it then.

– Pamela and I talked about this.

– Oh, if Pamela agreed the reason could not be that bad. Pamela likes me a lot you know, Styppas.

– Yes, yes I know. So, it is simply this. In my story about you bad things happen to many of your favorite people. Like the Corruptors and Stelios and Thales.

– What bad things?

– Like they die in the end.

– But everybody dies in the end, Styppas.

– True, but Pamela and I did not want you to know these bad ends now.

– Oh, Oh, Ohhh …

– Why are you 'Ohhing'?

– Because, I still want to see what you wrote about me.

– … OK, so here then is a counter-proposal to your 'deal'.

– Is a 'counter-proposal' the opposite, Styppas? I don't want an opposite deal of the deal that I told you about.

– You are still as pedantic as ever.

– Oh, thank you Styppas for the compliment.

– I will try not to get irritated. No a 'counter-proposal' is just a manner of speaking. It means that it would be a change, or modification of your proposal, big or small.

– OK, Styppas, what then is your 'counter-proposal'?

– That for now, my written story about you would stay locked in time. But when a bad end would actually happen and you would get to know about it, then that part of the story would be unlocked and you could read it.

– But would this not take a very long time?

– For sure it would take a very long time, Tasouli. And that is a good thing.

– But how would the story be unlocked, Styppas? Would you still be there to unlock it?

– I would still be here, Tasouli. But I would not have to unlock it. It would unlock itself anytime a bad thing happened to the people you liked in your story, your heroes.

– Ohh … that sounds like it is magical, Styppas.

– It is magical, Tasouli. But not really complicated. If something bad happened to one of your heroes the second you found out about it, it would unlock your story, just like you told it.

– Even though you wrote it?

– I wrote it exactly as you told it.

– By the light of the little wooden lamp, like the one I made in the wood shop at Hopewell?

245

– The very same.

– And would Pamela agree with unlocking your story like that?

– Oh yes. I am sure she would, Tasouli.

– I suppose it would be OK, then.

– So, Tasouli you must now keep up your part of the bargain, and tell me how you cured yourself from having the falling nightmare.

– It is not difficult, Styppas, but you have to be persistent and follow my method exactly.

– Go on then.

– First you have to understand my method. Because the method starts before you actually fall asleep. And you must do it every night before you fall asleep. That is because you do not know which night the falling nightmare will come to you.

– Makes sense.

– Second you must ask yourself the question, if you were really falling while awake and you could do anything at all, what would you try to do so you would not crash and be killed?

– One could do anything at all while falling?

– Yes, anything at all.

– I don't know. I would probably be flailing about trying to grasp something or to break my fall.

– And is that not what you might try to do in your falling dream, Styppas, before you crash? You would flail about, wouldn't you?

– So?

– So, you flail about because your reflexes tell you to. You are hoping to stop the fall like a young bird does when it falls out of the nest or from a branch.

– Who told you that?

– Stelios did when we lived in the Bastille. He was an engineer but he knew about everything. Like how birds fly and humans wanting to fly.

– But I can't fly, Tasouli. No human can fly on his own.

– You don't have to fly in reality, Styppas. Only in your dreams.

– Is that how you stopped having the falling dream, Tasouli? By flying?

– Once I mastered flying in my dreams, I could fly anywhere. It was so very beautiful.

– Oh?

– Oh Styppas, I would fly over green-blue waters and azure blue seas, and under bridges and over fields of anemones with blue, purple and deep red colors …

So, I took Tasouli's advice. Every night after I lay down and before I went to sleep I would make myself think I could fly. But I never could fly. I had a problem in knowing how to start. Was I supposed to pretend, when I was lying on my bed, that I climbed on a low tree branch and then jumped off while trying to fly? That certainly did not work. Neither did jumping from a high rock into a deep part of the sea or lake. I persisted nevertheless, because of Tasouli's enthusiasm about the end result. After about three months of these futile attempts, I was practically ready to give up.

Then it suddenly occurred to me that during these three months of trying to fly unsuccessfully when falling asleep, then something peculiar had happened to my sleep pattern. I never had the falling nightmare. Not once. I thought about it and I really wasn't sure how often I would have the nightmare, but three months seemed a long time to me. So, I figured that if nothing else, there was a benefit in trying to fly before falling asleep. Maybe it actually kept me from having the nightmare. Maybe there was something in a primitive human response, like a young bird like Tasouli had said. So, I continued my vain attempts to fly before I went to sleep for another few months. Nothing more happened — no flying and no nightmare.

And then totally unexpectedly one night it happened. The falling nightmare came back. But as I started to fall in my dream, all these months of practice of trying to fly must have paid off. I did not come crashing down in terror, waking up sweating and screaming. I had been able to slow down my fall so the terror abated somewhat. I woke up but I was not terrorized. I had only a feeling of a minor fear and I woke up much more gradually and was able to go back to sleep right away. And the reason was that I was able to put out my arms like wings and they broke my fall. I even glided a little bit.

Right after that night, I got this immense desire to have the falling nightmare come back, so I could try my nascent flying attempt again. But the nightmare did not come back. I even stopped my practice-flying before I would fall asleep and no nightmare came. Yet I knew I was not cured from the falling nightmare. And sure enough, unexpectedly as ever, the falling nightmare came back. And again I put out my arms like a bird, and this time I actually flew a little. It was the most exhilarating feeling I had ever experienced.

So my pattern of falling asleep changed. I was no longer practicing flying before falling asleep out of fear of falling. I would practice flying in the hope I could do it in my dream. It became a very pleasant sensation to think of flying and then going into a gentle, welcoming kind of sleep. And initially, for a few weeks, I would continue to start off with the falling dream which would turn into a flying dream, without ever me crashing or waking up. I think I would then go either into an unrelated dream or no dream at all that I could remember.

And then, the falling dream gradually faded away and disappeared. It was replaced by the flying dream. And what a gorgeous feeling this dream created! It was not just that I could fly at will. It was what I flew over and under; and the colors, the most beautiful colors. They were the colors of the *anemónes* of Tasouli. The colors he loved so much when he was in Pyrgos Vassilissis during the Occupation.

> Over green-blue waters I would fly
> And under magnificent bridges
> And over calm azure-blue seas
> Fields the color of anemones
> Blues and blue-purples
> Deep reds and deeper greens
> And soar at will and confident
> Gliding above the vales and dales
> Swooping up swooping down
> Hoping it would never end

And during that time I looked so much forward to going to sleep so I could fly again and again and again. But as a few years passed, gradually I could fly no more. I had no more falling nightmares either. I would have done anything to be able to fly again. But to no avail.

Tasouli had grown up too much to be able to teach me to fly again.

The End

... I would fly over green-blue waters and azure blue seas, and under bridges and over fields of anemones with blue, purple and deep red colors.

— Tasouli

Appendix

Apologia

These nineteen letters (including the two that Pamela had read) were picked more or less randomly to cover the period of summer of '39 to the spring of '41 from sixty-one surviving letters, and were translated. These letters were the wartime letters that were found in the 'Dinion', in a shopping bag, after Phoebus' death. They are mostly letters from Phoebus to Dina. There are a few from Sophia to Dina or to Phoebus and a few from other individuals. Only one letter from Dina was included among the sixty-one. Yet Phoebus had elevated Dina's wartime letters written to him as masterpieces of human relations, love and literature, as he often proclaimed in stentorian tones.

26 August 1939

My dear Dina,

We were waiting for an answer from the two letters of Thales that he sent to you but up to today we have not heard any news from you about the baby and we are worried. Also, we sent 1,000 drachmas to you for your trip if my[10] newborn continues to be sickly. In any case we are waiting anxiously for you to write to us details about the grandchild.

Here it's the same and the same for our private matters. Except we are very emotional because Thales leaves on Monday for the Albanian border and Phoebus will be drafted on September 10. We had a letter from him from the city of Alexandroupolis and a card from Drama. He is well. Have you communicated with him? I will send you my letter to the address of "Lower Gerakarion" while he has sent to you the 1,000 drachmas to "Gerakari". Have you received them?

We only stayed 14 days in Rafina and now we are staying in Athens. Yesterday Kouri and Elpida visited in the afternoon and they send you their greetings.

Kiss him for me very sweetly on his beautiful little bright eyes, my little newborn. Also from his Grandfather he has lots of kisses. Give my greetings to your mother, and my kisses to dear Nana. It was just the draw of luck for the grandchild to get sick again and to frighten you! And if you see the slightest illness in your baby, do not hesitate to come back and Voudouris[11] will see him and follow him; he will be back from Lamia in a few days.

I kiss you, your mother — Sophia

25 September 1939

My beloved Dina,

The boat left very late on Saturday about 11.30. I arrived in Patra at 5.30, 20 minutes before the departure of the train. I found Kefalinos in the Hotel. I woke him up and he was glad. I told him all the relevant matters. He told me that if the children do not come, he will resign from the Service and he will leave Greece deserting the children. Although we spoke only for a few minutes, I formed the impression that he has been considerably influenced by the attitude of his children. He did not speak aggressively against Tasia.[12] I have the impression that if Tasia were to write a letter to him that discusses the relevant matters and which conveys a tone of sincerity it is possible that Kefalinos

249

might wish to reconstruct their relations. Kefalinos does not think through his actions well and it is not impossible that he will carry out something similar to what he told me. The following is worth noting. Although, of course, he condemns severely the attitude (actions) of his children and talks about this through clenched teeth, he also justifies it from a point of view, because he says that the children do not know what is happening between himself and Tasia when the two of them are alone, and they only see what is going on in front of them. I think there is still a pathway to compromise.

However, here everything is very good. Gianis nearly came to Zakynthos to see you. I am stopping this letter here so it can be sent at once. I will write to you again tomorrow or the following day, I mean another letter that will include the photos which you will receive tomorrow.

Your Phoebus kisses you sweetly, sweetly.

Athens 30 September, 1939

My beloved Dina

I only received yesterday evening your letter of 23 of the month, Tuesday. Luckily I had calculated that you would have to be away, so the delay did not increase my anxiety. It is true that after Friday morning I was not specifically anxious about the throat of the child. But our uncertain separation has created in me as well as in you an idiosyncratic situation. Nevertheless, logically, we should be almost certain that at Christmas, or perhaps sooner, we will meet again at least for a week. So we should not let ourselves be carried away by our forebodings and the hatchet-killings of our imagination.

Your letter gave me an immense amount of joy. For a long time I had the false sense that I was near you and my little mite. It was as if we were talking to each other and that you had not simply written to me. I think that this letter of yours was entirely from your subconscious. You did not put anything in it because you thought about it, not even the date, (just) Saturday morning, and because of this it gave me great pleasure.

I believe that now you have begun to read. You must take advantage of the long months that you will stay alone. There are a few books on education there and it is possible for me to send you some others. I have not started anything yet (myself), and before I start I must finish the military service. I (now) take advantage only of the radio, trying to understand the news from French stations. Yesterday I went to Kouri's. Her school is going relatively well. She has registered forty-seven children up to now, more than the corresponding numbers from last year. Perhaps you could write to her a letter bringing up indirectly the possibility that she could take you on as a teacher. During the time that I was in Zakynthos, Beba (feminine) came also from the office. I am thinking that before I appear (for the army) I should ask for something and I will write to you accordingly.

I kiss you very sweetly, my Dina,
Your Phoebus.

Athens, 17 October 1939

My beloved Dina,

This letter is the last I will be writing to you before I present myself to the army. I had written to you yesterday an extensive letter, eight pages — the darn thing, about various small impressions (I had) in Athens. Mostly, I wrote to you about "The Persians" of Aeschylus, that I saw in the theater together with Stelios. But on rereading my letter I became convinced that it was rather a schoolchild's essay and I tore it up. Thus, I spared you the worry of having to read things that would not be worthy of the ideal human being that you have constructed in your mind.

Even if it were to be tomorrow that I would go as a soldier, I do not believe that anything would change in my life. I would continue to believe that every noon I would come home and find you and the child there.

You should continue to write to me to (the address of) the home. Yesterday I received your third letter. I had started to worry and the letter I tore up was full of these anxieties. Of course the intentions of the home would be impeccable towards your arrival, but I believe for you to come before December you should have secured at least some work. I did not go to Beba. I think it would be better if you wrote to her yourself. Relative to your arrival, if nothing happens with Kouri it would be better, that you come in December, when I will be able to have some leave and we will be able to see each other. Of course all of these things can change if I get a discharge or I continue to work at Evelepidis'. It is of course needless for me to note that if the child gets sick, even briefly, you must bring him at once here if it can be ascertained that the dampness is harmful for him.

From the army, I believe, that I will write to you more extended letters. But it is not time that I will mostly need. I can grasp the pen and write ... something. If it is nothing I just leave it. If it has any importance, I do not like it. I just rip up the letter and write another one about common, everyday things. Why is that? Intellectual decline! But until when will it last? Many times I base many of my hopes on you. I walk on the streets absent-minded, without any purpose. With many feelings and thoughts which are languid, bottomless. I become exasperated with myself — the only warm feeling — but then I revert to the old languid situation. At the bottom of it all, I think that something will help me. And this will be you. Because this morning I tore-up the eight pages I wrote about "The Persians". And I don't know. These lines were not meant for people in general to read. At most it would have been you that would have read them. Phoebus is no good as a critic. Why does he meddle in these things? And you would just turn over the page. In spite of all of this I tore the pages up and while tearing them I felt a small degree of satisfaction, because I threw that stuff I wrote where I should have. However, I cannot say that I am an indecisive person, but I breathe in with a deep self-contempt when it comes to my abilities. Not that I have any confidence in the dynamism of others. Neither can I say that I am a pessimist. On the contrary. But I hate the thoughtless optimism of the common man. Man is the most complex creation of nature. The psychological world is the most complex creation of man. How is it possible for anyone to recognize it at a glance? That is why routine is a deliverance from psychological exploration and, no doubt, psychopathology.

I close this letter without rereading it. I do not want to see what I wrote without thinking. It is a kind of super-realist art or artlessness.

I kiss you very, very sweetly, Your Phoebus

Athens, First Infantry Regiment, 23 of October 1939

My beloved Dina,

They have assigned me as a combatant in the Eleventh Regiment. However, this assignment is not final. Tomorrow I will have to visit the doctor again and most likely they will send me to the Hospital. In the meantime I have stretched out my legs in the Eleventh Regiment and I am resting my anxious and tortured self, to an extent that you can't even imagine.

The training maneuvers are very light. I feel my health is better than ever. The food they serve you is so much that I can't finish all of it and, while waiting for the developments of my case, I am processing this droplet of society that is gathered all around me in the Eleventh Regiment: The street-urchin chauffeur relating his feats and slithery escapes from the police; the boat engine fireman, a world traveled wanderer who knows about every port — but only their whorehouses; the peasant, who has come down to Athens for his first time, and is so amazed with what is happening that his mouth keeps dropping open; and the other peasant who is being tormented by trying to figure out the usage of the gun, and how to pronounce "repeating rifle"; the philosophy student from the Sorbonne, who when you ask him what his job is, he closes his eyes hedonistically, turns his head towards the infinite void and answers: "Philosopher"; the vagabond-intellectual, who states that his profession is "literature critic" — (can you figure out any of it?); the immigrant from Romania who knows how to spin tales about the beyond-mythical riches of his country and who boasts that he has swam in petroleum; the homophile[13] who came to serve his country and not the soldiers; the waiter, an unsuccessful restaurateur who knows how to serve everybody; the doctor, the fat guy educated in France who has taken seriously the pseudoscientific deceit of the twentieth Century; and the countless other types who altogether constitute this social droplet, which is so representative of the people.

The Regiment is located in the Northern slope of Lykavitos. Across from me is Ymitos and underneath it unfolds that entire so very attractive vista, which for years became the soil of our erotic flowering. The house of Zoklakogou can be seen face-on from our army camp. The end of Zographou, St. Thomas, all of the foothills of Ymitos induce my mind to spring-up again that small, little body which, with its compact and steady walk, would always come belated into my embrace. I have never admired Ymitos so much as from this continuing observation of its tableau and the memories simultaneously created in my mind.

As yet you should not write to me at the Regiment. Given that it likely is that I will go to the Hospital, it would be best to continue to send your letters to the house and they will continue to send them to me. I am now at the Regiment Club, they have a shadow play with Karagiozis[14] and everybody is laughing. They are not allowing me to continue my unrushed, and without thinking, letter. So, I am closing it and I send you all these sweet little kisses I used to give you in the foothills of Ymitos — all in one batch.

With all the love that you know, your Phoebus.
Always give greetings to Nana and your mother. Especially to Nana.
Phoebus.

First Infantry Regiment, Athens 27 October, 1939

My beloved Dina,

I have now received the entry ticket for the Hospital. I saw the physician on Tuesday and received the requisition to be placed under observation. However, I remain still outside because all of the Hospital beds are full and we are waiting for one to empty so I can be admitted. I am hoping that by Monday we will have managed it.

I have become more convinced that there is no hope for me to be discharged. The only question remaining is if the army would accept me as support personnel. Of course I will keep you updated in *the development of my case.*

Yesterday Stelios came to the Regiment and told me that Tzemos came to Zakynthos and he saw you and the baby and that both of you are well. In this way I learned your news. It is now ten days since you have written to me. Of course you would have been waiting to find out what happened with my case with respect to my military service, so you could send me a letter directly. But you could have written to me at the house, which would have calmed me if he had given it to me. Now you understand that one of your letters is twice as desirable as before.

The others are now doing military maneuvers. For me, because I have the Hospital entry requisition, I have been relieved of duties until I go to the Hospital.

After one month they will start giving us leaves of absence, so in a little while you can start to consider the issue of your return. What did you do with Kouri? Did she answer to you at all? Did you write to Beba?

Today, I do not have much appetite for writing. I am very bored. So, I greet you and kiss you so I will not transmit my boredom to you.

Your Phoebus

Athens, Third Military Hospital, 8 November '39

My beloved Dina,

Here I am again in the Hospital and actually the familiar one, the Sixth Hospital, which has now become the Third. I am this year on the lower level ward which is the same as the upper. Everything is amazingly the same as in the year before last, with the difference that my little Dinoula does not come every day to keep me such beautiful company.

The day before yesterday when the doctor examined me, he found nothing wrong. At that time also Zachopoulos arrived (the poor man is running around very much) and the doctor said from what he can hear and what he sees in particular from my good physical appearance and my nutritional state, it will not be possible for me to be assigned even as support personnel. In any case, tomorrow I will be going for an X-ray and we will see what happens after that. In spite of the opinion of the doctor that examined me, it is possible that my past pathological condition will be taken into account and I will come out assigned as support personnel. In any case, we will know in about ten days.

Yesterday my mother came and she brought me your letter. I enjoyed it very much, (or rather so much because) it has been so many days since you have written to me. Although I don't believe that we will remain many more days separated do not forget to write to me regularly as much as possible. In the meantime also Andoniades[15] arrived. Evelpides had given him, to bring to me my salary for November. I did not accept it, of course, because it is not correct to keep money while I am in the Hospital. Andoniades will put the money aside and he will give it to me as soon as I am released. This money, of course, is yours. However, I think it is better if I do not send it to you. I am answering this point which was in your letter. It is a shame that you will not come now to Athens to make an effort to find a job, which will be so good for you, and especially that we will able to stay together for a few months. I am, therefore, proposing that we use these 3,500 drachmas for your stay here. You would be giving, supposedly from your own work, 1,000 drachmas a month to the home from this money. In this way, you would be giving all of it to the home, I am certain, with your own hands. It is also not impossible that Evelpides will give me also another salary, or I could even continue working at the office, which seems rather difficult, but maybe with his help and if I end up being assigned as support personnel. For this reason, I think, that you should both come at the beginning of December. You have also the invitation from the home. You should also keep in mind that after the end of the first five month period, or even sooner, if I am declared fit to fight they will very likely send me up to the border, in which case it will not be possible to stay together. So I am waiting for you necessarily to come in the beginning of December or even sooner, if you are able to. If you want money write to me.

Waiting for you and the little mite to squeeze you in my arms, but for now I squeeze you instead on paper,

Your Phoebus.

P.S. Give always greetings to Nana and your Mother.

16 November 1939

My beloved Dina

Only yesterday I received your letter; I worried very much about the child. It passed through my mind to send to you a telegram and to notify you to come at once. I would have done if I had found someone to send it for me and if I was not afraid that you would worry. In any case I think, particularly since you are facing difficulties with the milk, you should come as soon as you get my letter with the first boat. In the meantime, I will have been released from the Hospital so we will be able to meet frequently. If you do not have money, send to me at the home the following telegram "I will be coming fastest". I will then understand that you need money. I am presuming that the child will be well and that his diarrhea would not continue. It is not impossible that it is due to the pregnant goats, since the diarrhea continues without any other obvious reason. For me, I have my little mite in my wallet next to your picture and I take it out and look at it each time I see you. Every time I think he is better than the previous. In this way I've begun to understand how love can be carried out through photographs, as for example the love of the Americans through photographed brides.

I am still staying at the Third Hospital. The things here suggest some evidence that I will come out as support personnel. However, nothing is certain. As it appears, it will not be likely that I will be disentangled in 2-3 days. I will still need another week. How good it would be if you were also here. From the home they come regularly, but your company would be worth so much.

For this past week I have thrown myself into reading. They have brought from the home 2 or 3 books and I have read all of them. The Archeologist by Kakavitcha, an old book, old like himself, (1901) it still has interest. It comprises one of the most live books of his era. Of course, the language issue cannot stir our emotions today, but it does make you recall in a pleasant manner all of the pre-war bloodiness. Zweig's Casanova is a wonderful book. I had read before a few novels by Zweig and I had formed the impression he is just an average author. Then we were reading in the newspapers a few of his historical studies (Magellan) and we formed the impression that he is a very observant, elegant and noteworthy historian. From random notes we knew him as a critic not to be scorned. His Casanova gave me the opportunity to form the opinion that he is a critic of great depth. In his general approach Zweig appears to be similar to Ludwick, preoccupied with a whole lot of themes: literature, critique and history. But the braggart and expansive Ludwick cannot be compared with Zweig. His Casanova is the first part of a three-part critique "Casanova, Stendhal, Tolstoy"; he has in the beginning of this small volume a general introduction for the examination of these three, who, at first glance, are such different authors. Rarely does one find in any writing such refined and deep observations. How this corrupted, swindler, gambler, untalented author can still claim a place in literature 150 years after his death? What comprises his literary value? Zweig carries out a first rate analysis of his life and work which describes this life. Its value is based on the literary value of his work. That which defines Casanova as an author worthy of attention is that he succeeded writing an autobiography telling all of the truth about his life (especially his love-life) and his environment.

Yet he is a liar. He has altered a pile of occurrences. But, at the bottom these lies do not change, do not offend the truth of his basic activities and do not interfere in any way from providing us with a picture of his male effectiveness as it appeared to himself. The others, the great ones, the artists that preoccupied themselves with their autobiographies, Rousseau, Tolstoy and many others did not lie, but they hid the truth where it was not to their advantage. In spite of the big-mouthed accusations against themselves in other matters, which were very important in themselves, they gave, in spite of their great value, a corrupted picture of their life. But the analysis of psychological phenomena, with advances in science, is that which is destined to be the focus of the art of tomorrow. Thus a Casanova is worth something as he gives us, without fear, another picture based either on the senses or the reality of any one soul. The comparisons that Zweig makes in his book with a series of other writers engaged in describing their lives, are those that have the greatest value compared to general observations. The comparison of Casanova with Don Juan is also very successful. As far as I can tell the title scandalized the soldiers of our Hospital ward, to see me reading this book. There are many educated boys amongst them. Two graduates from the Faculty of Commerce; others are Engineers, Journalists and Lawyers. Not one of them can read more than ten pages. In the meantime the fictional novels by Niezy and the "Bouquets" and the "Theates" have their bones picked right to the very last line. And you can't imagine with what elegance this cursed <u>Casanova</u> is written.

I also read Zola's <u>Doctor Pascal</u>. The literary works lose a lot in translation, especially a bad translation. From one point of view this work is an affirmation of Zweig's conception that with the progress of science, that literature will be confined to the sphere of psychology. Zola is famous for his ability to shadow-sketch psychological profiles. However, this book of his, owns primarily its fame to his cultivation, in an artistic whole, the biological conceptions of his day. If <u>Doctor Pascal</u> had value, from that point of view, it is largely due to the originality of such a direction. A family corrupted by alcoholism, crime and paralysis develops accordingly the dominant biological beliefs of the time, putting out all manner of types of people, which one can biologically classify. However, this family is not continually corrupted, but due to the power of life it also produces healthy members and biologically corrects itself. Simultaneously, Zola summarizes in this book most of ...

[This is the end of the last surviving page from this letter.]

Postal Section 490, 3 April 1940[16]

My beloved Dina

I received your letter of the 20th and I thank you for the warmth of your words. I am absolutely well in my health and now with the good weather we are enjoying the beginning of spring.

I received the two parcels that you all send to me. The one with the almonds and the raisins, etcetera, and the other with the flea ointment, the chocolates, etcetera.

From the boys, especially from Gianis, I receive letters very frequently.

From here, nothing else.

I greet you warmly,

Your Phoebus

Postal Section 490, 18 November 1940

Anastassiades

My beloved Dina

This is the second special letter that I am writing to you. I hope you received the previous one as well as the others that I sent to all of you.

These frequent letters of mine are an attempt to try to be in greater communication with you. You will not neglect, so I hope you will be sending me as much as possible frequent letters (without a postage stamp, of course). This I am expecting most of all from you. I don't believe that it will be difficult for you to write to me a couple of words not only for important matters, but also the details of your daily lives, yours, the child's, the home's, even those of outside people. Such letters will amuse me as they will give the illusion, at least the perception that I find myself always near you all, I breathe your air and hear your words. All of our common life the last six and a half years will come alive thus, through the little details of your frequent letters. Write to me particularly about the child. I had written to you in the previous letter that his little egotistical mite projects on my conscience with the bright halo of the most ethereal being, and I am certain with our help he will respond to all of our longings.

Vagelis Varikas told me that his brother Vasos told him that a decision has been taken that when two brothers are soldiers serving at the border, the third will be kept back behind the front. If this information is correct, every effort should be made to pull Gianis back, and who already has had a difficult time. Only if the fact that Gianis is an officer reservist, constitutes an insurmountable obstacle should then an effort be made for my case.

From here, nothing new[17]. If you want, wrap one or two newspapers in a piece of paper and send them to me.

I greet you and kiss you sweetly my love,

Your Phoebus

Kiss for me the child, sweetly and warmly.

My address always: Soldier Ph. Styppas, Unit 42/5 Postal Section 490

4 January 1941

My beloved Dina,

Thus '40 has also passed. And '41 finds us full of hopes and fears. Our hopes are more general, our fears familial. Our wishes for 1941 are for our hopes to come true and our fears to dissipate. Then all of our efforts and agonies will remain only as a pleasant memory. Which other New Year's day will be celebrated better and more pleasantly if in '42 (or even a later year) my paternal family, and particularly our family, is found gathered together with all of us alive and healthy.

Yesterday I received Mother's post-card dated the 25th. The last one from you that I have is the 20th. Like you I am agonizing over the delay about news from Gianis. But I don't believe it is anything. By the time my letter is in your hand, I believe that you will have had news from him.

Yesterday I received a post card and a parcel from Statha. I will thank her in a separate letter. I also received one from you all with cognac and some other edibles. For the edibles, I had written to you that if you send me any, you send them to me only in very infrequent intervals. And no figs or raisins, as they provide us with these. As far as the cognac goes you should definitely not send me any again, as they give us some every day, so much in fact, that for me who does not drink too much, I can't finish it all. I have also received the 500 drachmas. You can send me more when I write to you. I have now 1,300 drachmas.

The child, as you understand together with you, is continually in my mind. I am enthusiastic about the news that you are sending me about his development and I am full of satisfaction and peace that he has a mother like you. No matter what will happen, as long as you are there the child has secured the best development of his intellectual and psychological strengths.

I kiss you warmly and sweetly
Your Phoebus

16, January, '41

My beloved Dina

To my great surprise the days pass without having received a letter from you. I was expecting that after father's death you would have been writing to me very frequently so that I could learn how this misfortune happened and mainly to learn news from you. I have the fear that it will be difficult for mother to recover from the blow. We are all away except for you and Stelios. It is therefore necessary that the two of you, especially yourself to be the surrogate for all of us. And I believe that our child will help you in this. Now, truly, we will have to add all the love we had for his grandfather onto him. All of our hopes on him will be hung.

I am well in my health. From here on my letters might be briefer and less frequent. Don't worry about this. I also had a letter from Thales dated on the 30th.

You understand also now how much I have you continually in my mind.

I kiss you as you know, sweetly, my Dina

Your Phoebus

27 January '41

By beloved Dina

I received your card full of truthful sympathy for father's death and I thank you very much. Your words coming out of pain from your immeasurable heart have lightened my own pain. And this time, as always your presence, either nearby or far away is like a tonic and gives courage for life. I am sure that your warm heart would have found a way to respond also to the pain of my mother, which now and with your help will have become lighter. Let us hope at least that there will not be, even small, mishap to our family in the immediate future.

As for myself, I am well here, only that because of the change in my address I do not receive letters regularly from any of you. However, this is entirely a temporary matter. Here again it is mentioned persistently that there exists or it was recently enacted, an order that requires that if three brothers are serving in the zone of combat, one will be transferred behind the front. You must again research this matter. If it is true, then the responsible parties for the decision as to who will be transported (need to be appraised), as I had written to you before that every effort must be made that it is Gianis who must be transferred, who I believe has become more exhausted than any of us during the war.

Anastassiades

Only if in the case of Gianis, and following this also for Thales, it is impossible for this to happen because they are younger than me and both are officers then we can decide for me. In any case, if this notice is verified you must be informed specifically as to what documentation is necessary, if these documents need to be on plain paper or on stamped paper (and then you must send to each one of us the required stamped paper) and where they should be addressed — to the military office in Athens or to Unit of the individual who is to be transferred. Nothing new from here.

I kiss you sweetly and I greet you warmly my Dina
Your Phoebus

My address is now, soldier Ph.
Styppas, XVI Communications
Regiment, Postal Section 490

23 February 1941 Athens

My much-beloved child Phoebus

Yesterday I received your letter and I calmed down a little when I read it, as you wrote to me so consoling, warmly and sweetly, my child. How much, my Phoebus, I want to see you because in your face I would see him who loved you apart from the others and who secretly admired you as you resemble him in everything he was. My Child, I responded immediately after you wrote to me your first letter after the death of our beloved. I sent it to your other address and perhaps it was lost. The children, Phoebus, left again for the front. You were, all of my four children, the best children in the world for me. But, my child, why has fate stricken me so mercilessly? To lose in my old age my companion, my own self, my consolation, my life almost.

May you live my children, so that I can see you return. Maybe you will give me the little solace and life, which I am trying, full of sorrow, to pump-out from the great love that I have for you.

Our Tassos is growing up really well, he endlessly talks to you and calls you.

Dina is fine. Gianis has written a lot of letters to you.

Stelios has also written to you that when Giorgos comes we will show to him the postal cards you have written, as he has not written you anything.

I sweetly kiss you with great love

Your mother.

Postal Section 490, 25 February '41

My beloved Dina

It has been many days since I've received a letter from any of you. It seems that some of your letters have been lost before they reached my hands and because of this I beg of you to write to me again anything of substance that any of you had written in your letters during the first half of February. You understand that your letters here are the most precious thing that one can imagine.

You understand that I am still the same here in the war campaign. Have Gianis and Thales perhaps

258

left? Is it possible that they might have been able to stay longer in their leave but they left in order to facilitate my own return? You can imagine how heavily this question weighs on me. I am not writing more to you because you will think I have gone crazy.

Still spring has not arrived. But as winter ends, according to the calendar, my heart flies more and everyday to you. First time in my life I have felt so connected to the outdoors. First time I am just waiting for spring day by day, moment by moment. But this time spring is closely tied — united with you. Your return to winter is the obvious cause of your worship of fair weather. That you are the sun, the spring of life is the real cause. Even separated, miles apart we will celebrate together this year, more than any other time the spring that will come to us.

From here nothing that is new. My address has changed a little and has now become XVI.β Regiment Communications Postal Section 490. In each of your letters enclose maybe a postal card or a blank envelope.

If Gianis and Thales have left, write to me immediately their addresses.

I greet you warmly and kiss you very sweetly, my Dina, your Phoebus.

P.S. Just this moment I received letters from you, among which was yours, mother's and from Gianis. I thank you all very much. In the certification document from the municipality or the community, it must definitely state that I am the older brother of Gianis and Thales, or at least the dates of birth of each of the three of us and that we are all brothers.

I greet you again

Your Phoebus

Postal Section 490, 8 March '41

My beloved Dina

I received today your postal card of the 21st of January and your letters of the 22nd and 25th of February. As you understood from the letters that you have received later your complaints that I do not write to you privately are baseless. Not because I think about it and I write to you privately, but because an undefeatable power pushes me to correspond especially with you, to write something to you, to come with any kind of contact with you. If I do not write to you every day two or three letters it is because this is not possible and with sadness I limit this desire of mine and I write the few letters that I write to you. It is true that after the death of my father, I ensured that I would not send to my mother fewer personal letters than I sent to you, and this because I did not want the thought to even cross her mind even for an instant, during her mourning, that I am thinking more of you than her. As for you, I have no fear because I know that you are convinced that our love is superior the most valued thing that we can provide today are the letters that each of us receives from the other.

I received the certification document from the community. What the devil — these people do not know how to compose a certification document. For Gianis, who is older than Thales, they have put him last and even they have the date of birth for all of us for Gianis they have written how old he is. So, for one to find out who is the oldest, one needs to do calculations. I hope however they will not make it difficult for me due to these defects. If they do, I will write to you to send to me another one in which it will be adequate in which simply reference is made that me, Gianis and Thales who are serving in the army are brothers and the oldest of the three is me. In any case when I receive the certification document from Gianis I will undertake the relevant actions and I will write to you.

You can imagine what pleasure I get for every bit of news about the child and also every photograph from you. However, his first letters even if they were made by holding his hand, particularly moved me.

I wrote to mother a few words regarding our father's merit. I intend to write to you one day how I perceive, in all its breath, his work of fifty years. But I don't know when I will be able to do it. It is possible of course that my opinion is influenced from the fact that he is my father. But for one to understand his value one should not judge him with absolute measures. One should be transported to the environment of Smyrni towards the end of the last Century, and to understand how binding the influence of that retarded environment was on him. If one can understand this well he will then see, under a different light, not only his work but also his own development.

I don't have anything new from here.
I greet you warmly and
I kiss you sweetly

Your Phoebus.

23 March 1941

My beloved Dina

If I exclude your card of the 7th of the current month, it has been a long time since I have received a letter from you. Why is that? If on occasion I am slow in writing, and this has happened only once or twice, it can be justified. However, you should not interrupt your letters, even when you don't receive one from me. Luckily, I got the newspapers you had sent to me so I could see that you were OK. I also received two packages with woolens. One was very old with my previous address. For my transfer away from the front, I don't believe that anything will happen. It is said that there is a newer order which rescinds these types of transfers.

I've received a letter from Nana dated 2nd of February. During the period of the campaign I had thought about her many times, now that she will be isolated in Zakynthos. I had also written a postal card to her on the first of the year which it seems she finally received.

I have not yet received paper envelopes and you don't know how difficult it is to find any so I can write to you.

In the handkerchiefs I received I saw, made by your hand, my monogram. So simple and without superfluity as it is, it reminded me of all your being and all of our common life. When one is near to the other, small trifles of everyday life obstruct one from having a precise picture of the person next to them during every moment. Separation from this viewpoint has an advantage. In that it sets aside these small anomalies and it makes one imagine, with real perception, the entire contour of your nearness. Thus my deep appreciation of you increases every day since our separation when I look at you from a distance and I see you in your true magnificence. And you don't know how this thing does me good especially when I think about the child. No matter what happens he will have someone that stands by him and guides him and who will give him a breath of life that will make living worthwhile. How do I perceive my heart to beat together with yours! And how much this gives me strength and solace.

For the issue of transfer behind the front, I do not believe now that anything will happen. In fact they told me that a new order has arrived which recalls all similar previous transfers.

From here nothing else that is new.

I greet you warmly and kiss you sweetly my Dina

Your Phoebus

Send me the "New Worlds" that publish the English lessons.

A Relative Chronology for Tasouli and Styppas

The two sketches that follow are based on a family tree drawn up by Auntie Eleni, the oldest surviving relative into the post-World War II era. Direct descent of the family from Gregory the Vth can be considered as an embellishment by Auntie Eleni.

Tasouli and Styppas see events from different perspectives. Tasouli's narration starts from his first memories, probably in 1939, until he was 12 in 1950. Tasouli's closest circle in the Bastille is shown on the following pages. Styppas was much more influenced by the distant family history; his descent is shown on the right. Styppas' family history was driven by tumultuous events, which probably began in the 1700s. Central was the Greek revolution in 1821, followed by the massacre of the Greeks and the hanging of the Patriarch of Constantinople Gregory Vth (b. 1746) by the Ottoman Turks in 1821. Prior to becoming Patriarch of Constantinople, Gregory was Bishop of Smyrna (1785–1797). According to Yiayia Sophia, when Phoebus was a child in Smyrna he wanted to become a bishop. Phoebus considered this a venomous and factious charge by his mother, Sophia, and he vigorously denied it. Phoebus' father, Anastassios — the "great man of Smyrna", lived and taught in Smyrna in the later 1800s and then until the destruction of the City in 1922. He was certain that little Phoebus (b 1911) would become a pillar of the young Greek state as a great Naval Officer.

However, young Phoebus was dismissed from the Naval Academy due to health reasons. Styppas suspected that his father, Phoebus, became an Archeomarxist as a result of having failed to become either a great bishop or a naval officer. Of course, Phoebus vehemently denied that also.

Note that "cities past and present" include Smyrna which was destroyed in 1922 (shown by an asterisk).

The destruction of this most cosmopolitan of cities of the period also ended the Greek Ionian civilization, which had contributed immensely to ancient Greece and to Christianity.

Styppas' attitudes are undoubtedly colored by his family history including the close escape of his father and grandparents from the massacre that followed the destruction of Smyrna. Tasouli, on the other hand, is probably too immersed in his close circle in the Bastille to be as influenced by the events of Smyrna a couple of decades before.

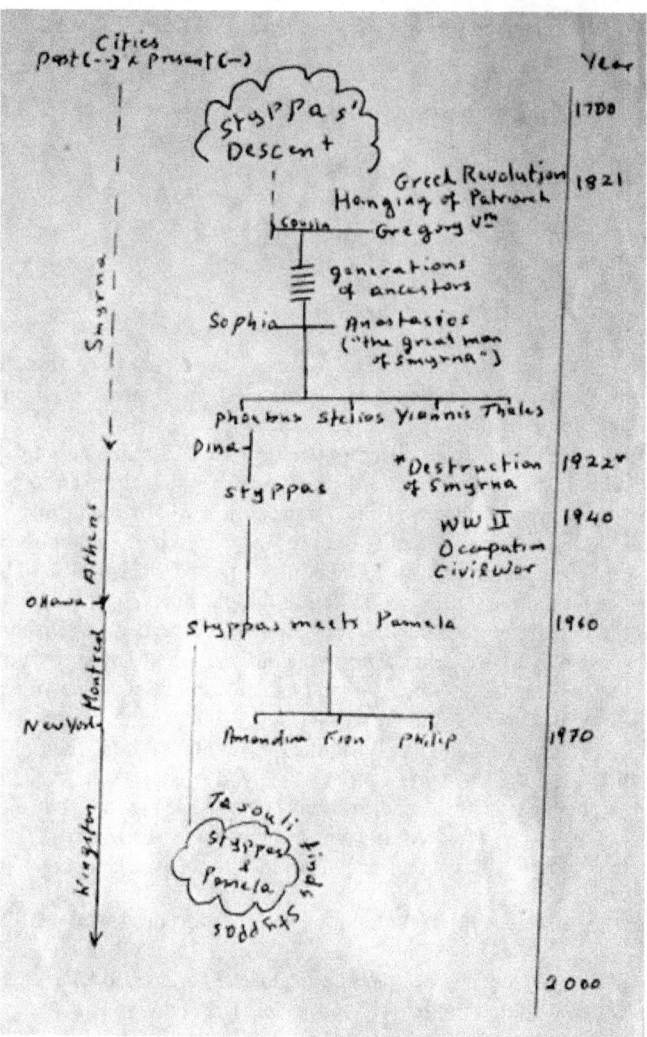

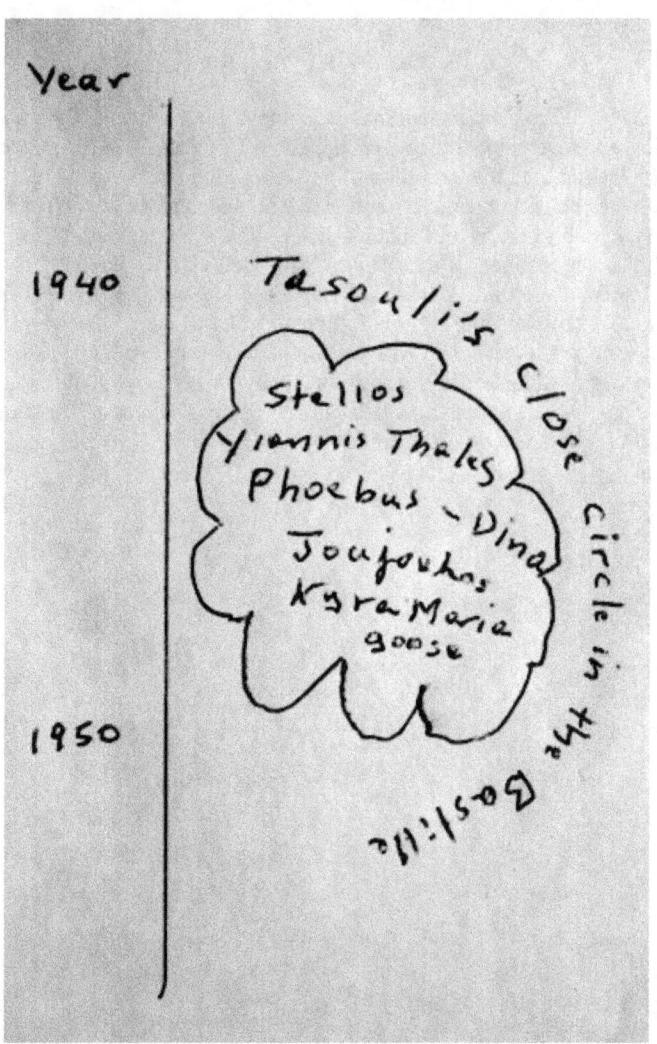

Acknowledgements

The sureness of Philip, Fion and Amandina that some of the story should be told in the voice of the child was critical for developing a theme for the book. Douglas Babington (Montreal) and Margaret Wigmore (Regina), with their strong literary backgrounds, provided much-appreciated reassuring commentary about the characters and plot. Toivo Roht (Ottawa), childhood friend since 1952, literary man and publisher, warned that my voice should not be altered. I would also thank the many others who read and commented on early drafts of the book.

I'm also very appreciative of the contributions of the following: Dimitris Filipou of Montreal for making CDs in Greek of the war-time letters of Phoebus to Dina, which greatly facilitated my translations of the letters for "Apologia"; Athena Moss (Athens) who created inspired sketches about a childhood long ago; and Danielle Aubrey of Petra Books for her careful and thoughtful editing.

I am also grateful to those who so impressed me during my childhood. While these individuals have mostly died, they still have not left Tasouli.

—T. Styppa

Notes

1. "Hairy" or "μαλιαροί" is a somewhat dated term for the strongly pro-demotic writers and poets of the time.

2. Evelyn Waugh, Brideshead Revisited, Book 1 (Chapman and Hall, 1945). See also "Nicolas Poussin – The Complete Works" French Painter. Accessed June 2017. http://www.nicolaspoussin.org/.

3. A. Stinas, "The Massacre of the Internationalist Communists in Greece, December 1944", extract from "Memoirs: A Revolutionary in 20th Century Greece", accessed June 2017. https://www.marxists.org/subject/greek-civil-war/ revolutionary-history/ stinas/memoirs.htm See
also a reference to Thalis (Thales) in Pagrati in this extract.

4. General election of February 1950 saw a much reduced Labour majority and the Tories back in power in October 1951.

5. Of course, Tasouli could not have remembered exactly what a particular Speaker said, but Styppas thinks that something along these lines was likely said and that the Speaker might have read this article quoting Stalin (in Pravda) published in the Manchester Guardian in August 1950. From the archive, 2 August 1950: "Stalin and the Soviet state". Manchester Guardian, accessed June 2017, www.theguardian.com/%20theguardian/2011/aug/02/%20archive-stalin-and-soviet-state

6. The term "Quebec sovereignist" would not have been in common use when the Occupation Child was on the Canberra in 1950. But it would have been for Pamela at the time of writing.

7. The affectionate diminutives of Phoebus and Dina are Phivaki and Dinaki.

8. Frank L. Miller, "ANDREW HALL MACPHERSON (1932–2002)", Obituary. ARCTIC : VOL. 55, NO. 4 (DECEMBER 2002) P. 403–406. Accessed June 2017. http://pubs.aina.ucalgary.ca/arctic/Arctic55-4-403.pdf

9. More letters can be found in the Appendix under "Apologia". These letters can also be viewed as an apology of sorts by Phoebus for his behavior, including his Archeomarxist rants in "The
Corruptors". "Apologia" is also the famous dialogue by Plato narrating Socrates' self-defense.

10. "my" is used here as affectionate for "our".

11. Voudouris was the highly trusted Pediatrician of the Styppas family dating back to their days in Smyrni. Among other feats, Voudouris was generally credited of having saved young Stelios' life from the tuberculosis that affected the bones of his shoulders.

12. The surname of the father of Litsa, described in "Family". Tasia was Litsa's mother. The
Kefalinos family lived in Zakynthos, near Gerakarion, and Dina and Litsa were cousins.

13. Phoebus uses here the word "κύναιδος". However, the use of ύ in "κύναιδος" suggests an ancient Greek derivation from dog. More common now seems the use of ί in writing "κίναιδος". Some commentary argues the origin of this spelling is from a myth: When Zeus formed man he imbedded positive attributes but he forgot to include shame. So, he stuck it in at the very end — as the rectum. So anyone passing through there "moves the shame" = "Κινεί την αιδώ=κίναιδος". Currently, the word "κίναιδος" often takes on a derogatory usage, particularly in the political and sports arenas.

14. The shadow plays of Karagiozis, the humped, huge nosed, ridiculous, irreverent and rude
characters were mostly working class entertainment for many generations. More recently Karagiozis has been elevated to a cultural icon, and his shadow theater antics remain genuinely popular with young children.

15. As described in "The Corruptors".

16. This letter is written on a post office card with stamped military markings illustrating a Soldier, a Marine and an Euzone with a bugle. The sender is soldier Phoebus Styppas, XVI β Communications Regiment Postal Section 490; the recipient is Mrs. Dina Styppas, Agiou Polykarpou 10, Nea Smyrni, Athens.

17. "Nothing new here" is a repeated message in the letters from the front as the fighting was raging. It would have been well understood by the recipient that it was all that could be said due to strict censorship. But it was also a reassuring message of survival.